CARBON-FREE SHIPPING AND SHIPPING CARBON

This book explores the private law implementation of the new international and EU regulatory framework targeting decarbonisation in the shipping industry.

Compared with other sectors, the shipping industry has traditionally been labelled a 'slow mover' concerning the sustainability agenda. However, new regulatory measures on carbon reduction both internationally and in the EU require fundamentally new developments in the industry. This book focuses on the goal of carbon reduction from a private law perspective and considers how the new regulatory framework can be implemented in the shipping industry.

This book studies existing contractual provisions in charterparties and bills of lading alongside new contractual model clauses designed to facilitate carbon reduction. It considers how the new clauses should be interpreted, whether they will transform traditional shipping contracts into more collaborative contracts, and how they will interact with other clauses in the contract and with other contracts in the supply chain. The contractual analysis is considered in context, reflecting on enforcement issues, such as Port State Control (PSC), the Poseidon Principles, and climate change litigation. The book also analyses the related topic of shipping contracts for carbon storage as a necessary means of meeting carbon reduction targets.

The book is intended to pave the way for understanding how core shipping contracts can work in this new context and the extent to which the new types of clauses will profoundly transform contracts.

It presents contributions by experienced and younger academics and practitioners from Asian, European, and Scandinavian legal systems.

Carbon-Free Shipping and Shipping Carbon

Contracts in Context

Edited by
Stephen Girvin
and
Vibe Ulfbeck

•HART•
OXFORD • LONDON • NEW YORK • NEW DELHI • SYDNEY

HART PUBLISHING

Bloomsbury Publishing Plc

Kemp House, Chawley Park, Cumnor Hill, Oxford, OX2 9PH, UK

1385 Broadway, New York, NY 10018, USA

29 Earlsfort Terrace, Dublin 2, Ireland

HART PUBLISHING, the Hart/Stag logo, BLOOMSBURY and the Diana logo are trademarks of Bloomsbury Publishing Plc

First published in Great Britain 2024

A catalogue record for this book is available from the British Library.

A catalogue record for this book is available from the Library of Congress.

Library of Congress Control Number: 2024937493

ISBN: HB: 978-1-50997-263-0
ePDF: 978-1-50997-265-4
ePub: 978-1-50997-264-7

Typeset by Compuscript Ltd, Shannon

PREFACE

This book is the follow-on to a Conference organised by Vibe Ulfbeck and hosted by the Shipping and Ocean Law Group (SHOC) at the University of Copenhagen, Faculty of Law on 10 November 2022. Members of SHOC and academic and practitioner colleagues from BIMCO and from Copenhagen, Hong Kong, London, Rotterdam, and Singapore were joined at the Conference by an audience of maritime lawyers and maritime professionals from both near and far, in person and virtually.

In early 2023, following the Conference, plans were put in place to generate written papers with a view to publication with a reputable publishing house. Following the example taken at an earlier conference of ours, which led to the publication of *Maritime Organisation, Management and Liability: A Legal Analysis of New Challenges in the Maritime Industry* (Hart Publishing, 2021), this new volume includes work by established and new scholars and practising lawyers. We thank, Aslı Arda, Simon Baughen, Sophia Hong Van Ang Cai, Ellen Johanne Eftestøl, Carola Glinski, Malthe Hersom Kløft, Jolien Kruit, Vincenzo Battistella Marinucci, Andreas Oxholm, Mikis Tsimplis, Yoshifumi Tanaka, and Maxim Usynin for their contributions. The gestation period for a book project such as this one inevitably involves a commitment over a significant timescale, and the editors would like to thank all the contributors for bearing with our queries and comments during this process.

Apart from the contributors to this volume, we record our thanks to our other Conference speakers: Rachel Hoyland, partner at Hill Dickinson LLP; Stinne Taiger Ivø, then Director for Contracts & Support (now Deputy Secretary General) at BIMCO; Kiki Larsen, Mærsk Mc-Kinney Møller Center for Zero Carbon Shipping; Søren G Nielsen, Blue Water Shipping; Krester Krøger Kjær, Senior Vice-President of Skuld; Niels Hemmingsen Schovsbo, GEUS (Geological Survey of Denmark and Greenland).

Vibe Ulfbeck, who took the lead in developing this volume, wishes to thank Stephen Girvin of the Centre for Maritime Law at NUS for agreeing to be her co-editor and for his effort in scrutinising and editing the contributions and proofs. She would also like to thank Aslı Arda for her assistance in editing the contributions in accordance with Hart Publishing's *House Style Guidelines for Authors and Editors* and for preparing the Tables. Vibe also thanks the Danish Orient's Fund for providing funding for the project on Green Law in Shipping (GreenLash), of which this book project is an important part.

Stephen Girvin would like to thank Vibe for her invitation to be involved in this project. He acknowledges the generous funding provided by the Ministry of Law through its NUS Law Vision Project, which enabled him to participate in the Conference on which this book is based. He also thanks Zenos Jin Haofeng, a JD student at NUS Law, for his acute and much-welcome research assistance during an exceptionally busy period.

Finally, both Stephen and Vibe would like to thank Roberta Bassi and Verity Stuart of Hart Publishing for agreeing to publish this collection and for their commitment to it. We are grateful to them for their support throughout the writing and production process.

Stephen Girvin
Centre for Maritime Law
National University of Singapore
Singapore
15 January 2024

Vibe Ulfbeck
CEPRI, Centre for Private Governance
SHOC, Shipping and Ocean Law Group
University of Copenhagen
Copenhagen
15 January 2024

CONTENTS

PART III
ENFORCEMENT ISSUES

PART IV
SHIPPING CARBON FOR CARBON STORAGE

LIST OF CONTRIBUTORS

Andreas Oxholm is Attorney-at-Law, Hafnia Law Firm, Copenhagen.

Aslı Arda is Assistant Professor, Centre for Private Governance (CEPRI) and Shipping and Ocean Law Group (SHOC), Faculty of Law, University of Copenhagen.

Carola Glinski is Professor in FB Umweltwirtschaft/-recht – FR Umweltrecht, Hochschule Trier and Associate Professor, Centre for Private Governance (CEPRI) and Shipping and Ocean Law Group (SHOC), Faculty of Law, University of Copenhagen.

Ellen Johanne Eftestøl is Professor of Law, BI Norwegian Business School, and Visiting Professor, School of Business, Administration and Law, Gothenburg University.

Jolien Kruit is Partner, Van Traa Advocaten NV, guest lecturer, Erasmus School of Law, and guest lecturer, Leiden University.

Malthe Hersom Kløft is Junior Associate, Bech-Bruun Law Firm, Copenhagen.

Maxim Usynin is Assistant Professor, Centre for Private Governance (CEPRI) and Shipping and Ocean Law Group (SHOC), Faculty of Law, University of Copenhagen.

Michael Tsimplis is Professor, School of Law, City University of Hong Kong.

Sophia Hong Van Anh Cai is Junior Associate, Accura Law Firm, Copenhagen.

Simon Baughen is Professor of Shipping Law, Institute of Shipping and Trade Law, Hilary Rodham Clinton School of Law, Swansea University.

Stephen Girvin is MPA Professor of Maritime Law, Director, LLM (Maritime Law), Director, Centre for Maritime Law, National University of Singapore.

Vibe Garf Ulfbeck is Professor, Head of Centre for Private Governance (CEPRI), Head of Shipping and Ocean Law Group (SHOC), Faculty of Law, University of Copenhagen.

Vincenzo Battistella Marinucci is PhD Fellow, Centre for Private Governance (CEPRI) and Shipping and Ocean Law Group (SHOC), Faculty of Law, University of Copenhagen.

Yoshifumi Tanaka is Professor, Centre for Private Governance (CEPRI) and Shipping and Ocean Law Group (SHOC), Faculty of Law, University of Copenhagen.

TABLE OF CASES

Belgium

Denmark

European Union

France

Germany

The International Court of Justice

Italy

Malaysia

Netherlands

Norway

Singapore

United Kingdom

United States of America

TABLE OF LEGISLATION AND INTERNATIONAL INSTRUMENTS

France

Germany

Norway

The Netherlands

United Kingdom

United States of America

International Instruments

1

Introduction

VIBE ULFBECK* AND STEPHEN GIRVIN**

I. Background: Regulatory Movement

The maritime sector accounts for three per cent of global carbon emissions and 28 per cent of GHG emissions in the EU. Nevertheless, the maritime sector was for a long time not taken into account in the general regulatory frameworks aimed at curbing emissions. It was not included in the Kyoto Protocol of 1997, and later amendments,[1] and it was not part of the EU Emissions Trading System (ETS) from 2003 establishing a trading system for carbon quotas.[2] Finally, the maritime sector was not included in the Paris Agreement of 2015.[3]

Instead, it has been left to the International Maritime Organization (IMO) to develop a strategy for curbing emissions in the shipping sector. The main issue is that critics complain that the IMO has not done enough.[4] In 2011, the IMO adopted a new amendment to the International Convention for the Prevention of Pollution from Ships (MARPOL),[5] which introduced the Energy Efficiency Design Index (EEDI),[6] energy efficiency design requirements for new ships. However, for a long time the focus was only on new ships. Regarding existing ships, the only initiative was the introduction of

* Professor, Head of Centre for Private Governance (CEPRI), Head of Shipping and Ocean Law Group (SHOC), Faculty of Law, University of Copenhagen.

** MPA Professor of Maritime Law, Director, LLM (Maritime Law), Director, Centre for Maritime Law, Faculty of Law, National University of Singapore.

[1] unfccc.int/kyoto_protocol.

[2] Directive 2003/87/EC of the European Parliament and of the Council of 13 October 2003 establishing a scheme for greenhouse gas emission allowance trading within the Community and amending Council Directive 96/61/EC (Text with EEA relevance) (2003) OJ L 275/32.

[3] unfccc.int/process-and-meetings/the-paris-agreement. See Tsimplis (ch 2) section II and, more generally, Erik Røsæg, 'GHG Emissions from International Shipping' (2022) 61 *Comparative Maritime Law* 63.

[4] See eg H Bach and T Hansen, 'IMO Off Course for Decarbonisation of Shipping? Three Challenges for Stricter Policy' (2023) 147 *Marine Policy* 105379. It appears the new IMO Secretary-General also recognises this issue: see '"Bring it on": IMO's New Head Prepared to Tackle Rifts, Wars and Shipping's Green Mission' *TradeWinds* (London, 2 January 2024).

[5] International Convention for the Prevention of Pollution from Ships (MARPOL) 73/78. Generally, see C de la Rue, CB Anderson and J Hare, *Shipping and the Environment*, 3rd edn (London, Informa Law from Routledge, 2022) 957ff.

[6] Res MEPC.203(62), reg 22.

the Ship Energy Efficiency Management Plan (SEEMP),[7] which has reporting requirements but no strong enforcement mechanisms.

However, the role of the industry is now changing. In 2018, the IMO adopted its initial strategy to curb emissions.[8] This led to an amendment of MARPOL Annex VI in 2021, which came into force on 1 November 2022.[9] The amendment included two new initiatives. First, it introduced a new technical energy efficiency requirement for existing ships (EEXI)[10] as a prerequisite for obtaining the International Energy Efficiency Certificate (IEE Certificate). Existing ships must comply with the new energy efficiency requirements from 1 January 2023.

Second, the amendment introduced the Carbon Intensity Indicator (CII), which applies from January 2024. The CII focuses on how ships are operated to achieve carbon emission reductions by requiring more operational efficiency. Under the CII, ships are subject to an annual rating based on the level of emissions from the preceding year.[11]

Despite these initiatives, the IMO has still been found wanting, and in 2023, a revised strategy was introduced aiming at achieving zero carbon emission around 2050.[12] One of the basic problems connected to the new regulatory initiatives is that they focus only on efficiency and not on the total amount of emissions. This means that while each ship may become more efficient if the total size of the fleet is at the same time enlarged, emissions may still not decrease. They may even increase. This is one of the reasons why it has been argued that carbon pricing is necessary if carbon reductions are to be ensured. However, although a global carbon pricing system has been on the agenda in the IMO for a while, there seem to be no concrete plans to adopt this measure.[13]

In contrast, at the EU level, a carbon pricing system for the maritime industry was introduced in 2023. Thus, with Directive 2023/959[14] amending the ETS Directive from 2003, the shipping industry has entered the EU Emissions Trading System from 1 January 2024 as regards CO_2 emissions.[15] This means that from 2024, shipping companies will have to trade for the necessary carbon allowances. This will put a cap on the amount of emissions each shipping company can emit and presumably, to some extent, incentivise the use of energy efficiency tools.

[7] See www.imo.org/en/OurWork/Environment/Pages/Improving%20the%20energy%20efficiency%20of%20ships.aspx.

[8] See www.imo.org/en/OurWork/Environment/Pages/Vision-and-level-of-ambition-of-the-Initial-IMO-Strategy.aspx#:~:text=The%20revised%20IMO%20GHG%20Strategy,points%20for%202030%20and%202040.

[9] The amendments to Annex VI were adopted as Res. MEPC.328(76). The amended Annex VI is available at wwwcdn.imo.org/localresources/en/OurWork/Environment/Documents/Air%20pollution/MEPC.328%2876%29.pdf.

[10] MARPOL, Annex VI, reg 23.

[11] ibid reg 28.

[12] The revised strategy can be found here: www.imo.org/en/OurWork/Environment/Pages/2023-IMO-Strategy-on-Reduction-of-GHG-Emissions-from-Ships.aspx?refresh=1.

[13] IMO's revised strategy includes no plans to introduce carbon pricing. See eg www.offshore-technology.com/news/imo-shipping-emissions-reduction-plan-revised/?cf-view.

[14] Directive (EU) 2023/959 of the European Parliament and of the Council of 10 May 2023 amending Directive 2003/87/EC establishing a system for greenhouse gas emission allowance trading within the Union and Decision (EU) 2015/1814 concerning the establishment and operation of a market stability reserve for the Union greenhouse gas emission trading system [2023] OJ L130/134.

[15] From 1 January 2026, emissions from two other greenhouse gases (GHGs), methane (CH_4) and nitrous oxide (N_2O) will be included.

For all of the described measures to work, they must be implemented at the operational level. Thus, whereas the green transition in shipping has often been studied from a public law perspective, the idea behind this book is to approach the topic from a private law perspective. The book's essential theme is questioning how the new regulatory measures can be transferred into the private law realm, putting the regulatory framework into action.[16]

Refitting ships, operating them efficiently daily and buying carbon quotas have costs, and the costs need to be distributed between the commercial actors in the maritime industry. Moreover, implementing efficiency measures usually requires the involvement of more than one party. Consequently, contracts become an essential tool.

This book focuses on commercial contracts as a tool for the green transition and brings in tort law when appropriate. It studies various contractual model clauses that have been developed and considers how they can be understood in the context of the regulatory framework they reflect and the overall objective of establishing carbon-free shipping. The objective is to pave the way for understanding how core shipping contracts can work in a new context and the extent to which the new type of clauses will transform the contracts more profoundly.

II. Contractual Responses

A. Contractual Clauses

The contractual response to the regulatory initiatives has been the development of new contractual clauses to be inserted into charterparties. Standard clauses have been developed by the Baltic and International Maritime Council (BIMCO).

As to the international regulatory initiatives, the energy efficiency requirements for existing ships embedded in the EEXI system imply that new and existing ships must live up to certain energy efficiency requirements concerning the way they are designed and built. This means that some ships must be re-built or refitted to obtain the required certificate. In some situations, it may be necessary to make the changes during the period when the ship is fixed on charter. In order to cater for this situation, the EEXI transition clause has been developed by BIMCO. It allows the shipowner to take the vessel out of service to carry out the necessary modifications, provided certain conditions are fulfilled. The provision requires close collaboration between the parties.[17] As existing ships are modified, the practical need for the clause will decrease.

In contrast, the CII system also creates new obligations for the shipowner after the ship has been modified. Thus, the system imposes on the shipowner an obligation to report annually on the emissions of a particular ship. On this basis, the ship will be rated by the relevant authority and placed in categories A, B, C, D or E (A being the most efficient). Tools for improving the efficiency score under the CII system are slow

[16] On the general theme of moving from public law enforcement of MARPOL to contract law aspects, see Tsimplis (ch 2).

[17] On the EXII transition clause, see Kløft and Cai (ch 4).

steaming, re-routing, and loading less cargo. Under the CII system, the obligation to maintain efficiency rests on the shipowner. However, under time charterparties, it is the time charterer which has the commercial control over the ship. To a large extent, it is, therefore, also the time charterer which controls the efficiency of the ship. BIMCO's CII Operations Clause for Time Charter Parties 2022 attempts to solve this problem. The clause specifies how the parties are to collaborate in good faith to keep down emissions and under which circumstances the shipowner may choose to slow steam or re-route, even in the absence of a consensus between the parties.[18] In the case of voyage charterparties, the shipowner controls the commercial operation of the vessel, but CII may still impact the performance of the voyage. The CII Clause for Voyage Charterparties 2023 provides for the adjustment of course, speed, or RPM without affecting the utmost or due despatch or any speed and consumption warranties under the charterparty.

At the EU level, the ETS has been extended to include the shipping sector. This means that from 2024, carbon emissions come with a price.[19] Shipping companies will have to buy and surrender the necessary allowances for each year. This will require using a new type of contract in the industry.[20] Furthermore, adaptations of charterparties will be needed. Again, the problem is that if a ship is under charter, it is not the shipowner but the charterer who has commercial control over the ship and, thereby, also the control over the amount of emissions. The time charter ETS clause, developed by BIMCO, tries to solve this problem by transferring the obligation to surrender the necessary amount of allowances to the time charterer. The clause requires close collaboration and data sharing between the parties. The ETS will also impact the management company's role, which is included in the definition of the 'shipping company' in the amended ETS Directive. This means the allocation of risks and liabilities connected with the duty to surrender allowances will need to be allocated between the shipowner and the manager in the ship management contract.[21]

B. General Contract Law Themes

i. Taking into Account Parties' External Interests

From a contract point of view, the new clauses have a main characteristic that makes them different from many other clauses used in charterparties. Thus, the clauses concern issues that are external to the parties' traditional commercial interests. Carbon reduction is a matter of societal interest and, as a starting point, not a matter of concern to the individual commercial interests of the parties to the contract. Indeed, handling societal interest matters is unfamiliar to contract law and, to some extent, challenges its fundamentals.[22] Indeed, contract law does not cater for societal interests but serves the interests of the parties, as reflected in the classic principle of

[18] On the CII clause, see Girvin (ch 3).

[19] On the system in general and some contractual issues, see Eftestøl (ch 5) and Baughen (ch 6).

[20] On this, see Oxholm (ch 7).

[21] On this, see Ulfbeck (ch 8).

[22] See eg V Ulfbeck and O Hansen, 'Sustainability Clauses in an Unsustainable Contract Law?' (2020) 16 *European R of Contract L* 186.

freedom of contract.[23] This conception of contracts is challenged by the market-driven corporate social responsibility (CSR) and sustainability movement, which argues that companies should take broader social considerations into account when doing business.[24] However, early attempts to incorporate CSR and sustainability requirements into contracts reflect the challenges in using contracts as a tool for this purpose.[25] Often, such requirements have been placed in a separate document, for example, a code of conduct, leading to discussions as to whether the CSR requirements were part of the contract or not.[26] Even if CSR requirements have been placed directly in the contract it has still been unclear whether to regard the requirements as legal or purely ethical. Furthermore, CSR requirements have often been formulated as broad or vague principles, giving rise to enforcement problems. Finally, the most basic problem has been the lack of incentive to enforce the CSR requirements for the parties to the contract since the interests protected by the requirements are external, third-party interests, and third parties themselves rarely have enforcement rights in contract law.

However, in recent years, commercial realities have changed. Today, not living up to sustainability requirements can cause severe reputational damage, and therefore, constitutes a real commercial risk. This in itself changes the dynamics of market-driven sustainability practices. In addition, the sustainability agenda is increasingly also being pushed as a state-driven agenda. A clear example of this is a recent proposal for an EU Directive on Corporate Sustainability Due Diligence (CSDDD proposal),[27] requiring companies over a certain size to consider sustainability requirements and to use contracts as a tool for this purpose. With regard to carbon emissions, the CSDDD proposal requires companies to have a company policy that is compatible with the Paris Agreement of keeping the rise of temperature below 1.5 degrees celsius.[28] The CSDDD proposal also covers shipping companies.

The use of carbon clauses in the shipping sector must be understood in this light. Whereas the shipping industry has been a latecomer to the CSR and sustainability movement,[29] the formulation of the carbon clauses already reflects the development described above. Thus, the requirements for carbon reductions are not written into an annex to the contract and kept in vague terms. Instead, the terms are inserted directly into the core of the contract. The commercial aspects of carbon reduction requirements have been recognised, and the formulation of the clauses clearly envisages an interaction between carbon clauses and the traditional commercial clauses of charterparties.

[23] See the classic work by PS Atiyah, *The Rise and Fall of Freedom of Contract* (Oxford, Clarendon Press, 1979) and the current assessment in H Beale (gen ed), *Chitty on Contracts* 35th edn (London, Sweet & Maxwell, 2023) para 2-003ff.

[24] See eg, V Ulfbeck and A Andhov, K Mitkidis, 'Introduction' in V Ulfbeck, A Andhov, K Mitkidis (eds), *Law and Responsible Supply Chain Management* (Abingdon, Routledge, 2019) 1, 3.

[25] On these problems in general, see ibid.

[26] On private law implications of the use of codes of contracts, see A Beckers, *Enforcing Corporate Social Responsibility Codes. On Global Self-Regulation and National Private Law* (Oxford, Hart Publishing, 2015).

[27] Proposal for a Directive of the European Parliament and of the Council on Corporate Sustainability Due Diligence and amending Directive (EU) 2019/1937, COM/2022/71 final.

[28] CSDDD proposal, Art 15.

[29] See eg J Skovgård, 'Responses to Institutional Processes: A Study of Corporate Social Responsibility in Danish Shipping Companies' in LL Froholdt (ed), *Corporate Social Responsibility in the Maritime Sector* (Cham, Springer International Publishing, 2018) 279.

ii. *Transforming the Contracts into More Collaborative Contracts?*

The above development does not mean that the introduction of carbon clauses into charterparties and other shipping contracts will not give rise to challenges. Historically, shipping contracts have been dominated by the common law tradition of formulating long contracts, spelling out the rights and duties of the parties to the contract in great detail. This tradition is mirrored in principles of interpretation, which relies on the contract wording as a starting point.[30] There is less inclination to take into consideration the context of the contract or accept implied terms of the contract.[31] In line with this, common law contract law tradition relies on the idea that the contracting parties are guardians of their own interests. As a starting point, and in contrast to the tradition in other legal systems such as Scandinavia, it is unfamiliar with the idea of a general principle of good faith obliging the parties to take into account the interests of the other party to the contract during the performance phase.[32] However, as something new to charterparties, the new carbon clauses contain good faith duties as express provisions.[33] The question is whether these duties can be confined to being applicable with regard to the specific duties they relate to according to their wording. Thus, the clauses also contain duties to collaborate and in general, it is anticipated that formal and informal collaboration will be essential in order to comply with the new requirements.[34] On this basis, it may be arguable that general good faith duties may need to be implied in the contracts more often than previously. Furthermore, it seems likely that a certain amount of 'contractual discretion' may need to be built into the contracts, for example, to determine in which situations the shipowner has the right to choose to slow steam or re-route.[35] The issue of contractual discretion has already been dealt with in a series of shipping law cases.[36] Also, contractual discretion can pave the way for implying good faith duties. Moreover, following the latest developments in UK case law, these good faith duties may take inspiration from administrative law principles[37] – principles that could be expected to prove particularly appropriate when dealing with the common interest subject matter of decarbonisation. On this basis, it does not seem unlikely that the 'decarbonising project' in the shipping sector will have effects on traditional

[30] For the common law approach, see *Lukoil Asia Pacific Pte Ltd v Ocean Tankers (Pte) Ltd (The Ocean Neptune)* [2018] EWHC 163 (Comm), [2018] 1 Lloyd's Rep 654, para 8; *Chitty on Contracts* (n 23) para 16-007.

[31] For a comparison of English law and Scandinavian law on these basic points, see A Møllmann, *Certepartifortolkning i nordisk og engelsk ret* (DJØF, 2007). For a recent English example on the implication of terms, see *Alpha Marine Corp v Minmetals Logistics Zhejiang Co Ltd (The Smart)* [2021] EWHC 1157 (Comm), [2022] 1 Lloyd's Rep 1.

[32] On good faith obligations in English contract law, see eg *Chitty on Contracts* (n 23) para 2-026ff and the references in Girvin (ch 3) section V(B)(ii). On good faith obligations in Scandinavian contract law, see eg LL Andersen and PB Madsen, *Aftaler og mellemmænd* (Stockholm, Karnov Group, 2022) 425.

[33] See the CII Operations Clause for Time Charter Parties 2022: Girvin (ch 3) section V.

[34] Collaboration is mentioned as a prerequisite in the Explanatory Notes to almost all of the new BIMCO clauses.

[35] On this, see Girvin (ch 3); Ulfbeck (ch 8).

[36] For example, *Abu Dhabi National Tanker Co v Product Star Shipping Ltd (The Product Star) (No 2)* [1993] 1 Lloyd's Rep 397 (CA), 404, dealt with the shipowner's right to choose a 'safe port' as contractual discretion.

[37] In *Braganza* it was expressed that 'the contractual implied term is drawing closer and closer to the principles applicable in judicial review': see *Braganza v BP Shipping Ltd* [2015] UKSC 17, [2015] 1 WLR 1661 [17]–[32] Lady Hale. Subsequently, this view seems to have been followed in other cases applying the administrative law principles established in *Wednesbury* to contractual discretion.

charterparties and their understanding that go beyond the insertion of specific new clauses but are rather more fundamental.

C. Interaction with Other Contracts in the Supply Chain and Broader Implications

The new carbon emission regulatory framework will directly affect the contractual relationship between shipowner and charterer, but quite clearly, it will also have implications for the bill of lading and indirectly for the entire maritime supply chain.[38] If the new frameworks are efficiently enforced, basically all the contracts in the maritime supply chain will need to be aligned with the new requirements. Most obviously, complying with the new regulatory systems may involve slow steaming and re-routing, which can cause delays throughout the chain. In addition, the ETS directly imposes costs on shipments that need to be allocated between the shipowner, the charterer, and the management companies but will, in the end, be passed on to cargo owners and buyers. The effect could be a general change of market expectations regarding how shipments can and should be carried out. This, in turn, may affect the understanding of general and open legal standards and concepts such as the concepts of 'reasonable despatch' and 'reasonable deviation'.

III. Enforcement Issues

A prerequisite for the system to work is efficient enforcement. At the moment, it is an open question how the new regulatory regimes and the contractual clauses will operate in practice. Indeed, the IMO initiatives have been criticised for 'lacking teeth'. Thus, at the moment, the only sanction for obtaining a poor CII rating is a requirement to report and explain plans for improvement.[39] Furthermore, past experience includes examples that illustrate a lack of will to enforce contractual obligations concerning external interests such as the environment.[40] On the other hand, the amended EU ETS directive provides for sanctions in the form of fines for not surrendering the required amount of allowances. It also provides the legal basis for ports to detain ships if they have surrendered the required allowances for a longer period of time.[41]

In addition to these state-based enforcement measures, it may also be considered whether market forces will drive the development. As mentioned above, today, not living up to sustainability requirements could cause reputational damage and, thereby also, commercial loss. In line with this, consumers may prefer goods that can be documented to

[38] Ulfbeck (ch 8).

[39] Girvin (ch 3).

[40] A recent example is *Begum v Maran (UK) Ltd* [2021]EWCA Civ 326, [2021] 2 Lloyd's Rep 505, concerning ship recycling, where Coulson LJ commented (at paras [68]–[69]) that '…. The problem is that, on the evidence, … the buyer, and the … seller of the vessel, knew that clauses like clause 22 would be entirely ignored …'.

[41] See the amended ETS directive at Art 11a. On the role of port states, see Battistella Marinucci (ch 9).

have been shipped in a carbon-neutral manner and 'Book and Claim' systems[42] are being developed that will enable cargo owners to prioritise carbon-free shipping of their goods. In addition, financial institutions may choose to charge a higher interest rate for granting loans to vessels that have been poorly rated.[43] Furthermore, big shipping actors that do not take the task of reducing carbon emissions seriously may risk being targeted in climate change litigation.[44] Finally, one could ask whether the potential gain of carbon reductions for all parties involved in the long run could become a driver for the development.[45]

IV. Context: Shipping Carbon for Carbon Storage

Not only must the shipping industry contribute to solving the climate crisis by reducing its own emissions, it also plays a role in the parallel strategy to decarbonise by storing carbon at sea. Specialised vessels need to be built to undertake the task of carrying carbon from land to deposits at sea. Carriage of carbon at sea raises new questions about the distribution of risks and liabilities between the shipowner and the cargo owner and of liability towards third parties.[46] Moreover, the storage of the carbon itself raises legal issues related to compliance with international conventions on the protection of the marine environment[47] and on EU regulations concerning the dumping of 'waste'.[48]

V. Overview of the Book

The book consists of four parts. Following this Introduction, Part I deals with contracts for carbon-free shipping from the international perspective and Part II deals with the same problem from the EU perspective. Part III deals with enforcement issues and Part IV deals with contracts for shipping carbon and carbon storage. An overview is provided below.

Part I: International Dimension

2. MARPOL to Contracts: Can Contract Law Support Green Shipping? (Michael Tsimplis)

The improvement in the environmental performance of ships is based on implementing new standards for new ships. This introduces delays of 10–20 years to environmental

[42] See eg www.globalmaritimeforum.org/press/major-maritime-companies-agree-to-develop-book-and-claim-approaches-in-order-to-accelerate-shippings-decarbonisation-transition and www.zerocarbonshipping.com/publications/maritime-book-claim.
[43] On the possible role of financial institutions, see Arda (ch 10).
[44] On this aspect, see Ulfbeck and Usynin (ch 11).
[45] On the potential in developing the traditional principles on general average for this purpose, see Kruit (ch 12).
[46] On these aspects, see Usynin (ch 13).
[47] On this, see Tanaka (ch 14).
[48] See Glinski (ch 15).

benefits. Several contractual clauses have been developed as supplementary methods for improving the environmental performance of ships. This chapter considers the legal character of such clauses and their capability to provide a more effective approach to assist in decarbonising shipping. The chapter also considers whether the increase in the commonality of such clauses, together with the need for sustainable development, affects the contractual matrix in a way which obligates the parties to consider the minimisation of the environmental impact of shipping operations as part of the standard of their contractual performance.

3. CII Clauses in Charterparties (Stephen Girvin)

One of several measures implemented to address Greenhouse Gases (GHG) in shipping is the Carbon Intensity Indicator (CII), a mandatory requirement in MARPOL, Art VI, Ch 4, reg 28, with effect from 1 January 2023. This chapter considers the implications of the new measure, which mandates an annual CII rating and depends upon the operation and trading of every vessel. It considers the implications for charterparties, such as time charterparties, and evaluates BIMCO's CII Operations Clause for Time Charter Parties, which was completed in November 2022, and has received much critical reaction from potential users and the CII Clause for Voyage Charterparties 2023.

4. EEXI: Navigating the New Regulation and its Implication for Time Charterparties (Malthe Hersom Kløft and Sophia Hong Van Anh Cai)

This chapter provides a short overview of the Energy Efficiency Existing Ship Index (EEXI) regulation introduced by the International Maritime Organization and what implications the EEXI regulation has for contractual obligations found under the most typically used time charterparties. On that basis, the chapter points out several irregularities resulting from the EEXI regulation. Finally, the chapter points out how the EEXI Transition Clause provided by BIMCO may counter such irregularities and what the parties should be on the lookout for.

Part II: EU Dimension

5. Mapping the EU ETS for Shipping: Functional, Geographical, and Personal Dimensions (Ellen Johanne Eftestøl)

Both climate change and international shipping are global in character and in need of global legal solutions. By tradition, these have developed through international collaboration by international institutions such as the United Nations. The EU has gradually expanded its legal activities to include international activities outside its own borders.

The exterritorial effect of EU legislation is by now an established term. With the 'Fit for 55' package, the EU aims to become a global leader in the Green Transition, and an accelerated shift to sustainable and smart mobility is taking place. For shipping, this includes an increased price on carbon fuels – among others – and an expansion of the EU ETS to national, inter-EU and international shipping. This chapter outlines the exterritorial effect of the EU ETS Directive, focusing on the political and historical development of the doctrine.

6. Shipping and the EU Emissions Trading Scheme and Maritime Transport: Its Effect on Shipping Contracts (Simon Baughen)

As part of the EU's 'Fit for 55' programme in 2021, the 2003 Emissions Trading Directive has been amended to cover international shipping on voyages into and out of ports in the Member States. This chapter describes the European Trading System (ETS) and considers the contractual implications of the system for participants in international shipping and its effect on contracts of carriage and charterparties, which involve calls to and from ports within the EU. The chapter discusses possible contractual clauses, such as BIMCO's ETSA Clause for Time Charter Parties 2022.

7. Contracts for Carbon Trading: Trading EU Allowances under the ETS (Andreas Oxholm)

From 2024, the maritime industry will be subject to the European Trading Scheme (ETS) for carbon allowances. This entails that shipowners will be required to submit carbon allowances each year based on their carbon emissions in the previous year. Carbon allowances can be acquired both through state-administered auctions as well as on the secondary market between private entities. This chapter describes and analyses the key aspects of contracts regarding the transfer of carbon allowances and the possible consequences of not adhering to the contractual obligations set out therein.

8. Carbon Clauses and Spill-over Effects on Bills of Lading and the Supply Chain (Vibe Ulfbeck)

This chapter investigates the spillover effects of the CII clauses on bills of lading and the supply chain. Whereas CII clauses may force charterers to take energy efficiency steps such as slow steaming, such choices may delay the delivery of the goods. A delay may have trickle-down effects throughout the entire supply chain. This raises the question whether such delays – that serve the purpose of compliance with international regulations – can give rise to liability under the bill of lading and in other contracts in the supply chain, disincentivising compliance with the CII system. The chapter seeks to shed light on these questions.

Part III: Enforcement Issues

9. Port State Control as a Mechanism to Ensure Compliance with Carbon Intensity Regulations (Vincenzo Battistella Marinucci)

This contribution explores the role of Port State Control in ensuring compliance with international environmental provisions concerning the Energy Efficiency Index (EEI), the Carbon Intensity Indicator (CII) and the EU ETS. The chapter analyses the amended regulation of Annex VI of the International Convention for the Prevention of Pollution from Ships (MARPOL), together with the revised Guidelines for Port State Control.

10. Environmental Targets as Mere 'Crowd-pleasers'? Enforcement of Green Targets through Ship Financing Contracts (Aslı Arda)

There are global environmental targets as well as legal tools to facilitate complying with trajectories that are designed to achieve these targets. A fundamental issue, however, is that environmental targets concerning the reduction of carbon emissions require wide collaboration. In the context of shipping, the 'rule of thumb' is that polluters must pollute less and financiers 'finance greenly'. The main difficulty, however, concerns how the rule of thumb is enforced. Environmental concerns have a contractual impact in ship finance. This chapter investigates the enforcement of environmental targets through green financing contracts. It adopts the perspective that these targets are realistic and achievable but they simply need to be internalised and commercial decisions should be taken by looking through a green lens.

11. Climate Change Litigation in the Maritime Sector as Enforcement Mechanism? (Vibe Ulfbeck and Maxim Usynin)

Strategic climate change litigation initially targeted states calling for more ambitious climate policies and regulations. However, large private companies, particularly oil companies, have recently become the target of such suits. In a recent Dutch case, an oil company has been held responsible and obliged to implement company policies to reduce carbon emissions based on tort law reasoning. This contribution asks whether the reasoning in the cases could be transferred to the maritime sector and whether large shipping companies and other maritime actors could also become the targets of such suits.

12. The future is General Average: General Average as Facilitator for Maritime Decarbonisation (Jolien Kruit)

One of the peculiarities of the maritime domain is the concept of general average, ie, a maritime burden-sharing mechanism, which provides that when actions are taken at a time of peril to safeguard the vessel and cargo, the costs thereof are to be shared by the parties interested in the properties involved in the maritime adventure. This chapter argues that suitably refurbished, general average can play an important role in maritime decarbonisation and may even energise the decarbonisation transition.

Part IV: Shipping Carbon for Carbon Storage

13. Shipping Carbon Dioxide as Dangerous Goods: Questions of Liability (Maxim Usynin)

Shipping of liquefied carbon dioxide will be central to the emerging carbon capture and storage industry. The chapter analyses its characteristics as dangerous cargo, looking at the different objects of legal protection and mapping the applicable regulatory framework. It displays the complexity of regulation, which comprises acts of different geographical scope, legal force and both public and private nature. While applied science demonstrates significant efforts in predicting the dangers of carbon dioxide shipping, the chapter advocates for appropriate legal support of the nascent industry.

14. Environmental Obligations Concerning Oceanic Carbon Capture and Storage in International Law: Toward the Long-term Sustainability of CO_2 Storage at Sea (Yoshifumi Tanaka)

Oceanic carbon dioxide (CO_2) capture and storage (CCS) is attracting growing attention as a technology for combatting climate change. However, the potential impact on the marine environment of leakage of CO_2 cannot be underestimated. An issue thus arises concerning the reconciliation of climate change mitigation and the protection of the marine environment. In considering this issue, the long-term sustainability of CO_2 storage in the oceans is key. This chapter examines the environmental obligations of international law concerning oceanic CCS with a view to securing the long-term sustainability of CO_2 storage at sea.

15. Carbon Storage and Waste Law (Carola Glinski)

This chapter analyses the relationship of carbon storage with European and international waste law and the subsequent requirements for carbon storage arising from European and international law. In principle, CO_2 to be captured and stored has to be regarded as waste according to European and international definitions. Thus, exclusion from the (general) waste law requirements in the respective regimes depends on the exceptions defined or specific requirements codified. The EU has set up a specific regime for CO_2 storage with Directive 2009/31/EC, which differs from those of Directive 1999/31/EC. However, storage in sub-seabed geological formations also has to comply with international agreements on the protection of the seas, such as the London, the OSPAR and the Helsinki Conventions, all of which prohibit the 'dumping of wastes and other matter'. The chapter considers the interplay between the EU regulation and the international agreements on the protection of the seas concerning carbon storage.

PART I

International Dimension

2

MARPOL to Contracts: Can Contract Law Support Green Shipping?

MICHAEL TSIMPLIS*

I. Introduction

Operational discharges and emissions from ships are regulated under the MARPOL Convention.[1] To put the operation of MARPOL in context, the general principle for discharges at sea, set by the London Dumping Convention 1972, must be mentioned.[2] The London Dumping Convention prohibits dumping some substances into the sea[3] and allows dumping for others with a permit from the relevant government.[4] This framework excludes operational discharges from ships.[5] MARPOL is the instrument which sets discharge standards for ships.

MARPOL consists of a main part, setting out the framework for its implementation and six Annexes, each dealing with a type of pollution, namely, oil pollution, noxious liquid substances in bulk, the carriage of hazardous and noxious cargoes in packaged form, sewage, garbage and air pollution from ships.[6] MARPOL deals with each type of pollution by implementing a combination of construction,[7] technical[8]

* Professor of Law, School of Law, City University of Hong Kong.

[1] The International Convention for the Prevention of Pollution from Ships 1973 as amended by its 1978 Protocol (MARPOL). MARPOL was not the first regulatory convention on pollution from ships. The International Convention for the Prevention of Pollution of the Sea by Oil 1954 was the first Convention.

[2] Convention on the Prevention of Marine Pollution by Dumping of Wastes etc, 1972, updated by the 1996 Protocol.

[3] ibid Art IV(I)(a) prohibits the dumping of all materials under Annex I. The complete prohibition includes oil and oily wastes and their mixtures (Annex I, s 5).

[4] ibid Art IV(I)(b)(c). Special or general permits are provided for under the Convention. The discharge of sewage sludge and incineration of other than industrial waste at sea are, under Annex I, to be dealt with through the provisions of permits where appropriate.

[5] ibid Art III(1)(b).

[6] For an analysis of the regulatory requirements by reference to environmental norms, see M Tsimplis, *Environmental Norms in Maritime Law* (Cheltenham, Edward Elgar, 2021).

[7] See n 1. See eg Annex I, reg 18 on the construction of segregated ballast tanks, regs 19 and 20 on the construction of double hull and double bottom requirements, reg 22 on the pump-room bottom protection, reg 27 on intact stability and reg 28 on subdivision and damage stability.

[8] ibid. For example, Annex I requires the installation of specific equipment for Oil discharge monitoring and control under reg 31, an oil/water interface detector under Reg 32 and a crude oil washing system under reg 33.

and operational[9] standards, and for some pollutants, by prescribing their maximum concentrations in ship discharges.[10] Compliance with MARPOL is usually confirmed through certification[11] by the flag state following appropriate surveys.[12] Enforcement is based on flag state surveys and on port state control based on confirming the existence of a certificate of compliance onboard and the inspection of that certificate.[13]

Each annex can be amended using the tacit amendment procedure.[14] An amendment to an Annex adopted by the Marine Environment Protection Committee (MEPC) becomes binding unless a state informs the IMO Secretary-General before the amendment becomes mandatory that its express approval is required before the amendment enters into force.[15] The tacit amendment procedure provides a quick and efficient way of updating the technical standards without needing an international convention and the relevant ratification complexities.[16] It does, however, exclude national legislators from the amendment process and restricts the discussion of each amendment within the relevant IMO committee dominated by shipping interests and governmental shipping and trade departments lobbied by national associations of shipowners.

The time scale for implementing an amended MARPOL standard could be a couple of years or longer from adoption.[17] Changes adopted in this way are notified and well advertised in advance. However, they can affect the trading ability of the ship because the flag state certification may not confirm compliance with the amended standards. As a result, the ship may be detained or excluded from particular trades.[18] An expected change like this cannot be considered a frustrating event, and, in any case, parties can provide in advance what should happen to the contract when such a change is expected. Contractual terms have been used to allocate the risk that the ship may not remain compliant with environmental regulations, particularly with MARPOL. Furthermore, efforts have been made to develop clauses that permit operational performance going

[9] ibid. For example, Annex I sets out the requirements for crude oil washing proceedings under reg 35, which, in essence, demands the provision of an Operations and Equipment Manual, which details the system and equipment and specifies the operational procedures. It further requires keeping an Oil Record Book (regs 17 and 36), and the development of an oil pollution contingency plan (reg 37).

[10] ibid. For example, reg 34 of Annex I permits the discharge of oily wastes from cargo tanks of tankers, provided that the ship is more than 50 nautical miles from the nearest land, the ship is en route, the discharge is less than 30 lt per nautical mile and the total discharge is less than 1/15,000 or the 1/30000 of the cargo, depending on the ship's age, and there is an oil discharge monitoring and control system in place as required by regulations 29 and 31. Different restrictions apply to Special Areas designated for each type of pollution, for example, in Annex I under Regulation.

[11] ibid. Under Annex I, this certification is the International Oil Pollution Prevention Certificate(see Annex I Regulation 7-10). The form of the certificate is provided under Annex I, Appendix II.

[12] ibid. For example, Annex I, reg 1.11.

[13] ibid Art 5 and, for Annex I, reg 11.

[14] ibid Art 16(2).

[15] ibid Art 16(2)(f)(ii).

[16] It is noteworthy that the relevant IMO Committee, the MEPC, in relation to MARPOL, can determine that an amendment has been accepted at the time of the decision or when it has been accepted by a two-thirds majority of the parties, present and voting, the combined merchant fleets of which constitute not less than 50% of the global tonnage. It follows that such amendments are controlled by flag state consent: see n 1, Art 16(2)).

[17] See n 1. The minimum required after the adoption under Art 16(2)(f)(iii) is 10 months.

[18] The sale of the ship may also be affected. See, eg, *Polestar Maritime v YHM Shipping Co Ltd (The Rewa)* [2012] EWCA Civ 153, [2012] 1 Lloyd's Rep 510.

beyond the regulatory standards and encourage environmentally better performance for shipping operations.[19]

This chapter discusses the use of contracts to ensure compliance with MARPOL and environmental regulations in general.[20] The use of contractual clauses to support compliance with environmental regulations hinges on whether a party to the contract has a financial reason to rely upon such a clause. In other words, a head of loss, entitling the innocent party to claim, must be present. Otherwise, no party will sue under the clause. A breach of a promise for compliance with environmental standards or for a better-than-the-standards environmental performance do not necessarily reflect in some financial loss for the contractual parties. This chapter discusses various ways this financial loss can be established. For example, non-compliance may lead to restrictions in the ship's operations or detention, in which case the loss of time and additional expenditure may be recoverable.[21] Economic loss may also be suffered because the non-compliant or polluting performance of one party affects the other party's environmental rating.[22] An economic loss could also be argued where the non-compliant or polluting performance of one party affects the Corporate Social Responsibility (CSR) undertakings of the other contractual party, which in turn may affect a company's value. A regulatory framework based on a market mechanism to improve environmental performance, for example, the imposition of a carbon price on ship emissions for each voyage, would also generate the economic loss required to make the plethora of contractual terms bite and ensure that contractual performance supports the environmental objectives included in the contract. Finally, the chapter argues that the direction of change in the regulatory regimes and the increase of environmental requirements in CSR could shift the standard of the reasonable person used to interpret contractual clauses towards the construction of clauses, ensuring the performance of the contractual tasks without environmental damage.

II. Decarbonisation of the Shipping Sector – The Obstacles on the Way

A relatively small number of states dominate maritime transport: most ships are built in three states[23] and recycled in four other states.[24] Ninety-five per cent of ships are owned

[19] An example is the BIMCO Sea Traffic Management (STM) Clause for Voyage Charterparties 2018, cl (g), which states: 'The Owners and Charterers shall give due consideration to environmental factors, including emission reductions, when determining the reasonableness of any orders given under this Clause'. *cf* also the BIMCO Recyclecon, where an obligation to 'recycle the vessel in a safe and environmentally sound manner' is introduced in the Preamble.

[20] See below, section II.

[21] See eg London Arb 11/23 (2023) 1139 LMLN 1, where the late redelivery of the ship led to the need to use better quality fuel as the regulatory regime changed.

[22] This could be the case where the Carbon Intensity Rating (CII) of a ship affects freight rates or, a value of it is used as providing a threshold for access to some ports. See the Guidelines adopted under Resolution MEPC 339(76).

[23] China, the Republic of Korea and Japan. These three countries account for 93% of the global number of ships built in 2022: *Review of Maritime Transport* (UNCTAD, 2023) 31.

[24] Bangladesh, India, Pakistan and Turkey. These four countries accounted for 92.7% of the recycled tonnage in 2022: ibid 37.

by 35 states. Greece, China and Japan own more than 42 per cent of the deadweight tonnage.[25] Eight ship registers each have more than five per cent of global tonnage registered under their flags, and they account collectively for around 68 per cent of the global tonnage, while 35 registers cover 93.4 per cent.[26]

The concentration of shipbuilding, ownership and registration, and the small number of ships create an expectation that guiding the shipping sector, or at least most of it, towards decarbonisation would be an easy task because there are relatively few decision-makers. Unfortunately, it has not worked like this. Instead, the shipping sector, buttressed by the procedures of its regulator, the International Maritime Organization (IMO), or, more correctly, the shipping industry expressed directly and through state representation, the ship registers, has successfully resisted change for the past three decades.[27] Shipowners have aimed to keep the operating costs for shipping low and to keep the value of older ships high. More expensive fuels, reduced operational freedoms, the reduction in profits from demurrage, and the need to retrofit increase operating costs. At the same time, new technology and requirements for more efficient ship performance undermine the resale price of existing ships.

Figure 1 The evolution of global atmospheric temperature anomalies. The reference period is 1900–2000. The values were obtained from NOAA.

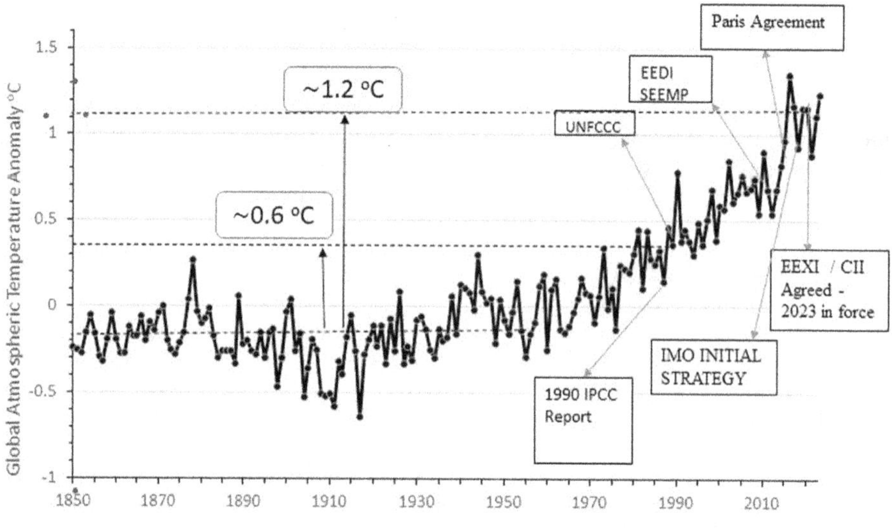

The policy developments are marked on the temperature curve in Figure 1. In 1990 the first Intergovernmental Panel of Climate Change Report was published, and the United Nations Framework Agreement on Climate Change was agreed two years later. At that

[25] ibid 34. Ships of 1000 grt or larger are counted in the ownership statistics. A total of about 56,591 ships are in this category. For comparison, Hong Kong alone has more than 900,000 cars.

[26] Panama, Liberia, Marshall Islands, Bahamas, Malta, Hong Kong (SAR), Singapore, China: ibid 35.

[27] See Figure 1.

point, the global atmospheric temperature increase was, by reference to the lower dashed line, about 0.6 °C. Shipping avoided the first effort for quantifiable emission reductions introduced by the Kyoto Protocol as this passed responsibility for emissions reduction for shipping to developed states through the IMO.[28] Emission reductions from shipping were also omitted from the 2015 Paris Agreement, even though little was done by the shipping sector under the Kyoto Protocol.

The first reaction to the Climate Change challenge by the international community at the IMO was in 2013 with the adoption of the EEDI (Energy Efficiency Design Index), which applied only to new ships, and with the development of the SEEMP (Ship Energy Efficiency Management Plan), which, in principle, required an examination of energy efficiency on ships but had little enforcement consequences. After the 2015 Paris Agreement and despite the omission of shipping emissions from the negotiations, in 2018, the initial IMO strategy was agreed. Within this, the Energy Efficiency Index for Existing Ships (EEXI) was agreed upon. This is designed to sanction the median operation of each group of ships irrespective of their emissions. Together with the EEXI, the Carbon Intensity Index was agreed upon. Both the EEXI and the CII apply to existing ships. Due to the way they are designed, they are predicted to contribute to a reduction of emission of about 1.5–2 per cent for existing ships through energy efficiency, although if the number of merchant ships or their fuel consumption increases, these may be reversed. A market-based mechanism was expected to be agreed upon in 2023, but its adoption has been pushed back once again.[29] The EU-ETS system will start operation in 2024 on ship emissions, and it is currently the only potentially efficient mechanism which can encourage significant ship decarbonisation.

At the time of the agreement on the IMO initial strategy, the global temperature increase was double the increase identified in 1992 (Figure 1). The time it took for the IMO to develop an initial strategy since the UNFCC agreement was 26 years. A generation of ships was allowed to operate as if nothing had been happening. The failure to adopt a market-based mechanism in the revised IMO Strategy adopted in July 2023 extends this period further for the sake of the invested capital in shipping. Because of the lack of efficient shipping policies during the past three decades, ships continued to emit greenhouse gases, undisturbed and indifferent to efforts to reduce emissions. Ship engine technology has not improved, and, as a result, it is unlikely that the IMO's strategy will be able to contribute to global efforts to control the greenhouse gas concentrations in the atmosphere.

Two statements can highlight the fundamentally institutional character of the resistance to reducing shipping emissions. The first is the Marshall Islands' characterisation of the IMO Secretary-General's views expressed in 2015 as 'a danger to the planet'.[30] The second statement made by the shipping industry states that '... the commercial

[28] See Art 2(2) of the Kyoto Protocol to the United Nations Framework Convention on Climate Change, 11 December 1997 entry into force, 16 February 2005.

[29] See Resolution MEPC 377(80): wwwcdn.imo.org/localresources/en/MediaCentre/PressBriefings/Documents/Resolution%20MEPC.377%2880%29.pdf.

[30] See the statement by RMI's Foreign Affairs Minister, Tony de Brum: 'His call is not just a danger to the planet, but as the research points out, also to the shipping industry's future prosperity, and therefore the future stability of world trade'. See www.offshore-energy.biz/marshall-islands-sekimizus-view-on-co2-emissions-danger-to-the-planet.

development of relevant technologies, fuels, propulsion systems and related infrastructure are the responsibility of other out-of-sector stakeholders rather than shipowners'.[31]

The first statement indicates dramatically that in 2015, the IMO, the UN body established to harmonise international shipping, had become isolated from, perhaps, the most critical global environmental challenge. Just before the negotiations leading to the Paris Agreement, the IMO Secretary-General called for shipping not to be included as the industry was already overregulated. The distancing statement by the Marshall Islands, a low-lying island facing extinction by sea level rise caused by climate change and one of the largest ship registers,[32] demonstrated that something was seriously wrong with the IMO's approach to the issue of climate change. The second statement suggests where the problem is. Shipowners do not wish to compete with each other on environmental standards because this will endanger their investment in existing, polluting ships. Since old technology is cheaper and old ships make the sector easier to enter, the association of national shipowner associations, the International Chamber of Shipping, protects the interests of existing shipowners by claiming that it is for other sectors and the taxpayers of the various states to invest and develop the technologies required for decarbonisation and then make them available as off-the-shelf solutions to shipowners. The disengagement with the global process is again evident.

This reactive approach results from the established process for regulating ships through a prescriptive, command-and-control regime, which, through certification of compliance, has removed from the sector innovation and competition with respect to environmental performance. Why should a shipping company invest in an environmentally better-performing ship if this involves costs which do not reflect in a profit or in better trading options? Unless and until the IMO changes its regulatory approach, there is no pressure for the shipping sector to effect change.[33] Decision-making in the IMO is dominated by existing shipowners, their associations, the shipowner-formed mutual-insurance associations, the P&I Clubs, and the technical experts in shipping, the classification societies. The regulatory approach concerns the emissions of each ship, not the emissions of the fleet or the national register. As a result, decision-making at the IMO is focused not on the level of reduction required to reduce greenhouse gas concentrations in the atmosphere and how the shipping sector can contribute. Instead, the IMO focuses on what the shipping sector can accept without reducing each ship's commercial and resale value.[34] This approach, probably appropriate from the financial point of view, shows the limitations of the IMO's governance when considering a multi-sectoral global crisis such as the concentration of greenhouse gases in the atmosphere. Each sector blames the other for the problem, requiring the other industries or governments to act and resist change to maximise the value of their existing investment.

[31] ISWG-GHG 10/5/2 3 September 2021, submitted by the International Chamber of Shipping and Intertanko.

[32] Above n 8.

[33] The way competition works in shipping even before international regulation was demonstrated in S Plimsoll, *Our Seamen: An appeal* (London, Virtue & Co, 1873) 38–39. Plimsoll's argument was that even if some shipowners did not wish to overload their ships and risk the loss of the ship with the crew, they were forced to do it or be thrown out of the market by the lower freight rates offered by competitors who chose to overload their ships. This created the need for international standardisation.

[34] See Tsimplis (n 6).

The weaknesses of this approach are evident in the adoption of the Energy Efficiency Existing Ship Index (EEXI)[35] and the Carbon Intensity Indicator (CII). The EEXI and the CII are the short-term measures adopted under the IMO's initial strategy. Both are presented as leading to improved environmental performance. However, their effect is expected to be very small, less than a two per cent reduction of emission of existing ships, which an increase in the number or the size of the ships trading may quickly reverse. Both these measures are inefficient because of how they are defined.[36] The performance indicators do not refer to an absolute standard of emissions because such a choice would have made the fastest and most polluting ships, the container ships, environmentally inefficient. Instead, the standards operate according to each ship category and, in some cases, within each category for each engine type. This means that the standard performance for a container ship is decided separately from that of a tanker. In addition, the normal performance of container ships using engine type A will be different from container ships using engine type B. The starting point is the median performance of each group or sub-group of ships. Starting from the median performer means that this is achieved already by half of the ships in that group or sub-group. At least half of the ships are not incentivised to improve, and only those seriously underperforming may have to adjust their performance. Thus, the median emissions rate is, at the beginning, legitimised, certainly not a pathway to decarbonisation. It is not surprising that this approach is inefficient, and the question that arises is whether the environmental benefit of implementing them is worth the costs involved in their implementation.

The implementation of the agreed measures can, however, affect the contractual performance of charterparties and any requirements concerning corporate responsibility[37] imposed on various stakeholders engaged in international trading and competing in international markets as promoters of green and sustainable development. The contractual performance aspects include, first, the promise that the ship will remain compliant so as to be allowed to trade. Second, any changes in the operational performance of the ship necessitated for the purpose of compliance should not be contradictory to other contractual undertakings. For example, slowing down the ship to reduce GHG emissions should not be in breach of a duty of due dispatch or an agreement speed performance.[38]

The issue of CSR, or environmental social governance (ESG) may affect the competition between shipping companies and the pricing of their services by reference to the adopted, by each company, emission or environmental standards. Transporting goods

[35] Resolution MEPC.334(76), adopted 17 June 2021. See respectively Kløft and Cai (ch 4); Girvin (ch 3).

[36] It has been noted that because ships already operate at speeds and engine loads that are unaffected by the technical efficiency targets set by EEXI, small reductions are likely to be achieved. See D Rutherford, X Mao and B Comer, 'Potential CO_2 reductions under the Energy Efficiency Existing Ship Index', Working paper 2020–27 (International Council on Clean Transportation, October 2020). It should also be noted that increased efficiency does not mean a reduction of emissions from shipping. If, in addition to efficiency standards, the total emissions were capped, improved energy efficiency would reward the shipowners achieving it by enabling them to perform more voyages.

[37] CSR is a broad concept normally referring to the voluntary assumption of responsibility by corporate entities with respect to the well-being of the various stakeholders, including the environment. For shipping, such duties can be found in the International Safety Management Code (ISM Code): see, eg, Tsimplis (n 6) 234. The legal component of CSR is evident in national company laws: see Anna Beckers, *Enforcing Corporate Social Responsibility Codes* (Oxford, Hart Publishing, 2015).

[38] The BIMCO clause aiming at resolving such an issue is discussed in Girvin (ch 3) section II(B).

in ships promising to minimise their environmental footprint and operating with lower or zero emissions may prove attractive to shippers using environmental friendliness as part of their brand. This way, and with the increased pressures for decarbonisation, a progressively clearer distinction between sustainable and unsustainable ships and practices is to be expected, with users and perhaps states having to explain any choice for selecting cost over pollution reduction when they use a ship. If such a differentiation becomes commercially important, investors and banks[39] may support the development of green ships and practices more efficiently and this process may overcome the slow and ineffective developments within the IMO. Though these processes have become more relevant as the need for decarbonisation has become more pressing, contractual arrangements to avoid the commercial consequences of non-compliance and changing regulatory standards have existed for several decades concerning other environmental requirements, in particular, the IMO standards for environmental performance included in MARPOL.[40]

III. Contractual Relationships and MARPOL

Each annex of MARPOL imposes direct obligations to prevent pollution from regulated substances but does not interfere with shipping contracts.[41] However, by requiring specific construction characteristics to be implemented, such as the requirement of a double bottom for oil tankers,[42] the installation of an oily water separator,[43] or the use of fuel with maximum sulphur concentrations,[44] MARPOL introduces significant changes in the operational characteristics of the ship. This affects charterers and other parties in the global transportation chain which have, voluntarily or involuntarily, an obligation to use compliant ships for their business.

[39] A private initiative with such aims is The Poseidon Principles: www.poseidonprinciples.org/finance/#home. See Arda (ch 10) section III(A).

[40] This was sometimes achieved indirectly, as, for example, in *Silverburn Shipping (IOM) Ltd v Ark Shipping Co LLC (The Arctic)* [2019] EWCA Civ 1161, [2019] 2 Lloyd's Rep 603, where a bareboat charterparty included a requirement that the ships will be '... with other required certificates in force at all times ...'. See also *The Rewa* (n 18) involving a contract for the sale of a ship under an amended Norwegian Saleform 1993. In other cases, express reference to MARPOL was made in the charterparty: see *Golden Fleece Maritime Inc v ST Shipping & Transport Inc (The Elli & The Frixos)* [2008] EWCA Civ 584, [2008] 2 Lloyd's Rep 119. BIMCO has developed ten clauses providing for compliance with various Annexes of MARPOL to enable compliance with MARPOL and avoid contractual disputes. In addition, several charterparties impose a general obligation of compliance with MARPOL and its amendments (for example, cl 40 of Shellvoy 6).

[41] By contrast, the 1989 Salvage Convention imposes environmental duties under Art 8 that cannot be undermined by contract. Art 32 of the Rotterdam Rules obliges the shipper to seek authorisation from the carrier before loading environmentally dangerous goods and permit the carrier or a performing party, to decline to receive or to load goods which may be so dangerous. Second, where there is cargo damage or delay caused or contributed by 'reasonable measures to avoid or attempt to avoid damage to the environment', the liability of the carrier and the performing parties is exempted. Thus, in such a case, the need for environmental protection norms overrides the commercial concerns of the cargo interests, despite the fact that the environmental risks are created by an external to the contract of carriage: see Tsimplis (n 6).

[42] See n 1, Annex 1, reg 19.

[43] ibid Annex I, reg 14.

[44] ibid Annex VI, reg 14.

A. Compliance with MARPOL and Contractual Terms

Shipping contracts may be illegal if environmental regulations are violated.[45] For example, where a ship containing hazardous materials is destined for scrapping, exporting it from a developed state to a developing state for recycling can violate the 1989 Basel Convention as amended by the 1995 Ban Protocol, thus making the contract illegal.

Non-compliance with the MARPOL Convention is not, in general, of a character that threatens the contract's enforceability. This is because, usually, non-compliance is difficult to detect as checking the certification is the first approach to port state control. Also, even where non-compliance is detected and the ship is detained until the deficiency is remedied, an appropriate off-hire clause in charterparties and an exception in laytime and demurrage for voyage charterparties[46] can resolve the issues. Violations of MARPOL regarding illegal discharges are also dealt with in the least interventionist way, by a fine, save where significant pollution damage is caused in the coastal state's territorial sea.[47] The coastal state is obliged to undertake the investigation swiftly so as not to affect the operation of the ship. Again, such delays can be dealt with by inserting appropriate exceptions.[48] Only where the MARPOL or other violations threaten damage to the environment is there an obligation on the coastal state to detain the vessel and, if this is practicable, to only allow it to go to the nearest repair yard.[49]

B. The Need for Contracts

Risks arising from general violations of MARPOL, whether or not remediable, are not the concern of the ship's users. Of greater concern are changes introduced via the tacit amendment procedure,[50] which may require expensive amendments or retrofits of the ship and result in substantial disruption to the service it provides. In some cases, the ship may be excluded from trading in particular areas.[51] Particular charterparty clauses

[45] This could be because the cargo carried is unlawful or the action of the shipowner is in direct violation of the way a state expects the shipowner to deal with the ship. The Convention on International Trade in Endangered Species of Wild Fauna and Flora 1973 may be the former case, while a ship sent to a scrapyard in violation of the 1989 Basel Convention and its 1995 Ban Protocol is an example of the latter case. See D Wall and M Tsimplis, 'Selling Ships for Scrap' [2004] *LMCLQ* 254 and Tsimplis (n 6) 221 for discussion.

[46] See eg *Golden Fleece Maritime Inc v ST Shipping and Transport Inc (The Elli & The Frixos)* [2008] EWCA Civ 584, [2008] 2 Lloyd's Rep 119.

[47] The EU has also imposed criminal liability under Directive 2005/35/EC. However, the available information on the implementation of the EU rules indicates that very few prosecutions take place every year: see SWD(2023) 159 Final Commission Staff Working Document Impact Assessment Report, Accompanying the document Proposal for a Directive of the European Parliament and of the Council, amending Directive 2005/35/EC on ship-source pollution and on the introduction of penalties, including criminal penalties, for pollution offences.

[48] Where compliance with MARPOL is contractually agreed breach of such a clause will lead to a breach by the owner (eg, cl 40 of Shellvoy 6). Other charterparties agree on half demurrage for 'arrest or restraint of princes, rulers or people': see, eg, Tankervoy 87, cl 10; BPVOY 4, cl 17.

[49] UNCLOS, Art 219.

[50] See n 1, Art 16(2).

[51] This, for example, could be the case where a MARPOL special area, under Annex I, II, IV and V or a new Emissions Control Area is designated, and the ship is unable to deal with the stricter standards: see www.imo.org/en/OurWork/Environment/Pages/Special-Areas-Marpol.aspx for the existing areas.

may entitle the charterer to claim damages and if classified as conditions or innominate terms, depending on the wording, may lead to the termination of the charterparty.[52] Such clauses provide a commercial incentive to the shipowner to perform in accordance with the applicable regulations. Contractual terms have also been used as the basis of the early implementation of international agreements.[53]

C. Contracts for Greenhouse Gas Emissions

Greenhouse gas emissions pose more complex problems. An easy way of reducing emissions is slowing down so that the ship attains maximum carbon efficiency.[54] In a voyage charterparty, this could result in reduced demurrage and the general loss of time if the port accepts ships on a first come, first served basis. As is noted elsewhere in this book, speed reduction usually means reducing bunker costs and will benefit either the shipowner or the charterer, depending on who is responsible for these obligations. Thus, there are incentives and disincentives for altering operational behaviour to reduce greenhouse emissions. Several contractual terms were developed to address slow steaming well before the EEXI and CII standards were agreed.

An example is the New York Produce Exchange (NYPE) 2015 charterparty,[55] which includes several requirements for complying with the IMO regulations concerning bunkers,[56] their sulphur content in the various areas of trading,[57] the use of non-polluting cleaning substances for the ship's holds,[58] options for slow and ultraslow steaming subject to the master's duty to the marine environment,[59] and a due diligence obligation on the shipowner to minimise fuel consumption, provided this is consistent with the safety of the ship, the crew, and protection of the marine environment.[60] Thus, the NYPE 2015 form reinforces environmental performance, as contractual performance, irrespective of whether these are statutorily compulsory. Thus, the developers of standard forms give increasing consideration to environmental performance. Standard

[52] See *Silverburn Shipping (IOM) Ltd v Ark Shipping Co LLC (The Arctic)* [2019] EWCA Civ 1161, [2019] 2 Lloyd's Rep 603 and *BS & N Ltd (BVI) v Micadao Shipping Ltd (Malta) (The Seaflower)* [2001] 1 Lloyd's Rep 341 (CA). The first concerns classification in a bareboat charter and the latter an oil Major's Approval clause in a time charterparty.

[53] The development of compensation regimes operating as agreements between carriers and traders of oil by sea through the TOVALOP (Tanker Owners Voluntary Agreement concerning Liability for Oil Pollution) and CRISTAL (Contract Regarding an Interim Supplement to Tanker Liability for Oil Pollution) in 1969 and 1971 provide the undertaking of strict liability arrangements which then became international law under the 1969 CLC and the 1971 IOPCF Conventions. See LG Cohen, 'Revisions of TOVALOP and CRISTAL: Strong Ships for Stormy Seas' (1987) 18 *JMLC* 525. These were not supported after February 1997. A second example is the partial contractual incorporation of the 1989 Salvage Convention in Lloyd's Open Form (LOF 2020). The Recyclecon form also purports to aim in an early implementation to incorporate aspects of the Ship Recycling Convention.

[54] See Girvin (ch 3); Ulfbeck (ch 8) section III(B)(iv).

[55] T Coghlin et al, *Time Charters*, 7th edn (London, Informa, 2014) preface.

[56] ibid cl 9(b).

[57] ibid cl 9(f).

[58] ibid cl 10(b).

[59] ibid cl 38(a).

[60] ibid cl 38(b).

clauses available provide compliance with the maximum sulphur content to bunkers,[61] may allow slow steaming,[62] and develop the concept of virtual and just-in-time arrival[63] to balance the financial consequences of slow steaming.

Following the adoption of the EEXI and the CII, each of which concerns improvements in energy efficiency that can be achieved by changing the operational behaviour of ships, several clauses were developed to facilitate the ship's compliance with the new standards.[64] Their major characteristic is that they facilitate the shipowner's business by allowing performance, which without the clause would have been a shipowner's breach of the charterparty.

D. Clauses Requiring Environmental Awareness in General

In addition to the clauses aimed at making the MARPOL provisions as painless as possible for shipowners, other pre-existing clauses reference environmental performance in more general terms. The BIMCO Sea Traffic Management clause[65] was designed to enable ships to participate in the Sea Traffic Management System, which aims to improve energy efficiency by developing just-in-time arrival. It includes the following clause under subsection (g): 'The Owners and Charterers shall give due consideration to environmental factors, including emission reductions when determining the reasonableness of any orders given under this Clause'. This clause broadens reasonableness to include environmental considerations, including emissions reductions. However, the scope of the clause is arguably broader because other environmental concerns, for example, a speed limit to avoid a collision with a sea mammal, would, arguably, fall under it.

E. Do Such Clauses Work?

Enforcing or broadening the environmental framework through shipping contracts does not necessarily mean that contractual performance is less damaging in environmental terms. It is not known whether the clauses discussed here have been inserted into the various maritime contracts and, if inserted, relied upon. There are very few cases concerning contractual obligations relating to MARPOL.[66]

[61] In particular, the Fuel Testing Programme Clause 2011, Bunkering Operations and Sampling Clause 2011, and Marine Fuel Sulphur Content Clause for Time Charterparties 2020.

[62] Slow Steaming Clause for Time Charter Parties 2011; Slow Steaming Clause for Voyage Charter Parties 2012.

[63] See eg the Virtual Arrival Clause for Voyage Charter Parties 2013 and the Sea Traffic Management (STM) Clause for Voyage Charter Parties.

[64] Examples include the EEXI Transition Cause For Time Charter Parties 2021, the ETS Emission Trading Scheme Allowances Clause for Time Charter Parties 2022, and the CII Operations Clause For Time Charter Parties 2022. See Girvin (ch 3) section V; Kløft and Tai (ch 4) section VII(A); Eftestøl (ch 5) section IV(C). These clauses already pose difficulties in the negotiations as shown in *Southeaster Maritime Ltd v Trafigura Maritime Logistics Pte Ltd (The Aquafreedom)* [2024] EWHC 255 (Comm).

[65] See also the Slow Steaming Clause for Time Charter Parties 2011, the Slow Steaming Clause for Voyage Charter Parties 2012, Virtual Arrival Clause for Voyage Charter Parties 2013, and the Just in Time Arrival Clause for Voyage Charter Parties 2021.

[66] See above (n 52).

In one recent case, however, the court commented on such a clause. In *Begum v Maran (UK) Ltd*,[67] an intermediary company *(Maran)* arranged to sell a ship destined for demolition to a cash buyer under a Memorandum of Agreement (MOA). The MOA included cl 22, obliging the buyer to sell the ship to a yard that would demolish the ship 'in accordance with good health and safety working practices'. The cash buyer sold the ship to a scrap yard in Bangladesh instead. During the demolition, a worker was killed, and his widow brought a claim in tort against Maran. Maran applied to the court to dismiss the claim. The Court of Appeal dismissed Maran's application. What is of interest here is Coulson LJ's comment on the contractual requirement in the MOA:[68]

> The evidence was that clauses like clause 22 were standard, so ensuring that they had real force might perhaps become standard too. The problem is that, on the evidence, both Hsejar, the buyer, and the Appellant, the seller of the vessel, knew that clauses like clause 22 would be entirely ignored. That appears to be part of the unhappy reality of the shipbreaking business: everyone turns a blind eye to what they know will actually happen. A seller in the position of the Appellant would have no interest in ensuring the performance of clause 22 as it stands, and a buyer in the position of Hsejar could therefore be in breach of that provision without any sanction. Even if it was in breach of clause 22, it would argue that the seller had suffered no loss as a result. However, if the payment arrangements had been different, then both buyer and seller would have had a very real interest in ensuring that provisions like clause 22 were more than words on a piece of paper.

This statement identifies well the crux of the matter. These types of clauses are only effective where there is a real interest and, correspondingly, an economic loss under the contract, which can work as an incentive. Thus, the question becomes how the contractual process can be supported by regulatory requirements to develop the relevant contractual losses or benefits which will make such clauses efficient.

IV. Developing a Contractual Interest in Decarbonisation

A party to a contract will enforce a promise where a financial incentive is in place. Thus, it is important that either the regulatory process or the market generates such a financial incentive. Otherwise, contractual clauses promising the facilitation of environmental performance are likely to be nothing more than words on a piece of paper. The development of such a financial incentive can be achieved in a variety of ways.

A. The Taxation of CO_2 Emissions and Unsustainable Performance

Taxing greenhouse gas emissions, for example, creates a direct financial loss when the ship operates by emitting more than it could. Similarly, surrendering emission

[67] [2021]EWCA Civ 326, [2021] 2 Lloyd's Rep 505.
[68] ibid paras [68]–[69].

allowances under an Emissions Trading System could also result in a financial loss for the party obliged to surrender the allowance,[69] if the ship exceeds the allowed emissions. Either way, the required contractual incentive would be generated. Pricing of the carbon emitted would also increase the demand for more efficient shipping operations as this way, the cost for the party paying the carbon price will be reduced. This will also benefit every other stakeholder because the party burdened with the payment would otherwise try to pass part of the cost to others. For an ETS system to operate efficiently, it must cover all voyages during a period of time. If emission efficiencies can be achieved by keeping the ship inactive and afterwards operating it at the usual polluting standards, the measure cannot be considered efficient. This follows because the cargo the ship would have carried during the inactive period would have to be carried by another ship. Thus, emissions overall are not affected, only particular emissions by the particular ship.

The IMO has been considering market-based measures for more than a decade.[70] Several new proposals are being discussed as part of the intermediate measures for the IMO's strategy. For example, in 2021, the ICS proposed a global levy for each ton of CO_2 emitted, with the money collected used to upgrade port infrastructure to provide alternative fuels. The uniform levy does not have the market variations of the EU Emissions Trading System (ETS), which is why shipowners prefer it: it can be predicted and included in the price. The efficiency of such a levy or any market-based measure would depend on the price it will have to motivate shipowners to invest in new fuels and technologies and explore more efficient operational arrangements. These arrangements do not necessarily create a contractual incentive unless contractually distributed between shipowners and charterers. For example, the BIMCO ETS Emission Trading Scheme Allowances (ETSA) Clause for Time Charter Parties 2022[71] transfers all the emission allowance obligations to time charterers but does not impose any obligation on the parties to improve the ship's environmental performance. Thus, it is unlikely to be able to create the required contractual incentive by itself although, assuming that the carbon price is high enough and the total allowances are effectively reduced year-on-year, there could be an effect in the long term.

[69] Under the consolidated version of the EU ETS Directive 2003/87/EC of the European Parliament and of the Council of 13 October 2003 establishing a system for greenhouse gas emission allowance trading within the Union and amending Council Directive 96/61/EC which has been extended to cover shipping form 2024 under Directive (EU) 2023/959 of 10 May 2023 amending Directive 2003/87/EC establishing a system for greenhouse gas emission allowance trading within the Union and Decision (EU) 2015/1814 concerning the establishment and operation of a market stability reserve for the Union greenhouse gas emission trading system, the party responsible for surrendering the allowances is the 'shipping company' defined as … 'the shipowner or any other organisation or person, such as the manager or the bareboat charterer, that has assumed the responsibility for the operation of the ship from the shipowner and that, on assuming such responsibility, has agreed to take over all the duties and responsibilities imposed by the International Management Code for the Safe Operation of Ships and for Pollution Prevention' (Art 3(w)).

[70] For an IMO summary, see www.imo.org/en/OurWork/Environment/Pages/Market-Based-Measures.aspx#:~:text=MBMs%20place%20a%20price%20on,in%2Dsector%20reductions%26%3B%20and.

[71] Emission Trading Scheme Allowances Clause for Time Charter Parties 2022, www.bimco.org/contracts-and-clauses/bimco-clauses/current/etsa_clause.

B. CSR and Environmental Social Governance (ESG)

The financial incentive for parties to a shipping contract may also be present where one party to the contract suffers a detrimental reputational and financial loss because of the other party's polluting behaviour. This can be argued on the assumption that the way a shipowner, a shipper or a logistics company conduct their business can affect their ability to market their services as ethical or environmentally friendly, thus achieving higher market prices or better access to markets demanding higher environmental standards.

i. What are CSR and ESG?

The social responsibility system adopted by each company is referred to as Corporate Social Responsibility,[72] while the impact on stakeholders is called Environmental Social Governance.

The context of such obligations can be legally imposed[73] but can also refer to voluntary assumption of responsibility. The simplest form of obligations concerns reporting on the social and environmental impacts of the company's activities and includes undertakings for compliance with relevant legislation.

ii. Social Responsibility and Profit

Socially responsible companies are thought to be in a better position to grow in terms of reputation and revenues. A negative relationship between CSR and profit identified in some studies has been attributed to other factors.[74] Shipping companies have not been particularly engaged with CSR.[75] The barriers identified include the lack of resources, the lack of strategic vision, high regulatory standards, and unwillingness to pay for CSR.[76]

[72] In COM(2011) 681 final, The European Commission defines Corporate Social Responsibility as 'the responsibility of enterprises for their impacts on society'. It further states: 'Respect for applicable legislation, and for collective agreements between social partners, is a prerequisite for meeting that responsibility. To fully meet their corporate social responsibility, enterprises should have in place a process to integrate social, environmental, ethical, human rights and consumer concerns into their business operations and core strategy in close collaboration with their stakeholders, with the aim of: – maximising the creation of shared value for their owners/shareholders and for their other stakeholders and society at large; – identifying, preventing and mitigating their possible adverse impacts.'

[73] The legal component of CSR is prescribed in national company laws. In the UK, for example, company directors must, among other things, have regard to the impact the company has on the environment: see Companies Act 2006, s 172(1)(d). The directors' report must include environmental matters reported against key performance indicators: Companies Act 2006, s 417(5) and s 417(6). *cf* also G Wang, KX Li and Y Xiao, 'Measuring Marine Environmental Efficiency of a Cruise Shipping Company Considering Corporate Social Responsibility' (2019) 99 *Marine Policy* 140 who compare CSR on the basis of compliance with regulations.

[74] W Drobetz et al, 'Corporate Social Responsibility Disclosure: The Case of International Shipping' (2014) 71 *Transportation Research Part E: Logistics and Transportation Review* 18.

[75] I Fafaliou, M Lekakou, and I Theotokas, 'Is the European Shipping Industry Aware of Corporate Social Responsibility? The Case of the Greek-owned Short Sea Shipping Companies' (2006) 30 *Marine Policy* 412; T Pawlik, P Gaffron and PA Drewes, 'Corporate Social Responsibility in Maritime Logistics' in D-W Song and PM Panayides (eds), *Maritime Logistics: Contemporary Issues* (Bingley, Emerald Group Publishing Ltd, 2012) 205–226.

[76] KF Yuen and JM Lim, 'Barriers to the Implementation of Strategic Corporate Social Responsibility in Shipping' (2016) 32 *The Asian J of Shipping and Logistics* 49.

The same study argues that because the IMO regulations adequately address environmental and safety standards, which are frequently updated, there is no benefit for shipping companies in exceeding the relevant standards by developing CSR.[77] The analysis of MARPOL indicates that the lack of an incentive arises from the uniformity of the minimum standards and not from their adequacy.[78]

There are, however, suggestions that stakeholder pressure can force the shipping industry into developing better CSR.[79] Indeed, parts of the shipping industry appear willing to move beyond the regulatory standards to improve their image[80] and the company's balance sheet.[81] By improving CSR these companies aim to become preferred carriers for products claiming minimum environmental impact and shippers claiming the use of green transport services.

A company which uses CSR or ESG as part of its market positioning if it is proven not to comply with its promises may, theoretically, suffer market losses in the sense of the company's price, the markets it can access and the price for its services. Where the inconsistency between the CSR undertakings and the environmental performance standards is caused by the breach of performance standards contained in a shipping contract then a claim against the other party may be possible, although quantifying the damage may prove challenging. This is because, causation of the loss suffered may be difficult to substantiate in the volatile shipping market.

C. Does the Reasonable Person Support Decarbonisation?

Perhaps the most radical argument is that the 'reasonable person',[82] the standard underpinning contractual construction,[83] includes environmental standards. The reasonable person's expectation arguably is that contractual performance would not lead to the violation of legal requirements. A more challenging proposition is that the construction of a contractual clause which leads to reduced environmental impact would be supported by the reasonable person test.

[77] ibid.

[78] ibid. The economic costs appear to be the major barrier across industries: see R Saha, RC Shashi, R Singh and R Dahiya, 'Effect of Ethical Leadership and Corporate Social Responsibility on Firm Performance: A Systematic Review' (2020) 27 *Corp Social Responsibility and Env'l Mgt* 409. The transport sector has been identified where the primary concern for shippers is transport cost, and this leads to low willingness to pay for CSR.

[79] T Parviainen, A Lehikoinen and S Kuikka, 'How can Stakeholders Promote Environmental and Social Responsibility in the Shipping Industry?' (2018) 17 *WMU J Marit Affairs* 49.

[80] See eg the EU Eco-Management and Audit Scheme (EMAS) originally based on Council Regulation (EEC) No 1836/93 of 29 June 1993 allowing voluntary participation by companies in the industrial sector in a Community eco-management and audit scheme. A survey on the image of shipping companies by H Jang, H Park, SY Kim and P Piboonrungroj, 'Corporate Image and Reputation in the Shipping Industry in Four Asian Countries: Republic of Korea, China, Japan, and Thailand' (2019) 8 *Int'l J of Supply Chain Mgt* 1065, 1070, found that 'shipping companies are environmentally responsible' was not within the top three attributes of the shipping industry in any of these countries.

[81] See the discussion of the relationship between CSR and economic and operational performance in Drobetz et al (n 74).

[82] In contract law, the test of the reasonable person represents the legal and commercial externalities to the agreement: see LA Di Matteo, 'Counterpoise of Contracts: The Reasonable Person Standard and the Subjectivity of Judgment' (1997) 48 *South Carolina LR* 293.

[83] J Gardner, 'The Many Faces of the Reasonable Person' (2015) 131 *LQR* 563.

To support this assertion, reliance can be placed on analyses suggesting that the reasonable person should be defined by normative standards rather than empirically observed practice and perception.[84] Such standards evolve with time, and thus, the reasonable person's views may evolve accordingly. Such an interpretation is also indirectly supported by the view that the reasonable person's expectation is only an excuse for judicial discretion.[85] Whatever the correct justification for the use of the reasonable person in contract law is, it is submitted that it would be increasingly difficult to argue that the reasonable person may ignore greenhouse gas emissions when interpreting a contract, provided, of course, that there is an ambiguity which can be resolved by alternatives with different GHG emissions outcomes. Where the contracting parties have adopted sustainability targets or given pledges for reducing greenhouse gas emissions, it may be easier to establish that performance inconsistent with such pledges damages the other party. Thus, remedies may be granted.

The problem that such an argument faces is that contractual construction has not considered the risks for third parties or society in general as a parameter necessary for the interpretation of a contract,[86] except where the contract violates a particular law or where express environmental obligations are imposed by statute.[87]

An example of how contract law usually focuses on the contract as a pure arrangement for the contracting parties without consideration for third parties and externalities can be given in relation to the safe port warranty in voyage charterparties. It is evident to any observer that instructing a ship to enter an unsafe port may damage the ship and possibly also cause loss of life and pollution. However, the contractual construction by English Courts does not accept an implied obligation of safety because it is easy for the parties to contract expressly as to the safety of the port.[88] This suggests that it is for the contract to allocate liability but not to pursue public policy objectives. Thus, English contract law does not involve considerations of public policy or public good in determining the intention of the parties. Instead, it considers only the allocation of risks of damage to third parties and the environment.[89]

[84] AD Miller and R Perry, 'The Reasonable Person' (2012) 87 *New York University LR* 323.

[85] See the review on the reasonable person in non-contractual contexts in M Moran, 'The Reasonable Person: Conceptual Biography in Comparative Perspective' (2010) 14 *Lewis & Clark LR* 1233.

[86] In *Sembcorp Marine Ltd v PPL Holdings Pte Ltd* [2013] SGCA 43, [2013] 4 SLR 193 [85], the Singapore Court of Appeal held that: 'Depending on the nature of and the parties to the contract, for instance, one between family members, there could conceivably be some other external normative standards which may be more appropriate than business efficacy in distilling the parties' presumed intentions.' Thus, other normative requirements can be relevant.

[87] For example, Art 8 of the Salvage Convention 1989 imposes on the parties to a salvage operation a duty to the other party to exercise due care to prevent or minimise damage to the environment. There is no relevant case law, but it is submitted that a breach of such an obligation may create an indemnity right where the innocent party has to pay for environmental damage arising from such a breach.

[88] The only English case where a judge suggested the possibility of implying a safe port warranty concerned a time charterparty is *Vardinoyannis v The Egyptian General Petroleum Corp (The Evaggelos Th)* [1971] 2 Lloyd's Rep 200, 204. The argument for an implied term does not concern public or environmental safety but simply an issue of allocation of liability for the property of the shipowner.

[89] The position is likely to be different in the approaches adopted by other legal systems where public and moral norms are considered differently in contract formation and performance. See eg C Valcke, 'On Comparing French and English Contract Law: Insights from Social Contract Theory' (2009) 4 *J Comp L* 69.

An implied obligation is imposed on the carrier in contracts of carriage to provide a seaworthy ship.[90] Such an obligation, which is supportive of public interests of safety and environmental protection, can and is routinely[91] overwritten by express clauses reducing the obligation to one of 'due diligence'.[92] Thus, again, it is difficult to argue that broadening the reasonable person's environmental awareness could lead to an implied obligation of contractual performance consistent with greenhouse gas emission reduction.

Suppose that a contractual clause obliging the parties to reduce emissions was agreed. In such a case, a breach of the clause may lead to orders for specific performance, and damages suffered, reputational or other, are likely to be recoverable if they were in the contemplation of the parties.[93] Arguably, none of the currently available clauses imposes such a general obligation.

New regulatory requirements for emission reductions mean that the reasonable person's standard is likely to shift towards considering such requirements.[94] However, the effect is likely to be the broadening of the type of losses which may become recoverable, what is under the reasonable contemplation of the parties, and not by implying contractual performance obligations, at least not under English law. Thus, express clauses will need to be developed to impose such duties, although the broadening of the views of the reasonable person would arguably extend the scope of damages that can be claimed.

D. Green Financing

Green financing concerns investment or credit provision to companies that account for or actively manage their environmental footprint, including carbon emissions.[95] It can be argued that if such a company, whether it is a shipping company or a trading company utilising shipping services, loses the opportunity to obtain or retain green financing due to contractual performance by the other party which is inconsistent with the requirements for green financing, a loss recoverable in damages may exist. Such loss will operate as an incentive for one of the contractual parties to bring a claim against the contractual party which made it lose the green financing opportunity by breaching a relevant contractual clause.

[90] See Stephen Girvin, *Carriage of Goods by Sea*, 3rd edn (Oxford, Oxford University Press, 2022) para 24.03.

[91] For example, by the incorporation of the Hague-Visby Rules. See Girvin, ibid para 27.15.

[92] See also Gencon 1994, cl 2; Gencon 2022, cl 2(a)(i).

[93] In line with the rules of remoteness: see *Hadley v Baxendale* (1854) 9 Ex 341; *Transfield Shipping Inc v Mercator Shipping Inc (The Achilleas)* [2008] UKHL 48, [2009] 1 AC 61.

[94] Note also that the 'reasonable person' may note that imposing carbon prices on bunkers might increase the import prices of goods marginally and, if done uniformly across transport, may even increase maritime transport: see RA Halim, T Smith and DP Englert, 'Understanding the Economic Impacts of Greenhouse Gas Mitigation Policies on Shipping: What is the State of the Art of Current Modeling Approaches?', World Bank Policy Research Working Paper No 8695 (9 January 2019), available at SSRN: ssrn.com/abstract=3320893.

[95] An interesting point is that equity markets appear to be more successful in reducing GHG emissions than the banking system, probably because innovative sectors grow faster in countries with deeper equity markets. See R De Haas and A Popov, 'Finance and Decarbonisation: Why Equity Markets Do it Better' (Research Bulletin 2019 – ecb.europa.eu). See www.ecb.europa.eu/pub/economic-research/resbull/2019/html/ecb.rb191127~79fa1d3b70.en.pdf.

However, in such a case, the degree of knowledge the contracting party has in this respect and the express contractual arrangements between the parties will matter. Thus it matters that green financing includes requirements for the company obtaining the investment and due diligence duties concerning contractors and subcontractors because it pushes commercial parties to acquire such knowledge. In this way, contractual undertakings may be utilised to ensure the required information is provided. The inclusion of specific duties for decarbonisation in shipping and logistics contracts would facilitate the discharging of due diligence that is required and may be the basis for claiming opportunities for green financing.

E. Vetting Systems by Trading Companies

Private vetting systems can achieve a different type of contractual control. Such systems are implemented by large oil companies and ensure that ships engaged by them meet the required standards. They were developed in the wake of major oil spills amid accusations and lawsuits that oil companies only looked at the cost of carriage and did not play their part in ensuring that the ships selected were safe for the environment.

These vetting systems operate in addition to the flag state compliance requirements and are a private standard-setting and enforcement system. Failure to comply with the requirement to hold a major's approval may be considered a breach of a condition of the contract.[96] The role of the private vetting requirements in improving the standards for shipping is difficult to distinguish from the improvements achieved through the enforcement of improved IMO standards for tankers. Whether one believes that the vetting arrangements rather than the improvement of the IMO standards caused the reduction in oil pollution incidents depends on the trust one has in the flag state and port state control standards, known to be deficient in many parts of the world, or the surveys by chartering oil companies which are controlled by the relevant company.

For the present discussion, it suffices to say that if the charterers of ships require disclosure of the emissions per unit of cargo (or per passenger) and themselves confirm maximum emissions per unit to their customers, a private system through which cargoes sold would be comparable, and easy for financiers and investors to identify 'green' operators. Furthermore, depending on the progress on meeting the Paris Agreement targets, carriage of goods on lower or minimum emission standards could be achieved without the need for IMO regulations. Notably, the contractual incentive that would be created would reflect the loss of business to those operators if they fail to deliver the promised reductions and perhaps the dismissal of polluting ships from the service for breach of a condition, provided there is a properly worded clause.

V. Conclusions

Contractual arrangements have been an efficient supplementary way of enforcing established and evolving regulatory standards. In shipping, contractual arrangements

[96] See *The Seaflower* (n 52).

have routinely allowed shipowners to comply with public law requirements and arrange the distribution of risk between themselves and other parties in cases of delay, detention and exclusions of the ship due to non-compliance.

Contractual clauses have been developed to allow performance consistent with the EEXI, CII and the EU ETS system. These are permissive and do not improve the regulatory system's potential for decarbonisation. Within the context of the current, rather ineffective, IMO initial strategy, they are an additional cost for small, minimal efficiency improvements. The existing clauses reflect an effort to expand shipowners' flexibility to do the little required under the IMO strategy rather than an opportunity to require substantially improved performance.

Freedom of contract permits the shipowners' customers to demand better performance and push for green shipping.[97] The problem is that without interventions which will directly or indirectly generate a financial loss a contractual clause is likely to be words on a paper without any incentive for the parties to ensure enforcement.

Most existing shipowners do not wish for competition on environmental standards.[98] Such competition will devalue their existing investment and may exclude shipowning entities that operate opportunistically from entering the market at a minimum cost. Indeed, this is the crux of the matter. Efforts to achieve minimum standards by consensus at the IMO have led to the compromise that these are only to be applicable to the next generation of ships. In turn, this has created an expectation that the same will be done with decarbonisation. Minimum standards have their place in avoiding a race to the bottom, and the IMO's regulatory system has achieved that much. However, at the same time, it has removed incentives for competition and innovation. There is no reason why a shipowner should choose to perform more efficiently if there is no financial benefit.

Contractual arrangements can overcome these problems if they provide financial incentives. Taxation of greenhouse gas emissions per voyage payable and controlled either by reducing emission allowances or increasing the price of carbon is one way of doing this.[99] Reporting of emissions under ESG or CSR commitments,[100] private vetting systems and standards for access to green financing may also create incentives which can be quantified as losses in cases of a contractual breach. These have to be imposed indirectly or directly on the customers and users of shipping services and in ways which oblige them to transfer the need for compliance down their chain of customers.

[97] Shipowners are unlikely to do so. The International Chamber of Shipping (ICS) and Intertanko, both eminent shipowner associations, have repeatedly stated that: '… the commercial development of relevant technologies, fuels, propulsion systems and related infrastructure are the responsibility of other out-of-sector stakeholders rather than shipowners'. See ISWG-GHG 10/5/2, 3 September 2021.

[98] The position is different for large logistics companies in Europe involved in liner shipping. For them, the EU ETS is already providing them with the incentive to reduce emissions, and they see this as an opportunity to increase their share over their competitors.

[99] Thus, the application of the EU ETS to shipping is more important than the negotiations in the IMO. It provides the incentive to shipowners trading in EU ports, and, in this way, it is to their benefit that the IMO finally agrees on a carbon tax, at least as effective as the EU ETS system. Of course, whether anything adopted by the IMO would be efficient would depend on the detail which is, at the time of writing, unclear.

[100] This is notoriously difficult, though, because there are issues of attributing losses in the company's value but also with the standardisation of information disclosed: *cf* V Ho, 'Modernizing ESG disclosure' (2022) *U of Illinois LR* 277.

Such changes are already in place in parts of the world. They are unavoidable actions for governments aiming for emissions reduction or energy efficiencies as part of their pledges under the Paris Agreement. The urgency to achieve emission reductions has changed consumers in many parts of the world, making, for example, electric cars, efficient light bulbs and renewable energy central in decarbonisation policies. In non-legal terms, it is not easy to argue that a reasonable person can consider the performance of contractual obligations without considering the environmental footprint of the contractual performance. Even oil-producing companies claim to do so. However, in legal terms, it has been argued that the reasonable person may only support the insertion of public policy requirements for decarbonisation if the law sets them as the framework limiting commercial performance. This is a significant and necessary improvement in the contractual framework, which can be made either in the form of an implied or expressly imposed obligation of best endeavours to minimise greenhouse gas emissions and environmental impacts. Such an obligation and a duty to pay for the emitted GHG emissions would create enough incentive to make contractual performance supportive of the decarbonisation efforts.

The final point is that the international shipping governance in the IMO has been developed with a different aim in mind, namely the imposition of minimum standards. It is deficient in dealing with rapid changes in environmental requirements because existing investments dominate the governance process. The choice for governments is either to push for a change in the IMO or to overtake it by establishing efficient decarbonisation systems and providing incentives for green shipping. The IMO's strategy is inefficient and can be viewed as a distraction technique from the reality of shipping: the few state actors which determine shipping emissions have been failing systematically in guiding the shipping sector towards global sustainable development. Why this happens is perhaps best summarised by saying that the IMO does not protect the environment from shipping – but saves shipping from environmental regulation.[101] By contrast, contract law does not care about the niceties of compromise and consensus in international organisations. It can utilise financial values created by social and legal processes locally or regionally and through them may help in developing efficient and clean shipping globally.

[101] This pithy statement was made by Dr Michael Prehn, Counsellor to IMO for Solomon Islands High Commission. It is used here with his permission.

3

CII Clauses in Charterparties

STEPHEN GIRVIN*

I. Introduction

In 2022, ships emitted around 700 million metric tons of carbon dioxide ($MtCO_2$) into the atmosphere,[1] around 4.7 per cent higher than in 2020, and attributable to increases in trading by container vessels, dry bulk carriers, and general cargo vessels.[2] During the past five to ten years, there has been a flurry of regulatory activity by the IMO[3] and the EU,[4] responding to pressure to reduce greenhouse gas (GHG) emissions from ships.[5] New regulatory provisions[6] introduced by the IMO concerned with energy efficiency cover EEDI (Energy Efficiency Design Indices of New Ships), EEXI (Energy Efficiency Indices for Existing Ships),[7] and SEEMP (the Ship Energy Efficiency Management Plan) are discussed elsewhere in this book.[8] This chapter focuses on CII

* MPA Professor of Maritime Law, Director, LLM (Maritime Law), Director, Centre for Maritime Law, Faculty of Law, National University of Singapore.

[1] See 'Carbon Dioxide Emissions from International Shipping Worldwide from 1970 to 2022' (Statista, 6 February 2023). See also 'Carbon Dioxide Emissions by Main Flags of Registration, 2012 and 2022' in *Review of Maritime Transport 2023* (UNCTAD, 2023) 59.

[2] *Review of Maritime Transport 2022* (UNCTAD, 2022) 107.

[3] For an exploration of some of the challenges of the IMO's regulatory role, see H Bach and T Hansen, 'IMO Off Course for Decarbonisation of Shipping? Three Challenges for Stricter Policy' (2023) 147 *Marine Policy* 105379.

[4] See Eftestøl (ch 5); Baughen (ch 6).

[5] See Tsimplis (ch 2); H Ringbom, 'Regulating Greenhouse Gases from Ships: Some Light at the End of the Funnel' in E Johansen et al, *The Law of the Sea and Climate Change: Solutions and Constraints* (Cambridge, Cambridge University Press, 2020) ch 6; S Baughen, 'Shipping and Climate Change' in B Soyer and A Tettenborn (eds), *Disruptive Technologies, Climate Change and Shipping* (London, Informa Law from Routledge, 2022) ch 10. See also N Khalid and A Aai, 'Greening and Bearing It' (2010) 24(5) *MRI* 14.

[6] These are found in Annex VI of MARPOL 73/78, the International Convention for the Prevention of Pollution from Ships. On MARPOL generally, see C de la Rue, CB Anderson and J Hare, *Shipping and the Environment*, 3rd edn (London, Informa Law from Routledge, 2022) 957–994. See also *MARPOL – 25 years* (IMO, October 1998), available at www.imo.org/en/KnowledgeCentre/ConferencesMeetings/pages/Marpol.aspx. On MARPOL, ch 4, see M Tsimplis, *Environmental Norms in Maritime Law* (Cheltenham, Edward Elgar, 2021) 142.

[7] MARPOL, Arts 23; 25.

[8] See Kløft and Cai (ch 4).

(the Carbon Index Indicator),[9] which, together with the other measures, came into force on 1 November 2022 and is applicable from 1 January 2023.

The interface between these new regulatory provisions and commercial shipping law is not within the contemplation of the regulators and has left those most affected, shipowners and charterers, scrambling to adapt and adjust their contractual arrangements. Indeed, the latest regulatory changes, especially CII, contradict traditional cargo vessel operating patterns where the typical pattern is for vessels to travel at optimal speeds, albeit with the risk of congestion or longer waiting times at the discharging port. This practice – known as 'Sail Fast, Then Wait' (SFTW)[10] – means that sea journeys are not optimised,[11] leading to unnecessary fuel consumption. It also follows that vessels waiting to enter port continue to burn fuel and emit emissions.

This chapter considers the legal requirements for CII as laid down in MARPOL Annex VI and the impact of these requirements on the performance of time charterparties and voyage charterparties. Particular attention is given to the controversial BIMCO CII Operations Clause for Time Charter Parties 2022 and the companion BIMCO CII Clause for Voyage Charter Parties 2023.

II. Regulatory Requirements for CII

A. Application

MARPOL reg 28.1 (the CII Regulation) applies 'after the end of calendar year 2023 and after the end of each following calendar year'. It attaches to ships of '5,000 gross tonnage and above …', namely, bulk carriers, combination carriers, container ships, cruise passenger ships, gas carriers, general cargo ships, LNG carriers, refrigerated cargo carriers, ro-ro cargo and passenger ships, and tankers.[12] Each ship of these types is required to calculate an attained annual operational CII over 12 months from 1 January to 31 December during the preceding calendar year using data collected under reg 27,[13] taking into account the guidelines developed by the IMO.[14]

[9] Implemented in Singapore in the Prevention of Pollution of the Sea (Air) Regulations 2022 No S 837 (and made pursuant to Prevention of Pollution of the Sea Act 1990 (2020 rev ed), s 34).

[10] See M Heider et al, 'The Wrong Speed for All the Wrong Reasons' (Nautilus Labs and BIMCO Whitepaper, 22 May 2023) 2, downloadable from www.bimco.org/insights-and-information/general-information/20230522-sail-fast-then-wait; EP Martin, 'Can Nautilus Labs Unlock Commercial Efficiencies for Cutting Carbon?' *TradeWinds* (London, 23 June 2023) 20. See also H Zografakis et al, 'Decarbonize Shipping or Decarbonize International Maritime Trade: The Present Contractual Framework and the Need for a New Contractual Architecture' in M Lind, W Lehmacher and R Ward (eds), *Maritime Decarbonization: Practical Tools, Case Studies and Decarbonization Enablers* (Cham, Springer, 2023) 201, 215.

[11] For an alternative model, see I Sung, H Zografakis and P Nielsen, 'Multi-lateral Ocean Voyage Optimization for Cargo Vessels as a Decarbonization Method' (2022) 110 *Transportation Research Part D: Transport and Environment* 103407.

[12] As defined in regs 2.2.5, 2.2.7, 2.2.9, 2.2.11, 2.2.14–2.2.16, 2.2.22, and 2.2.26–2.2.29.

[13] 'Collecting and reporting of ship fuel oil consumption data'.

[14] See also reg 2.2.

The required annual operational CII is calculated by the methodology specified in the Regulations and the ancillary guidelines.[15] This involves a 'Z factor', the 'annual reduction factor to ensure continuous improvement of the ship's operational carbon intensity within a specific rating value', and a 'CII_g value', the 'reference value',[16] which measures grams of CO_2 emitted per cargo-carrying capacity, and nautical miles travelled.

Linked with CII each ship must have a Ship Energy Efficiency Management Plan (SEEMP) – which may form part of the ship's Safety Management Plan (SMS)[17] – and which, on or before 1 January 2023, must contain: (i) a description of the methodology used to calculate the ship's attained annual operational CII and the processes that will be used to report this value to the ship's Administration; (ii) the required annual operational CII for the next three years; (iii) an implementation plan documenting how the required annual operational CII will be achieved during the next three years; and (iv) a procedure for self-evaluation and improvement.[18] Where a ship is rated D for three consecutive years or E, the regulations provide that the SEEMP must be reviewed to include a 'plan of corrective actions to achieve the required annual operational CII'.[19] However, there is no indication of the consequences of failing to do so.

B. Rating

Once developed, the attained annual operational CII is documented and verified against the required annual operational CII to determine an operational carbon intensity rating as follows: A (major superior), B (minor superior), C (moderate), D (minor inferior), and E (inferior performance).[20] Administrations, port authorities, and other stakeholders are encouraged to incentivise ships to achieve an A or B rating.[21] The Regulations also spell out the consequences of obtaining a particular rating. In particular, any ship rated as D for three consecutive years or rated E must develop a plan of corrective actions to achieve the required annual operational CII.[22] Again, as also noted above, there is no indication of the consequences of failing to do so.

[15] See also reg 28.4. See 2022 Guidelines on Operational Carbon Intensity Indicators and the Calculation Methods (CII Guidelines, G1), Resolution MEPC.352(78); 2022 Guidelines on the Reference Lines for Use with Operational Carbon Intensity Indicators (CII Reference Lines Guidelines, G2), Resolution MEPC.353(78).

[16] ibid.

[17] ie, pursuant to the ISM Code, mandatory under SOLAS Ch IX, and also relevant for the EU ETS (see Eftestøl (ch 5)). For ISM, see H Honka, 'The Standard of the Vessel and the ISM Code' in J Schelin (ed), *Modern Law of Charterparties* (Stockholm, Axel Ax:son Johnson Institute of Maritime and Transport Law, 2003) 105; P Anderson, *ISM Code: A Practical Guide to the Legal and Insurance Implications* (London, Informa Law, 2015) para 3.3. For an example of a charterparty clause, see NYPE 2015, cl 44.

[18] Reg 26.3.1.

[19] Reg 26.3.2.

[20] Reg 28.6.

[21] Reg 28.10.

[22] Reg 28.7.

C. Reaction

The CII methodology is controversial. On the one hand, it has generated considerable adverse reactions,[23] such as being a 'flawed example of what can go wrong'.[24] On the other hand, there is a view that, although imperfect, it can be applied 'to a majority of vessels and is a good yardstick to measure the performance of operations'.[25] Particular issues with CII include that CII does not consider the specific cargo carried on board, the weather conditions during the service, or vessels travelling on shortsea routes or getting stuck in port.[26] An unintended consequence of CII is that an individual ship may achieve a more favourable rating by undertaking ballast[27] legs, which will not reduce emissions overall.

Meanwhile, negotiating a medium- to long-term charterparty is fraught with difficulty: most shipowners want the ship, when returned, to have a rating similar to that upon delivery. In such conditions, charterers are reluctant to commit because of numerous commercial factors beyond their control.[28] Designing precise round voyages and slick triangulation voyages[29] – particularly when chasing cargo – will be challenging. However, this will become essential when trying to maximise the benefits of different routes.

There are likely to be particular issues with the CII ratings. In the tanker trade, for example, if a particular tanker were E-rated, oil majors[30] would likely be reluctant to approve the vessel through the OCIMF Ship Inspection Report Programme (SIRE).[31] In the dry markets, there will be similar issues for traders in the coal and iron ore markets.[32]

[23] See eg EP Martin, 'Dieleman Warns Carbon Intensity Indicator "Doesn't Make Sense"' *TradeWinds* (London, 7 October 2022) 18–19; H Birkett, 'Oldendorff Rubbishes CII for being a "Flawed Formula"' *TradeWinds* (London, 9 December) 6; H Papachristou, 'Intercargo Joins the Chorus Criticising "Flawed" CII Benchmark' *TradeWinds* (London, 9 December 2022) 6; P Peachey, 'CII is Too "Simplistic" Say London Greek Owners' *TradeWinds* (London, 27 January 2023) 23; H Papachristou, 'Olivi and Zacharidis Fail to see Eye to Eye on CII' *TradeWinds* (London, 17 February 2023) 20; A Olivi, 'CII Score is a Fantastic Concept Clouded by a Suboptimal Metric' *TradeWinds* (London, 31 March 2023) 12; E Tunagur, 'Economou Calls for Flawed CII to be Scrapped' *Lloyd's List* (London, 5 June 2023); MW Bockmann, '"Shipping Carbon Intensity Indicator Fundamentally Flawed" Says d'Amico International Shipping' *Lloyd's List* (London, 22 June 2023).

[24] R Meade, 'The Case for a More Holistic Approach to Regulation' *Lloyd's List* (London, 6 May 2023).

[25] P Berrill, '"Imperfect" CII Demands Joined-up Thinking to Fill Gaps' *TradeWinds* (London, 17 March 2023) 24. See also G Dixon, '"Is CII Perfect? No, But Let's Give It a Go", Says Cerup-Simonsen' *TradeWinds* (London, 16 December 2022) 18.

[26] See eg I Short, 'CII – Time for a Rethink?' (2022) 37(5) *MRI* 14; Enes Tunagur, 'ABS Expects Carbon Intensity Indicator Amendments from MEPC 80' *Lloyd's List* (London, 16 May 2023).

[27] ie non-revenue earning voyages.

[28] See eg C Shen, '"Flawed" CII Rating Complicates Charterparty Talks and Trade Designs' *Lloyd's List* (London, 3 May 2023).

[29] Such as booking a tanker to carry North American gasoline to South America, where upon discharge it loads a soybean oil cargo for shipment to Asia, predominantly heading to China.

[30] Such as BP, Chevron, Eni, ExxonMobil, Shell, and TotalEnergies.

[31] See, generally, DW Martowski, 'Vetting Clauses' (2001) 26 *Tulane Mar LJ* 123, 125; C Eason, 'Digital Readiness Crucial for SIRE 2.0 Vetting Regime' *TradeWinds* (London, 8 December 2023) 22. See also *Transpetrol Maritime Services Ltd v SJB (Marine Energy) BV (The Rowan)* [2012] EWCA Civ 198, [2012] 1 Lloyd's Rep 564.

[32] BHP Billiton, Cargill Ocean Transportation, and Rio Tinto Shipping.

Indeed, RightShip[33] has already updated its algorithm behind its GHG ratings methodology in line with the CII methodology.[34] Difficulties should be anticipated even for shipping tonnage rated at D; traders could exclude such vessels in a weak ('soft') freight market, particularly in certain trades.[35]

III. Time Charterparty Clauses

A. Background

It is customary for time charterparties to be fixed on well-known standard forms;[36] it is trite that the most well-known and utilised general form by some distance is the New York Produce Exchange (NYPE) form.[37] As 'one of the legal backbones of the deployment of vessels in international maritime commerce',[38] such contracts for services[39] involve the shipowner putting 'the profit earning capacity of the ship at the disposal of the charterer … only … against advance payment'.[40] Standard form charterparties have become increasingly sophisticated and detailed when dealing with the industry's changing landscape. Modern revised standard forms drafted solely by or in collaboration with BIMCO, such as NYPE 2015, increasingly reflect BIMCO's standard clauses.[41] However, as noted by BIMCO, current standard form time charterparties are 'not geared' to deal specifically with the CII regime[42] or, as remarked by another commentator, many shipowners and charterers 'are still trying to push the square peg of CII through the round hole of a time charterparty'.[43]

[33] See *Seagate Shipping Ltd v Glencore International AG (The Silver Constellation)* [2008] EWHC 1904 (Comm), [2008] 2 Lloyd's Rep 440, para 7; *DHL Project & Chartering Ltd v Gemini Ocean Shipping Co Ltd (The Newcastle Express)* [2022] EWCA Civ 1555, [2023] 1 Lloyd's Rep 245, para 19.

[34] See H Papachristou, 'RightShip Updates Algorithm to Compare "Apples with Apples"' *TradeWinds* (London, 15 September 2023) 8. See also rightship.com/technical-information?nid=538.

[35] See Shen (n 28).

[36] See generally S Girvin, *Carriage of Goods by Sea* 3rd edn (Oxford, Oxford University Press, 2022) para 34.02 (available online at olrl.ouplaw.com/); Sir D Foxton, 'Why Shipping Law Still Matters' [2021] *LMCLQ* 440, 444.

[37] ibid paras 1.55; 34.03; M Davies, 'When was the Last Time you were Restrained by a Prince? Conservatism and the Development of Maritime Law' in PK Mukherjee (ed), *Maritime Law in Motion* (Cham, Springer, 2020) 153, 157.

[38] *Reiter Petroleum Inc v The Ship 'Sam Hawk'* [2016] FCAFC 26, [2016] 2 Lloyd's Rep 639, para 76 (Allsop CJ and Edelman J).

[39] See eg *Scandinavian Trading Tanker Co AB v Flota Ecuatoriana (The Scaptrade)* [1983] 2 AC 694 (HL), 700; Girvin (n 36) para 1.55.

[40] ibid 702. See also *Mardorf Peach & Co Ltd v Attica Sea Carriers Corp of Liberia (The Laconia)* [1977] AC 850 (HL), 854 (John Hobhouse QC).

[41] See eg NYPE 2015, cl 30 (Hull Fouling Clause for Time Charter Parties); cl 32 (Electronic Bills of Lading Clause); cl 34 (War Risks Clause CONWARTIME 2013); cl 38 (Piracy Clause for Time Charter Parties 2013); cl 47 (Designated Entities Clause for Charter Parties); cl 48 (North American Advance Cargo Entities Clause for Charter Parties).

[42] See www.bimco.org/contracts-and-clauses/bimco-clauses/current/cii-operations-clause-2022.

[43] See eg N Austin, 'CII Six Months On: A Plague on Both Your Houses?' *TradeWinds* (London, 30 June 2023) 20.

B. Time Charterparty Clauses Affecting Performance

This part of the chapter outlines the primary time charterparty clauses affecting performance and which are most likely to be affected by CII.

i. Employment of the Ship

The standard time charterparty wording concerning employment, represented by cl 8(a) of the NYPE 93 form, states that 'the master shall … be under the orders and directions of the Charterers as regards *employment* …'.[44] In the NYPE 2015 form, the employment term is qualified by the words 'subject to Clause 38 (Slow Steaming) …'[45] but it otherwise uses the same wording, as do other standard form time charterparties, including the oil forms.[46] The import of this wording[47] is that the time charterer

> agrees to pay hire for the vessel because he wants to make use of it. Crucial to the bargain, for him, are the terms which … provide that the master (although appointed by the owner) shall be under the orders and directions of the charterer as regards employment and which require the charterer to furnish the master from time to time with all requisite instructions and sailing directions.[48]

The charterer may give the master orders relating to the vessel's employment because it 'wants the vessel to be well positioned for a commercial opportunity or other commercial reason'[49] but not navigational orders, which are 'in the control of the owner through his master'.[50]

As noted below, the most significant sticking point with CII is that the rating depends almost entirely on how the time charterer decides to use the vessel as an economic asset.[51] In these circumstances, the shipowner may request the time charterer to adjust its voyage orders, which may involve reducing speed or switching to a more fuel-efficient route if there is a likelihood that the vessel's CII rating will fall below the agreed levels. Most time charterers will see such demands as a non-negotiable interference with their rights under the charterparty employment clause.

[44] Lines 100–103 (emphasis provided). See also the still heavily used NYPE 1946 form, cl 8, lines 76–77, and *cf* also Baltime 1939, cl 9, lines 69–71. Generally, see H Bennett (gen ed), *Carver on Charterparties*, 2nd edn (London, Sweet & Maxwell, 2021) para 7.170.

[45] Line 130.

[46] BPTime 3, cl 10, line 239; ExxonMobil Time 2005, cl 14(a), lines 1035-1038; Gastime, cl 15, line 176; Shelltime 4 (v 1.02), cl 10.1, lines 226–227.

[47] *cf* the wording in the Danish Merchant Shipping Act (consolidation) Consolidated Act no. 1505 of 17 December 2018, s 378 (first sentence) and the discussion in T Falkanger, H Jacob Bull and L Brautaset, *Scandinavian Maritime Law: The Norwegian Perspective*, 4th edn (Oslo, Universitetsforlaget, 2017) para 16.4.3.

[48] *Whistler International Ltd v Kawasaki Kisen Kaisha Ltd (The Hill Harmony)* [2001] 1 AC 638 (HL), 641 (Lord Bingham). See also *Hyundai Merchant Marine Co Ltd v Gesuri Chartering Co Ltd (The Peonia)* [1991] 1 Lloyd's Rep 100 (CA), 107 (Bingham LJ).

[49] *The Hill Harmony*, ibid 654.

[50] *New A Line v Erechthion Shipping Co SA (The Erechthion)* [1987] 2 Lloyd's Rep 180, 185.

[51] See eg Austin (n 43).

ii. *Congestion and Other Factors Affecting Ports*

On average, vessels spend 15 per cent of total voyage time at ports in deep-sea shipping and as much as 60 per cent in short-sea shipping.[52] Congestion in port is part and parcel of ship operations and is a regular occurrence in the trading of any ship,[53] and highlighted throughout the COVID-19 pandemic.[54] In *The Maratha Envoy*,[55] a leading voyage charterparty case, Lord Diplock characterised congestion as a 'misfortune risk':

> Among the most prevalent of misfortune risks is congestion at a loading or discharging port causing the vessel to wait idly until a berth falls vacant at which her cargo can be loaded or discharged. If it is to wait at the shipowners' expense he will endeavour to secure that this risk is covered in the freight rate that he charges. If it is to wait at the expense of the charterer and paid for as demurrage or by reduction in dispatch money he will expect this to be reflected in a lower freight rate charged.

In time charterparties, the time charterer bears the cost of delay in port.[56] The NYPE 93 form, for example, expressly states that 'the Charterers … shall pay for port charges (including compulsory watchmen and cargo watchmen and compulsory garbage disposal) …'.[57] In voyage charterparties, the charterer bears the risk of any waiting time at anchorage to enter the port, at least from the point at which the vessel is an 'arrived ship'[58] or activated by an appropriately drafted clause.[59]

Port congestion is considered a 'ratings killer' for CII because it can vastly increase idling time in proportion to voyage time.[60] For this reason, perhaps more so than ever before, most shipowners will keep an eagle eye on port conditions, and if there appears a risk of a lengthy wait in the 'roads'[61] pending the availability of a berth, the shipowner may insist on alternative arrangements at a different port.

iii. *Speed and Consumption of Bunkers*

Most classic time charterparty standard forms contain an undertaking by the shipowner that the vessel can perform voyages at a stated speed,[62] which has a material impact on

[52] See X Bai et al, 'Identifying Port Congestion and Evaluating its Impact on Maritime Logistics' (2022) *Mar Pol'y & Mgmt* doi.org/10.1080/03088839.2022.2135036.

[53] See eg Port Congestion: Report of the Group of Experts (UNCTAD, 1976) TD/B/C.4/152, paras 19–23.

[54] *Review of Maritime Transport 2022* (n 2) 81–91. See also Andras Komaromi, Diego A Cerdeiro and Yang Liu, 'Supply Chains and Port Congestion Around the World' WP/22/59 (IMF, March 2022).

[55] *Federal Commerce and Navigation Co Ltd v Tradax Export SA (The Maratha Envoy)* [1978] AC 1 (HL), 8.

[56] In voyage charterparties, congestion is built into the charterparty in the form of an agreed number of laydays, failing which the charterer has to pay demurrage. For the leading case on the latter, arising out of port congestion at Longkou in China, see *K Line Pte Ltd v Priminds Shipping (HK) Co Ltd (The Eternal Bliss)* [2021] EWCA Civ 1712, [2022] 1 Lloyd's Rep 12.

[57] Cl 7, lines 84–87. *cf* also NYPE 2015, cl 7(a), lines 114–116; Baltime 1939, cl 4, lines 29–30.

[58] Girvin (n 36) para 33.04.

[59] Ibid para 33.14. See particularly S Baughen, *Summerskill on Laytime*, 7th edn (London, Sweet & Maxwell, 2022) ch 4.

[60] E Martin and B Rust, 'Tug of Law' *TW+* (London, Autumn 2022) 22, 25.

[61] Ie the normal sheltered waiting area for ports, usually an area where ships can anchor and ride safely. Whether this area falls within or outside the port area can become particularly fraught in voyage charterparties: see eg *EL Oldendorff & Co GmbH v Tradax Export SA (The Johanna Oldendorff)* [1974] AC 479 (HL), 535 and the discussion in Baughen (n 59) paras 4–15.

[62] Girvin (n 36) para 34.13. *cf* also Falkanger (n 47) para 16.2.3(a).

the time charterer's voyage planning. Taking NYPE 93 as an example, this provides: 'Speed about … knots, fully laden, in good weather conditions up to and including maximum Force … on the Beaufort wind scale …'[63] The more elaborate cl 12(a) in the NYPE 2015 form provides that:

> … the Vessel shall be capable of speed … rates as stated in Appendix A in good weather and on all sea passages with wind up to and including Force four (4) as per the Beaufort Scale and sea state up to and including Sea State three (3) as per the Douglas Sea Scale (unless otherwise specified in Appendix A).[64]

The reason for such elaborate clauses is that even minor differences between the ship's stated speed and its actual speed may significantly affect the overall profitability of the charterparty, directly impacting the period it takes to complete any given voyage and the time charterer's voyage planning pending the redelivery of the vessel. As highlighted in *The Divinegate*:[65]

> Speed and performance claims very commonly arise out of the performance of time charters … [and] there is a very significant industry involving everyday practice and expertise in the assessment of routes, weather, performance and consumption, and where scientific advances (including GPS) have introduced considerable sophistication in the assessment of these claims. Where these disputes arise they commonly raise questions of law, fact and practice. The charter provisions are to be applied … in light of the fact that the parties … will generally have expected to achieve certainty and commercially pragmatic solutions.

Speed is, therefore, certainly an area in which disputes will occur particularly where this is warranted by the shipowner or supported by a guarantee that a particular warranted performance will be achieved during the whole term of the charterparty.[66] This will be closely watched especially where the shipowner proposes changes or variations in the light of CII performance.

As there is a direct correlation between speed and consumption of bunkers,[67] this tends to be reflected as such in standard clauses,[68] particularly in time charterparties, where the time charterer pays for the consumption of bunkers, which become its property.[69] Bunkers are a key cost element when calculating the overall profitability of its trade. Modern time charterparties contain sophisticated bunkering clauses,[70] especially during periods of unstable bunker prices and following the introduction of mandatory reductions in the sulphur content of bunker fuels.[71] In the CII context, this is significant

[63] Lines 18–19. NYPE 1946 refers to the vessel as '… capable of steaming, fully laden, under good weather conditions about … knots …' (lines 9–10). As to 'good weather conditions', see *Polaris Shipping Co Ltd v Sinoriches Enterprises Co Ltd (The Ocean Virgo)* [2015] EWHC 3405 (Comm), [2018] 1 Lloyds Rep Plus 101, para 3; *Eastern Pacific Chartering Inc v Pola Maritime Ltd (The Divinegate)* [2022] EWHC 2095 (Comm), [2023] 1 Lloyd's Rep 442, paras 93–94.

[64] Lines 315–319.

[65] *The Divinegate* (n 63) para 90 (Clare Ambrose, sitting as a Deputy High Court Judge).

[66] As in *SK Shipping Europe plc v Capital VLCC 3 Corp (The C Challenger)* [2022] EWCA Civ 231, [2022] 1 Lloyd's Rep 521.

[67] For bunkers, see Girvin (n 36) para 34.21. *cf* also Falkanger (n 47) para 16.2.3(b).

[68] See eg NYPE 93, lines 18–20 (NYPE 2015, cl 12(a), lines 312–23).

[69] See eg *The Saint Anna* [1980] 1 Lloyd's Rep 180, 182; *The Span Terza* [1984] 1 Lloyd's Rep 119 (HL), 122.

[70] On the cost of bunkering, see eg NYPE 93, cl 7, lines 84–85 (NYPE 2015, cl 9(a), lines 140–157).

[71] MARPOL, Annex VI, reg 14. See Girvin (n 36) para 34.25.

for the shipowner, because the consumption of bunkers directly impacts the measurable emissions of the vessel.

iv. Slow Steaming

Slow steaming, which entails performing at lower speeds in a bid to reduce fuel consumption, first became attractive when the cost of oil (and bunker fuels) accelerated after the Global Financial Crisis (GFC), accounting for a much larger share of the operating cost of vessels and cutting significantly into the earnings of shipowner (and, potentially, time charterers), particularly in container vessels which operate at relatively higher speeds.[72]

Older charterparty forms do not elaborate on the scenario where the charterer orders slow steaming. However, to assist shipowners, BIMCO drafted the Slow Steaming Clause for Time Charter Parties 2011,[73] giving the time charterer the option of asking, in writing, for 'slow steaming'[74] or 'ultra-slow steaming',[75] and focused on minimising fuel consumption,[76] which as noted already,[77] is a key element in the charterer's bottom line. In line with this priority, NYPE 2015, cl 12(a) states that

> Any period during which the Vessel's speed is deliberately reduced to comply with the Charterers' orders/requirements (unless slow steaming or eco speed warranties have been given in Appendix A) … shall be excluded from performance calculations.[78]

The principal clause is, however, cl 38, which states that the charterer can give orders to the master to 'reduce speed or Revolutions Per Minute (main engine RPM) and/or instructions to adjust the Vessel's speed to meet a specified time of arrival at a particular destination'.[79] As with the BIMCO clause, the master must comply, subject to his

> obligations in respect of the safety of the Vessel, crew and cargo and the protection of the marine environment … provided that the engine(s) continue(s) to operate about the cut-out point of the Vessel's engine(s) auxiliary blower(s) and that such instructions will not result in the Vessel's engine(s) and/or equipment operating outside the manufacturers'/designers' recommendations as published from time to time.[80]

The above clauses have a specific purpose, fuel consumption. However, it is clear that some shipping companies have adopted a slow steaming strategy in response to CII, slowing their ships down to 'an optimised, economical speed'.[81] One leading shipping

[72] See P Cariou et al, 'Slow Steaming in the Maritime Industry' in Photis M Panayides, *The Routledge Handbook of Maritime Management* (London, Routledge, 2019) 140. See also the discussion in Ulfbeck (ch 8) section III.

[73] For consideration in sale contracts, see T Nikaki, 'Slow Steaming Clauses and International Sales Contracts: A Successful Marriage?' in B Soyer and A Tettenborn (eds), *International Trade and Carriage of Goods* (London, Informa Law from Routledge, 2017) ch 2.

[74] Subcl (a)(i).

[75] Subcl a(ii). These two subclauses are alternatives.

[76] See eg subcl (b).

[77] Above, section III(B)(ii).

[78] Lines 319–323.

[79] Cl 38(a), lines 663–665.

[80] Cl 38(a)(i), lines 667–672.

[81] H Birkett, 'Rindbo Cautions Maritime About Kicking Carbon Down the Road' *Tradewinds* (London, 22 September 2023) 22.

services provider, Clarksons,[82] has warned that the effect of speed reductions in improving a shipowners' CII ratings are 'grossly overestimated' being based on 'textbook speed-consumption curves' and that once all of the consumers of a vessel and the variables of real-world sailing conditions are factored in, 'the curve becomes less exponential (or flatter) at lower speeds'.[83]

v. Reasonable Despatch

Standard form time charterparties usually embody an express undertaking by the shipowner that the master will 'perform the voyages with due despatch'[84] or 'utmost despatch'.[85] This is discussed further below in the context of voyage charterparties.[86]

vi. Off–hire

The fundamental principle underlying all time charterparties, as stated by MacKinnon LJ,[87] is that:

> … [T]he charterers have, during each month and part of a month, to pay to the shipowners the agreed sum, and their continuous liability to pay that sum would … only be interrupted if there were a provision in the charterparty for some period during which there is to be no payment notwithstanding the other terms of the contract. Such a clause is [the off-hire clause] in this contract …

The NYPE 93 and NYPE 2015 charterparty each provide, in the relevant off–hire clause,[88] that:

> Should the vessel deviate or put back during a voyage, contrary to the orders or directions of the Charterers, for any reason other than accident to the cargo or where permitted in lines 257 to 258[89] hereunder, the hire is to be suspended from the time of her deviating or putting back until she is again in the same or equidistant position from the destination and the voyage resumed therefrom.[90]

The standard principle is that because off-hire runs counter to the charterer's obligation to pay hire continuously, the charterer must prove that a relevant event falls within

[82] See www.clarksons.com/home/green-transition/carbon-intensity-indicator/.

[83] G Dixon, 'Shipowners "Grossly Over-estimating" Effect of Slow Steaming on CII, Clarksons Warns' *TradeWinds* (10 May 2023).

[84] NYPE 93, cl 8(a), line 100; NYPE 2015, cl 8(a), line 130. See generally, Girvin (n 36) ch 26. *cf* also the Danish Merchant Shipping Act (n 47), s 405(3), which in translation uses the phrase 'due despatch'. See the further discussion in Falkanger (n 47) para 15.3.3.

[85] NYPE 1946, cl 8, line 76; Baltime 1939, cl 9, line 69, Shelltime 4 (v 1.2), cl 2(b)(i), line 69.

[86] See section IV(B)(ii).

[87] *Sea and Land Securities Ltd v William Dickinson & Co Ltd* [1942] 2 KB 65 (CA), 70. See also *Leolga Compania de Navigacion SA v John Glynn & Son Ltd* [1953] 2 QB 374, 382–3; *Mareva Navigation Co Ltd v Canaria Armadora SA (The Mareva AS)* [1977] 1 Lloyd's Rep 368, 381.

[88] See J Weale, *Off-hire: A Study* (London, Steamship Mutual Underwriting Association Ltd, 2016).

[89] This is a reference to NYPE 93, cl 22, where there is '… the liberty to sail with or without pilots, to tow and be towed, to assist vessels in distress, and to deviate for the purpose of saving life and property'. *cf* also NYPE 2015, cl 22, lines 409–10.

[90] NYPE 93, cl 17, lines 226–230; NYPE 2015, cl 17, lines 380–384.

the charterparty off–hire clause. As the NYPE 93 and NYPE 2015 clauses state, 'in the event of loss of time … the payment of hire and overtime, if any, shall cease for the time thereby lost'.[91] Thus, in the event of an adjustment to the vessel's performance ordered by the shipowner, the time charterer must point to a specific named breach of the off–hire clause by the shipowner to put the vessel off–hire.[92]

IV. Voyage Charterparty Clauses

A. Background

As with time charterparties, voyage charterparties are often fixed on well-known standard forms,[93] particularly the 'Uniform General Charter', better known as Gencon, and revised in 1994 and, following root and branch revision, in 2022.[94] Voyage charterparties, which are historically more ancient,[95] are generally fixed on the spot market for a single agreed voyage from a loading port to an agreed discharging port or range of ports,[96] with the disponent owner or charterer using the vessel to trade on its own account.[97] Such charterparties are characterised by provision for payment of demurrage[98] by the charterer if loading or discharging is prolonged beyond the agreed laydays, specified in the charterparty as the period during which the vessel is available to the charterer for that purpose and paid for in the freight.[99] Lord Diplock so stated in *The Maratha Envoy*:[100]

> … [T]here is an inter-relationship between rates of freight, demurrage and dispatch money and clauses of the charterparty which deal with the allocation between the charterer and shipowner of those risks of delay in the prosecution of the adventure contemplated by the charterparty [and] which [are] beyond the control of either party … If [the vessel] is to wait at the shipowner's expense he will endeavour to secure that this risk is covered in the freight rate that he charges. If it is to wait at the expense of the charterer and paid for as demurrage or by reduction in dispatch money he will expect this to be reflected in a lower freight rate charged.

[91] ibid cl 17, lines 220 and 225–226; cl 17, lines 372 and 379–380.

[92] As occurred in *Bulk Ship Union SA v Clipper Bulk Shipping Ltd (The Pearl C)* [2012] EWHC 2595 (Comm), [2012] 2 Lloyd's Rep 533 (slow steaming within the wording of cl 15 of an amended NYPE charterparty).

[93] There is a large number of specific forms for particular trades: see Girvin (n 36) para 32.08.

[94] See J Weale, 'A new GENCON: Transforming a Standard Charter for the Modern World' in B Soyer and A Tettenborn (eds), *Ship Operations: New Risks, Liabilities and Technologies in the Maritime Sector* (London, Informa Law from Routledge, 2021) ch 12.

[95] See eg the *Charter party of Our Lady of Lyme* (later *Saint Marie*) (1323); R Ward, 'A Surviving Charterparty of 1323' (1995) 81 *The Mariner's Mirror* 387.

[96] There may also be a series of consecutive voyage charterparties: see eg *Anglo-Saxon Petroleum v Adamastos Shipping Co (The Saxon Star)* [1957] 2 QB 233 (CA) paras 275–276.

[97] See eg *The Hill Harmony* (n 48) 652.

[98] For demurrage, see *K Line Pte Ltd v Priminds Shipping (HK) Co Ltd (The Eternal Bliss)* [2021] EWCA Civ 1712, [2022] 1 Lloyd's Rep 12.

[99] *The Johanna Oldendorff* (n 61) 553.

[100] *The Maratha Envoy* (n 55) 8. See also above, section III(B)(ii), in relation to congestion.

B. Voyage Charterparty Clauses Affecting Performance

Unlike time charterparties, which are driven by the need of time charterers, as disponent owners, to make a profit, the risks of delay during the voyage in a voyage charterparty fall on the shipowner. However, where the delay is causative of loss to the charterer, it may be able to rely on an express breach by the shipowner of one or other express clauses, discussed below.

i. Deviation Clauses

A deviation[101] is a breach of the obligation 'to proceed without unnecessary deviation in the usual and customary course',[102] which entails taking the usual route between two ports.[103] The usual presumption is that this is 'the direct geographical route [that] may be modified in many cases, for navigational or other reasons …'[104] and a deviation is the 'intentional adoption of a route that differs from the contract route'.[105] While the consequences of a breach of the obligation can be severe for the shipowner,[106] most contracts of carriage, including many voyage charterparties, provide 'liberty' clauses which seek to remove the sting from these consequences. A classic example in the Gencon 1994 form, cl 3, states that:

> The Vessel has liberty to call at any port or ports in any order, for any purpose, to sail without pilots, to tow and/or assist Vessels in all situations, and also to deviate for the purpose of saving life and/or property.

The latest Gencon 2022 charterparty, cl 22(a) states that:

> The Vessel shall have liberty to sail with or without pilots, to tow or go to the assistance of vessels in distress, to deviate for the purpose of saving life or property and *for any other purpose reasonably necessary to the safe continuation of the voyage*, including calling at any place for bunkers, taking on board spares, stores or supplies, repairs to the Vessel, crew changes, landing of stowaways or persons rescued at sea, medical emergencies and ballast water exchange, and the Owners shall not be liable for any loss or damage (including delay) arising or resulting therefrom.

[101] Generally, see Girvin (n 36) ch 25. *cf* also the Danish Merchant Shipping Act (n 47) s 405(3), which provides that 'deviation may only be to save life or to salvage ship or goods or for some other reasonable ground'. See the further discussion in Falkanger (n 47) para 15.3.3.

[102] *Davis v Garratt* (1830) 6 Bing 716, 725 (Tindal CJ).

[103] Sometimes stated to be 'the usual and customary course' (see eg *Compagnie Primera de Navagaziona Panama v Compania Arrendataria de Monopolio de Petroleos SA* [1940] 1 KB 362 (CA), 374) or 'the ordinary track of the voyage from one place to the other' (*Leduc & Co v Ward* (1888) 20 QBD 475 (CA), 481). In *Alianca Navegaceo e Logistica Ltda v Ameropa SA (The Santa Isabella)* [2019] EWHC 3152 (Comm), [2020] 1 Lloyd's Rep 603, the court held that the Cape Horn route from Topolobampo (Mexico) to Durban and Richard's Bay (South Africa), was a usual and reasonable route for the purposes of identifying the contractual route, and did not amount to a deviation. See also Ulfbeck (ch 8).

[104] *Reardon Smith Line Ltd v Black Sea & Baltic General Insurance Co (The Indian City)* [1939] AC 562 (HL), 584.

[105] *The Santa Isabella* (n 103) para 58.

[106] Although just how serious is subject to the reasoning in *Joseph Thorley Ltd v Orchis Steamship Co Ltd* [1907] 1 KB 660 (CA) and *Tate & Lyle Ltd v Hain Steamship Co Ltd* (1936) 55 Ll L Rep 159 (HL): see the important obiter comments of Moulder J in *Dera Commercial Estate v Derya Inc (The Sur)* [2018] EWHC 1673 (Comm), [2019] 1 Lloyd's Rep 57, paras 107–108.

While such liberty clauses, which are also prevalent in time charterparty forms,[107] are standard, it is also well established that these must be interpreted consistently with the contemplated voyage.[108] So, for example, whether 'any other purpose' would extend to changes of voyage orders mandated by the shipowner is doubtful, and it would be prudent to spell this out if it is intended to extend to changes put in place because of the CII Regulation. Where incorporated by a paramount clause, such as in NYPE 93, cl 31(a),[109] the Hague and Hague-Visby exception in Article IV, rule 4, for a 'reasonable deviation' will be incorporated and may be relevant.[110] In the leading English case, *Stag Line Ltd v Foscolo, Mango & Co Ltd*,[111] Lord Atkin[112] held that:

> A deviation may … may be reasonable, though it is made solely in the interests of the ship or solely in the interests of the cargo, or indeed in the direct interest of neither … The true test seems to be what departure from the contract voyage might a prudent person controlling the voyage at the time make and maintain, having in mind all the relevant circumstances existing at the time, including the terms of the contract and the interests of all parties concerned, but without obligation to consider the interests of any one as conclusive … The decision has to be that of the master or occasionally of the shipowner …

It is fair to say that it is distinctly arguable whether a change of voyage orders instigated by the shipowner to fulfil its CII obligations will fall within the scope of such an exception.[113]

ii. Reasonable Despatch

As noted earlier,[114] time charterparties usually contain an express clause requiring the time charterer to proceed on the voyage with 'reasonable despatch'. Such clauses are also standard in some voyage charterparty forms, although not the Gencon form (or its 2022 revision). Elsewhere, 'all convenient speed'[115] or 'all convenient despatch'[116] are not

[107] See eg NYPE 93, cl 22, lines 256–258; NYPE 2015, cl 22, lines 408–410.
[108] See eg *Frenkel v MacAndrews & Co Ltd* [1929] AC 545 (HL), 562.
[109] See also NYPE 2015, cl 33(a).
[110] See Girvin (n 36) para 27.55.
[111] [1932] AC 328 (HL).
[112] ibid 343–344. Wright J (later Lord Wright) in *Foreman & Ellams Ltd v Federal Steam Navigation Co Ltd* [1928] 2 KB 424, 431, stated that: 'I think it is clear that a deviation would not be reasonable *merely because it was convenient to the shipowner*. Its reasonableness must depend upon what would be contemplated reasonably by both parties having regard to the well-known exigencies of the route, known, or assumed to be known, to both parties …'. Lord Atkin expressly rejected his reasoning that such a deviation should 'be contemplated reasonably by both cargo owner and shipowner …' (ibid 343) but without saying whether convenience to the shipowner is a factor. See also *Thiess Bros (Queensland) Pty Ltd v Australian Steamships Pty Ltd* [1955] 1 Lloyd's Rep 459 (SC NSW).
[113] The existing case law does not assist. See eg *Rey Banano del Pacifica CA v Transportes Navieros Ecuatorianos (The Isla Fernandina)* [2000] 2 Lloyd's Rep 15, where the bosun died, and the vessel deviated for the purpose of disembarking his body. However, Langley J (at 33) held that the resulting grounding was not a reasonable deviation as competent navigation 'would and should have avoided the grounding. The want of competence was the effective cause not the fact that the vessel happened to divert before it occurred'. *cf*, however, Ulfbeck (ch 8) section III(B)(ii).
[114] Above, section III(B)(v).
[115] ie, promptly. See eg *Dimech v Corlett* (1858) 12 Moo PC 199, 225; *CHS Inc Iberica SL v Far East Marine SA (The MV Devon)* [2012] EWHC 3747 (Comm). See also Amwelsh 93, cl 1, lines 16–17; Synacomex 2000, cl 2, line 8 (and Synacomex 2023, cl 2).
[116] See eg Asbatankvoy, cl 1.

unheard of. Sometimes, stronger wording, '*utmost* despatch', is used.[117] The undertaking is '... a merchants' clause with the object of giving effect to the mercantile policy of saving time'.[118] It is considered 'an important obligation ... intended to give comfort to a charterer'.[119] The shipowner is in breach if, without good reason, the master sails at a reduced speed[120] or delays at a port of refuge unnecessarily.[121] However, if there is no evidence that a particular voyage took longer than such a voyage should take, no breach of the obligation has occurred.[122] In the event of changes in the course of the voyage, the shipowner may find itself in difficulty, particularly if this has a knock-on effect on the vessel's arrival at the discharging port. On the other hand, if the charterparty contains the wording of the BIMCO Slow Steaming clauses, then, provided the shipowner exercises due diligence, this is not a breach of any obligation requiring 'the Vessel to proceed with utmost and/or due despatch (or any other such similar/equivalent expression)'.[123]

iii. Speed and Consumption

We have noted the close interrelationship concerning speed and bunker consumption in the context of time charterparties.[124] Such clauses are not the norm in voyage charterparties – see, for example, the Gencon form, where there is no such clause – but some specialist oil voyage charterparty forms contain such statements[125] and, of course, such undertakings may be added as a rider to any standard form. As we will see in due course, provision for such changes is included in the BIMCO clause.[126]

V. BIMCO's CII Operations Clause for Time Charter Parties 2022

A. Background

When published in November 2022, BIMCO's CII Operations Clause for Time Charter Parties was one of the longest ever produced by the BIMCO Documentary Committee. In setting out to draft a clause for incorporation by the parties to a time charterparty, the Committee saw its task as providing 'the necessary building blocks for the parties

[117] See eg Shellvoy 6, cl (A)(I)(vii), line 25.

[118] *The Hill Harmony* (n 48) 653 (Lord Hobhouse).

[119] *CSSA Chartering and Shipping Services SA v Mitsui OSK Lines Ltd (The Pacific Voyager)* [2018] EWCA Civ 2413, [2019] 1 Lloyd's Rep 370, para 13 (Longmore LJ).

[120] *The Pearl C* (n 92).

[121] *Owner of Steamship Istros v FW Dahlstroem & Co* [1931] 1 KB 247.

[122] *Univeg Direct Fruit Marketing DFM GMBH Univar v MSC Mediterranean Shipping Co SA (The MSC Stella)* [2013] EWHC 2962 (Comm), para 28.

[123] BIMCO Slow Steaming Clause for Time Charter Parties 2011, subcl (e). *cf* also the BIMCO Slow Steaming Clause for Voyage Charterparties 2012, subcl (b), which contains no reference to compliance with the charterer's orders.

[124] Above, section III(B)(iii).

[125] See eg BPVOY4, line 55; Shellvoy 6, cl (L); LNGVOY, cl 18.

[126] Below, section VI(B).

to operate ships in accordance with the new CII playing field'.[127] Although striving to provide a fair and balanced clause,[128] the clause has not attracted praise from the get-go; quite the reverse, as elaborated later.[129] Before looking in more detail at the criticisms, we begin with an examination of the provisions of the clause.

B. The Provisions in the Clause

i. Definitions

The first part of the BIMCO clause contains nine definitions. These do not all travel controversial ground, cross–referencing CII, 'CII Rating', 'Agreed CII',[130] 'the effective date',[131] and the 'MARPOL Carbon Intensity Regulations'. More significantly, the 'Required CII' is defined as:

> … the middle point of CII rating level C equivalent to the required annual operational CII set out in Regulation 28.6 of the MARPOL Carbon Intensity Regulations or as otherwise specified in the Guidelines for the MARPOL Carbon Intensity Regulations.

On the one hand, this links with the 'C/P Attained CII', which is

> The CII value in gCO_2/(dwt.nmile) attained by the Vessel, applying any regulatory correction factors and voyage adjustments applicable to the Vessel and excluding fuel consumed and distance travelled during off-hire periods in excess of [ ] accumulated days … measured in the relevant calendar year from the start of the calendar year to date or, if the Charter Party begins during a calendar year, from date of the Vessel's delivery under the Charter Party to date.

On the other hand, the 'Delivery Attained CII' is 'the CII value in gCO_2/(dwt.nmile) attained by the Vessel for the calendar year to date as calculated at the time of delivery into the Charter Party'. This definition is important because the information has to be passed to any new time charterer. The 'Projected Attained CII' is 'the C/P Attained CII extrapolated over the remainder of the relevant calendar year (or the charter period should redelivery be sooner than the end of the calendar year) and used to demonstrate the trajectory of the Vessel's C/P Attained CII'.

ii. Introductory Clause

By subclause (a), the parties acknowledge and accept that from the 'effective date', as defined,[132] the vessel must comply with the Carbon Intensity Regulations and that the clause governs the relationship between the parties and their 'obligations' relating to those Regulations. This causes potential difficulty in two respects. The first is that

[127] See www.bimco.org/contracts-and-clauses/bimco-clauses/current/cii-operations-clause-2022.

[128] B Rust and EP Martin, 'Drafting a CII Time-charter Clause is a Balancing Act, Says BIMCO's Ivo' *TradeWinds* (London, 30 September 2022) 23.

[129] Below, section V(c). *cf* also P Rebelo, 'BIMCO's Carbon Intensity Indicator Clause (CII) for Time Charters: Towards a New Era of Climate Drafting' (2022) 28 *JIML* 240.

[130] ie, the values in gCO2/(dwt.nmile) set out in subclause (d), below section V(B)(v).

[131] ie, 1 January 2023.

[132] Above, section V(B)(i).

although stating that the vessel must 'comply' with the Regulations, this falls within the shipowner's remit, not the time charterer. The second difficulty is it is unclear what types of 'obligations' the time charterer has, save as specified in the clause. In so far as the MARPOL Carbon Intensity Regulations are concerned, the Guidance Notes emphasise that this includes the SEEMP[133] and that, since the SEEMP may include operational measures which the shipowner should follow, 'the charterer should seek sight of the ship's SEEMP'. There is, however, no express obligation on the shipowner to make this available to the charterer, other than subcl (b), discussed next.

iii. Cooperation and Working Together in Good Faith

Subclause (b) contains a central but awkward component of the BIMCO clause. It underscores the belief that CII is 'inevitably a shared responsibility for the owners and the charterers in a time charter party context and requires the parties to collaborate and cooperate'.[134] Most charterers and shipowners will see this as aspirational, but subclause (b) makes such cooperation mandatory ('*shall* cooperate and work together …) and links acting 'in good faith' with sharing 'any' findings and best practices that they may identify or potential improvements to the vessel's energy efficiency'.[135] Arguably, there are difficulties with the mandatory wording ('shall'), notably in determining what such cooperation might involve and the consequences of failure to cooperate. Moreover, invoking 'good faith' in a contractual setting is notoriously elusive to define.[136] Although good faith in contractual settings is familiar in civil law jurisdictions, EU legislation,[137] international instruments,[138] and domestic statutes,[139] the exact meaning is still underdeveloped in many common law settings, and no general standard exists in English law.[140]

The clause requires the parties to 'collect, share and report on a daily basis' any relevant data that may assist in monitoring and assessing the vessel's compliance with the

[133] Above, section II(A).

[134] See www.bimco.org/contracts-and-clauses/bimco-clauses/current/cii-operations-clause-2022.

[135] Subcl b(i). *cf* also the Slow Steaming Clause for Time Charter Parties 2011, subcl (d), where 'owners and the charterers shall share any findings and best practices that they may have identified on potential improvements to the Vessel's energy efficiency'.

[136] See especially M Bridge, *The International Sale of Goods* 5th edn (Oxford, Oxford University Press, 2023) paras 2.21–2.22.

[137] See HG Beale, *Chitty on Contracts*, 35th edn (London, Sweet & Maxwell, 2023) para 2-002.

[138] Notably, the United Nations Convention on Contracts for the International Sale of Goods (Vienna, 1980) (CISG), Art 7(1). See uncitral.un.org/en/texts/salegoods/conventions/sale_of_goods/cisg. See the discussion in Bridge (n 136) paras 10.42–10.43; I Schwenzer and UG Schroeter (eds), *Schlechtriem & Schwenzer, Commentary on the UN Convention on the International Sale of Goods (CISG)*, 5th edn (Oxford, Oxford University Press, 2022) Pt 1, Ch II, paras 16–19.

[139] A standout example in English (and Singaporean law) is the Carriage of Goods by Sea Act 1992, c 50, s 5(2), concerning the meaning of 'holder' under the Act, which has been interpreted as meaning no more than 'honest conduct': see *Aegean Sea Traders Corporation v Repsol Petroleo SA (The Aegean Sea)* [1998] 2 Lloyd's Rep 39, 60; *The Yue You 902* [2019] SGHC 106, [2019] 2 Lloyd's Rep 617, paras 104–108.

[140] See eg *Yam Seng Pte Ltd v International Trade Corp Ltd* [2013] EWHC 111 (QB), [2013] 1 Lloyd's Rep 526, para 131. See the discussion in the case concerning other common law jurisdictions (including Australia, Canada, New Zealand, and Scotland): ibid paras 126–130. See E McKendrick, *Goode and McKendrick on Commercial Law*, 6th edn (London, Penguin Books, 2020) para 3.74 and *cf* M Chen-Wishart and V Dixon, 'Good Faith in English Contract Law: A Humble "3 by 4" Approach' in PB Miller and J Oberdiek (eds), *Oxford Studies in Private Law Theory*, vol I (Oxford, Oxford University Press, 2020) ch 8; Bridge (n 136).

regulations and planning prospective voyages.[141] It is, however, difficult to determine the consequences of not doing so from this and, as noted by one commentator, not all trading involving ships takes place between known parties, and some shipowners and operators charter out vessels to customers they do not know or brokers they have not dealt with previously.[142] Such difficulties are likely to be particularly evident in the spot charter market.[143]

iv. Time Charterer's Duties

Subclause (c) must also be approached with care. It outlines the charterer's duty to operate and employ the vessel, extending to 'planning of voyages and the supply and selection of fuel' and 'consistent with' the Regulations. As drafted, this may require adopting alternative or adjusted voyage or employment orders, instructions or sailing during the charter period.[144] This makes significant inroads into the charterer's contractual employment choices. Further, the charterer must not 'permit' the 'C/P Attained CII' to exceed the 'Agreed CII' by the end of each relevant calendar year or, if the charter period or period remaining is less than a full calendar year, by the time of redelivery.[145] Again, many charterers will view such requirements as a significant imposition, requiring them to take unexpectedly heavy responsibility for the operational aspects of the vessel's performance. This also does not comfortably sit with the statement that the shipowner's existing despatch, speed and consumption[146] warranties continue to apply. However, where there is a breach of such warranties, the time charterer is entitled to pursue a separate claim against the shipowner, save that any such breach cannot be relied upon by the charterer as a basis to avoid meeting its obligations under this clause, including where subcl (g) is validly invoked.

v. Agreed CII by Calendar Year

Subclause (d) provides that the 'Agreed CII'[147] by calendar year must be set out in a table for each year to 2026.[148] If this is not agreed in writing, the clause states that the parties agree and acknowledge that the default 'Agreed CII' for the ship will be the 'Required CII'.[149] Where the charterparty extends outside 31 December 2026,[150] the parties must review and incorporate the 'Agreed CII' under any new annual carbon intensity targets set by the IMO for any remaining calendar years under the charterparty.[151] At the time of delivery, the shipowner must provide the charterer with the 'Delivery Attained CII'

[141] Subcl (b)(ii). *cf* also the BIMCO Slow Steaming Clause for Time Charter Parties 2011, subcl (d).

[142] B Rust, 'Lawyer Up Now as Looming CII Charter Wars Could Last Years' *TradeWinds* (London, 25 November 22) 11.

[143] ibid.

[144] Subcl c(i)(1).

[145] Subcl c(i)(2). This is also subject to subcl (g).

[146] Above sections III(B)(iii); III(B)(v).

[147] See above, section V(B)(i).

[148] Subcl (d)(i).

[149] Subcl (d)(ii). But subject to subcl (d)(iii).

[150] ie, the date of review of the existing Regulations.

[151] Subcl (d)(iii).

and details of the types and quantities of fuels consumed and distance travelled to date for the current calendar year. To the best of the shipowner's knowledge, this data must be accurate and complete.[152]

vi. Speed/RPM Adjustments

Subclause (e) is an echo of the BIMCO Slow Steaming Clause for Time Charters.[153] It permits the charterer to provide written orders or instructions to the master to adjust the ship's speed or RPM[154] to meet a specified arrival time at a particular destination or to proceed at a specified main engine fuel consumption. The master must comply with such orders, subject to the charterer's compliance with its obligations and the master's overriding obligations for the safety of the ship, crew and cargo and the protection of the marine environment. The charterer cannot request adjustments outside the existing safe operational limits of the ship or those that result in the engines or equipment operating outside the manufacturers' or designers' recommendations. As already noted, speed reduction is likely to be one of the principal ways in which the shipowner will seek to meet its CII responsibilities.[155]

vii. Shipowners' Duties

Subclause (f) is the converse to subcl (c).[156] It provides that the shipowner must exercise 'due diligence' to ensure the ship operates to minimise fuel consumption.[157] The clause essentially requires the due diligence[158] standard of seaworthiness, which modifies the absolute standard in most standard forms, such as the NYPE 93 charterparty, which states that the vessel must be 'tight, staunch and strong and in every way fitted for ordinary cargo service …'.[159] The BIMCO clause highlights that the required standard extends to maintaining the ship, its engines and hull, and any equipment relevant to the ship's energy efficiency under the charterparty and the Regulations, including SEEMP, subject to provisions placing maintenance obligations on the charterer. Any deficiencies must be notified to the time charterer.[160] In the case of passage planning,[161] the shipowner must ensure that the ship's trim is adjusted while operating its main engine and auxiliary engine.[162] The shipowner must also make optimal use of the ship's navigation equipment and additional aids provided by the charterer, such as weather routing, voyage

[152] Subcl (d)(iv).
[153] Above, section III(B)(ii).
[154] Main engine revolutions per minute.
[155] Above.
[156] Above, section V(b)(iv).
[157] Subcl (f)(i).
[158] Echoing the wording in Art III, rule 1 of the Hague-Visby Rules. See Girvin (n 36) para 27.20. See also the Danish Merchant Shipping Act (n 47), s 276(2), which uses the same phrase, and the discussion in Falkanger (n 47) para 14.3.7.
[159] Lines 33–35. See also cl 2(b) of NYPE 2015 and the discussion in Girvin, ibid para 24.32ff.
[160] Subcl (f)(i)(1).
[161] As to which, see *Alize 1954 v Allianz Elementar Versicherungs AG (The CMA CGM Libra)* [2021] UKSC 51, [2021] 2 Lloyd's Rep 613, paras 124–128; *Astimewa Sdn Bhd v Budget Marine Ltd* [2023] MLJU 2010 (H Ct, Kota Kinabalu) paras 83–84.
[162] Subcl (f)(i)(2).

optimisation and performance monitoring systems,[163] which have become routine in recent years.[164] Unless the time charterer otherwise orders, the vessel must proceed by the most fuel-efficient route, but the master may deviate where he has reasonable grounds to believe that such a route will compromise the ship's safe navigation or the safety of the ship, crew or operation of equipment,[165] which is always an overriding consideration.[166]

The shipowner must monitor and calculate the actual consumption of the ship daily and provide the time charterer with details of the types and quantities of fuels consumed, the distance travelled, and any other relevant data it may reasonably request.[167] This data is used to calculate the charterparty 'Attained CII' value and must be compared against the 'Agreed CII' for the relevant calendar year or charter period and shared with the charterer. The shipowner undertakes that the data provided to the time charterer is, to the best of its knowledge, accurate and complete.[168] Finally, the shipowner must comply with the SEEMP, provided the time charterer adheres to its obligations.[169]

viii. Advance Warning in Case of Deviating from the Agreed CII

The next clause goes to the heart of the relationship between the shipowner and the time charterer. Under subcl (g), the shipowner is required to give the charterer advance warning where the expected trajectory of the 'C/P Attained CII' deviates from the 'Agreed CII'. If, despite this, the 'C/P Attained CII' continues to deviate and there is a reasonable likelihood that the charterer may fail to meet its obligations, the charterer must provide the shipowner with a written plan[170] detailing any proposed commercial operation of the ship for at least the next voyage.[171] Suppose the shipowner can reasonably show that the time charterer will fail to meet its obligations under subclause (c), and the 'Agreed CII' for the relevant calendar year will be exceeded. In that case, the shipowner must communicate this in writing to the charterer.[172] The parties must cooperate 'and work together in good faith'[173] to agree on an adjusted written plan for the next voyage or voyages to bring the 'C/P Attained CII' in line with the 'Agreed CII'. Any adjusted written plan agreed between the parties constitutes orders by the time charterer as if given by it at the outset.[174]

Until an adjusted written plan is agreed, the shipowner is entitled not to follow the charterer's orders, and such does not breach its obligations under the charterparty, the

[163] Subcl (f)(i)(3).

[164] For weather routeing, see eg, *The Hill Harmony* (n 48) 643; *The Santa Isabella* (n 103) para 15; *The Divinegate* (n 65) para 17. See also IMO's Recommendation on Weather Routeing, Res A.528(13) (17 November 1983).

[165] Subcl (f)(i)(4).

[166] Deviation to save life or property is always an exception: see Girvin (n 36) para 25.08 and the discussion above, section IV(B)(i).

[167] Subcl (f)(ii).

[168] ibid.

[169] Subcl (f)(iii).

[170] Within two working days.

[171] Subcl (g)(i).

[172] Subcl (g)(ii). Also, within two working days.

[173] See the earlier comments on good faith: above, section V(B)(iii).

[174] Subcl (g)(ii).

vessel remaining on hire.[175] Where a speed reduction is considered insufficient, the shipowner can require the charterer to provide all requisite instructions, orders and sailing directions to the ship, which bring the 'C/P Attained CII' in line with the 'Agreed CII' for the relevant calendar year.[176]

ix. Breach

Under subclause (h), compliance with any order by the charterer, its written plan or an adjusted written plan is not deemed a breach by the shipowner of any of its obligations but is considered due fulfilment of the charterparty. However, this does not lessen the charterer's responsibility to comply with its own obligations under the clause.

x. Terms of Bills of Lading, Waybills, and Other Documents

Subclause (i)[177] provides that the charterer must ensure the terms of any documents that evidence contracts of carriage issued by (or on behalf) of the shipowner must provide that compliance by the shipowner does not constitute a breach of the contract of carriage. The clause gives the shipowner an express indemnity against all consequences and liabilities that may arise where these impose or result in a breach of the shipowner's obligation to proceed with due despatch or amount to a deviation or impose more onerous liabilities on the shipowner than those arising under this subclause.[178] Such an express indemnity provision should be included particularly, for example, in the NYPE form, as there is no express indemnity provision in the charterparty.[179]

xi. Damages

Finally, subclause (j) provides that the shipowner is entitled to claim any losses, damages, liabilities, claims, fines, costs, expenses, actions, proceedings, suits or demands suffered by the ship and the shipowner where caused by any breach by the time charterer of its obligations. This clause is extensive, but the BIMCO Guidance Notes state that it should only need to be invoked on limited occasions. That, however, assumes that the parties cooperate in line with subcl (b).[180]

xii. Things Left Unsaid …

Inevitably, there are gaps in coverage in the clause, and these do not assist in making the clause any more palatable. While, as noted above, there is a detailed damages clause, it is not, for example, clear how potential earnings losses resulting from slower steaming or changes in the voyage will be compensated.

[175] Cl (g)(iii)(1).
[176] Cl (g)(iii)(2).
[177] This is not applicable in the liner trade and mirrors the similar provision in the BIMCO Slow Steaming Clause for Time Charters 2011.
[178] For further discussion of this clause in the context of bills of lading, see Ulfbeck (ch 8).
[179] Generally, see Sir N Hamblen, 'Under Charterer's Orders – To Indemnity, Or Not to Indemnify' [2019] *LMCLQ* 200.
[180] See above, section V(B)(iii).

C. Reaction

On 20 December 2022, soon after the release of the BIMCO clause, a group of 23 major companies sent an open letter to BIMCO stating that the CII clause was 'unworkable' because it disproportionately affected charterers and was detrimental to achieving a good outcome for each vessel.[181] It removed an incentive for shipowners to do their fair share for decarbonisation efforts and failed to recognise that shipowners were primarily responsible under the Regulations and 'unbalanced and unusable'.[182] All the indications, therefore, are that uptake of the BIMCO clauses 'has been low to non-existent'.[183] For this reason, specific bespoke ('home-grown') clauses for particular trades and counterparties will certainly become the norm.[184] Some parties may wish to borrow particular provisions from the BIMCO clause but with changes, achieving a balance with which shipowners and time charterers can live. BIMCO has indicated that it will only instigate an automatic review of the clause following the publication of the first ratings in 2024.

VI. BIMCO CII Clause for Voyage Charterparties 2023

A. Background

While working on a clause for time charterparties, BIMCO also indicated that it planned to draft a similar clause for voyage charterparties.[185] As already noted that was published in late 2023.[186]

B. The Provisions in the Clause

As noted in the earlier discussion on voyage charterparties,[187] the shipowner is largely in the driving seat when controlling performance under a voyage charterparty, save where the vessel is in port. Even then, it can earn substantial agreed liquidated damages in demurrage[188] should the charterer exceed any agreed lay days for loading and discharging.[189] This relatively short clause largely reflects the nature of a voyage charterparty.

[181] See N Bakhsh, 'Big Names Slam BIMCO's CII Clause as "Unusable"' *Lloyd's List* (London, 21 December 2022). See also D Osler, 'Time Charterers to Take Responsibility for Carbon Intensity Indicator Compliance' *Lloyd's List* (London, 17 November 2022).

[182] ibid.

[183] Austin (n 43).

[184] ibid.

[185] *cf* also the BIMCO Slow Steaming Clause for Voyage Charter Parties 2012.

[186] See D Osler, 'BIMCO Adopts New CII Clause for Voyage Charterparties' *Lloyd's List* (London, 13 October 2023).

[187] Above, section IV(B).

[188] And hence why, following the insolvency of the charterer, the shipowner may seek to recover such damages from the holder of a bill of lading. For an unsuccessful example, see *Miramar Maritime Corp v Holborn Oil Trading Ltd (The Miramar)* [1984] 1 AC 676 (HL). See also Ulfbeck (ch 8) section V(B)(ii).

[189] See above, section IV(A).

First, taking into account that the shipowner and master control performance during the voyage from the loading to the discharging port, subcl (a) provides that the shipowner is entitled to adjust course or reduce speed or RPM provided that the vessel's speed, 'basis good weather conditions' does not fall below the stated knots during any voyage performed under the charterparty. As noted above, not all standard form voyage charterparties contain such express undertaking, and this clause may not be that useful to most charter charterparties unless such undertakings are adopted in a rider clause or an Addendum to the main terms.

Second, subcl (b) states that any actions taken under subcl (a) do not constitute a breach of the utmost or due despatch or any speed and consumption warranties under the charterparty[190] but that the agreed 'laycan' remains unaffected. This echoes the same wording in the BIMCO Slow Steaming clause.[191]

Third, subcl (c) echoes the earlier subclause (i) in the BIMCO Time Charterparty clause.[192]

Fourth, subcl (d) provides that the clause is without prejudice to any other express or implied rights which entitle the vessel to proceed at speeds below the minimum speed stated in subcl (a).

Finally, subcl (e) provides that within an agreed number of days after completion of the final discharge of the cargo, the shipowner must make available to the charterer: (i) details of the types and quantities of fuels consumed under the charterparty, and (ii) distance travelled with respect to both the ballast and laden voyages. This may not be a direct concern for many voyage charterers, who do not pay directly[193] for bunkers, which fall for the shipowner's account.

VII. Conclusions

The CII provisions in MARPOL and the indicative BIMCO clauses covering their implementation in charterparties have endured a rough passage since they were published. There are two interrelated problems. On the one hand, there is unhappiness with the methodology set out in the CII Regulation. On the other hand, responding to the draft clauses for time charterparties, it is clear that most charterers are so opposed that they will not adopt them, at least in their present form, and this will continue so long as market conditions are in their favour.

While one can always hope that draft clauses, particularly by a reputable organisation such as BIMCO, will attract buy-in from the industry, it appears that this is not the case and that chartering counterparties will draft their own bespoke clauses, which will then not be open to general scrutiny as private contractual arrangements. Indeed, one should assume that most charterers will insist on bespoke clauses, either using some of the more palatable BIMCO provisions as a starting point or starting from scratch.

[190] See the earlier discussion.
[191] Slow Steaming Clause for Voyage Charter Parties 2012, subcl (b).
[192] Above, section V(B)(x).
[193] The cost of such bunkers invariably features when the shipowner calculates the charterparty freight.

By way of response, it is becoming evident that Rightship's GHG rating is emerging as a key benchmark for shipping emissions.[194]

On the positive side, a factor that CII may influence is as a trigger for shipowners to scrap older tonnage that does not meet the requirements[195] in favour of newer, more fuel-efficient and less polluting vessels.[196] However, the difficulty with any rush to new tonnage is that the prices of newbuilds have risen and the yards are 'facing challenges in labour, steel pricing, and the inflationary economic environment' and that the forward order book for new tonnage is advancing, currently 3.6 years, compared with 2.5 years before COVID-19.[197]

Whatever steps are taken by shipowners, it seems clear that the CII provisions will have the capacity to influence trade patterns in the future, particularly when or if maintaining a decent rating becomes a priority in commercial decision-making. Standing still or, worse, not doing anything, will not be possible in a new CII world.

[194] See Enes Tunagur, 'RightShip GHG Rating Emerging as Emissions Benchmark Amid CII Concerns' *Lloyd's List* (London, 1 March 2024) and above, section II(C).

[195] See eg I Ang, 'Union Maritime Swells Fleet with Eight NewBuildings in a Fortnight' *TradeWinds* (London 14 April 2023) 3.

[196] Although it has been suggested that there 'is no straight-line relationship between age and fuel consumption': B Rust, 'NYK's Saga Shipholding Faces Renewal Dilemma' *TradeWinds* (London, 24 February 2023) 22.

[197] See L Hine, 'Decarbonisation Demands Drive Fleet Renewals' *TradeWinds* (London, 20 October 2023) 20–21.

4

EEXI: Navigating the New Regulation and its Implication for Time Charterparties

MALTHE HERSOM KLØFT* AND SOPHIA HONG VAN ANH CAI**

I. Introduction

In recognition of the shipping industry's impact on the climate, the International Maritime Organization (IMO) has implemented a range of regulations and measures aimed at promoting the greater energy efficiency of ships. The IMO's regulation of ships' energy efficiency started with the Energy Efficiency Design Index (EEDI)[1] and the Ship Energy Efficiency Management Plan (SEEMP)[2] and aimed to encourage the development and use of more energy-efficient ships.

Building on these efforts, the IMO introduced the Energy Existing Ship Index (EEXI),[3] establishing a minimum energy efficiency baseline for ships. The introduction of the EEXI is a step closer towards reducing the climate impact of the shipping industry and advancing more sustainable practices in the shipping industry.

The EEXI requirement mandates that all ships, regardless of age or type, meet a minimum level of energy efficiency based on their size, type, and other factors. The EEXI requirement came into force on 1 January 2023 and will significantly impact the shipping industry, which is responsible for approximately 3 per cent of global greenhouse gas emissions.[4]

A contract that may be at risk due to the changed regulation is the time charterparty. A key feature of time charterparties is the transfer of operational control over the ship from the shipowner to the charterer.[5] However, legal ownership and possession remain

* Junior Associate, Bech-Bruun Law Firm, Copenhagen.
** Junior Associate, Accura Law Firm, Copenhagen.

[1] MARPOL 1973 (The International Convention for the Prevention of Pollution from Ships 1973, as amended by the 1978 Protocol). See *MARPOL Consolidated Edition 2022* (IMO 2022), Annex VI, reg 22 (Attained Energy Efficiency Design Index) and reg 24 (Required EEDI).

[2] ibid reg 26.

[3] ibid reg 23 (Attained EEXI) and reg 25 (Required EEXI).

[4] A King, 'Emissions-free sailing is full steam ahead for ocean-going shipping', (*Horizon – The EU Research & Innovation Magazine*, 6 September 2022) ec.europa.eu/research-and-innovation/en/horizon-magazine/emissions-free-sailing-full-steam-ahead-ocean-going-shipping.

[5] See eg *Whistler International Ltd v Kawasaki Kisen Kaisha Ltd (The Hill Harmony)* [2001] 1 AC 638 (HL), 641 (Lord Bingham); 652 (Lord Hobhouse). See also Girvin (ch 3) section III(A).

vested in the shipowner.[6] Any changes in regulations that affect the ship's operation, such as new climate or environmental regulations, will likely impact the parties' ability to perform as agreed under the contract. Time charterparties may cover a longer period. Therefore, any changes in the law are more likely to occur during the contract term.

Specifically, the regulation may result in decreased performance of already chartered ships, making the shipowner unable to comply with performance figures given under the time charter party. This may impact shipowners' profitability and ability to fulfil their contractual obligations.

To address these concerns, the Baltic and International Maritime Council (BIMCO) has developed an EEXI Transition Clause that can be included in time charterparties. The clause provides a framework for managing the transition to the new energy efficiency standards. It outlines the parties' responsibilities regarding compliance, cost-sharing, and dispute resolution.[7]

However, including the EEXI Transition Clause in time charterparties raises several legal and practical issues that need to be carefully considered by the parties. For example, the clause may conflict with existing contractual provisions or require amendments to the contractual terms.[8] Furthermore, the clause may not apply to all types of time charterparties or may not fully address all potential disputes and liabilities arising from non-compliance.

This chapter aims to guide shipowners and charterers in navigating the complexities of the EEXI regulation and the associated contractual implications. It discusses the potential risks and opportunities for both parties and highlights the key considerations when negotiating and implementing the EEXI Transition Clause. By doing so, the chapter aims to contribute to a more efficient and sustainable shipping industry that can meet the challenges of a changing regulatory landscape while maintaining a fair and equitable contractual balance between the parties.

II. Background

In 2011, the IMO adopted a new amendment to the International Convention for the Prevention of Pollution from Ships (MARPOL).[9] This introduced the first international regulation of the energy efficiency of ships.

The amendment introduced a requirement for an energy-efficient design of new ships (EEDI).[10] A new ship is understood as a ship of over 400 gt and above,[11] for which the building contract was placed on or after 1 January 2013.[12] In the absence of a building contract, a ship is considered new if the keel of the ship was laid or was at a similar stage of construction on or after 1 July 2013.[13] A ship is also considered new if the delivery of

[6] ibid. See also *Timber Shipping Co SA v London & Overseas Freighters Ltd (The London Explorer)* [1972] AC 1 (HL), 13–14.

[7] See below, section VII.

[8] Similar difficulties arise with the CII clause. For discussion, see Girvin (ch 3) section V(B).

[9] See above (n 1) and *MARPOL Consolidated Edition 2022* (IMO, 2022).

[10] ibid reg 22.

[11] ibid reg 19.1.

[12] ibid reg 2.2.18.1.

[13] ibid reg 2.2.18.2.

the ship was placed on or after 1 July 2015.[14] In addition, the ship must also fall under one of the categories under reg 22.1 as defined by reg 2.2, which includes bulk carriers, combination carriers, containerships, cruise passenger ships with non-conventional propulsion, gas carriers, general cargo ships, LNG carriers, refrigerated cargo carriers, ro-ro cargo ships (including vehicle carriers), ro-ro passenger ships and tankers.

Furthermore, under reg 26, a new requirement is provided for all ships to have a ship-specific energy efficiency plan (SEEMP) on board.

In 2018, the IMO adopted its initial strategy to reduce greenhouse gas emissions from ships (Initial GHG Strategy). This established several short-, medium-, and long-term strategies and ambitions to reduce the shipping industry's carbon footprint. This led to a proposal to amend the MARPOL Annex VI, Chapter 4, in 2021.[15]

The amendment introduced a new technical energy efficiency requirement for existing ships (EEXI)[16] as a prerequisite for obtaining the International Energy Efficiency Certificate ('IEE Certificate').[17] The EEXI requirement sets out energy efficient requirements for the design of existing ships, in most areas expanding the current EEDI requirement to apply to existing ships.

Contrary to the Carbon Intensity Indicator (CII),[18] the EEXI requirement was adopted as a mandatory requirement for existing ships to obtain the IEE Certificate. The amendments to MARPOL Annex VI came into force on 1 November 2022. After this date, existing ships must comply with the new energy efficiency requirements from 1 January 2023 at the earliest, depending on the ship's age and when the ship's next periodic survey takes place.

III. Technical Functionality and Legal Compliance with EEXI

A. Technical Requirements

The purpose of the EEXI is to calculate a ship's CO_2 emissions per ton of cargo and nautical mile. This is done firstly by calculating the ship's current attained EEXI.[19] The method of calculation is technical and is laid down by guidelines.[20]

The parameters included in calculating the ship's attained EEXI share many similarities with the calculation of the attained EEDI.[21] The three main parameters in the calculation are the power of the main and auxiliary engines, the ship's reference speed and certified specific fuel oil consumption.[22] If a ship is required to live up to the EEDI requirement,

[14] ibid reg 2.2.18.3.
[15] See Resolution MEPC.328(76).
[16] See *MARPOL Consolidated Edition 2022* (n 1) reg 23.
[17] ibid reg 6.4 and Annex VIII.
[18] See Girvin (ch 3).
[19] *MARPOL Consolidated Edition 2022* (n 1) reg 23.1.
[20] See 2022 Guidelines on the method of calculation of the attained Energy Efficiency Existing Ship Index (EEXI), Resolution MEPC.350(78).
[21] As to which, see also the 2018 Guidelines on the method of calculation of the attained Energy Efficiency Design Index (EEDI) for new ships, Resolution MEPC.308(73), as amended by Resolution MEPC.322(74) and MEPC.332(76).
[22] See 2022 Guidelines (n 20).

the calculated attained EEDI[23] may also be used for the ship's attained EEXI. The ship's calculated attained EEXI must be equal to or below the ship's required EEXI, which will constitute the maximum passable attained EEXI of the ship as calculated after reg 25.[24]

Shipowners are not entirely on their own to adapt to these compliance measures. IMO has proposed two technical ship modifications to enable the ship to meet the EEXI requirement.[25] The first proposed modification is a limitation of the ship's propeller shaft power (SHaPoLi), the 'mechanical power transmitted by the propeller shaft to the propeller hub'.[26] The other proposed modification is a limitation of the engine power (EPL), the 'mechanical power transmitted from the engine to the propeller shaft'.[27]

SHaPoLi is defined as a verified and approved system for the limitation of the maximum shaft power by technical means that can only be overridden by the ship's master or the officer in charge of the navigational watch to secure the safety of a ship or save life at sea.[28] The definition of the EPL is almost identical but covers a limitation of maximum engine power.[29]

The implementation of SHaPoLi is done by installing a system which should consists of the main arrangement set forth by IMO while the implementation of EPL is done by installing a sealing device.[30] Therefore, it should be possible to introduce SHaPoLi and EPL modifications during the regular maintenance of the ship, after which the time loss would be substantially limited. Both measures cap the ship's maximum speed of around 25 per cent for normal operations,[31] which is only possible to override if the purpose is to secure the safety of a ship or save life at sea. The actual decrease in available maximum speed depends on the individual ship concerning its current attained EEXI rating.

The core principle of the EEXI is reducing ship fuel consumption by limiting the accessible output speed of the ship.[32] It is, therefore, essential to bear in mind that a requirement for the ship's energy efficiency under EEXI is set on this basis.

B. Legal Compliance

The necessary information for verifying the attained EEXI and other relevant background documents must be kept in English under an EEXI Technical file.[33] Compliance with the EEXI requirement will be noted in the IEE certificate.[34]

[23] ie under reg 22. See also the 2018 Guidelines, as amended (n 21).

[24] Reg 25.1.

[25] 2021 Guidelines on the shaft/engine power limitation system to comply with the EEXI requirements and use of a power reserve, Resolution MEPC.335(76).

[26] ibid para 1.1.

[27] ibid para 1.2.

[28] ibid para 1.3.

[29] ibid para 1.4.

[30] 2021 Guidelines on the shaft/engine power limitation system to comply with the EEXI requirements and use of a power reserve, Resolution MEPC.335(76).

[31] See the 2022 Guidelines (n 20).

[32] See 2021 Guidelines (n 25), para 1, figure 1.

[33] 2021 Guidelines on survey and certification of the attained energy efficiency existing ship index (EEXI), Resolution MEPC.334(76), para 4.2.

[34] See *MARPOL Consolidated Edition 2022* (n 1), Annex VI, app VIII.

In practice, classification companies oversee inspections and certificate issuance on behalf of the port states.[35] The port state will only verify that the visiting ship holds valid certificates. Consequently, the ship may be physically detained until the necessary certification is obtained and/or fined for lack of compliance. Therefore, the ship must hold the required certification to perform its voyages.

IV. Compliance Measures: Shipowners' Obligations

IMO has proposed two technical ship modifications to meet the EEXI requirement. These consist of either retrofitting the ship with a shaft power limitation (ShaPoLi) or an engine power limitation (EPL).[36]

In the context of existing time charterparties, meaning time charterparties negotiated before the implementation of the EEXI requirement, such measures may give rise to several conflicts between the charterer and shipowner. The parties may, for instance, dispute whether the shipowner must retrofit its ships to comply with the EEXI requirement and question who is responsible for any time lost.

A. In the Context of Charterparties

The question of which party is contractually obligated to retrofit the ship to live up to the EEXI requirement must be answered with reference to the parties' obligations under a time charterparty.

Most standard time charterparties contain an express clause requiring the shipowner to maintain the chartered ship to ensure that the ship is in an efficient state for its intended service. The wording of such maintenance clauses may differ, depending on the standard form time charterparty used and any modifications or rider clauses.

The shipowner's general obligations under the Baltime 1939 (rev 2001) form follow from cl 3:

> **3. Owners' Obligations**
>
> The Owners shall provide and pay for all provisions and Wages, for insurance of the Vessel, for all deck and Engine-room stores and maintain her in a thoroughly efficient state in hull and machinery during service.

As drafted, this clause embraces two sets of duties, one relating to 'payment' and the other concerning a 'duty to maintain'. Under the maintenance clauses, the shipowner has an ongoing obligation to maintain the ship in 'a thoroughly efficient state in hull and machinery', which leaves no doubt regarding which physical parts the owner must maintain.[37] Similar wording is found under cl 6 of the well-known NYPE 2015 form,[38] as well as other time charterparty forms fitted for more specific voyages.[39]

[35] See Code for Recognized Organisations (RO Code), Resolution MEPC.237(65).

[36] See section III above.

[37] H Bennett et al, *Carver on Charterparties*, 2nd edn (London, Sweet & Maxwell, 2020) 7–805ff; T Coghlin et al, *Time Charters*, 7th edn (London, Informa Law from Routledge, 2014) 11.

[38] See also NYPE 1946 (cl 2) and NYPE 1993 (cl 6).

[39] See Boxtime 2004 (cl 2) and Gencon 2022 (cl 21(2)).

However, the precise understanding of 'a thoroughly efficient state' and whether this entails an obligation to retrofit a ship in order to be EEXI compliant remains unclear. In order to determine this, the clause will have to give effect to the parties' objective intentions, including reference to the remaining context of the clause and the time charterparty as a whole.[40]

Under cl 1 of Baltime 1939 (2001 revision), the shipowner must deliver 'the Vessel being in every way fitted for ordinary cargo service'. The clause is also to be understood to contain a requirement for the owner to deliver a ship in a seaworthy state.[41] The reasoning for such an obligation is that the ship delivered must be 'fit to meet and undergo the perils of the sea and other incidental risks to which she must of necessity be exposed in the course of the voyage'.[42] The assessment of whether a ship can be deemed seaworthy depends on several factors, such as the type of ship being chartered and the known intended usages of ship.[43]

Clause 2 of NYPE 2015 states that 'the Vessel on delivery shall be seaworthy'; this provides an express requirement for the ship to be delivered in a seaworthy state. In comparison, cl 5 of NYPE 46 states that the ship must delivered 'with hull, machinery and equipment in a thoroughly efficient state …' and cl 2 of NYPE 93 states that 'The Vessel on her delivery shall be ready to receive cargo with clean-swept holds and tights, staunch, strong and in every way fitted for ordinary cargo service …'. While NYPE 46 and NYPE 93 do not have the same express requirement, the shipowner still has an implied obligation to deliver a seaworthy ship under these standard time charterparties.[44]

In practice, the seaworthiness of a ship is documented through surveys that attest to its seaworthiness.[45] Recognised organisations, such as classification societies, typically conduct these surveys.[46] The consequences of missing certificates depend on the flag state's laws and enforcement carried out by port states. However, it is to be expected that the port state will detain the ship until the necessary certification is obtained.

As previously stated, the EEXI requirement was introduced as a part of the mandatory International Energy Efficiency Certificate (the 'IEE Certificate').[47] If a ship does not obtain the IEE certificate, it may lead to the ship being detained in port, as the ship would no longer be considered seaworthy.

Under the obligation to maintain the ship, the shipowner is obligated to maintain the ship's seaworthiness throughout the time charterparty.[48] Therefore, the shipowner will, in most instances, also have an obligation to implement EEXI compliance measures, as

[40] Bennett et al (n 37) 2-079-2-081.

[41] Bennett et al (n 37) 3-075. T Falkanger et al, *Scandinavian Maritime Law*, 4th edn (Oslo, Universitetsforlaget, 2017) 450–451.

[42] *Kopitoff v Wilson* (1876) 1 QBD 377 (Div Ct), 380 (Field J). See also ibid.

[43] S Girvin, 'The Obligation of Seaworthiness: Shipowner and Charterer' (NUS Working Paper 2017/019, 2017) 17.

[44] Bennett et al (n 37) 3-074-3-075. Under Danish law, these wordings will not be considered an express implication of seaworthiness, *cf* Falkanger (n 41) 451.

[45] See also s 372 of the Danish Merchant Shipping Act.

[46] T Falkanger, H Bull and L Overby, *Søret*, 5th edn (Karnov Group Denmark, 2019) 49.

[47] See above, section II.

[48] Falkanger et al (n 41) 452. An implied obligation in this regard is also found under s 384(1) of the Danish Merchant Shipping Act.

the ship can otherwise be considered unseaworthy due to missing the mandatory IEE Certificate. However, the option as to which measures are taken to comply with the EEXI requirement remains with the shipowner. As such, the charterer is not entitled to demand a certain measure over another.[49]

NYPE 2015 includes a detailed regulation of the parties' obligations and rights. Under cl 6(b), the shipowner has a duty to ensure documentation, which is needed for the ship to sail within the agreed areas under the standard time charterparty. Several specific certificates, which the shipowner is obligated to ensure that the ship obtains, are mentioned. However, the obligation to provide such documentation is not limited to the specific certificates mentioned as cl 6(b) states 'including but not limited to'. Therefore, cl 6(b) supports the principle that the shipowner must ensure the ship is retrofitted to ensure that the ship complies with the EEXI requirement, which is a prerequisite for obtaining the IEE Certificate.

A more express regulation may be found in some of the specialised time charterparty forms. For instance, Bimchemtime 2005, cl 15(b), establishes a general obligation for the shipowner during the entire time charterparty period to ensure the ship's compliance with new legal requirements unless it would require a significant structural change or addition to the vessel. In case of significant structural changes or additions to the ship, it follows from cl 15(c) that the time charterer has the right to introduce such changes and additions at their own expense and under normal hire payment arrangements. Further, if the time charterer does not want to introduce the change, the shipowner can choose to introduce such changes or additions to the ship. Suppose neither party can agree on who should undertake the obligation to ensure compliance. In that case, the parties have 60 days to negotiate a solution, after which the time charterer, in the absence of agreement between the parties, has seven days to maintain or terminate the time charterparty with the effect of 30 days before the new regulatory change takes effect. The parties have the option when entering into the time charterparty to define when a change or addition, based on cost considerations, should be deemed significant.[50] Gastime contains a similar clause, but the parties may also request the arbitral tribunal to allocate the costs between them.[51]

V. Off-hire

A. In the Context of Charterparties

The charterer pays the hire for the entire time that the ship is at its disposal.[52] However, during the charterparty period, situations may arise when the time charterer cannot use the ship, for example, as a result of required maintenance of the ship. The question as

[49] Resolution MEPC.328(76) [2021], reg 25.
[50] See Gastime, cl 15(d).
[51] ibid cl 15(c) para 3.
[52] See Girvin (ch 3) section III(B)(vi).

to who must bear the costs for the time lost will generally be regulated under the time charterparty in an off-hire clause, where the parties agree under which circumstances the charterer is not to pay hire.[53] The following off-hire clause is found in Baltime 1939 (2001 rev):

> **11. Suspension of Hire etc.**
>
> **(A)** In the event of drydocking or other necessary measures to maintain the efficiency of the Vessel, deficiency of men or Owners' stores, breakdown of machinery, damage to hull or other accident, either hindering or preventing the working of the Vessel and continuing for more than twenty-four consecutive hours, no hire shall be paid in respect of any time lost thereby during the period in which the Vessel is unable to perform for the service immediately required. Any hire paid in advance shall be adjusted accordingly.
>
> **(B)** In the event of the Vessel being driven into port or to anchorage through stress of weather, trading to shallow harbours or to rivers or ports with bars or suffering an accident to her cargo, any detention of the Vessel and/or expenses resulting from such detention shall be for the Charterers' account even if such detention and/or expenses or the cause by reason of which either is incurred, be due to, or contributed to by, the negligence of the Owners' servants.

This off-hire clause specifies a detailed list of events that result in the ship being off-hire, after which the time charterer is not required to pay time charter hire for that period. This will include under cl 11(a) 'necessary measures to maintain the efficiency of the Vessel' if it prevents commercial use for more than 24 hours. As the clause contains a 24-hour threshold, meaning that if one of the listed events does not prevent the ship's use for more than 24 hours, the charterer is not exempted from its obligation to pay hire. Thereby, the shipowner will not be liable for insignificant time loss. If, on the other hand, an event covered by the clause extends over 24 hours, the charterer is not obligated to pay hire for the full loss of time, including the first 24 hours.[54]

A loss of time may occur if the shipowner does not implement EEXI compliance measures and obtain an IEE Certificate. The absence of the IEE Certificate may also mean the ship is detained by port state control and ordered to obtain the relevant certificate before leaving the port. However, the clause must be understood according to its wording, and as such, the ship will not be off-hire during detention.[55]

With regards to the time loss resulting from implementing EEXI compliance measures, Baltime cl 11(A) must be considered 'necessary measures to maintain the efficiency of the Vessel' if the *ejusdem generis*[56] interpretation rule is used.

The same is not necessarily true for time loss due to port authority detention due to missing IEE Certificates. Baltime, cl 11(B) provides that detention of the ship for ship deficiencies due to the ship being driven into port or to anchorage through stress of weather, trading to shallow harbours or to rivers or ports with bars or suffering an accident to her cargo shall be for the charterer's account, even if the detention is 'incurred, be due to, or contributed to by' the negligence of the shipowner's servants. However, the

[53] See further Coghlin et al (n 37) para 25.2.

[54] Falkanger et al (n 41) 477; P Gram, *Chartering Documents* (London, Lloyd's of London Press Ltd, 1981) 71.

[55] See below, section V(B) for the position under Danish law.

[56] ie, 'of the same class (kind)': see *Andre & Cie SA v Orient Shipping (Rotterdam BV (The Laconian Confidence)* [1997] 1 Lloyd's Rep 139.

clause does not deal with the scenario where the detention is directly due to the shipowner, including the lack of ensuring the needed certificates. Thus, a ship chartered on the Baltime form will not be considered off-hire in case of detention by port authorities due to missing certificates (such as the IEE Certificate), as the clause otherwise contains an explicit regulation of which time loss events are the responsibility of the owner.

By contrast, the off-hire clause in NYPE 2015 reads as follows:[57]

> **17. Off-Hire**
>
> In the event of loss of time from deficiency and/or default and/or strike of officers or ratings, or deficiency of stores, fire, breakdown of, or damage to hull, machinery or equipment, grounding, detention by the arrest of the Vessel, (unless such arrest is caused by an event for which the Charterers, their sub-charterers, servants, agents or sub-contractors are responsible), or detention by Port State control or other competent authority for Vessel deficiencies, or detention by average accidents to the Vessel or cargo, unless resulting from inherent vice, quality or defect of the cargo, drydocking for the purpose of examination, cleaning and/or painting of underwater parts and/or repair, or by any other similar cause preventing the full working of the Vessel, the payment of hire and overtime, if any, shall cease for the time thereby lost.

The clause will be effective if the ship is off-hire during maintenance because the clause provides that the ship is off-hire during 'drydocking for the purpose of examination, cleaning and/or painting of underwater parts and/or repair, or by any other similar cause'.[58] Also, the wording explicitly states that the ship will be off-hire due to the time lost caused by 'detention by port state control'. Accordingly, detention of the ship because of the lack of an IEE Certificate entails the ship being off-hire.[59] For charterparties concluded on the earlier NYPE 93 or NYPE 46 forms, detention by port state control would also constitute an off-hire event, as this would be considered as 'any other cause preventing the full working of the vessel'.[60]

It should be noted that the lost time during the implementation of EEXI compliance measures, namely, ShaPoLi or EPL, may be reduced if the implementation is made in connection with the scheduled maintenance of the ship.

B. In the Context of Danish Law

Under Danish law, off-hire clauses that are unclear or cannot be considered exhaustive can be interpreted or supplemented under section 392 of the Danish Merchant Shipping Act.[61] Section 392 provides that in the event of loss of time due to conditions for which the shipowner bears the risk, the charterer will be exempted from paying hire for the lost time. As it is unclear whether the charterer would also bear the costs during the ship's detention caused directly by the shipowner, a standard form off-hire clause

[57] See also Coghlin et al (n 37) 25.

[58] Such an understanding of the clause is in line with both Danish law as well. See s 392 of the Danish Merchant Shipping Act, A Møllmann, *Certepartifortolkning – i nordisk og engelsk ret* (Copenhagen, Jurist- og Økonomiforbundets Forlag, 2007) 65.

[59] This also holds true under Danish law.

[60] *The Laconian Confidence* (n 56) 150.

[61] ND 1952.442 ('M/S Hakefjord') [1952]; ND 1962.68 ('NV Hindanger') [1962]; ND 1950.398 ('M/S Karnøy') [1950].

must be interpreted under section 392 of the Act. A detention due to missing certificates must be considered an event for which the shipowner bears the risk, and as such, the ship will be off-hire during such detention under section 392 of the Act.

However, the same does not hold true under English law, as the principle of interpreting or supplementing off-hire clauses does not apply.[62]

VI. Implications for Speed Warranties

A. In the Context of Charterparties

Retrofitting the ship with a ShaPoLi or an EPL may prevent the use of the ship's actual maximum speed.[63]

In the context of existing time charterparties, the shipowner and the charterer will always agree that the chartered ship is able to sail with a certain speed, written into the time charterparty as a speed warranty.[64] Accordingly, retrofitting the ship with a ShaPoLi or an EPL will result in the vessel being unable to perform at the warranted speed. This can have major financial consequences for the charterer, as the charterer considers the ship's speed when estimating the expected commercial exploitation of the ship.

Under Baltime 1939 (rev 2001), the ship's speed is regulated in Box 12, in which the parties indicate the speed in knots that the ship is capable of sailing and its estimated fuel consumption. The following appears from the preamble:

> It is agreed between the party […] [that the ship shall be] fully loaded capable of steaming about the number of knots indicated in Box 12 in good weather and smooth water on a consumption of about the number of tons fuel oil stated in Box 12.

The decision in *The Al Bida*[65] establishes that the term 'about' cannot be determined precisely but must take into consideration the specific circumstances. Parker LJ stated in this regard that 'the margin imported in the word "about" cannot be fixed as a matter of law. The margin must, as the arbitrators rightly held, "be tailored to the ship's configuration, size, draft and trim, etc"'. In practice, when disputes arise in connection with speed performance, the parties will often agree to set a threshold of 0.5 knots.[66]

If the parties have indicated that the chartered ship can sail at a given speed and the ship cannot do so, this can be considered a breach of an intermediate term[67] of the charterparty.[68] If ShaPoLi or EPL measures are implemented under existing time charter parties, the same will apply if the speed of the vessel is affected. A breach of contract in this scenario would typically result in damages unless the charterer can demonstrate

[62] Møllmann (n 58) 72–75.

[63] Resolution MEPC.351(78) [2022]. See also Girvin (ch 3) section III(D)(iii).

[64] See below, section VI(A) and under NYPE; See Coghlin et al (n 37) 61.

[65] *Arab Maritime Petroleum Transport Co v Luxor Trading Corporation (The Al Bida)* [1987] 1 Lloyd's Rep 124 (CA).

[66] Coghlin et al (n 37) 3.79.

[67] See also the discussion in Arda (ch 10) section III(A).

[68] ibid 3.77.

that the reduction in speed was a crucial factor, particularly if the vessel has been chartered for a specific service where its speed is a significant requirement.[69]

However, the question remains as to when the speed warranty must be fulfilled. The decision handed down in 2002 in *The Pamphilos*[70] established that a ship must comply with the agreed speed capabilities at the time of delivery.[71] However, the issue in that case was also whether the ship's reduced speed may have been due to fouling on the hull and whether the overgrowth had occurred during the charter period or upon delivery. In this regard, the arbitrators stated the following:[72]

> The vessel did not have a record of underperformance during the period of trading between drydocking and her delivery at Sepetiba under the time charter as was to be inferred from inter alia the absence of claims by charterers to make deductions from hire. … It was to be inferred from that fact and from the vessel's performance on the ballast approach voyage from Piombino to Sepetiba via Algeceris that the vessel had been kept in a thoroughly efficient state in hull, machinery and equipment and was capable of complying with the speed and consumption warranty at the date of delivery.

The *Pamphilos* decision could be interpreted to suggest that events occurring after the ship's delivery, which diminishes its performance due to the shipowner's failure to fulfil its maintenance obligation, might constitute a breach of the speed warranty under the Baltime charterparty. However, the implementation of EEXI compliance measures is carried out to fulfil the shipowner's obligation to keep the ship seaworthy. Consequently, it remains uncertain whether retrofitting a ship with EEXI compliance measures that affect the vessel's speed would be considered a violation of the speed warranty stipulated in the Baltime form.

Under NYPE 2015,[73] the ship's speed is to be provided in knots under Appendix A. Further regulation of the ship's speed appears from cl 12, where the following is stated:[74]

> **12. Speed and Consumption**
>
> (a) Upon delivery and throughout the duration of this Charter Party the Vessel shall be capable of speed and daily consumption rates as stated in Appendix A in good weather on all sea passages with wind up to …

In other words, the charterparty specifically states that the ship must be able to sail at the speed specified in the speed warranty throughout the entire charterparty.[75] The wording of the clause leaves no doubts as to the shipowner's warranty concerning the speed of the ship.

A test will be made to establish whether the chartered ship complies with a given speed warranty. The test is made by looking at the ship's speed for the performed

[69] ibid.

[70] *Bulfracht (Cyprus) Ltd v Boneset Shipping Co Ltd (The Pamphilos)* [2002] EWHC 2292 (Comm), [2002] 2 Lloyd's Rep 681.

[71] See also *Cosmos Bulk Transport Incorporated v China National Foreign Trade Transportation Co (The Apollonius)* [1978] 1 Lloyd's Rep 53.

[72] Above (n 68) 684.

[73] Under NYPE 46, line 4, an obligation is undertaken in respect of the horsepower of the engine.

[74] See further Coghlin et al (n 37) 3.67.

[75] NYPE 46, line 4, and the preliminary vessel description under NYPE 93 does not contain a continuous obligation.

voyages during a certain period of time under good weather conditions.[76] Such a test will most likely establish that the ship has not sailed with the guaranteed speed due to the impact of the EEXI compliance measures, and the test would reflect the ship's speed at the time of delivery.

Shipowners may argue that the test cannot be used as evidence of performance as the EEXI compliance measure is to be considered a 'special circumstance' affecting the logged speed entries of the ship. However, such arguments must be refuted as the EEXI compliance measure would require deliberate and planned action by the shipowner to ensure compliance with EEXI compliance measures. For that reason, implementing EEXI compliance measures would not be considered a special circumstance, in contrast to events such as adverse weather conditions.

Accordingly, due to the implementation of EEXI compliance measures, eg EPL or ShaPoLi, the shipowner may be in breach of its speed warranty, as the implementation hereof may reduce the ship's speed capability. This will affect the log's speed entries, which is the basis for the speed at the time of delivery.

B. In the Context of Danish law

Under Danish law, the ship's speed entries will also be used to determine the speed at the time of delivery.[77] In what may be considered contrary to English law, when the shipowner has provided a speed warranty that states the vessel must achieve a speed performance of 'about' a certain speed, a deviation of approximately 0.5 knots will be within the tolerated margin.[78] In order for a charterer to determine a breach of the speed warranty due to the implementation of EEXI compliance measures, the charterer would thus have to determine that the maximum speed has been decreased by over half a knot.

VII. Contractual Adjustment Measures

A. BIMCO Clauses

There is a tradition of negotiating new clauses to overcome issues that could otherwise hinder or change the parties' obligations throughout the charterparty.[79] Following the general principles of contract law, it is up to the parties to negotiate and adopt the additional clauses to supplement their contract.

Regarding compliance with the technical energy efficiency requirement (EEXI), BIMCO has developed the EEXI Transition Clause for Time Charter Parties 2021 (the 'EEXI Transition Clause'). The clause aims to clarify the allocation of responsibilities and economic consequences that may arise from EEXI compliance measures between

[76] Coghlin et al (n 37) 3.79.

[77] HP Michelet, *Håndbok i tidsbefraktning* (Oslo, Sjørettsfondet, 1997) 34.

[78] ND 1958-8 (M/S Ole Bratt), see also Falkanger et al (n 41) 505.

[79] Currently, BIMCO has more than 160 active supplementary clauses that parties may adopt to adjust their contract. See www.bimco.org/contracts-and-clauses/bimco-clauses.

the parties. In particular, the clause regulates a limitation of propeller shaft power (ShaPoLi) or a limitation of engine power (EPL).[80]

Under the EEXI Transition Clause, cl(b), the shipowner commits to comply with the EEXI requirement before the next relevant survey of the ship. Subsequently, cl(c) exhaustively regulates how the parties should act when introducing a ShaPoLi or an EPL. If the shipowner wishes to take other measures to comply with the EEXI requirement, this requires the charterer's acceptance, as per cl(d).

As previously illustrated, the retrofitting of ships with either ShaPoLi and EPL will, under most standard time charterparties, leave the shipowner unable to comply with the agreed speed and performance figures. Clause (c)(i) of the EEXI Transition Clause provides a solution by stipulating that the ship's estimated maximum speed and fuel consumption after such measures must be calculated and communicated to the charterer without undue delay.

Under cl(c)(ii), the shipowner must make reasonable efforts to implement the measures during regular maintenance of the ship and without causing any delay for the charterer. However, the shipowner has the right to take the ship out of service to implement the needed modifications. In addition, the shipowner may demand to be informed of the planned sea routes during the time charter period, and the charterer must notify the shipowner of any changes pursuant to cl(c)(iii) of the EEXI Transition Clause. The clause states the shipowner must inform the charterer of the timing, location, and duration of a planned introduction of EPL and ShaPoLi no later than three weeks before.

Under cl(c)(iv), the shipowner will bear all costs associated with the introduction of either EPL or ShaPoLi, and the ship will also be considered off-hire during the introduction. After installing the EEXI compliance measures, the shipowner must inform the charterer of the vessel's new maximum speed and fuel consumption. Suppose the figures reported to the charterer are lower than the original values in the time charterparty. In that case, in accordance with cl(c)(v) of the EEXI Transition Clause, the new figures will replace these. According to the EEXI Transition Clause, this also applies to other changes to the ship's description resulting from the introduction of EPL and ShaPoLi.

Finally, the charterer will undertake an obligation not to sail faster than the ship's new maximum speed limit according to cl(c)(vi) of the EEXI Transition Clause.

Thus, the EEXI Transition Clause solves the two significant contractual problems related to retrofitting ships to comply with the EEXI requirement, including introducing the IMO's recommended compliance measures, ShaPoLi or EPL. This concerns: (i) compliance with the EEXI requirement under the shipowner's maintenance obligation, and (ii) the impact of the EEXI requirement for the shipowner's speed warranty. Under the EEXI Transition Clause, the shipowner is responsible for all costs and releases the charterer from paying hire during the implementation of ShaPoLi or EPL. Furthermore, the ship's new maximum speed and fuel consumption will replace the values that may appear in the original time charter party. Therefore, if the additional clause is adopted, the charterer cannot invoke the original maximum speed warranty under the time charterparty when the ship is no longer able to sail at that speed due to the introduction of EEXI compliance measures.

[80] See above, section V.

BIMCO's EEXI Transition Clause distributes the consequences of complying with the EEXI requirement proportionally between the parties. First, the shipowner will have to pay for the introduction, after which the charterer must bear the change for the commercial use of the ship. Compared to Baltime 1939 (rev 2001) and NYPE 2015, the EEXI Transition Clause may arguably put the shipowner in a more favourable position. This is because the shipowner will not be in breach of its speed warranty. For time charterparties of longer duration, a replacement may be burdensome for the charterer.

B. Long-term Contractual Adaptions

Including the BIMCO Clauses into current charterparties entails that the parties may agree on including the clause in its current form. The shipowner will have little leverage under such negotiations, especially under existing time charterparties. This is partly due to the shipowner being required to ensure compliance with the EEXI requirement and, at the same time, being met with possible non-conforming claims with reference to the performance figures if the EEXI Transition Clause is not adopted. On the other hand, it is vital that both parties distribute equal responsibility when it comes to ensuring compliance with new sustainability regulations. In the spirit of the polluter pays principle, it would only be considered fair that the charterer also contributes to ensuring that the ship under his operational control may operate sustainably.

In any event, in order to successfully implement the EEXI Transition Clause in any form or shape will require collaboration between the shipowner and the charterer. This exercise will most likely not be the last when it comes to new climate regulation, as it must be expected that further regulations will be introduced to ensure that the climate impact of shipping is further reduced.

The parties may even consider finding inspiration for a long-term solution under other standard contracts such as Bimchemtime and Gastime.[81] The Bimchemtime and Gastime forms open for the parties to make a fairer allocation of significant costs that a regulatory change may entail. The background for this allocation of the risk of regulatory changes can, among other things, be found in the fact that Bimchemtime and Gastime are used when entering into time charter agreements to transport dangerous goods, such as harmful chemicals. The transport of dangerous goods is more heavily regulated, which makes the risk of regulatory changes more unpredictable. However, with the increased focus on climate action in the shipping industry, the same may, to some extent, be said to apply in general for all types of long-term time charterparties. The parties to time charterparties concluded on other forms, such as NYPE or Baltime, may find comfort in a predictable contractual regulation when it comes to the introduction of new climate demands to ships.

[81] See above, section IV(A).

VIII. Conclusion

As noted, the EEXI requirement in MARPOL Annex VI entered into force on 1 November 2022, with compliance on the next survey placed after 1 January 2023.[82] Under the most commonly used general time charterparties, such as Baltime 1939 and NYPE, the shipowner has an obligation to the charterer to ensure that the ship complies with the EEXI requirement.

While the shipowner is obliged to implement EEXI compliance measures, the shipowner may at the same time risk being in breach of its speed warranty since retrofitting the ship with a ShaPoLi or an EPL puts the agreed maximum speed under the time charterparty below the agreed performance figures of the ship.

This issue can be solved by adopting a transition clause such as the EEXI Transition Clause prepared by BIMCO. The EEXI Transition Clause considers the problems and challenges that the parties may face due to the EEXI regulation. The EEXI Transition Clause balances the consequences related to EEXI compliance measures by placing an obligation on the shipowner to ensure the retrofitting of the ship with a ShaPoLi or an EPL. The shipowner is obligated to bear the costs associated with such measures. However, the charterer will, in turn, be compelled to accept the ship's new performance figures due to the measures.

The risk of disputes may be mitigated by including the EEXI Transition Clause under new and existing time charterparties, which will provide clarity and predictability over the matters of EEXI compliance and the impacts on the time charterparty.

Incorporating the EEXI regulation into existing time charterparties may present challenges on its own, but by considering either the EEXI Transition Clause or an alternative distribution of risks and/or obligations, shipowners and charterers can work together to navigate this complex regulatory landscape and ensure a sustainable future for the shipping industry.

[82] See above, section II.

PART II

EU Dimension

5

Mapping the EU ETS for Shipping: Functional, Geographical, and Personal Dimensions

ELLEN JOHANNE EFTESTØL*

I. Introduction and Background

After long discussions and several legal proposals, the European Union (EU) on 10 May 2023 managed to agree on how to expand the European Union Emission Trading System (EU ETS) to shipping starting from 2024.[1] The extension takes place by amendments to the ETS Directive on establishing a system for greenhouse gas emission allowance trading within the Union (ETS Directive)[2] as well as to the 2015 regulation on monitoring, reporting and verification of carbon dioxide emissions from maritime transport, the 2015 MRV Regulation.[3] The amendments are published in Directive (EU) 2023/959.[4]

The consequence of the expansion is that starting from 1 January 2024 it will be illegal, for any shipping company calling at an EU port, to emit CO_2 without a permit.[5] The permits are limited and come with a price. The price is a market price which varies according to supply and demand. According to the European Central Bank (ECB), the price on allowances has grown from €8 per tonne in 2018 to around €40 per tonne in 2021.[6] In February 2023, the price reached a record high of €100,34 per metric ton of CO_2.[7]

* Professor of Law, BI Norwegian Business School; Visiting Professor, School of Business, Administration and Law, Gothenburg University.

[1] Directive (EU) 2023/959 of the European Parliament and of the Council of 10 May 2023 amending Directive 2003/87/EC establishing a system for greenhouse gas emission allowance trading within the Union and Decision (EU) 2015/1814 concerning the establishment and operation of a market stability reserve for the Union greenhouse gas emission trading system [2023] OJ L130/134 (the 2023 amendments).

[2] Directive 2003/87/EC of the European Parliament and the Council of 13 October 2003 establishing a system for greenhouse gas emission allowance trading within the Union and amending Council Directive 96/61/EC [2003] OJ L275/32.

[3] Regulation (EU) 2015/757 of the European Parliament and of the Council of 29 April 2015 on the monitoring, reporting and verification of carbon dioxide emissions from maritime transport, and amending Directive 2009/16/EC [2015] OJ L123/55.

[4] As of 25 September 2023. Referred to in this chapter as 'the 2023 amendments' (n 1).

[5] Below, section II.

[6] www.ecb.europa.eu/pub/economicbulletin/focus/2021/html/ecb.ebbox202106_05~ef8ce0bc70.en.html.

[7] EU ETS carbon pricing 2023, www.statista.com/statistics/1322214/carbon-prices-european-union-emission-trading-scheme/.

As of September 2023, the price was approximately €80 per metric ton of CO_2.[8] The system applies to all commercial cargo and passenger vessels above 5,000 gross tonnage calling at EU ports, and also those flagged outside the EU.[9]

Expanding the EU ETS to international shipping is considered a necessary step to fulfil the emission reduction target of the 'Fit for 55' package, where the goal is at least 55 per cent emission reduction compared to 1990 levels.[10] The reason is that shipping, due to its large dependence on fossil fuels, is considered a major polluter: global shipping is estimated to be responsible for around 2–3 per cent of total global greenhouse gas emissions. The situation is even worse at the EU level, where shipping accounts for 13 per cent of emissions from transport.[11] According to a study from the International Maritime Organization (IMO), the Fourth IMO GHG Study 2020, emissions from shipping will continue to increase.[12]

When the current EU ETS legislation was revised in 2018, it was predicted to deliver a 43 per cent reduction of EU ETS emissions by 2030 compared to 2005. This would have been coherent with the previous target of at least a 40 per cent reduction by 2030 compared to 1990.[13] However, according to the Commission, if the legislation had remained unchanged, the sectors covered by the EU ETS would achieve only a reduction of 51 per cent compared with 2005, which is not satisfactory considering the new target of at least 55 per cent reduction compared to 1990 levels. To reach the latter goal, the sectors covered by the EU ETS need an emission reduction of 61 per cent.[14] If international shipping were left outside, this would be difficult to attain.

After lengthy debates with the stakeholders and the EU Parliament, the Commission came up with a proposal for the needed regulatory changes to include emissions from international shipping to the system in 2021.[15] After this, interinstitutional negotiations followed, and the Council made several adjustments particular to the scope provisions. These adjustments are now incorporated in the 2023 amendments.

This chapter outlines the inclusion of international shipping in the European Union's Emissions Trading System (EU ETS), focusing on the scope provisions after the latest amendments.[16] Section III outlines the functional and geographical provisions, whereas the personal scope provisions are discussed in section IV. A summary and some reflections will be obtained in section V. First, however, the EU ETS system will be outlined.

[8] See eg Carbon Price Tracker (ember-climate.org).

[9] See below, section III.

[10] Communication from the Commission to the European Parliament, the Council, the European Economic and Social Committee and the Committee and the Committee of the Regions 'Fit for 55': delivering the EU's 2030 Climate Target on the way to climate neutrality. COM(2021) 550 final.

[11] ibid.

[12] Fourth IMO GHG Study 2020 (London, IMO, 2021).

[13] Proposal for a Directive of the European Parliament and of the Council amending Directive 2003/87/EC establishing a system for greenhouse gas emission allowance trading within the Union, Decision (EU) 2015/1814 concerning the establishment and operation of a market stability reserve for the Union greenhouse gas emission trading scheme and Regulation (EU) 2015/757, COM/2021/551 final (p 1).

[14] ibid.

[15] ibid.

[16] This chapter is an updated version, with the latest developments, of EJ Eftestøl, 'The Proposed Extension of the EU-ETS to Shipping – BIMCO's ETS – Allowances (ETSA) Clause for Time Charter Parties 2022 Filling a Legal Gap' in Lia Athanassiou (ed), *Protecting Maritime Operators in a Changing Regulatory and Technological Environment* (Athens, Nomiki Bibliothiki, 2023) 321. Many thanks to Anders Rønningen, Nordic Defence Club, for valuable comments on this version.

II. The EU ETS

A. A 'Cap and Trade' System

The EU Emissions Trading System (EU ETS) is defined as a cornerstone of the EU's policy to combat climate change and is considered a key tool for reducing greenhouse gas emissions cost-effectively.[17] It is the world's first major carbon market and remains the biggest one. It currently covers around 40 per cent of the EU's greenhouse gas emissions.

The main legal instrument governing the EU ETS is the ETS Directive on establishing a system for greenhouse gas emission allowance trading within the Union from 2003 with its multiple amendments.[18] The ETS Directive provides a scheme for greenhouse gas emission allowances within the community, with the aim of promoting the reduction of greenhouse gases in a cost-effective and economically effective manner.[19] It is a 'cap and trade' system. This means that a cap, a maximum, is set for the total amount of certain greenhouse gases that can be emitted by the entities covered by the system.[20] This maximum is reduced over a period so that the total emissions fall. Within the set maximum, the participants covered by the system can buy or receive emission allowances, which they can trade with one another as needed. The fact that the total number of allowances available is capped ensures that they have a value. For the EU ETS to work it is important that the emissions can be measured, reported and verified with a high level of accuracy.

It is obligatory for the sectors covered by the directive to participate in the system. The entities subject to the ETS Directive are named 'installations', and the persons in charge are 'operators'. According to Article 4 of the ETS Directive, the operator of an installation needs a permit issued by a competent authority to legally undertake activities covered by the directive. This means that any person who operates or controls[21] a technical unit where the activities listed in Annex I and the emissions listed in Annex II of the ETS Directive are carried out needs to have a permit to perform the activity.[22] The permit gives the operator allowance to emit. However, the right to emit is coupled with an obligation to surrender allowances equal to the total emissions of the installation each calendar year within four months following the end of that year.[23] As an example, this means that the deadline for paying the emissions for 2023 is 30 April 2024. By surrendering allowances, the participants compensate for their emissions from the

[17] Above (n 10) 2.2.

[18] ETS directive (n 2).

[19] ibid Art 1.

[20] ibid Art 3(e).

[21] Or, if provided for in national legislation, to whom decisive economic power of the technical functioning of the installation has been delegated: see ETS Directive (n 2) Art 4.

[22] The greenhouse gases and activities listed in Annex I and II to the ETS Directive include: Nitrous oxide (N_2O) from production of nitric, adipic and glyoxylic acids, glyoxal; perfluorocarbons (PFCs) from production of aluminium and carbon dioxide (CO_2) from electricity and heat generation, energy-intensive industry sectors including oil refineries, steel works, and production of iron, aluminium, metals, cement, lime, glass, ceramics, pulp, paper, cardboard, acids and bulk organic chemicals and commercial aviation within the European Economic Area.

[23] ETS directive (n 2) Art 6(e).

previous year, concluding that year. It is a precondition for the system to work that the operator is capable of monitoring and reporting the emitted emissions. Guidelines for monitoring and reporting emissions are provided by the Commission and ensured by the Member States.[24]

An allowance means allowance to emit one tonne of carbon dioxide equivalent during a specified period, which shall be valid only for the purpose of meeting the requirements of the ETS Directive and shall be transferable.[25] The transferability provides a right to trade the allowances and is hence a precondition for the cap-and-trade system to work. The total amount of allowances, 'the cap' under the ETS is set by the EU and divided between the Member States.[26] Allowances can thereafter be obtained through a mixture of free allowances and allowances acquired by auction. From 2021 onwards, 57 per cent of the allowances are auctioned.[27] The Member States auction their allowances in accordance with the ETS Directive Chapter II and the Auctioning Regulation.[28] Auctions are held by auction platforms. One of the auction platforms is the European Energy Exchange AG (EEX), which serves as a joint auction platform for 25 Member States and separately as auction platforms for Germany and Poland, respectively.[29]

The Member States are responsible for keeping a registry to ensure the accurate accounting of the issue, holding, transfer and cancellation of allowances.[30] It is important that the registers are public.[31] By 30 June every year, the Member State must report to the Commission on the application of the ETS Directive and the Commission must evaluate the system.[32] The results are published in an annual (technical) report from the Commission. The latest report was published on 26 July 2023.[33] It considers the reports from all countries that have implemented the EU ETS. For the reporting year 2021, these were the EU Member States, as well as Liechtenstein, Iceland, Northern Ireland and Norway. The total emissions reported increased 6.6 per cent from 1 253 mt CO_2 (eq) in 2020 to 1 335 mt CO_2 (eq) in 2021 but are still below pre-pandemic emission levels of 2019.[34]

In line with Article 16 of the ETS Directive, all countries have some form of penalty in place for different types of infringements. An overview of the sanctions and infringements across the EU ETS Member States is provided in Annex 6 of the report. Most penalties concern fines with a defined financial minimum or maximum,[35] but a prison

[24] ibid Arts 14 and 15.

[25] ibid Art 3(a).

[26] ibid Art 10.

[27] ibid Art 10 nr. 1 second para.

[28] Commission Regulation (EU) No 1031/2010 of 12 November 2010 on the timing, administration, and other aspects of auctioning of greenhouse gas emission allowances pursuant to Directive 2003/87/EC of the European Parliament and of the Council establishing a system for greenhouse gas emission allowances trading within the Union [2010] OJ L302/1.

[29] European Energy Exchange AG (EEX): see www.eex.com/en/.

[30] ETS Directive (n 2) Art 19 nr. 2.

[31] ibid.

[32] ibid Art 21.

[33] European Commission, Directorate-General for Climate Action, Application of the European Union Emissions Trading Directive – Analysis of national responses under Article 21 of the EU ETS Directive (reported data in 2022), Publications Office of the European Union, 2023 www.data.europa.eu/doi/10.2834/576137.

[34] ibid 2.

[35] The variation in fines among countries is high. The report from 2022 does not contain any number, but according to the previous report, the minimum fines range from €63 (Hungary, per day) to €75,000 (France)

sentence may also be imposed.[36] In addition, some countries provide the option to impose penalties other than fines and prison sentences. This can, for example, be an option to shut down an installation for a period.[37] All countries have a defined penalty for infringements such as not having a permit or not complying with permit conditions, not submitting an emission report, and not monitoring in line with the approved monitoring plan. The fines for these categories are usually also higher than for other types of infringements.[38] In addition to the general penalties, the Member States have additional tools for Shipping Companies not complying with the system.[39]

B. The Extension of the EU ETS to Shipping

i. The Obligations

Starting in 2024, and with some modifications, the EU ETS will apply to shipping. The extension to shipping is well prepared. Since 1 July 2015, when it entered into force,[40] the 2015 EU MRV regulation has been EU law. According to the regulation, from 2018 all companies[41] with vessels subject to the regulation, must monitor, verify and report their emissions in a yearly report.[42] The emission report is to be submitted to the Commission and the authorities of the flag States involved by 30 April each year, starting from 2019.[43] The information is submitted in an electronic inspection database called THETIS[44] and used for calculating the amount of allowances each ship must surrender.[45] The required data is therefore already available.

THETIS is developed, maintained, and hosted by the European Maritime Safety Agency (EMSA). EMSA has developed a new module in THETIS, namely THETIS-MRV, enabling companies responsible for the operation of large ships using EU ports to report their CO_2 emissions under the 2015 MRV regulation. THETIS-MRV includes

per infringement and the maximum ranges from €102 plus the allowance price (Liechtenstein per tonne CO_2) to €16 million (Estonia). In some countries, the size of fines also differs between the 14 types of infringements reported under Art 21. M Oudenes et al, *Application of the European Union Emission Trading Directive: Analysis of National Responses under Article 21 of the EU ETS Directive in 2020* (Luxembourg, European Union, 2021) 94.

[36] Cyprus, Denmark, Estonia (for some infringements), Ireland, Luxembourg, Norway and Sweden (for some infringements) provide for the possibility of a prison sentence of up to 120 months (Ireland) for some or all types of infringements. France is the only country that has indicated a minimum prison sentence: a period of 12 months for operating without a permit or failure to comply with the conditions of the permit. See ibid.

[37] In Greece the authorities have the option to shut down installations for a period between 5 and 20 days: ibid.

[38] ibid.

[39] See below, section B(ii).

[40] MRV Regulation (n 3) Art 26.

[41] According to the MRV Regulation (n 3) Art 3(d), 'company' means 'the shipowner or any other organisation or person, such as the manager or the bareboat charterer, which has assumed the responsibility for the operation of the ship from the shipowner'.

[42] The MRV Regulation, ibid, furthermore applies to ships above 5,000 gross tonnage calling on EU ports, with certain exemptions mentioned in 2.2. See more on the scope provisions below, section III.

[43] ibid Art 11(1).

[44] See mrv.emsa.europa.eu/#public/eumrv.

[45] See the 2023 amendments (n 1) Arts 3gd and 3ge.

a mandatory and a voluntary module. Through the mandatory module, companies will generate Emission Reports, which is assessed by Verifiers who issue an electronic Document of Compliance in the system.[46]

From 2024, the Commission is required to publish and regularly update a list of shipping companies covered by the Directive and their respective administering authority.[47] If the shipping company is registered in a Member State, the administering authority is the Member State.[48] In other cases, it will be the Member State with the greatest estimated number of port calls from voyages performed by a shipping company not registered in a Member State in the last four monitoring if falling within the scope set out in Article 3ga.[49] Lastly, if the shipping company is not registered in a Member State and did not carry out any voyage falling within the scope set out in Article 3ga in the preceding two monitoring years, the administering authority shall be the Member State from where the shipping company's ship has started its first voyage falling within the scope set out in Article 3g.[50] Where appropriate, the responsible administering authority in respect of a shipping company must be updated every other year.

ii. Penalties for Infringements

In the event that a shipping company fails to comply with the requirements, such as by missing the deadlines for surrendering emissions allowances, it runs the risk of triggering enforcement procedures according to Article 16 of the ETS Directive. As a starting point, this provision sets out that the Member States are responsible for laying down rules on penalties applicable to infringements of the national provisions adopted pursuant to the Directive. The penalties must be effective, proportionate and dissuasive.[51]

In addition to penalties decided on by the Member States, the Directive imposes a penalty fee of €100 on all responsible entities covered by the Directive, including the shipping company, for each tonne of carbon dioxide equivalent emitted for which the responsible entity has not surrendered allowances.[52] This comes on top of the obligation to surrender an amount of allowances equal to those excess emissions when surrendering allowances in relation to the following calendar year.[53] Furthermore, the directive provides for a 'name-and-shame' sanction. According to Article 16(2) of the 2023 amendment, 'Member States shall ensure publication of the names of operators, aircraft operators and shipping companies who are in breach of requirements to surrender sufficient allowances under this Directive'.

[46] The system has been available from 7 August 2017 and is available at mrv.emsa.europa.eu.
[47] The 2023 amendments (n 1) Art 3gf, 2(a).
[48] ibid Art 3gf 1(a).
[49] ibid Art 3gf 1(b).
[50] ibid Art 3gd 1(c).
[51] ibid Art 16(1).
[52] ibid Art 16(3). According to the 2023 amendments, Art 16(3) also applies to shipping companies.
[53] ibid.

As a last resort measure, the Member States should be able to refuse entry to the ships under the responsibility of the shipping company concerned, except for the Member State whose flag the ship is flying, which should be able to detain that ship.[54] A precondition in both situations is that the shipping company has failed to comply with the surrender requirements for two or more consecutive reporting periods and other enforcement methods have failed. Also, the shipping company should be allowed to submit its observations before an expulsion order is issued or the ship is detained. When an exculpation order is issued, all Member States, except the Member State whose flag the ship is flying, are required to deny the ship access to its ports until the allowances are surrendered.[55] These rules are, however, overruled by international maritime rules applicable in the case of ships in distress.[56]

III. The Functional and Geographical Scope of the Rules

A. The Functional Scope

i. Emissions and Vessels Covered by the System

The EU ETS applies to maritime transport activities covered by the MRV Regulation.[57]

The greenhouse gas currently covered by the system is carbon dioxide (CO_2).[58] Both methane and nitrous hydrogen are, however, to be included in the systems. The duty to monitor, report and verify these gases starts from 2024 onwards,[59] and from 1 January 2026, shipping companies will also need to surrender allowances for these gases under the EU ETS.[60] As regards carbon dioxide, however, the 2023 amendments contain an exemption for permanently captured greenhouse gases. For these, there will be no obligation to surrender allowances. The precondition is that the gases are permanently chemically bound in a product so that they do not enter the atmosphere under normal use, including any normal activity taking place after the end of the life of the product.[61] What permanently chemically bound entails will be outlined by the Commission through a delegated act in accordance with Article 23.[62]

[54] ibid Art 16 (11a). This is in line with a Port States right to take administrative measures to prevent the vessel from sailing if the ship is in violation of applicable international rules and standards relating to seaworthiness of vessels and thereby threatens damage to the marine environment, see Art 218 (1), Enforcement by port States, of the United Nations Convention of the Law of the Sea (UNCLOS).

[55] ibid.

[56] ibid.

[57] ibid Art 2.1 with reference to its Annexes I and III. The list of activities to which the EU ETS apply is, according to amendment (ix) Maritime transport activities covered by the MRV regulation, with the exemption of transport activities covered by Art 2(1a) and until 31 December 2026, Art 2(1b) of that regulation.

[58] ibid Art 2, 1 with reference to Annex I and II, which again has a reference to the 2015 MRV Regulation, Art 2.

[59] The MRV Regulation (n 3) Art 2, 1c.

[60] The 2023 amendments (n 1), preamble at 20 and Annex I (ix).

[61] ibid Art 12.3b para 1.

[62] ibid para 2.

The EU ETS is limited to ships transporting cargo or passengers for commercial purposes. Warships, naval auxiliaries, fish-catching or fish-processing ships, wooden ships of a primitive build, ships not propelled by mechanical means or government ships used for non-commercial purposes are exempt.[63]

Obviously, the scope provisions have been subject to political discussions. Following the interinstitutional discussions during the legislative process, the Council suggested that including smaller vessels in the EU ETS in the future would improve the effectiveness of the ETS and potentially reduce evasive behaviours with the use of vessels below the 5,000 gross tonnage threshold.[64] Hence, it was decided that the Commission should present a report to the European Parliament and to the Council no later than 31 December 2026 in which it should examine the feasibility and cost-effectiveness of the inclusion of emissions from ships below 5,000 gross tonnage but not below 400 gross tonnage.[65] In the report, the Commission should also consider whether off-shore vessels should be included in the system.

The outcome of the discussions are now implemented in the ETS directive through its 2023 amendment. From 2024 the EU ETS will apply to ships of 5000 gross tonnage and above that are transporting cargo or passengers for commercial purposes. Off-shore vessels of the same size will be included in the system from 2027.[66] There is still no agreement on whether or not the ETS should apply to vessels between 5000 and 400 gross tonnage, but from 1 January 2025, these vessels will be included in the scope of the MRV regulation.[67] In addition the agreed 2023 amendment contains several exemptions from the system.

ii. Exemptions for Voyages to Certain Islands and Routes

Until 31 December 2030, Member States can request for exemptions from the ETS obligations for voyages performed by passenger ships,[68] and by ro-pax ships, between a port of an island under the jurisdiction of that requesting Member State, with no road or rail link with the mainland and with a population of fewer than 200,000 permanent residents.[69] The Commission must publish a list of the islands referred to in the first subparagraph and the ports concerned and keep that list up to date.[70]

Two Member States can also within the same time frame, apply – jointly – for exemptions from the ETS obligations providing that one of the Member States have no land border with another Member State and the other Member State is the geographically closest Member State to the Member State without a land border with any EU Member State. This exemption only applies to voyages performed by passenger or ro-pax ships in the framework of a transnational public service contract or a transnational public service obligation.[71]

[63] The 2015 MRV Regulation (n 3) Art 2.2.
[64] The proposed changes 19 b) by the Council to the 2003 Directive of 30 July 2022: pdf (europa.eu) 14.
[65] The 2023 amendments (n 1), Art 3 gg (5).
[66] The ETS directive (n 2) Art 2, the 2023 amendment (n 1) Annex 1(1)(c)(ix).
[67] The MRV Regulation (n 3) Art 2, 1a and 1b.
[68] This does not include cruise passenger ships.
[69] The 2023 amendments (n 1) Art 3d.
[70] ibid second para.
[71] ibid Art 3c.

Lastly, an obligation to surrender allowances does not arise in respect of emissions released from voyages between a port located in an outermost region of a Member State and a port located in the same Member State.[72]

B. The Geographical Scope

i. The Port of Call Concept

The geographical scope of the EU ETS is extracted from the geographical scope of the EU, which equals the jurisdiction of the Member States, as well as the definition of 'port of call' in both the 2015 MRV Regulation and the 2023 amendments.[73] Under both the regulation and the directive, a 'port of call' means '… the port where a ship stops to load or unload cargo or to embark or disembark passengers'. In addition, the 2023 amendments prepare for including offshore ships by adding to the port of call definition, '… the port where an offshore ship stops to relieve the crew …'.[74]

There is, however, a list of exemptions from the scope provisions. Under the 2015 MRV Regulation, the following is excluded:[75]

> … stops for the sole purposes of refuelling, obtaining supplies, relieving the crew, going into dry-dock or making repairs to the ship and/or its equipment, stops in port because the ship is in need of assistance or in distress, ship-to-ship transfers carried out outside ports, and stops for the sole purpose of taking shelter from adverse weather or rendered necessary by search and rescue activities.

The same exemptions, and a few more, apply under the EU ETS. Excluded from the 'port of call' definition are:

> … stops for the sole purposes of refuelling, obtaining supplies, relieving the crew of a ship other than an offshore ship, going into dry-dock or making repairs to the ship, its equipment, or both, stops in port because the ship is in need of assistance or in distress, ship-to-ship transfers carried out outside ports, stops for the sole purpose of taking shelter from adverse weather or rendered necessary by search and rescue activities, and stops of containerships in a neighbouring container transhipment port listed in the implementing act adopted pursuant to Article 3ga(2).

Whilst the inclusion of 'offshore vessels relieving the crew of a ship' to the EU ETS is feasible, considering that carrying crew is a major task of these vessels, the exemption for 'stops of containerships in a neighbouring container transhipment port' must be read considering the exterritorial scope of the system.

Obviously, the port of call definition mentioned above includes voyages within the European Union, including both EU national and EU international voyages. In addition to this, based on the 2023 amendments Article 3ga, the EU ETS for shipping apply to '… ships performing voyages departing from a port of call under the jurisdiction of a Member State and arriving at a port of call outside the jurisdiction of a Member State …'.

[72] ibid Art 3b.
[73] The 2015 MRV Regulation (n 3) Art 3(b), and the 2023 amendments (n 1) Art 3(z).
[74] The 2023 amendments (n 1) Art 3(z).
[75] The 2015 MRV Regulation (n 3) Art 3(b).

The abovementioned exemptions from the port of call concept are made to mitigate the risk of evasive stops outside the EU. The exclusion is targeted to ports in the Union's vicinity where the risk of evasion is the largest. Following the suggestion of the Council, a limit of 300 nautical miles is seen to constitute a proportionate response to evasive behaviour, balancing the additional burden and the risk of evasion. The idea is that if the ship calls on a port closer than 300 nautical miles from the EU, this port will not be considered a port of call in relation to the shipping companies' duty to surrender allowances for the voyage. If the vessel departs from Singapore, stops at the Port of Felixstowe to unload, and tranship containers, and continues to Rotterdam, the ports of call will be Singapore and Rotterdam. The emissions which the shipping company will have to surrender, will be the emissions from the entire voyage, and not limited to the voyage from Port of Felixstowe to Rotterdam. The stop at Felixstowe could be considered an evasive stop outside the EU. This does not apply if the UK 'effectively applies measures equivalent to … [this] directive'.[76]

The exclusion from the concept of port of call does not, however, target all ports within 300 nautical miles from the EU. Only 'containerships and ports whose main activity is the transhipment of containers' are subject to the exception. The share of transhipment of containers, measured in 20-foot equivalent units, '[must] exceed […] 65% of the total container traffic of that port during the most recent twelve-month period for which relevant data are available'.[77] This means that all other vessels than large containerships can make evasive stops outside the EU and reduce their numbers of emissions considerably. In the Port of Felixstowe example, the decision depends on the features of the port – or for more practical purposes, whether the port in the example will be on the list of neighbouring ports, which is to be published by the Commission by 31 December 2023. The list will make the system transparent and should be updated by 31 December every two years thereafter.[78]

ii. The Extraterritorial Scope

The extension of the EU ETS to international shipping includes a duty to surrender allowances as described above.[79] This duty will cover carbon emissions that occur not only inside the EU, but even emissions related to voyages outside the EU. This exterritorial extension of the system gives rise to both political and legal concerns. From a legal perspective, the question of whether the EU has the competence to include emissions from third-country vessels entering EU territory as regards CO_2 gases emitted outside the EU, arises. The EU itself advocates that it has this competence. A decision of the European Union Court of Justice (CJEU) in the *ATA* case[80] also suggests that the EU has such competence under EU law. Even though the case directly concerned the external dimension of a Directive from 2008 on including international aviation to the EU ETS,

[76] The 2023 amendments (n 1) Art 3ga(2), second para.
[77] ibid.
[78] ibid first para.
[79] See section II(B)(i).
[80] Case C-366/10 *Air Transport Association of America and Others v Secretary of State for Energy and Climate Change* ECLI:EU:C:2011:864.

the problem is parallel for international shipping.[81] It seems also that an inclusion of CO_2 gases emitted outside the EU into the EU ETS for vessels calling at EU ports, does not violate public international law.[82]

In order to comply with the praxis of the CJEU and the raised concerns related to the exterritorial effect of the extension of the EU ETS to international shipping, the EU has limited the exterritorial effect of the system: Only 50 per cent of the emissions from voyages between a port of call under the jurisdiction of a Member State and a port of call under the jurisdiction of a third country (or the other way around) is included in the EU ETS.[83] This solution gives third-party countries a possibility to decide on appropriate actions in respect of the 'free' half of emissions from voyages between it and the EU.[84] The solution also opens for other countries to adopt similar systems.

IV. Personal Scope: Who Takes Responsibility?

A. The Shipping Company, the Charterer or the Ship Management Company?

Both the 2015 MRV Regulation[85] and the 2023 amendments[86] point to the 'shipping company' as the legal entity 'liable to surrender allowances' according to the schedule provided in Article 3gb. The shipping company is also the entity responsible for monitoring and reporting the relevant parameters during the one-year reporting period. It is in other words paramount to define the term 'shipping company'. According to the agreed Article 3(w), it includes the

> … shipowner or any other organisation or person, such as the manager or the bareboat charterer, that has assumed the responsibility for the operation of the ship from the shipowner and that, on assuming such responsibility, has agreed to take over all the duties and

[81] See Directive 2008/101/EC of the European Parliament and of the Council of 19 November 2008 amending Directive 2003/87/EC so as to include aviation activities in the scheme for greenhouse gas emission allowance trading within the Community [2009] OJ L8/3. For a thorough analysis, see G De Baere and C Ryngaert, 'The ECJ's Judgment in Air Transport Association of America and the International Legal Context of the EU's Climate Change Policy' (2013) 18(2) *European Foreign Affairs Rev* 389.

[82] See DP Rodríguez, 'The Inclusion of Shipping in the EU Emissions Trading Scheme: A Legal Analysis in the Light of Public International Law' (2012) 3(2) *Revista Catalanade de Dret Ambiental* 1, available at www.ssrn.com/abstract=2210858. The position is however questioned by H Ringbom, 'Global Problem – Regional Solution? International Law Reflections on an EU CO_2 Emissions Trading Scheme for Ships' (2011) 26 *Int'l J of Marine and Coastal Law* 613.

[83] The 2023 amendment (n 1) Art 3ga, 1.

[84] See the proposed Art 3g on scope of application to maritime transport activities: '1.The allocation of allowances and the application of surrender requirements in respect of maritime transport activities under the jurisdiction of a Member State and arriving at a port outside the jurisdiction of a Member State, fifty per cent (50%) of the emissions from ships performing voyage departing from a port outside the jurisdiction of a Member State and arriving at a port under the jurisdiction of a Member State, one hundred per cent (100%) of emissions from ships performing voyages departing from a port under the jurisdiction of a Member State and arriving at a port under the jurisdiction of a Member State and one hundred per cent (100%) of emissions from ships at berth in a port under the jurisdiction of a Member State. '.

[85] The MRV Regulation (n 3) Art 3(d).

[86] The 2023 amendments (n 1) Art 3gb.

> responsibilities imposed by the International Management Code for the Safe Operation of Ships and for Pollution Prevention set out in Annex I to Regulation (EC) No 336/2006 of the European Parliament and of the Council.

The latter is the International Safety Management (ISM) Code.[87] The purpose of the ISM Code is to provide an international standard for the safe management and operation of ships and for pollution prevention.[88] The ISM Code applies directly in the EU through the abovementioned regulation from 2006.[89] It requires that companies establish safety objectives as described in the Code and, in addition, develop, implement and maintain a safety management system (SMC) which includes functional requirements as listed in the Code. The intention is that the ISM Code should support and encourage the development of a safety culture in shipping.[90]

B. What about the Charterer?

The responsibility allocated to the ship management company is, however, normally limited, leaving the commercial operation of the vessel to a third party, the time charterer or demise charterer. Under a time charterparty, the charterer oversees the commercial operation of the ship. The time charterer has quite wide authority and can use the vessel for almost any purpose and route pursuant to the 'employment' clause and subject to any express trading restrictions in the charterparty.[91] In the case of a time charterparty, the time charterer makes all decisions on fuel, route, speed, and the amount of cargo and/or passengers. Under a voyage charterparty, the authority of the charterer is more limited as the voyage performed is agreed upon at the time of fixing the charterparty.[92] Depending on the type of charterparty, the person who decides on the parameters that influence the amount and quality of fuels (and hence of emissions) spent by the vessel and the person responsible for surrendering the allowances will not always be the same. This solution is not in line with the polluter pays principle and is accordingly challenged by shipowners. The argument is that if the responsibility is placed on the shipowner, the charterer will not have any incentive to implement measures for fuel efficiency.[93] Hence, lengthy negotiations have been ongoing concerning who will be responsible for surrendering allowances as the 'shipping company'.

[87] P Anderson, *ISM Code: A Practical Guide to the Legal and Insurance Implications*, 3rd edn (London, Informa Law from Routledge, 2015).

[88] The ISM Code in its current form was adopted in 1993 by Resolution A.741(18) and was made mandatory with the entry into force, on 1 July 1998, of the 1994 amendments to the SOLAS Convention, which introduced a new chapter IX into that Convention. It has been amended five times since then (2000, 2004, 2005, 2008, 2013).

[89] Regulation (EC) No 336/2006 of the European Parliament and of the Council of 15 February 2006 on the implementation of the International Safety Management Code within the Community and repealing Council Regulation (EC) No 3051/05 [2006] OJ L64/1.

[90] See eg Resolution A.1118(30), adopted on 6 December 2017 (Agenda item 9), Revised Guidelines on the Implementation of the International Safety Management (ISM) Code by Administrations, 1.1.

[91] See, eg, Girvin (ch 3) section III(B)(i).

[92] ibid section IV.

[93] The 2023 amendments (n 1) preamble (32).

The EU is, of course, aware of the discussion and has arrived at a solution where the problem is to be solved by contractual agreements. According to the preamble of the 2023 amendments, the EU suggests that

> … the shipping company should […] be entitled, under national law, to claim reimbursement for the costs arising from the surrender of allowances from the entity that is directly responsible for the decisions affecting the greenhouse gas emissions of the ship.[94]

It is a bit unclear what this obligation contain. Is it enough that the Member States ensure that the shipping company can make a claim for reimbursement of costs under the EU ETS or do the Member States have an obligation to assert a mandatory right for the shipping company to claim such reimbursement? When reading the instruction in context with the explanation on how the right should be ensured; '… such a mechanism of reimbursement could be subject to a contractual arrangement',[95] it is my opinion that the duty for the Member States is to ensure that the shipping company can make a claim (that there are no hinders for third party claims, eg) but that it is up to the parties (the shipping company and the entity responsible for the relevant decisions, normally the charterer) to negotiate the terms of these contracts. The question will probably be clarified by the Commission, and if not, eventually by the European Court of Justice.

C. BIMCO's Contractual Arrangement, the ETSA Clause for Time Charter Parties

With its ETS Emission Trading Scheme Allowances (ETSA) Clause for Time Charter Parties 2022, BIMCO has proposed a contractual solution to the problems addressed above.[96] According to BIMCO, the ETSA Clause follows the 'polluter-pays' principle by ensuring the pass-through of ETS costs to the commercial operators of vessels – in this case, time charterers. The fundamental principle behind the clause is that it requires both parties to the charterparty to cooperate and collaborate.

This means that both the shipowner and the charterer agree to cooperate and exchange all relevant data and information necessary to facilitate compliance with 'any applicable Emission Scheme'. An emission scheme is defined in the clause to include a 'greenhouse gas emission trading scheme … that regulate the issuance, allocation, trading or surrendering of emission allowances'. As stated in the clause, this obviously includes the EU ETS. The data and information shared must enable the shipowner and the time charterer to calculate the amount of emission allowances to be surrendered to the relevant authorities in respect of the vessel subject to the charterparty (cl (a)). The shipowner must monitor and report the relevant greenhouse gas emissions of the vessel for verification by an independent verifier in accordance with the applicable emission scheme (cl (b)). All information, including information on the aggregated emissions,

[94] ibid.

[95] ibid.

[96] ETS – Emission Trading Scheme Allowances Clause for Time Charter Parties 2022 (www.bimco.org).

must be exchanged between the parties in a timely manner to facilitate compliance with the system.[97]

As mentioned above, it is the shipping company, the shipowner, the bareboat charterer or a ship management company that will be responsible for surrendering allowances under the EU ETS. In line with the polluter pays principle, the ETSA clause redirects this cost to the Charterer. According to the clause, the shipowner must notify the charterer, in writing and within the first seven days of each month of the quantity of emission allowances for the previous month.[98] The shipowners' notification must include the relevant calculations and the data used to establish the quantities.

Although it is the shipowner who is responsible for monitoring, reporting and surrendering emissions under the MRV regulation, BIMCO's ETSA clause shifts the financial burden from the shipowner to the charterer. According to clause (c)(i), '… the Charterers shall provide and pay for the Emission Allowances corresponding to the Vessel's emissions under the scope of the applicable Emission Scheme' throughout the charterparty period. The money must be transferred to an account nominated by the shipowners within the seven-day notification period mentioned above. If the estimated quantity is higher or lower than the actual quantity, any difference in emission allowances must be transferred by the charterer or returned by the shipowner within seven days of notification from the receiving party. Likewise, if the vessel is off-hire, the charterer has the right to offset against any emission allowances that it otherwise would have been responsible for. The ETSA clause also gives the charterer a right to claim the shipowner to return already submitted emission allowances for the off-hire period (cl (c)(iv)).

If the charterer fails to transfer allowances in accordance with the above (ETSA Clause c), the shipowner has the right, according to cl (d), after five days' notice, to suspend the performance of any or all their obligations under the charterparty until the allowances are received in full by the shipowner. The vessel will, regardless of this, be on hire, and the shipowner is exempted from any responsibility for the action taken. Furthermore, such action does not impact any other rights or claims that the shipowner might have against the charterer under the charterparty.

V. Conclusions

Imposing an emission trading system on shipping to combat emissions from the industry has been a difficult task. On a global level, there is still no consensus behind such a system. The EU has accordingly implemented its existing regional system on the shipping industry, including ships calling at EU ports to or from a port outside the EU. The shipping company responsible for such a vessel will have to surrender allowances to an administering authority within the EU for emissions emitted not only within but also outside the jurisdiction of the Union. To ease the international criticism of this, the EU has decided that only 50 per cent of the emissions on these voyages are included in the system. Also, within the EU, voices have been raised against the consequences of the

[97] See cl (a).
[98] Cl (c)(1).

system. Hence, several exemptions from the ETS are made in the agreed rules, which will enter into force in 2024. The plan is to expand the ETS to other greenhouse gases as well as to smaller ships (above 400 gross tonnage). Further research is needed to evaluate the environmental effect of the system as well as the impact it has on the industry.

Post Scriptum

On 22 November 2023, the Commission Implementing Regulation (EU) 2023/2599 on the administration of shipping companies[99] was implemented in the EU. At the same time the discussion on who will be responsible for surrendering allowances under the ETS ended. According to the Regulation Article 1(4), 'the shipowner shall be considered as the entity responsible for ETS-obligations'. Shipowners can agree contractually that the bareboat charterer or other holders of the ISM-document takes over this responsibility. Such an agreement must, however, be certified by a notary public or other similar person, Article 1(2 and 3).

[99] Commission Implementing Regulation (EU) 2023/2599 of 22 November 2023 laying down rules for the application of Directive 2003/87/EC of the European Parliament and of the Council as regards the administration of shipping companies by administering authorities in respect of a shipping company.

6

Shipping and the EU Emissions Trading Scheme and Maritime Transport: Its Effect on Shipping Contracts

SIMON BAUGHEN*

I. Introduction

The EU's Emissions Trading Scheme is a carbon market based on a system of cap-and-trade of emission allowances for energy-intensive industries and the power generation sector. It requires the surrender of one emissions allowance for every ton of CO_2 emitted in a calendar year. It was established under Directive 2023/959 and introduced in 2005. It did not then cover CO_2 emissions from shipping. On 1 January 2024 that has all changed. On 16 May 2023, the Official Journal published Directive 2023/959,[1] amending the ETS Directive, and Regulation 2023/957, and the Monitoring, the Reporting and Verification (MRV) Regulation 2015/757. Shipping entered the ETS from 1 January 2024 as regards CO_2 emissions and from 1 January 2026 as regards emissions from two other greenhouse gases (GHGs), methane (CH_4) and nitrous oxide (N_2O). The reporting obligations under the MRV Regulation will be extended from CO_2 to these other two greenhouses gases as from 1 January 2024.

The EU's first legislative foray into addressing greenhouse gas (GHG) emissions from shipping was the MRV Regulation, which started on 1 January 2018. This applies to all voyages into and out of ports in the European Economic Area (EEA) and requires reporting of three items: actual cargo carried onboard, fuel consumed and CO_2 emitted. Reporting is the responsibility of the company defined as the shipowner or any other organisation or person, such as the manager or the bareboat charterer, which has assumed the responsibility for the operation of the ship from the shipowner. In the event of a change of company, the new company should only be responsible for the monitoring and reporting obligations related to the reporting period during which

* Professor of Shipping Law, Institute of Shipping and Trade Law, Hilary Rodham Clinton School of Law, Swansea University.

[1] Directive (EU) 2023/959 of the European Parliament and of the Council of 10 May 2023 amending Directive 2003/87/EC establishing a system for greenhouse gas emission allowance trading within the Union and Decision (EU) 2015/1814 concerning the establishment and operation of a market stability reserve for the Union greenhouse gas emission trading system [2023] OJ L130/161.

the change of company has taken place. The MRV calculations have to be verified by an accredited verifier and sent to a central European Commission (EC) database, and the information is to be publicly available.

The International Maritime Organization (IMO) has produced its own fuel consumption reporting measure through amendments to the Ship Energy Efficiency Management Plan (SEEMP) guidelines for fuel-consumption data collection. The measure, which started on 1 January 2019, requires reporting only of fuel consumed and requires verification by the flag ship administration under national procedures. The resulting raw data is restricted to the IMO and flag states, and aggregated anonymised data is made public.

In the IMO in 2012, there had been extensive consideration of possible market-based mechanisms (MBMs) to reduce GHG emissions, but no measures were adopted. In 2017 slow progress on GHG reduction by the IMO prompted the EU Parliament to propose the inclusion of shipping in the EU ETS. That was followed by the IMO's MEPC 72 in April 2018, in which the IMO stated its ambition to reduce greenhouse gas emissions from shipping by 50 per cent over 2008 levels by 2050, while, at the same time, pursuing efforts towards phasing them out entirely.[2] The strategy sets a carbon intensity reduction target – the amount of emissions relative to each tonne of shipping cargo – of at least 40 per cent by 2030, rising to 70 per cent by 2050. The strategy includes a specific reference to 'a pathway of CO_2 emissions reduction consistent with the Paris Agreement temperature goals'. Notwithstanding this, the EU has pressed ahead with legislative initiatives directed at reducing GHG emissions from shipping.

II. The Amendment of the ETS Directive and the MRV Regulation

On 16 September 2020, the European Parliament voted in favour of a 40 per cent reduction in CO_2 by 2030 for all maritime transport and for the inclusion of ships of 5,000 grt and over in the EU Emissions Trading System (ETS), with the establishment of an 'Ocean Fund' to run from 2022–2030 to contribute to protecting marine ecosystems. This was to be done by amending the MRV Regulation 2015/757 and including ships of 5,000 grt and over in the ETS for all voyages into and out of a port in the EU, including from and to ports outside the EU, starting on 1 January 2022. The responsibility for surrendering allowances would fall on the 'shipping company', which was defined to include the shipowner, bareboat charterer, manager, and time charterer, all of whom were to be responsible under the ETS for the costs of acquiring and surrendering ETS allowances.

In 2021 the EU adopted a binding target under the European Climate Law[3] of a reduction in GHG emissions economy-wide and domestically of at least 55 per cent

[2] On 7 July 2023 at MEPC 80 the IMO revised its strategy with a new target for international shipping reaching 'net zero' close to 2050 and indicative checkpoints of a cut in total greenhouse gas emissions of at least 20% by 2030, but 'striving' to reach cuts of 30% by then, and 70% in 2040 but 'striving' for 80%.

[3] Regulation (EU) 2021/1119 of the European Parliament and of the Council of 30 June 2021 establishing the framework for achieving climate neutrality and amending Regulations (EC) No 401/2009 and (EU) 2018/1999 (European Climate Law).

by 2030 compared to 1990 levels. On 14 July 2021, the Commission released its 'Fit for 55' package of proposals for achieving that target.[4] One of the legislative proposals was an amendment to the 2003/87/EC directive establishing the Emissions Trading Scheme (ETS Directive)[5] to include intra-EU voyages within the ETS and emissions occurring at berth in an EU port, but with only 50 per cent cost for CO_2 emissions on a voyage from or port outside the EU to one in EU, and to a voyage from the EU to a port outside the EU. There would be a phase-in period between 2023 and 2026 for the surrender of allowances, according to the following schedule: (a) 20 per cent of verified emissions reported for 2023; (b) 45 per cent of verified emissions reported for 2024; (c) 70 per cent of verified emissions reported for 2025; (d) 100 per cent of verified emissions reported for 2026 and each year thereafter. Only the shipowner, bareboat charterer or manager that had assumed responsibilities under the ISM Code would be the shipping company responsible for allowances.[6] Regarding other GHG gases, the Commission left the extension of the 2015 MRV from CO_2 to other gases to a later phase once the monitoring approaches and emissions factors of these gases had been agreed upon. The proposed amendment was considerably less extensive than the EU Parliament's proposed amendment to the 2015 MRV Regulation, in its phase-in period, the 50 per cent cost for extra-EU voyages, and the restriction to CO_2 emissions.

The Parliament proposed various counter-amendments on 22 June 2022, as did the Council on 29 June. On 18 December 2022, the Parliament and Council issued a press release stating that they had reached a provisional agreement regarding the amendments to the ETS Directive, with the formal proposal being released on 8 February 2023. On 18 April 2023, the Parliament voted to adopt the amended ETS Directive. The legislative process concluded on 10 May 2023 with Directive 2023/959,[7] and Regulation 2023/957 making the necessary amendment to the MRV Regulation.[8]

Maritime shipping emissions for vessels over 5,000 gross tonnage for transporting for commercial purposes cargo or passengers would come within the scope of the EU ETS from 1 January 2024,[9] with a phased introduction of obligations for the shipping

[4] See above, Eftestøl, ch 5.

[5] Pursuant to inserted Arts 3g to 3ge.

[6] The proposed amending directive included new definitions for 'shipping company' and 'administering authority in respect of shipping companies' in Art 3(w) and Art 3(y) respectively. The person or organisation responsible for the compliance with the EU ETS should be the shipping company, defined as the shipowner or any other organisation or person, such as the manager or the bareboat charterer, that has assumed the responsibility for the operation of the ship from the shipowner and that, on assuming such responsibility, has agreed to take over all the duties and responsibilities imposed by the International Management Code for the Safe Operation of Ships and for Pollution Prevention. This definition is based on the definition of 'company' in Art 3(d) of Regulation (EU) 2015/757, and in line with the global data collection system established in 2016 by the IMO.

[7] Directive (EU) 2023/959 of the European Parliament and of the Council of 10 May 2023 amending Directive 2003/87/EC establishing a system for greenhouse gas emission allowance trading within the Union and Decision (EU) 2015/1814 concerning the establishment and operation of a market stability reserve for the Union greenhouse gas emission trading system [2023] OJ L130/161.

[8] Regulation (EU) 2023/957 of the European Parliament and of the Council of 10 May 2023 amending Regulation (EU) 2015/757 Directive (EU) 2023/959 of the European Parliament and of the Council of 10 May 2023 amending Directive 2003/87/EC establishing a system for greenhouse gas emission allowance trading within the Union and Decision (EU) 2015/1814 concerning the establishment and operation of a market stability reserve for the Union greenhouse gas emission trading system [2023] OJ L130/161.

[9] Under amended Art 3a 'Scope', which provides: '… Articles 3ga to 3gg shall apply in respect of the maritime transport activities listed in Annex I'.

company to surrender each year 100 per cent of allowances for verified CO_2 emissions for intra-EU voyages within the ETS and emissions occurring at berth in an EU port. The shipping company would also be required to surrender 50 per cent of verified CO_2 emissions for extra-EU voyages from and to a port within the jurisdiction of a Member State. Emissions are calculated on a tank-to-wake basis[10] as defined in amended Article 3(b): '"emissions" means the release of greenhouse gases … from ships performing a maritime transport activity listed in Annex I of the gases specified in respect of that activity …'

Offshore vessels of 5,000 gross tonnage and above will be included in the MRV Regulation from 2025 and in the EU ETS from 2027. General cargo vessels and offshore vessels between 400–5,000 gross tonnage will be included in the MRV regulation from 2025 and their inclusion in EU ETS will be reviewed in 2026. Non-CO_2 emissions (methane and nitrous oxide) will be included in the MRV regulation from 2024 and in the EU ETS from 2026. The reporting obligations for in-scope ships under the amended MRV Regulation remain on a tank-to-wake basis, being 'greenhouse gases released during their voyages'.[11]

The surrender of allowances will be subject to the following phase: 40 per cent for verified emissions from 2024, 70 per cent for 2025 and 100 per cent for 2026. There will be no free allocation of allowances to shipping companies. Allowances will have to be purchased by the shipping company from either the primary market through auctions arranged by the European Energy Exchange (EEX) or through the secondary market. Participation in the primary market will require the shipping company to hold a nominated holding account in the Union registry and hold a nominated bank account. A third party, such as a charterer, must be registered in a Member State; otherwise, it will have to purchase through the secondary market.[12] To take account of the inclusion of shipping in the ETS, approximately 80 to 100 million additional emission allowances will be put on the market. Auction revenues from 20 million of these emission allowances will go to the Innovation Fund and the Climate Investment Fund to be used for shipping-specific projects,[13] with the remaining revenues going to the Member States to be used for climate and energy-related activities. The shipping company' is defined in art 3(w) as

> … the shipowner or any other organisation or person, such as the manager or the bareboat charterer, that has assumed the responsibility for the operation of the ship from the shipowner and that, on assuming such responsibility, has agreed to take over all the duties and responsibilities imposed by the International Management Code for the Safe Operation of Ships and for Pollution Prevention, set out in Annex I to Regulation (EC) No 336/2006 of the European Parliament and of the Council(*)

[10] Tank-to-wake emissions are those solely derived from on-board fuel combustion.

[11] Art 3(b).

[12] Eligible participants according to the EU Auctioning Regulation are: Compliance buyers, investment firms and credit institutions, business groupings of compliance buyers, and other intermediaries specifically authorised by the home Member State. Under EU and EEX rules these participants must be: established in the EU (except for compliance buyers); hold a nominated holding account in the Union registry; hold a nominated bank account.

[13] Previously it had been proposed that 75% of emissions revenues from shipping should go into an Ocean Fund for these purposes.

This is the same definition used for 'the Company' in the MRV Regulation.[14] However, on 22 November 2023 the Commission introduced an Implementing Regulation whereby the 'shipping company' for the purposes of the ETS will be the shipowner unless there is a clear written delegation to either the demise charterer or the ship's manager, satisfying certain specified criteria.[15] On 31 January 2024 the EU Commission published their list showing which shipping companies are to be associated with the different administering authorities of the member states under the EU ETS.[16] The list will be updated every two years.

Unlike the initial proposal of the Parliament time charterers are not included in the definition, but the Directive also provides for the application of the 'polluter pays' principle to direct the costs of surrendered allowances from the 'shipping company' to the party with ultimate responsibility for the operation of the vessel 'when the ultimate responsibility for the purchase of the fuel and/or the operation of the ship is assumed by a different entity than the shipping company pursuant to a contractual arrangement'.[17] Operation of the ship means 'determining the cargo carried and/or the route and the speed of the ship' and so clearly encompasses time charterers. Recital (32) states:

> While such a mechanism of reimbursement could be subject to a contractual arrangement, Member States should, to reduce administrative costs, not be obliged to ensure or control the existence of such contracts, but should instead provide, in national law, a statutory entitlement for the shipping company to be reimbursed and the corresponding access to justice to enforce that entitlement.

Under Article 3gc, Member States are required to

> take the necessary measures to ensure that when the ultimate responsibility for the purchase of the fuel and/or the operation of the ship is assumed by a different entity than the shipping company pursuant to a contractual arrangement, the shipping company is entitled to reimbursement from that entity for the costs arising from the surrender of allowances'.

This will secure a pass-through of ETS costs borne by the 'shipping company' to the time charterer of the vessel in creating a statutory right of recovery to the 'shipping company' of these costs from the entity that has assumed the ultimate responsibility for the purchase of the fuel and/or the operation of the ship. However, this it does not affect the primary liability of the 'shipping company' to pay for the necessary carbon allowances'.[18]

[14] Regulation (EU) 2015/757 of the European Parliament and of the Council of 29 April 2015 on the monitoring, reporting and verification of carbon dioxide emissions from maritime transport, and amending Directive 2009/16/EC [2015] OJ L123/55.

[15] Implementing Regulation (EU) 2023/2599 of 22 November 2023.

[16] All shipping companies now have 40 days from the publication of the list to open a maritime operator holding account (MOHA) used to deliver and trade emission allowances within 40 days, and shipping companies that are not on the list must open an account within 65 working days of the first port of call falling within the scope of the EU ETS Directive. The 'shipping company' must nominate at least two 'authorised representatives' when opening the account.

[17] Art 3gc.

[18] Art 3 gc states that 'Member States shall ensure that shipping companies under their responsibility comply with their obligations to surrender allowances, notwithstanding their entitlement to be reimbursed by the commercial operators for the costs arising from the surrender.'

The pass-through provisions stop at the time charterer, and BIMCO's Emissions Trading Scheme Allowance clause for Time Charterparties 2022 likewise only concerns the position regarding ETS allowances between owner and time charterer. One may wonder why the time charterer is singled out in that voyages in and out of the EU will involve commercial operations involving a chain of participants, all of whom are involved in the pollution to which the 'polluter pays principle' applies.

The pass-through provision in the ETS amended Directive will conflict with the contractual position under a standard form time charter that, absent a specific clause, there is no mechanism for the shipowner to recover the costs of surrendered allowances relating to trips to and from EU ports.

The onus of claiming the statutory right of reimbursement will be on the 'shipping company' be it the shipowner, the bareboat charterer, or the ship manager, which will probably be in the courts of the Member State with jurisdiction over them under the ETS, although not necessarily so. In response, assuming a charter subject to English law and English jurisdiction or London arbitration, the time charterer could then respond by arbitrating for a declaration of non-liability. It may consider applying to the English High Court for an anti-suit injunction, which has become possible again following the conclusion of Brexit on 1 January 2021. When the owner seeks to enforce the judgment of the courts in which it has claimed the statutory reimbursement, it can do so easily against assets of the time charterer within the EU, but enforcement in England will be possible only where the defendant was present in the foreign country at the time the claim was served or had submitted to the foreign country's jurisdiction. If those conditions are met, enforcement may be challenged on various grounds, such as: the foreign court did not have jurisdiction according to the English rules; the proceedings were brought contrary to a jurisdiction or arbitration agreement; inconsistency with a prior judgment on the same subject matter and between the same parties, such as an arbitral declaration of non-liability that has been converted into a High Court judgment prior to the final judgment in the courts of the EU Member State.

The administering authority for a shipping company in the EU will be the Member State in which it is established. For a non-EU shipping company, it will be the Member State in which it has the largest amounts of ports of call through the verified data of previous years. If a non-EU shipping company has not yet traded, the administering authority will be the EU Member State of their first EU port of call. In the event of non-compliance by the shipping company for two or more consecutive reporting periods, the competent authority of the Member State of the port of entry may issue an expulsion order, and an EU flag state may also order a ship that flies its flag to be detained if its obligations are not fulfilled. Where the shipping company is a manager dealing with several ships in different ownership, there is a risk that an expulsion order relating to a failure to surrender allowances for one particular vessel will also affect other vessels under the same management. A penalty of €100 for each tonne of CO_2 equivalent emitted that has not been surrendered will be levied on the shipping company, in addition to the shipping company remaining liable for surrendering the required allowances.

The relevant time frame for the MRV is that three months from adoption on 5 June 2023, an updated ship EU MRV monitoring plan describing the method for monitoring and reporting methane and nitrous oxide must be verified by an accredited verifier and submitted to the administrating authority of the company. From 1 January 2024, each ship needs to start reporting according to the revised monitoring plan. By 31 March each year from 2025, a verified company emission report needs to be submitted to the administering authority. This must aggregate the emissions within the scope of the ETS reported and verified for each ship under the responsibility of the shipping company during the reporting period of the calendar year. So, on 31 March 2025, and thereafter, the shipping company must report tank to wake emissions from CO_2, methane and nitrous oxide. By 30 September each year, the necessary emission allowances for the previous calendar year then have to be surrendered to the administering authority. For calendar years 2024 and 2025, that will be CO_2 emissions, but by September 2027, emissions allowances to be surrendered for the calendar year 2026 will include allowances in respect of methane and nitrous oxide emissions, as well as CO_2 emissions.

The Directive contains provisions to review its consistency with possible future market-based shipping measures to avoid a double burden. Article 3gg provides for review of the Directive in the light of any future adoption by the IMO of a global market-based measure to reduce greenhouse gas emissions from maritime transport, and the Commission is to present a report to the Parliament and the Council within 18 months of the adoption of the IMO measure examining it in the light of:

(a) its ambition in light of the objectives of the Paris Agreement;
(b) its overall environmental integrity, including compared to the provisions of this Directive covering maritime transport; and
(c) any issue related to the coherence between the EU ETS and that measure.

If the IMO does not adopt such a measure by 2028, the Directive provides that the Commission is to present a report to the European Parliament and to the Council in which it must examine the need to apply the allocation of allowances and surrender requirements in respect of more than fifty per cent of the emissions from ships performing voyages between a port of call under the jurisdiction of a Member State and a port of call outside the jurisdiction of a Member State, in light of the objectives of the Paris Agreement. This goes on to say that

> In particular, the Commission shall consider progress at IMO level and examine whether any third country has a market-based measure equivalent to this Directive and assess the risk of an increase in evasive practices, including through a shift to other modes of transport or a shift of port hubs to ports outside the Union. Where appropriate, either report shall be accompanied by a legislative proposal to amend the Directive.

The current IMO strategy for reduction of GHG emissions from shipping was set out at MEPC 80 on 7 July 2023.[19] The IMO adopted a new target for international shipping reaching 'net zero' close to 2050 and indicative checkpoints of a cut in total greenhouse gas emissions of at least 20 per cent by 2030, but 'striving' to reach cuts of 30 per cent by then, and 70 per cent in 2040 but 'striving' for 80 per cent. GHG emissions are now to be calculated on a 'well to wake' basis. There is also a target that at least 5 per cent

[19] wwwcdn.imo.org/localresources/en/MediaCentre/PressBriefings/Documents/2023%20Strategy%20%20on%20Reduction%20of%20GHG%20emissions%20from%20ships%20as%20adopted%20subject%20to%20any%20final%20editorials_.pdf.

of the energy used for international shipping by 2030 should be zero carbon, or near zero carbon, but 'striving' to reach 10 per cent by then. There is no change to the 2018 target of reducing the carbon intensity (emissions produced per cargo and distance travelled) of international shipping by 40 per cent by 2030, compared with 2008 levels. No decision was made on the proposal for a carbon levy, but the proposal lives on for future discussion. Discussion on the application of on-board carbon capture and storage or utilisation, has been postponed to the next intersessional meeting of the Working Group on GHG reductions. The IMO has set a deadline of 2025 for the development of mid-term measures to support its GHG strategy, with them to come into effect in 2027. The candidate measure(s), delivering on the reduction targets, should comprise both: a technical element, namely a goal-based marine fuel standard regulating the phased reduction of the marine fuel's GHG intensity; and an economic element, on the basis of a maritime GHG emissions pricing mechanism.[20] These mid-term measures may well include some form of market-based measure equivalent to the Directive and will need to be considered by the Commission within 18 months of its adoption in 2025. The amended Directive also addresses possible evasion of the ETS by transshipping containers outside EU countries (which could include the UK) in Article 3ga(2), which provides:

> The Commission shall by 31 December 2023 by means of implementing acts establish a list of the neighbouring container transhipment ports and update this list before 31 December every two years thereafter.
>
> Those implementing acts shall list neighbouring container transhipment ports where the share of transhipment of containers, measured in twenty-foot equivalent unit, exceeds 65 % of the total container traffic of that port during the most recent twelve-month period for which relevant data are available located outside the Union but less than 300 nautical miles of a port under the jurisdiction of a Member State. For the purpose of this paragraph containers shall be considered as transhipped when they are unloaded from a ship to the port for the sole purpose of loading them on another ship. The list shall not include ports located in a third country that effectively apply measures equivalent to this Directive.

Article 3(z) defines 'port of call' to exclude various activities, including stops of containerships in a neighbouring container transhipment port listed in the implementing act adopted pursuant to Article 3ga(2).

The amended Directive also takes into account geographical specificities with transitional measures up to 31 December 2030 for small islands, ice-class ships and journeys relating to outermost regions and public service obligations.[21]

The amended Directive will also have an impact on Carbon Capture and Storage (CCS) within the EU. Previously, a registered emitter was under no obligation to surrender allowances in respect of emissions which are verified as captured and transported by pipeline to a storage facility, authorised in accordance with the CCS Directive. The amended ETS Directive now removes the previous requirement that CCS had to be transported by pipeline to a storage facility. This means that captured carbon from a

[20] MEPC 80/WP.12 Annex 1: Draft Resolution, adopted 7 July 2023, para 4.5.
[21] Art 12(3)(b)–(e).

registered emitter can now be transported to a permitted storage facility by ship without the emitter being obliged to surrender allowances in respect of its captured emissions.[22]

III. Other EU Measures

In its 'Fit for 55' communication of 14 July 2021, the European Commission proposed additional measures to reduce GHG emissions from shipping. First, there is the Fuel EU Maritime Regulation[23] which introduces increasing limits on the intensity of the energy used by vessels from 2025 through to 2050, gently at first, with increasing stringency in the 2040s, which should promote the adoption of alternative fuels. The Regulation entered into force 20 days after publication in the Official Journal of the European Union on 22 September 2023 and will apply from 1 January 2025 with the exception of Articles 8 and 9 which shall apply from 31 August 2024.[24]

FuelEU Maritime sets maximum limits on the yearly greenhouse gas intensity of the energy a ship uses, with targets becoming increasingly ambitious over time to stimulate and reflect the expected developments in technology and the increased production of renewable and low-carbon fuels. The targets cover not only CO_2 but also methane and nitrous oxide emissions over the full lifecycle of the fuels, which includes emissions related to the extraction, cultivation, production, and transportation of the fuel and contains provisions for crediting ships using wind-assisted propulsion. The Regulation applies to commercial vessels of 5,000 gross tonnes and above, regardless of flag, with exemptions for naval vessels, fishing vessels, and ships using non-mechanical propulsion. It covers all energy used on board when the ship is at the port, all energy used on voyages between EU ports and 50 per cent of the energy used on voyages departing from or arriving at an EU port.[25] The reduction schedule from a 2020 baseline is −2 per cent from 2025; −6 per cent from 2030; −14.5 per cent from 2035; −31 per cent from 2040; −62 per cent from 2045; −80 per cent from 2050. Offsetting emissions credits are given to those ship owners who use renewable fuels of non-biological origin (RFNBO) from 2025 to 2034, and a 2 per cent renewable fuels usage target as of 2034 will be set if the

[22] The reference to CCS in the table to Annex I to Directive 2003/87/EC is amended so as to read 'Transport of greenhouse gases for geological storage in a storage site permitted under Directive 2009/31/EC, with the exclusion of those emissions covered by another activity under this Directive.' Article 69 of the Preamble states: 'As CO2 is also expected to be transported by means other than pipelines, such as by ship and by truck, the current coverage in Annex I to Directive 2003/87/EC for transport of greenhouse gases for the purpose of storage should be extended to all means of transport for reasons of equal treatment and irrespective of whether the means of transport are covered by the EU ETS. Where the emissions from the transport are also covered by another activity under Directive 2003/87/EC, the emissions should be accounted for under that other activity to prevent double counting.'

[23] REGULATION (EU) 2023/1805 OF THE EUROPEAN PARLIAMENT AND OF THE COUNCIL of 13 September 2023 on the use of renewable and low-carbon fuels in maritime transport, and amending Directive 2009/16/EC. OJ L 234/48 22 September 2023.

[24] Under which shipping companies must submit to verifiers a standardised emissions monitoring plan for each of their vessels by 31 August 2024.

[25] Article 1 provides: 'This Regulation lays down uniform rules imposing: (a) a limit on the greenhouse gas (GHG) intensity of energy used on board by a ship arriving at, staying within or departing from ports under the jurisdiction of a Member State; and (b) an obligation to use on-shore power supply (OPS) or zero-emission technology in ports under the jurisdiction of a Member State.'

Commission reports that in 2031 RFNBOs amount to less than 1 per cent in the fuel mix. There are also similar provisions to those in the ETS regarding evasive container transhipments from ports less than 300 nautical miles from an EU port, with the Commission to provide the first list of such ports before 31 December 2025.

From January 2030, container ships and passenger ships at EU ports will also have to connect to the onshore power supply and use it for all energy needs while at berth at the quayside in TEN-T core and comprehensive network ports or use alternative zero-emission technologies. From January 2035, this will apply to container ships and passenger ships at the quayside in all EU ports where the quay is equipped. Whether this onshore power supply will be provided from green sources remains to be seen.

The responsibility for compliance lies with the shipping company, as defined in the MRV Regulation and the ETS Directive. Shipping companies must submit to verifiers a standardised emissions monitoring plan for each of their vessels by 31 August 2024. Their records must contain the 'well to wake' emissions factors for each type of fuel used at berth and sea.[26] At the end of April each year, shipping companies must submit their data, including that already reported for MRV regulation. There are harmonised penalties for non-compliance with the requirements on both the greenhouse gas intensity content and the connection to onshore electricity. Revenues generated from the penalties under the FuelEU regulation are to be allocated to projects to support the decarbonisation of the maritime sector.[27] The Regulation provides for a voluntary pooling mechanism under which ships will be allowed to pool their compliance balance with one or more other ships, thereby making it the overall pool that has to meet the greenhouse gas intensity limits on average.

FuelEU Maritime also recognises the 'polluter pays' principle, providing:

> The Regulation allows for the possibility that contractual arrangements could be made between the company and the entity responsible for the choice of fuel, route and speed of the ship, and also the company and fuel suppliers, so that in the event of compliance deficit, those entities be put under the obligation to reimburse or otherwise compensate the company with respect to the cost of the FuelEU penalties resulting from the operation of the ship.[28]

[26] The emission intensity of biofuels and biogas, among others, will be determined using the RED Directive, whereas fossil fuels should be assessed using FuelEU's default emission factors.

[27] Article 23(11) provides: 'Member States shall endeavour to ensure that the revenue generated from the FuelEU penalties, or its equivalent financial value, is used to support the rapid deployment and the use of renewable and low-carbon fuels in the maritime sector, by stimulating the production of greater quantities of renewable and low-carbon fuels for the maritime sector, facilitating the construction of appropriate bunkering facilities or OPS infrastructure in ports, and supporting the development, testing and deployment of the most innovative technologies in the fleet to achieve significant emission reductions.' By 30 June 2030, and every five years thereafter, Member States shall make public a report on the use of revenue generated from the Fuel EU penalties over the five-year period preceding the year of every such report, including information on the beneficiaries and the level of expenditure concerning the objectives listed in the first subparagraph.

[28] Recital 63 provides: 'While the company should remain responsible for fulfilling monitoring and reporting obligations under this Regulation, as well as for paying the FuelEU penalties, in line with the "polluter pays" principle and in order to promote the uptake of cleaner fuels, the entity responsible for purchasing the fuel or for taking operational decisions that affect the GHG intensity of the energy used by the ship could, through contractual agreements with the company, in the event of compliance deficit, be put under the obligation to reimburse or otherwise compensate the company with respect to the cost of the FuelEU penalties resulting from the operation of the ship. That company should be able to, on a contractual basis, request the verifier to calculate the amount of the FuelEU penalties corresponding to the operation of the ship by the other entity during the reporting period. Within this context, operation of the ship should be understood to

However, there is no provision for a mandatory pass-through of compliance costs to such entities, as there is under the amended ETS Directive, and irrespective of any such contractual arrangements being entered into the company remains responsible for the payment of Fuel EU penalties.[29]

Second, there is a Regulation (EU) 2023/1804 of the European Parliament and of the Council of 13 September 2023 on the deployment of alternative fuels infrastructure, and repealing Directive 2014/94/EU (AFIR).[30] This amends the Directive on the Deployment of Alternative Fuels Infrastructure 2014/94/EU (DAFI) to require Member States to take necessary measures to ensure that minimum shore-side electricity supply for seagoing container and passenger ships is provided in maritime ports by 1 January 2030. Member States must also ensure that an 'appropriate' number of refuelling points for Liquefied Natural Gas (LNG) are put in place at TEN-T core maritime ports by 31 December 2024.[31]

Third, there is the proposed revision of the Energy Taxation Directive 2003/96/EC (ETD) to introduce varying tax rates used for intra-EU ferry, fishing and freight vessels under a ten-year transition period starting from 1 January 2023.[32] The proposed Directive would require unanimous approval by all Member States. In November 2023, the Council took stock of progress on the revision of the Directive and concluded that positions among delegations were still 'divergent on several crucial issues'.

As for the UK, on 20 April 2021, the Government announced that the Sixth Carbon Budget would include the UK's share of international shipping emissions, as recommended by the Climate Change Committee (CCC). The projections for international shipping emissions represent the estimated emissions from fuel sold in the UK for use

mean determining the cargo carried, the route and the speed of the ship. Similarly, while the company should remain responsible for fulfilling monitoring and reporting obligations under this Regulation, as well as for paying the FuelEU penalties, companies and fuel suppliers should be able to, by means of contractual agreements, agree on mutual commitments to produce, supply and purchase predetermined quantities of certain fuels. Such contractual agreements could provide for the liability of fuel suppliers to compensate the company for the payment of penalties in cases where fuels were not made available to the company as agreed.'

[29] Article 23 8 as regards contractual agreements with commercial operators that have assumed responsibility for the purchase of the fuel or the operation of the ship – defined as determining the cargo carried, the route and the speed of the ship. Article 23.9 as regards contractual agreements with fuel suppliers.

[30] The Regulation entered into force twenty days after its publication in the Official Journal on 22 September 2023 and applies from 13 April 2024.

[31] Article 14.1 provides that: By 31 December 2024, each Member State shall prepare and transmit to the Commission a draft national policy framework for the development of the market as regards alternative fuels in the transport sector and the deployment of the relevant infrastructure. Article 14.2 (k) provide that the national policy framework should contains: (k) an overview of the state of play, perspectives and planned measures in respect of the deployment of alternative fuels infrastructure in maritime ports other than for liquefied methane and shore-side electricity supply for use by seagoing vessels, such as for hydrogen, ammonia, methanol and electricity.

[32] Brussels, 14.7.2021 COM (2021) 563 final 2021/0213 (CNS) Proposal for a Council Directive restructuring the Union framework for the taxation of energy products and electricity (recast). The proposed tax rates are: –0.9 Euros per Gigajoule gas oil for heavy fuel oil, kerosene and non-sustainable with no reduction during the Transition Period; –0.6 Euros per Gigajoule during the Transition Period and 0.9 Euros per Gigajoule afterwards for LPG, LNG, non-sustainable biogas and non-renewable fuels of non-biological origin; –0.45 Euros per Gigajoule during the Transition Period and 0.9 Euros per Gigajoule afterwards for sustainable food and feed crop biogas and sustainable food and feed crop biofuel; –0.15 Euros per Gigajoule during the Transition Period and 0.45 Euros per Gigajoule afterwards for low carbon fuels; 0.15 Euros per Gigajoule both during and after the Transition Period for renewable fuels of non-biological origin, advanced sustainable biofuels, biogas and electricity.

in international shipping. However, shipping is not currently included in the UK's ETS. On 25 March 2022, BEIS launched a consultation on developing the UK Emissions Trading Scheme (UK ETS). This included proposals for widening the scope of the UK ETS to include the CO_2 emissions of the domestic maritime industry. 3 July 2023 the UK government announced that: domestic shipping for vessels above 5000 grt will be required to participate in the UK's Emissions Trading Scheme starting in 2026.[33] The government would also: expand the existing scope of the scheme to create a level playing field between operators who use pipeline and non-pipeline modes of transportation of CO2, working with key regulatory partners to establish how Non-Pipeline Transport (NPT) should best be integrated into the existing UK ETS framework; and review its policy of expanding the UK ETS to methane emissions from upstream oil and gas and other traded sectors.

At the IMO level, the current measures on GHG reduction are the Energy Efficiency Existing Ship Index (EEXI)[34] and Carbon Intensity Indicator (CII)[35] regimes under MARPOL, which entered into force on 1 November 2022 and applied to relevant vessels from 1 January 2023. However, the GHG reduction strategy, amended at MEPC 80, aims for further mid-term measures will emerge in 2025 to come into force in 2027.

IV. The Costs to Shipping of the EU ETS

As of 1 January 2024, shipping will enter the EU's ETS. This will entail added costs to voyages into and out of the EU, which will fall on the shipping company (owners, bareboat charterers, ship managers). It should be noted that although the UK has established its own ETS, this does not currently include shipping, although this will cover domestic shipping from 2026.

An example of these coming ETS costs was given by Safety4Sea in late September 2022,[36] who posited the example of a voyage from Brazil to Rotterdam, using a carbon credit price of US$85 per metric tonne of carbon emitted.[37] The example has been updated in line with the phase-in period in the amended Directive and takes a Capesize dry bulk voyage carrying iron ore from Ponta da Madeira in Brazil to Rotterdam (4,100 nm) for 2024, the first year in which shipping will be subject to the ETS. Assuming a Capesize speed of 14 knots, this would take around 12 days: at 62 tonnes per day, this corresponds to 744 tonnes of fuel consumed, emitting 2,300 tonnes of CO_2. As the voyage starts outside Europe, only half the emissions qualify for allowances – 1,150 tonnes. Forty per cent of this will need to be covered for 2024, 460 tonnes. Therefore, at a carbon credit price on 13 December 2022 of just over €85/mt of carbon emitted, the total cost for the carbon allowance would be €39,100, plus a small addition for consumption in port. This compares with a fuel cost for the voyage of around €520,000 (equivalent to 8 per cent). But two years later, in 2026, the cost for the carbon allowance

[33] assets.publishing.service.gov.uk/government/uploads/system/uploads/attachment_data/file/1166812/uk-emissions-trading-scheme-consultation-government-response.pdf.

[34] See Kløft & Hong (ch 4).

[35] See Girvin (ch 3).

[36] safety4sea.com/prepare-for-higher-shipping-costs-but-the-eu-ets-should-be-a-manageable-change.

[37] As of 21 May 2023, the price is slightly higher at US$87.06.

would rise to 100 per cent for half the emissions, almost €100,000 – equivalent to 20 per cent of the total fuel bill for the voyage.

V. The Extra Costs and Charterparties

For voyage charters to and from the EU, these costs will likely be reflected in increased freight rates for voyages in and out and within the EU. For time charters, although charterers bear the cost of bunkering the vessel during the currency of the charter, that does not mean that owners will be able to recover the costs of ETS allowances from them. Assuming that the EU is a permitted trading area, owners have no mechanism under the standard form time charters to recover these additional costs. For example, in NYPE 1946, there is no provision which would make charterers responsible for allowances surrendered by the shipping company in respect of voyages involving the EU. Clause 2 provides:

> That the Charterers shall provide and pay for all the fuel except as otherwise agreed, Port Charges, Pilotages, Agencies, Commissions, Consular Charges (except those pertaining to the Crew) and all other usual expenses except those before stated, but when the vessel puts into a port for causes for which vessel is responsible, then all such charges incurred shall be paid by the Owners.

Surrendered EU Allowances (EUAs) will not constitute 'Port Charges' as these refer to all charges that a ship has to pay before she leaves a port, even if some of those charges relate to benefits which will accrue to the ship only after she has left the port.[38] However, surrender of allowances relating to the trip involving the EU would not be required until 30 September in the following calendar year. Nor would it fall under the umbrella of 'all other usual expenses'. In *The Dimitris L (No 2)*[39] Christopher Clarke J rejected an argument that payments levied on owners under the US Gross Transportation Tax would fall within a similar clause which he held[40]

> is designed to deal with the payments that need to be made to third parties (such as port authorities, canal operators, providers of fumigation services or dunnage equipment) to enable the vessel to be able to transport a cargo from port to port and to carry out the charter service; and not with a levy imposed on the contractual reward for the charter service, or a liability to reimburse someone higher in the charter chain in respect of that levy.

Nor would surrendered EUAs fall under Baltime form cl 4, which expressly provides that the charterers are to pay 'all dock, harbour and tonnage dues at the ports of delivery and redelivery (unless incurred through cargo carried before delivery or after redelivery)'.

Nor could the costs of surrendered EUAs be recovered by way of an express or implied indemnity under the time charter, as these costs will be regarded as the natural costs of trading, as was the case in *The Dimitris L (No 2)*,[41] where Christopher Clarke J

[38] *Newman & Dale v Lamport & Holt* [1896] 1 QB 20.

[39] *Global Maritime Investments Ltd v STX Pan Ocean Co Ltd (The Dimitris L) (No 2)* [2012] EWHC 2339, [2012] 2 Lloyd's Rep 354.

[40] ibid [54].

[41] ibid.

held that the BIMCO US Gross Transportation Tax clause which was incorporated in a chain of charters only operated as regards reimbursement by the head charterer to the owner on whom the tax had been levied. He then considered that the disponent owner would not be able to recover by way of indemnity because the costs it had incurred under the head charter flowed from sub charterers' orders to proceed to the United States. He stated:[42]

> As to clause 8, in a broad sense the tax was incurred in consequence of the order to proceed to the US. But owners are not entitled to recover from charterers under the implied indemnity the ordinary expenses and losses of trading or those of which the owner has accepted the risk: *The Island Archon*, page 235; *Antiparos ENE v SK Shipping Co Ltd (The Antiparos)* [2008] 2 Lloyd's Rep 237, page 243. In the case of voyages to or from the USA USGTT is, as it seems to me, an ordinary expense of trading and not an unusual feature. In any event the risk of incurring or being liable for this very tax has been dealt with by clause 112 and, to the extent that the owners are not entitled to recover under that clause, the risk of having to bear the cost of the tax is one which they must be taken to have accepted.

On this analysis, with charters concluded after 1 January 2024 the cost of surrendered EUAs by reason of the time charterer's order to proceed to or from a port in the EU would be an ordinary expense of trading to a permitted area under the time charter.[43] As such it would not be recoverable under the express or implied indemnity since the owner will have voluntarily accepted the risks of such trading. With a time charter concluded before 1 January 2024 these costs would still be regarded as a risk which the owners must be taken to have accepted as the extension of the ETS to shipping has been an imminent prospect since the Parliament kicked off the legislative process in September 2020.[44] Nor will there be an indemnity from the fact that the charterer is responsible for paying for the vessel's fuel during the currency of the time charter. True, the time charterer is responsible for paying for fuel, but there is no real choice of fuel as this will depend on the fuel used to power the vessel, something within the owner's province. Further, if there is a failure in two consecutive years to surrender allowances, a vessel sailing to a port in the EU would likely be unseaworthy in that its default means it is at risk of detention in or exclusion from the port.

VI. BIMCO's Emissions Trading Scheme Agreement for Time Charterparties 2022

Specific clauses may be developed to deal with the apportionment of ETS costs. One such clause is BIMCO's Emissions Trading Scheme Agreement for Time Charterparties

[42] ibid [55].

[43] Similarly, in *Actis Co Ltd v The Sanko Steamship Co Ltd (The Aquacharm)* [1980] 2 Lloyd's Rep 237 there was no right to recover the costs of transshipment at the Panama Canal by way of indemnity as these were an ordinary expense incurred in the course of navigation.

[44] In *Triad Shipping Co v Stellar Chartering & Brokerage Inc (The Island Archon)* [1994] 2 Lloyd's Rep 227, 236 Evans LJ stated, 'What risks the shipowner has agreed to bear must depend upon the true construction of the charter-party and therefore upon the situation when the charter-party was entered into.' For charterparties entered into after September 2020, the situation has been such that it has been highly likely that the EU would legislate to include shipping in the EU ETS within a matter of a few years.

released on 31 May 2022. The clause is not explicitly limited to time charters, but its language is that of time charters with references to off-hire and redelivery. With voyage charters, the owner can calculate emissions costs in advance and take that into account in the freight rate.[45] The clause deals with any emission scheme and is not limited to the EU scheme.[46] The obligation to acquire Emissions Allowances (EAs) falls on the time charterer, who is then obliged to transfer them to the owners' nominated Emissions Account. For this reason, the clause is not appropriate for inclusion in sub-charters to pass the cost of time charterer's transferred emissions allowances down the chain of charters. If this is desired, a simpler clause could be used requiring indemnification of the disponent owner in respect of the payments it has made in respect of EAs surrendered to the account of the shipping company in respect of the vessel.

Co-operation between owners and time charterers is mandated in working out how to calculate the amount of EAs that need to be surrendered for the period of the charter. Owners are to monitor and report GHG emissions, and just CO_2 emissions, by an independent verifier:

(a) Owners and charterers to co-operate and exchange all relevant data and information in a timely manner to facilitate compliance with any applicable Emission Scheme and enable the Parties to calculate the amount of Emission Allowances in respect of the Vessel that must be surrendered to the authorities of the applicable Emission Scheme for the period of the Charter Party.

(b) The Owners shall monitor and report the relevant greenhouse gas emissions of the Vessel for verification by an independent verifier in accordance with the applicable Emission Scheme.

Charterers then have to provide and pay for emission allowances monthly. Within seven days of notification, the relevant amount of allowances must go into the owners' nominated Emission Scheme account. Provision is made for adjustment on redelivery if the actual quantity of allowances is higher or lower than that estimated. Charterers may offset allowances during any period of off-hire.

(c) (i) Throughout the Charter Party period the Charterers shall provide and pay for the Emission Allowances corresponding to the Vessel's emissions under the scope of the applicable Emission Scheme:

(1) Within the first seven (7) days of each month, the Owners shall notify the Charterers in writing of the quantity of Emission Allowances for the previous month; and

(2) No later than fourteen (14) days prior to the expected date of redelivery the Owners shall notify the Charterers in writing of the estimated quantity of Emission Allowances for the final month or part thereof.

[45] On 8 December 2023 BIMCO released three ETS clauses for voyage charterparties: ETS-Emission Scheme Freight Clause for Voyage Charter; ETS – Emission Scheme Surcharge Clause for Voyage Charter Parties 2023 (www.bimco.org/contracts-and-clauses/bimco-clauses/current/~/link.aspx?_id=DFE2D36892E44FF99F6BACA2A9BB62A3&_z=z); ETS – Emission Scheme Transfer of Allowances Clause for Voyage Charter Parties 2023 (www.bimco.org/contracts-and-clauses/bimco-clauses/current/~/link.aspx?_id=0A80B939A65040E98F8200C3FADC0844&_z=z).

[46] 'Emission Scheme' means a greenhouse gas emissions trading scheme which for the purposes of this Clause shall include the European Union Emissions Trading System and any other similar systems imposed by applicable lawful authorities that regulate the issuance, allocation, trading or surrendering of Emission Allowances.

(ii) The Owners' notifications in subclause (c)(i) shall include the relevant calculations and the data used to establish the quantities.

(iii) Within seven (7) days of notification under subclause (c)(i), the quantity of Emission Allowances notified by the Owners above shall be transferred by the Charterers and received into the Owners' nominated Emission Scheme account. If the estimated quantity of Emission Allowances for the final month or part thereof is higher or lower than the actual quantity calculated by the Owners as at the time and date of redelivery, any difference in Emission Allowances shall be transferred by the Charterers or returned by the Owners, as the case may be, and received into the nominated account of the receiving Party within seven (7) days of written notification from that Party.

(iv) During any period of off-hire, the Charterers shall have the right to offset against any Emission Allowances due or require the Owners to return a quantity of Emission Allowances equivalent to the emissions that the Charterers would otherwise have been responsible for, had the Vessel remained on hire.

The clause then provides owners' remedies for breach by the time charterers. Owners' obligations will be suspended without prejudice to other rights or claims owners may have under the charter, and the vessel will stay on hire. Owners will not be responsible for the consequences of exercising this right.

> (d) If the Charterers fail to transfer any of the Emission Allowances in accordance with subclause (c), the Owners shall, by giving the Charterers' five (5) days' notice, have the right to suspend the performance of any or all of their obligations under this Charter Party until such time as the Emission Allowances are received in full by the Owners. Throughout any period of suspended performance under this subclause, the Vessel shall remain on hire and the Owners shall have no responsibility whatsoever for any consequences arising out of the valid exercise of this right. The Owners' right to suspend performance under this Clause shall be without prejudice to any other rights or claims they may have against the Charterers under this Charter Party.

Unlike many BIMCO clauses, there is no provision for incorporation into any bills of lading or waybills issued under the charter. This makes sense as ensuring the time charterers bear the financial consequences of acquiring ETS allowances required during the currency of the charter will not directly impact on third-party holders of bills of transport documents. This may happen, though, with delay due to owners operating their rights to suspend services under the clause. This will directly impact on third-party holders of bills of lading, and lead to liabilities for breach of the obligation to proceed to the discharge port with reasonable dispatch, and not to deviate. The clause enables owners able to be indemnified by charterers in respect of resulting liabilities incurred to such third parties by reason of suspending services under the charter, such as delaying discharge.

VII. How will Ships Reduce their GHG Emissions, and How will this Affect their Contracts?

The aim of including shipping in the ETS is to push for a reduction in CO_2 emissions, at first, and from 2026, methane and nitrous oxide emissions from vessels coming into and out of port in the jurisdiction of Member States. It is important to remember that CO_2 and GHG emissions are not synonymous. The MRV and the initial Commission proposal for the Directive were directed only at the reduction of CO_2 emissions. However, other gases, such as methane, have a potent impact on global warming and a focus just on CO_2 reduction is likely to encourage a switch to LNG a fuel which trades a 25 per cent reduction in CO_2 emissions against an increase in methane emissions due to 'methane slip'. This is the unburned fuel that is not fully combusted in ships' engines which releases methane into the atmosphere (on a tank to wake basis) and also the methane leakage that happens throughout the LNG supply chain (on a well to wake basis). Such a switch is encouraged by the inclusion of gas and nuclear as transitional fuels in the 2020 Taxonomy Regulation,[47] under which criteria applicable to investment in shipping are currently being prepared with a view to coming into force in 2026. The amended MRV Regulation and ETS Directive recognise this and provide for first the extension of the MRV to other methane and N_2O from 2024 and then to the ETS from 2026. And among the 'Fit for 55' EU measures that affect shipping, there is also the Fuel EU Maritime Regulation to consider, which mandates increasingly stringent energy reductions over the 2020 baseline from 2025 onwards to 2050. It will not be an option to make no reductions and accept the costs of purchasing and then surrendering ETS allowances with the hope of passing them down to the shipowner's contractual counterparties.

Recognising this, what can a shipping company do to reduce the GHG emissions of its vessels trading to and from the EU? First, there are efficiency measures, involving alterations to the vessel's engines. This is something shipowners already need to take account of due to the IMO's EEXI measures which came into effect on 1 January 2023 and which have given rise to a new BIMCO clause for time charters.[48] Second, there is slow steaming. Contractually, shipowners cannot safely adopt this measure. Under time charters, there will be speed and consumption warranties which they are obliged to meet, and under voyage charters and bills of lading, there are implied obligations to proceed with reasonable despatch that will be broken. Slow steaming needs to be justified by specific contractual clauses. Similarly, re-routing may contribute to a reduction in GHG emissions, but this too, needs contractual justification if shipowners are not to be in breach of charterers' routing directions in time charters or in breach of the obligation not to deviate from a customary route from the loading to the discharge port implied into voyage charters and bills of lading. Specific liberty clauses can be used to achieve these ends, and they will not be struck out by Article III, r 8 of the Hague and Hague-Visby Rules,[49] but the clauses need to be included in the respective contracts.[50]

Ideally, there should be a transition to fuels which involve no, or substantially lower, emissions of GHGs. The current principal candidates are ammonia; hydrogen;

[47] Regulation (EU) 2020/852 of the European Parliament and of the Council of 18 June 2020 on the establishment of a framework to facilitate sustainable investment, and amending Regulation (EU) 2019/2088 [2020] OJ L198/13.

[48] See Kløft & Hong (ch 4).

[49] *GH Renton & Co Ltd v Palmyra Trading Corp of Panama* [1957] AC 149 (HL).

[50] As the rerouting would amount to a breach of the obligation to proceed to the discharge port on a usual and reasonable route without deviation.

fuel cells; LNG; biomethane. All have problems concerning their immediate adoption for large cargo vessels on international voyages. Batteries have been used successfully with some ferries but are not currently viable for such voyages. The are three other considerations. The first concerns the means of producing such alternative fuels – will the energy used to effect this be derived from renewable sources? The production of hydrogen, for example, can involve the use of fossil fuels (grey hydrogen), the use of fossil fuels with carbon capture and storage (blue hydrogen) and the use of renewable sources (green hydrogen). Second, will there be adequate supplies of alternative fuels, given that shipping is only one of many industries needing to make this green switch? Third, will there be adequate bunkering facilities for these new fuels? This is something which the FuelEU Maritime Regulation addresses with its requirement for container ships to use onshore electricity while at berth from 2030. There is also the need for adequate bunkering facilities for alternative fuels, such as LNG, Hydrogen and Ammonia, and the AFIR addresses this with the requirement for the provision for bunkering facilities for these fuels within EU ports from 2025.

The inclusion of shipping in the EU taxonomy rules also needs to be considered, particularly their impact on retrofitting vessels with LNG duel fuel capacity. The rules provide a classification system to determine which investments can be environmentally sustainable. The European Commission is currently finalising the criteria for shipping to be included in the taxonomy rules.[51] Under its draft proposal of Delegated Act, from 2026 onwards, there are three options for sea and coastal freight and passenger vessels to be eligible for a green label: (i) have a zero-direct (tailpipe) CO_2 emission; or (ii) demonstrate a low GHG intensity per unit of energy use and minimum energy efficiency performance; or (iii) overachieve by 20 percentage points the reduction rates applicable for IMO's Phase 3 EEDI targets applicable from 1 April 2022.[52] Analysis by T&E of the third criterion is that it would create a loophole in the taxonomy framework by labelling 'green' ships still running entirely on fossil fuels for an indefinite period in that fossil fuel-powered vessels that are certified as having a dual fuel LNG propulsion system would be eligible for a green label even if they do not, in fact, use LNG.[53]

VIII. Conclusion

Although the IMO is the UN organisation responsible for shipping, the EU is ahead of the game when it comes to environmental measures. For instance, both the IMO and the EU have adopted measures regulating the maximum sulphur content in fuel oil used on board ships. Until 2016 the IMO's global cap of 0.50 per cent was planned to be introduced between 2020 and 2025, but from 1 January 2020 under the EU's Sulphur

[51] ec.europa.eu/finance/docs/level-2-measures/taxonomy-regulation-delegated-act-2022-climate-annex-1_en.pdf.

[52] The first two options are similar to the proposal issued by the Platform on Sustainable Finance in October 2022. The third option was introduced by the Commission after that proposal.

[53] www.transportenvironment.org/wp-content/uploads/2023/04/TE-shipping-taxonomy-explainer_v3.pdf.

Directive,[54] the same global limit was to apply for vessels within EU waters[55] which would have left a period of up to five years when different caps would have applied for EU waters and non-EU waters. However, the IMO position was harmonised with that under the Sulphur Directive with its decision in October 2016 at the 70th meeting of the Marine Environment Protection Committee (MEPC70) to introduce a global cap of 0.50 per cent on 1 January 2020.[56] There is now parallel regulation directed at reducing GHG emissions from shipping globally in the IMO with EEXI and CII and in the EU, with the Fit for 55' agenda now bearing legislative fruit as regards voyages into, within, and out of the EU.

Nor will 1 January 2024 for the ETS and 1 January 2025 see the end of the story as regards the EU measures. There will be a review in 2026 by the Commission as to whether general cargo vessels between 400 and 5,000 grt should be brought into the ETS, at which date the ETS will expand to encompass emissions from methane and nitrous oxide. Then there is another review by the Commission no later than 2028 monitoring developments in the IMO. If a global bunker tax is introduced, then changes will be needed to the ETS to avoid double liabilities. Alternatively, nothing substantial may have come out of the IMO and the Commission may propose amending the ETS and FuelEU Maritime to ensure 100 per cent coverage as regards voyages to and from ports outside the EU.

In the short term, the inclusion of shipping in the amended ETS Directive, and the amendments to the MRV Regulation, are of immediate concern to the shipping community. The focus has shifted from the reduction in CO_2 emissions to include two other potent greenhouse gases, methane and nitrous oxide, which will need to be reported under the MRV as from 1 January 2024 and will become subject to the ETS Directive two years later. The emissions in question will be assessed on a tank-to-wake basis, although this may change when the ETS Directive is reviewed in 2026. However, there is a different basis of assessment in the other major EU measure directed at reducing GHG emissions from shipping, and that is the FuelEU Maritime Regulation, which will take effect on 1 January 2025. This assesses emissions on a wake-to-wake basis, which will take into account the emissions attributable to the creation of the fuel, something particularly significant as regards methane emissions associated with LNG, until recently the pin-up fuel to replace heavy fuel oil. Hydrogen and Ammonia made from fossil fuels will also have those emissions counted, not just the emissions coming out of the vessel's smokestack. This opens up a discrepancy with the treatment of GHG emissions under the ETS. The Commission's recent proposal regarding shipping and the Taxonomy Regulation as of 2026[57] also opens up a further discrepancy as regards green finance for shipping in its third option for vessels to be labelled as 'green', if they overachieve by 20 percentage points the reduction rates applicable for IMO's Phase 3 EEDI

[54] Directive 1999/32/EC and subsequent amendments, most recently Directive 2012/33/EU.

[55] Defined as the Economic Exclusive Zone (EEZ) which stretches 200 nautical miles from shore of its member states, except where that encroaches on the EEZ of non-EU countries.

[56] A further ban on carriage of fuel with a sulphur content in excess of 0.5% by 1 March 2020 was introduced in October 2018.

[57] Above (n 53).

targets applicable from April 1, 2022. Vessels with a dual fuel LNG propulsion system would be eligible for a green label even if they do not, in fact, use LNG.

Contractual issues are also going to be in the front of the minds of owners and charterers. Who will pay for acquiring the Emissions Allowances that will have to be surrendered for trading within the EU for calendar years 2024 and 2025 for CO_2 and, additionally, for methane and nitrous oxide for calendar years 2026 and onward? BIMCO's ETSA clause has a simple answer. The time charterer. That answer will be entirely consonant with the pass-through in the Directive whereby Member States must legislate to provide a right for the shipping company to claim reimbursement for surrendered allowances from the time charterer. Shipowners may also, or as well, seek to modify their voyage operations to reduce emissions, something that can be done by slow steaming and re-routing. This is fine if shipowners have contractual liberty to do so, but otherwise, they will find themselves in breach of express obligations under time charters to proceed on the route ordered by charterers and to meet the provisions of the speed and consumption warranties. For a voyage charter and the bill of lading, there will be a breach of the implied obligations to proceed with reasonable despatch and not deviate from a usual route on the voyage.

Ship managers and demise charterers may also be affected by the new Directive if there has been a clear written delegation to them by the registered shipowner satisfying the criteria specified in the Implementing Regulation,[58] in which case they will become responsible for surrendering allowances for the vessels they manage in respect of their voyages into, within, and out of the EU. This needs to be taken into account in the contract with the shipowner, not just regarding funding for the acquisition of allowances for vessels under their management trading to the EU, but also regarding penalties. Two years of non-compliance for one ship under their management could lead to detention or expulsion of any ship under the management when it attempts to enter a port in the EU. They will need to include provision in their management contract for dealing with reimbursement from the shipowner for emissions allowances they incur, which forms the subject of BIMCO's ETS – Shipman Emission Trading Scheme Allowances Clause 2023.[59]

[58] Implementing Regulation (EU) 2023/2599 of 22 November 2023.

[59] www.bimco.org/contracts-and-clauses/bimco-clauses/current/ets-shipman-allowances-clause.

7

Contracts for Carbon Trading: Trading EU Allowances under the ETS

ANDREAS OXHOLM*

I. Introduction

From 2024, the maritime industry will be subject to the European Trading System (ETS) for carbon allowances. This change will require shipowners to submit carbon allowances each year based on the previous year's carbon emissions. Carbon allowances can be acquired through auctions of carbon allowances issued by member states and freely on the secondary market between private entities.

This chapter aims to describe and analyse the key aspects of contracts regarding the transfer of carbon allowances and the possible consequences of not adhering to the contractual obligations set out in them. The chapter will focus on the ETS and trading EU emissions allowances (EUA) and evaluate how including the maritime industry in the ETS may affect the shipping industry and the particular challenges the shipping industry might face when trading EUAs. The chapter will also provide guidance for trading carbon allowances under different systems.

II. What are EUAs

In order to discuss contracts for trading EUAs, it is necessary to understand what EUAs are.[1] They serve one purpose: to pay for the carbon emissions of the entity subject to surrendering EUAs under the ETS (Compliance Entities).[2] The EUAs do not have any other purpose and cannot be used for anything else save for investment purposes.[3] Unlike most other commodities, they do not have multiple uses. The EUAs serve as a permit that the Compliance Entity must acquire to emit certain greenhouse gasses.

* Attorney-at-law, Hafnia Law Firm, Copenhagen.

[1] For a discussion of The European Trading System (ETS) for EUAs, see Eftestøl (ch 5), Baughen (ch 6).

[2] As laid down in Directive 2003/87/EC of 13 October 2003 establishing a scheme for greenhouse gas emission allowance trading within the Community and amending Council Directive 96/61/EC [2003] OJ L275/32 (the 'ETS Directive').

[3] See Baughen (ch 6).

Unlike other goods and tradeable assets, the EUAs ultimate purpose is to be surrendered to a relevant national authority and then deleted.

The EUAs are not represented by any physical instrument (loan document, share, bill of lading or similar) but are registered on the respective Compliance Entity's online account with the Union Registry.[4] The documentation for ownership lies solely with the proof that the EUAs are featured on the accounts with the Union Registry.

EUAs are a hybrid between an administrative right and a property right.[5] They resemble an administrative right as they represent a permit issued by a national authority to emit a certain amount of greenhouse gasses without being fined. Moreover, the EUAs are issued by the respective national authorities, who decide how many EUAs will be issued and when. The EUAs are also a finite and decreasing resource which cannot be created privately (ie they cannot be mined, grown or otherwise produced independently) but merely through legislation. They are subject to full government control in the sense that the government can at any time decide that EUAs are no longer needed or valid for compensating for carbon emissions.

They also resemble property rights as they are freely transferable and represent an economic value that changes depending on market fluctuations.[6] An entity's excess EUAs can be transferred to the following year or sold to a third-party buyer. The owner of the EUAs can, to a full extent, exercise an owner's right over the EUAs, including, ultimately, deciding to delete them.

Thus, they represent both an economic asset (potential resale and freeing of capital) and a necessity so shipowners and operators can undertake their business in the future without penalties and interruption from national authorities.

The EUAs further share similarities with commodities; they are freely transferable, generic in nature, and freely priced and can be transferred in all quantities down to one single EUA.[7] The EUAs are not individualised, are consequently not numbered or marked, and are therefore traded in bulk.

The EUAs are further classified as financial instruments under the MiFID II[8] directive. Classifying them as financial instruments affects how they can be traded and places additional compliance requirements on entities trading EUAs, with exemptions in place regarding Compliance Entities.

III. The Union Registry

EUAs are traded and returned through a central European registry, the so-called Union Registry.[9] Each member state provides access to the Union Registry under its

[4] See Baughen (ch 6).

[5] *Legal Nature of EU ETS Allowances: Final Report* (European Commission, 2019) 44, downloadable from op.europa.eu/en/publication-detail/-/publication/9d985256-a6a9-11e9-9d01-01aa75ed71a1.

[6] ibid 42.

[7] It is not possible to transfer EUAs.

[8] Directive 2014/65/EU of the European Parliament and of the Council of 15 May 2014 on markets in financial instruments and amending Directive 2002/92/EC and Directive 2011/61/EU (recast) [2014] OJ L173/349.

[9] As laid down in Commission Delegated Regulation (EU) 2019/1122 supplementing Directive 2003/87/EC of the European Parliament and of the Council as regards the functioning of the Union Registry [2019] OJ L177/3 ('the Union Registry Reg').

jurisdiction. Compliance Entities and other individuals or companies wishing to trade EUAs may apply for one or more accounts in the Union Registry through the designated national administrator. Each member state must appoint a national administrator to create and administer accounts in the Union Registry for entities under its jurisdiction.[10] Thus, the individual member state administers the accounts and transactions from the accounts for account holders and Compliance Entities in the jurisdiction of the national administrator.

EUAs are 'stored' in the Union Registry, appearing as a number on the relevant accounts. It is not possible to store, trade or acquire EUAs elsewhere. It is through the accounts in the Union Registry that a Compliance Entity will return the EUAs mandated under the ETS as compensation for its carbon emissions. It is through the Union Registry that an account holder will receive new EUAs when they acquire them through the European Energy Exchange (EEX). The Union Registry is a closed system where all transactions with respect to the transfer of EUAs take place. As will be further described below, the trade and acquisition of EUAs follow contracts negotiated and concluded separately from the Union Registry. However, the EUAs can only be transferred within the Union Registry.

Anyone can apply to open an account in the Union Registry, provided they meet the documentation requirements set out in the annexes to the regulation. Companies subject to surrendering EUAs under the ETS will, in most instances, be invited to open an account, but other prospective account holders may apply to the national administrator for an account.

It is also through the Union Registry that parties can transfer its EUAs to other account holders.[11] EUAs (under the ETS) cannot be stored anywhere else, and it is thus only through the Union Registry that parties may transfer EUAs. The registry itself merely assists in the transfer of EUAs, but other than that does not have legal power over the transfer of the EUAs between the parties. Once the EUAs have been transferred between the parties, the Union Registry cannot return the EUAs or cancel the transfer.[12] This also applies to fraudulent transfer contracts or if payments have not been made in a timely fashion or at all.

At this stage, it is unclear how non-EU Compliance Entities will be able to set up an account with the Union Registry. It must be expected that they will be able to set up an account either directly through the central EU administrator or through one of the national administrators.

IV. The European Energy Exchange – Auctioning of EUAs

The primary way to obtain EUAs is by acquiring the EUAs issued by the EU member states and auctioned on a weekly basis. As described in an earlier chapter,[13] it is not envisioned that Compliance Entities in the maritime sector will be granted free EUAs

[10] *cf* ETS Directive, Art 7(1).
[11] *cf* Union Registry Reg, Art 55.
[12] *cf* Art 58(2).
[13] See Baughen (ch 6).

under the EU ETS. All EUAs must be obtained through auctions of new EUAs or bilateral agreements.[14]

Most EU member states auction EUAs through the European Energy Exchange (EEX). The EEX is a marketplace for trading energy-related products and environmental commodities in Europe and, for the purpose of this chapter, the central trading place for EUAs.

To understand how EUAs are priced (and traded), it is important to understand how the EEX operates.

The auctioning process on EEX involves several stages, which in detail is regulated by EU Regulation 1031/2010 on the timing, administration and other aspects of auctioning of greenhouse gas emission EUAs pursuant to Directive 2003/87/EC of the European Parliament and of the Council establishing a scheme for greenhouse gas emission EUAs trading within the Community (the 'Auctioning Regulation').

The European Commission sets an annual emission cap, determining the total number of EUAs available for the trading period. These EUAs are then allocated to participating member states, who distribute them to installations under their jurisdiction which still receive free EUAs.[15] A portion of these EUAs are auctioned on EEX. As it is not envisioned that the maritime industry will receive any free EUAs, all EUAs will have to be initially acquired through the EEX.

A. Registration

To participate in the auction, interested parties must register with EEX and meet the eligibility criteria. The admissions process includes taking a course in trading EUAs on the EEX, providing proof of sufficient liable equity, a commercial relationship with a pre-approved clearing bank and providing KYC documentation to the EEX and other admission documentation. The admission process is doable, but the process might appear cumbersome for smaller shipowners without a large group administration.

B. Bidding

Once registered, participants can submit bids through the electronic trading platform during specific auction sessions. The bids consist of the quantity of EUAs desired and the price the bidder is willing to pay. Concerning auctioning of EUAs, the EEX employs an auction format described as uniform price auction. In uniform price auctions, all successful bidders pay the same price, which is set as the lowest successful bid.

The bids are submitted confidentially.[16] Each auction will indicate the amount of EUAs offered in the given auction. Each bid must indicate the price envisioned per EUA

[14] See below, section V.

[15] As described in more detail in Eftestøl (ch 5); Baughen (ch 6).

[16] Commission Regulation (EU) No 1031/2010 of 12 November 2010 on the timing, administration and other aspects of auctioning of greenhouse gas emission allowances pursuant to Directive 2003/87/EC of the European Parliament and of the Council establishing a scheme for greenhouse gas emission allowances trading within the Community [2010] OJ L302/1 ('Auctioning Regulation') Art 5.

and the number of EUAs in multiples of lot sizes of 500 EUAs.[17] Once all bids have been submitted, the bids are ranged in order from highest to lowest bid. The lowest bid, which is accepted, will determine the clearing price for all the EUAs sold during that auction in accordance with the uniform price auction model.

If the amount of EUAs represented by the submitted bids is lower than the amount of EUAs offered for auction in the given auction, the entire auction will be annulled.[18] The EEX may also annul the auction if the clearing price is significantly lower than the second market price.[19] EU legislators found that an auction not being able to collect enough bids or delivering a clearing price significantly under the second market price would evidence an ineffective auction.[20] They assessed that allowing such an auction to stand would significantly affect both the market for EUAs and the incentives intended with the ETS. A bona fide bidder may thus find himself in a situation where a genuine bid over the second market price gets annulled due to a lack of other bidders. The EUAs offered on an annulled auction will roll over to the following auctions.

Following a successful bid, the payment will have to be effectuated. The EEX acts as a clearinghouse between the issuer of the EUAs and the buyer. Bidders must provide collateral for default on payment risks,[21] thus ensuring effective payment. Once the payment is received, the EEX transfers the EUAs to the buyer's account, completing the transaction, and the EUAs are available to the buyer for submission to the authorities or further trade.

If the successful bidder fails to pay the clearing price for the auctioned EUAs, the EEX has various remedies available. EEX may charge the bidder a penalty fee or interest for late payment[22] but may also choose to either cancel the bid or use the placed collateral to pay the owed amount (including any late payment fees and interest).[23] If the bid is cancelled, the EUAs will be returned to the EEX for auctioning on the subsequent auctions.

The EEX ensures a fast and secure way to acquire EUAs through a clearinghouse process. The principal risk of acquiring EUAs through the EEX is not placing a successful bid and thus missing out on the auction or placing a bid in an auction that gets annulled due to insufficient bids.

For smaller Compliance Entities, it may be too cumbersome to set up an account with the EEX and it will instead be easier to acquire the EUAs from third-parties or intermediaries.

V. The Mechanics of EUA Trading

In addition to acquiring EUA through the EEX platform, it is possible to acquire EUAs on the secondary market. The ETS directive requires member states to ensure that

[17] ibid Art 6.
[18] ibid Art 7(5).
[19] ibid Art 7(6).
[20] Preamble no 20.
[21] Auctioning Regulation, Art 49(1).
[22] ibid Art 45(3).
[23] ibid Art 45(4).

EUAs can be freely transferred between parties.[24] The Union Registry allows account holders to transfer EUAs to one another freely, and these are referred to as over-the-counter transactions or OTC transactions.

A. The EUA Contract

EUA contracts in the secondary market can take the form of forward contracts or spot contracts. Forward contracts involve an agreement between the buyer and the seller to trade carbon quotas at a specified future date and price, allowing participants to hedge against price volatility and manage long-term compliance obligations. Spot contracts, on the other hand, involve the immediate transfer of carbon EUAs.[25]

While the transfer of EUAs between two parties occurs within the Union Registry, the remainder of the transaction, including the contract negotiations and conclusions, takes place independently of the Union Registry on a free-market basis. The EUAs are registered as financial instruments and the contract for acquiring EUAs are therefore excluded under the CISG.[26] However, the local sale of goods statutes in many EU member states do not exclude contracts for sale of financial instruments such as shares or EUAs.[27] Thus, depending on what choice of law the parties to a contract might decide on, local rules governing the sale of goods (or financial instruments) may act as default rules in the absence of a contract.

The parties to a contract for transferring EUAs are free to decide on the terms for the transfer of EUAs, including any remedies and restrictions concerning the transfer. This includes both price as well as terms concerning transfer date, delivery in instalments, damages, and other terms the parties may agree to. Trading EUAs is not subject to specific mandatory rules other than what applies to all other transactions (unconscionability, fraud defences, etc.).

As described above, EUAs are generic, not individualised, rights to emit a certain amount of carbon. EUAs do not differ in quality. They do not expire and are completely identical. For these reasons, the contract itself can be straightforward. The contract will resemble standard, generic commodities contracts except that, unlike other commodities, the risk of the EUAs suffering loss or damage during the transaction is very low.

The contract will have to identify the quantity of EUAs and the price for the EUAs. Further, the contract should identify a time for the transfer of EUAs. Notwithstanding other purposes of a transfer of EUAs, the delivery date should be set well in advance of the deadline for surrendering the EUAs to the relevant authorities, allowing the parties to remedy any issues with the transaction before the buyer becomes subject to the draconic late-surrender fees set out in the ETS directive.[28]

The contract should stipulate the account to which the EUAs can be transferred to govern when the seller has fulfilled its obligations under the contract. Some standard

[24] ETS Directive, Art 12.

[25] For a detailed description on forward contracts and price hedging see: M Bridge, *The International Sale of Goods*, 5th edn (Oxford, Oxford University Press, 2023) para 1.49ff.

[26] *cf* Art 2(d) to the United Nations Convention on Contracts for the International Sale of Goods.

[27] See for example Art 19 to the Danish Sales of Goods Act.

[28] *cf* ibid Art 16(3).

contracts for trading carbon quotas stipulate that the seller should specify the account from which it is transferring its EUAs.[29] This, however, will be superfluous in most cases, given that the seller's primary obligation is to deliver EUAs as specified in the contract. The EUAs are all identical and do not carry any individual traces.[30] For the Compliance Entity buyer who needs them for surrendering to the national authorities, the EUAs are equally valuable independent of which account they are transferred from. Moreover, the IETA contract – for instance – does not stipulate any consequence of transferring the EUAs from a different account. The buyer will not suffer any loss from receiving EUAs from an account not specified in the contract. Most contracts ought to simply stipulate that the seller is to procure the transfer of a specific number of EUAs on the buyer's designated account at a specific date. It will thus be up to the seller to procure the transfer of the EUAs.

In two instances, specifying the specific account from which the seller is to transfer the EUAs might be worthwhile. From a buyer's perspective, the purpose of determining a specific account would be to correctly identify the EUAs subject to the contract in case of competing rights to the EUAs. From a seller's perspective, specifying the account from which the EUAs are to be transferred will limit the seller's obligations. In the event of a force majeure event,[31] theft or hacking targeting the specified account, the seller will not necessarily be obligated to deliver EUAs stored in other accounts, as the contract only governs the EUAs listed on a specific account.

Save from the description above, two factors make the carbon contract stand out. One is the lack of simultaneous transfer and the limited powers of the Union Registry to enforce contracts. The other is the ultimate purpose of acquiring EUAs – to surrender them to the relevant authority for deletion.

B. Lack of Simultaneous Transfer

Since the Union Registry does not allow for any transfer of funds but only the transfer of EUAs, it is impossible to ensure simultaneous transfer of funds and EUAs within the Union Registry. A contract for the transfer of carbon EUAs will determine that the primary obligation of the seller of the EUA is to transfer a specific number of EUAs within the registry to an account specified by the buyer. The seller will typically have fulfilled its obligations when the EUAs are identified on the buyer's designated account.

The International Emissions Trading Association (IETA) have drafted templates for a standard carbon trading contract.[32] The suggested wording for the seller's main obligations is as follows:

> With respect to each Delivery Date referred to in column (A) of the delivery schedule in clause 3.2, *the Delivering Party shall Transfer* (or procure the Transfer of) *the corresponding*

[29] For instance, cl 3.3 and cl 3.4 of the IETA's Standard Emissions Allowances Single Trade Agreement for Phase IV of the EU ETS: www.ieta.org/Trading-Documents.

[30] Aviation EUAs aside.

[31] As might be defined in the contracts.

[32] Available at www.ieta.org/Trading-Documents.

> *Periodic Quantity of Allowances referred to in column* (B) of the delivery schedule in clause 3.2 by no later than that Delivery Date *from any Account in any Registry to the relevant Receiving Party's Account* (as set out in the table below)…[33]

The sample contract further specifies that the transaction is concluded when the buyer has received the EUAs:

> The Transfer *shall be considered to be completed* for the purposes of this Agreement *when the Allowances are received in the Receiving Party's Account* in accordance with the Registries Regulation, whereupon risk of loss, related to the Allowances, or any portion thereof, shall transfer from the Delivering Party to the Receiving Party[..][34]

The sample contract stipulates that following receipt of the EUAs, payment of the agreed purchase sum must be transferred 5 banking days later. The IETA contract thus suggests placing the risk of a party's non-performance on the seller, who will have to accept payment after transferring the EUAs. The parties are naturally free to decide on how to manage the non-performance risk. It will vary from transaction to transaction, and the relationship between the parties, who are closest to bear the risk of a non-performing counterparty.

EUAs are a scarcer resource than money, and non-performance of the party transferring the EUAs could not only result in a financial loss from having to acquire potentially more EUAs at a higher price somewhere else, it could also result in hefty fines if the buyer is a Compliance Entity which is not able to submit EUAs to cover its emissions. It would, in most instances, be more burdensome for the buyer of the EUAs to release the purchase sum prior to receiving the EUAs, than having the seller release the EUAs before receiving the purchase sum. The risk of not having sufficient EUAs to submit to the national authorities and the risk of fines or even limitation in trade would normally outweigh the credit risk of the seller.

However, international shipping is a volatile industry and credit risks in trading with shipowners and other industry players should not be neglected. Unlike the current Compliance Entities under the ETS, which are heavy production and industry companies, shipping companies often operate through one ship companies, trade all around the world and sell and acquire new vessels often.

There are several ways for a seller of EUAs to manage the credit risk of a non-performing buyer. The seller may require a letter of credit issued by a reputable financial institution as collateral. These letters guarantee that the issuing bank will pay the non-defaulting party if the obligated party fails to fulfil its payment obligations. Along the same lines, the seller can require a bank guarantee ensuring performance. Suppose the buyer is a single-purpose company with only one vessel as is often seen amongst shipowners. In that case, the seller may also consider a parent company guarantee or a shareholder guarantee.

Both Letters of Credit and bank guarantees can be costly to facilitate and, depending on the buyer's bank or parent company, might not even be attractive for the seller.

[33] Cl 3.3 to the IETA's standard Emissions Allowances Single Trade Agreement for Phase IV of the EU ETS v 6.0 (2019), available at www.ieta.org/Trading-Documents. Emphasis added.

[34] ibid cl 3.5. Emphasis added.

Another option widely used in the maritime industry for the sale and purchase of vessels is the use of an escrow agent. The escrow agent is a third-party intermediary who receives the buyer's purchase sum before the seller transfers the EUAs. This arrangement removes the seller's credit risk while the buyer is still certain that the purchase sum is not released before they receive the EUAs.

For large transactions of EUAs, the parties may decide to use a central clearing counterparty, which can act as a counterparty to both the buyer and the seller. As the EEX acts as a clearing house for auctioning the EUAs offered by the national government, a central clearing counterparty manages the credit risk associated with the transaction by acting as an intermediary between the parties and clearing the transaction. Thus, the clearing counterparty administers the distribution of the EUAs and the purchase sum, which are all cleared through them.

The parties to a contract for trading should carefully consider including mechanisms for securing a safe exchange of EUAs and funds.

C. The Nature of the EUAs

The contracting parties to a contract for trading EUAs should remember that the ultimate purpose of acquiring EUAs is to surrender them to the relevant authority as compensation for carbon emissions. Failure to submit the EUAs within the deadline will lead to a fine of 100 euros per missing EUA, while the party in default will still have to submit the missing EUAs the following year.[35] Failure to surrender the EUAs will lead to public 'naming and shaming' in a central registry and expose the Compliance Entity to potential arrests and detentions of its vessels by local authorities.

EUAs do not serve any purpose or have other traits that give them inherent value. They might be traded for a profit purpose – as the EUAs get scarcer every year, the price of them is expected to go up, provided, of course, that the industry is not lowering emissions faster than the global number of EUAs is decreasing. But ultimately, they only serve the purpose of being deleted as compensation for greenhouse gas emissions.

The single-purpose nature of the EUAs makes questions on mitigation and remedies relatively straightforward. All actors in the transaction know precisely what the purpose of the transaction is and how non-performance might affect the other party. In terms of discussing mitigation, it is similarly quite simple. There are no alternatives or substitutions for EUAs; either the buyer uses its own excess EUAs or undertakes a cover purchase. The remedies for non-performance are further explored below.

D. Risks and Remedies

In contracting for EUAs, the most significant risk for the seller is the buyer's non-performance in paying the purchase price. The previous sections describe how the payment-default risks might be handled.

[35] *cf* the ETS Directive, Art 16(3) and 16(4).

i. Seller's Remedies

It seems moot to discuss specific performance instead of damages for the sellers' remedies. The seller's loss will arise when the buyer reneges on its promise to acquire the EUAs at the agreed price and the market price of EUAs is lower than the contract price. EUAs can be surrendered for deletion by anyone holding a Union Registry account, which means that in the somewhat unlikely event that the seller cannot sell the EUAs to a third party, the seller can delete the EUAs and claim damages for loss from the buyer, which would be the contract sum plus any additional cost incurred in this respect.[36] It would make little sense to insist on the buyer taking possession of EUAs that the buyer does not desire.

The seller's damages will likely be calculated based on the difference between the current secondhand market price and the agreed price in the contract.

ii. Buyer's Risk and Remedies

From a buyer's perspective, the main risk is non-delivery of the EUAs, either due to the seller's unwillingness to deliver, insolvency, double sale or fraud.

In case the seller becomes insolvent before the EUAs have been duly transferred, but after the purchase sum has been transferred, the buyer will, in most jurisdictions, be left with the option of filing a claim with the estate. The trustee will likely have to sell the EUAs on the secondary market to acquire funds to pay the estate's creditors.

If the agreement for the transfer of EUAs stipulated that *all* the EUAs in one specific account[37] were to be transferred to a buyer, in some jurisdictions the buyer may have a right to receive the EUAs because the EUA's on the specified account is a secured claim. This will, to a large extent, depend on the insolvency laws in the jurisdiction of the estate. It will further rely on whether or not the seller has entered into several contracts for the same EUAs on the same specified account.

Concerning a double sale, defined as a situation where the seller has sold more EUAs than available to him to different buyers who have paid in advance for the EUAs, it will vary from jurisdiction to jurisdiction how to deal with this property right's issue. First in time will, in most cases, be first in right,[38] but also actual possession, and exercising an owners' right may protect a bona fide buyer.[39] Similarly, as in cases of insolvency, if the contract specifies that the seller is to deliver all EUAs in a specific account, the buyer may also be entitled to receive the EUAs on the basis of them being a secured claim.

Aside from these property issues arising from non-performance of the seller, the buyer will have access to contractual remedies, specifically either damages or specific performance.

[36] See eg *Benjamin on Sale of Goods*, 12th edn (London, Sweet & Maxwell, 2024) para 15-112.

[37] With proper identification of said account.

[38] Also known as the *nemo dat quod non habet* principle, by which a seller cannot transfer title that he does not have (because the goods have already been sold), see *Benjamin on Sale of Goods* (n 36) para 7-001ff.

[39] See eg ibid para 7-053ff.

The events giving rise to remedies are either: (1) the price of the EUAs has gone up since the conclusion of the contract for EUAs, or (2) the buyer is not able to obtain new EUAs before having to submit them to the relevant national authorities.

E. Specific Performance

The question whether the buyer has a right to specific performance depends on the law that governs the contract. As a general rule, in most common-law jurisdictions, specific performance is only available to the buyer where its claim for damages is inadequate to compensate the buyer fully.[40] Many civil law countries have an at least de jure general rule that the buyer has access to specific performance.[41] However, in most cases, there are significant exceptions to this rule. Whilst the question of whether or not the buyer may demand specific performance ultimately relies on local courts and arbitrators, some considerations must be made.

Assuming that the buyer is a shipowner or another Compliance Entity subject to submitting EUAs, the buyer needs the EUAs to undertake its ordinary business. Failure to submit the EUAs in time will lead to severe fines and public naming and shaming.[42] EUAs are or at least will be a scarce resource and especially for minor or non-EU shipowners and operators acquiring the EUAs through the EEX may not be practically possible due to the significant compliance requirements for setting up an account with EEX. They will thus be left with acquiring the EUAs on the secondary market in over-the-counter transactions. As discussed below, it is not clear how the secondary market for EUAs will form, but it must be expected that some companies will acquire large portions of EUAs and sell them to industry actors and Compliance Entities. This will allow industry actors to acquire EUAs from these traders without having to acquire EUAs through the denser process in the EEX. Moreover, industry actors can hedge against risk by entering into long-term contracts with these EUA traders.

Provided the seller is such a larger trading house which (also) deals in EUAs and the buyer is a smaller ship-owning entity, the question of whether the buyer should be allowed to claim specific performance could, on a balance of equities, easily fall out in the buyer's favour. Between the two parties, in this case, the seller would appear to be the party closest to acquiring further EUAs to be delivered to the buyer, as opposed to the buyer, who will have to identify and negotiate a purchase contract with a third-party seller.

The problem regarding enforceability remains, ultimately becoming the problem with specific performance for EUAs. In order to undertake its duty of mitigation, it is unlikely that – at least as long as there is a large number of EUAs available – it will result in a better outcome for the buyer to insist on specific performance than to acquire the EUAs somewhere else and claim a potential loss for damages from the defaulting seller.

[40] See eg the Uniform Commercial Code (UCC), para 2-716(1), and for UK references see H Beale (ed), *Chitty on Contracts, volume 1: general principles*, 35th edn (London, Sweet & Maxwell, 2023) para 31-015.

[41] See eg H Lando and C Rose, 'On Specific Performance in Civil Law and Enforcement Costs' 2000, Working Paper – Copenhagen Business School No. 2000-10, p 12 and Bridge (n 25) para 12.47.

[42] *cf* ETS Directive, Art 16(2).

F. Calculating Damages

As stated in the previous section, specific performance will likely not be an available remedy in practice. If the non-performing seller is not a professional intermediary who deals in trading EUAs it might not be practically or commercially possible to insist on specific performance, and a wronged buyer might obtain the EUAs somewhere else (or have hedged themselves by having acquired excess EUAs) and insist on claiming damages instead.

The calculation of damages in itself is a fairly easy task to do and will follow the general principles for calculating damages. The damages will be calculated based on the difference in the price stipulated in the contract and the market price for EUAs.[43] The determining time for calculating the difference will, in most instances, be at the time of performance under the contract.[44] The seller should not be able to benefit from fluctuating prices by reneging on its contract. The buyer will likely be able to collect any extra fees or costs incurred (brokerage fees, transaction costs, fees to the EEX) in acquiring the new EUAs in addition to the difference between the contract price and market price.

G. Fines

The second question is whether the wronged buyer may collect any fines and claim damages for reputable damage caused by not being able to surrender a sufficient amount of EUAs.

Parties trading in the maritime industry will be aware that each year, on 30 September, EUAs must be surrendered to the relevant national authority.[45] Failure to surrender will lead to a fine of 100 EUR per missing EUA and being featured in the official list of companies not complying with the submission requirements.[46] The question then arises whether the buyer may claim the fines issued by the authorities from the seller and whether any documented losses arising from being on the list of non-complying companies are recoverable.

In terms of causation and foreseeability, there are good arguments to the point that these costs are linked to the seller's breach of contract. The question then arises whether the seller can provide the defence that the buyer has failed in its duty to mitigate the loss. The closer the seller's breach is to the relevant cut-off date of 30 September 2023, the stronger the buyer's argument may be that the seller's breach has caused the buyer to suffer a loss in paying the 100 EUR fine in addition to the fluctuation in the price. Similarly, if the seller reneges on the contract for EUAs being delivered in mid-October it will definitely be more difficult for the buyer to argue that they could not acquire the needed EUAs before the following 30 September.

[43] See *Benjamin on Sale of Goods* (n 36) para 16-064.
[44] See J Beatson et al, *Anson's Law of Contract*, 31st edn (Oxford, Oxford University Press, 2020) 533ff.
[45] ibid Art 12(3)(c).
[46] ibid Art 16(2) and Art 16(3).

The breaching seller is, if this line of argument is to be followed, placed in very different situations depending on when the breach occurs. It is not in itself controversial; parties must be expected to honour their obligations, and in failing to do so, they must remedy their breach as an overriding principle unless the parties have opted for limitations in liability. But there are modifications to this, most notably considerations with respect to mitigation and foreseeability.

The buyer will know on 31 December with fair certainty how many EUAs they will have to surrender nine months later on 30 September. A buyer may thus already, on 1 January, acquire the EUAs needed to cover the emissions of the previous year. The party claiming that the breach of one contract for the transfer of EUAs has caused the party to suffer an additional loss in the form of a public fine will likely have to document that the seller ought to have realised that the EUAs in the contract were to be submitted the coming deadline.

The EUAs do, however, only serve one single purpose – permitting the emission of a certain amount of CO_2 or CO_2 equivalents. A seller claiming that they did not foresee that the buyer needed the EUAs for submitting them to the authorities will likewise have to show that the contract in question was not needed for the buyer to meet its immediate compliance needs.

It is not given how the balance of equities will fall when the courts hear cases like this, and parties may do well in dealing with this in their contract for trading EUAs.

The IETA's emissions trading master agreement for the EU scheme[47] has a mechanism for letting the parties decide whether the seller is to be liable for paying excess emissions penalties following failure to transfer the EUAs. The suggested clause is structured as such that if the parties have opted to not apply the excess emissions penalty clause, the seller will be liable for the difference in contract price and market price in addition to interests and affiliated expenses incurred by the buyer in obtaining replacement EUAs.

If the parties have opted to apply the excess emissions penalty clause, the seller will, in addition to the difference in market and contract price, also be liable to pay any excess emissions penalties that the buyer incurs as a result of the seller's non-performance. The buyer will have to show: (1) that they did not have EUAs available to them that they could have used to surrender to the authorities, and (2) that it was the seller's non-performance that caused the buyer to incur the excess emissions penalty. Further, the buyer will have to show that they have made reasonable efforts to avoid being liable to pay the excess emissions penalty. The contract provides that the buyer must allocate the penalties pro rata between all (if more than one) sellers that have failed to make a proper transfer.

It is clear that if the parties have agreed on a contract format by which they actively exclude the excess emissions' penalties from the remedies under the contract eg, by using the IETA contract and using the opt-out option, the parties have actively decided not to make the costs of the excess emissions' penalties part of the buyer's remedies and claim for damages.

If the parties, on the contrary, decide to opt in or use another mechanism for making the seller liable for potential excess emissions penalties, disputes may still arise. While

[47] www.ieta.org/resources/trading-documents/.

the buyer – whether or not it is explicitly stated in the contract – of course, will always have to mitigate the loss and avoid being subject to penalties, there are limits to what can be expected of the buyer. To the extent that the buyer has EUAs available to them for surrendering, they will have to surrender those to minimise the loss. The buyer will generally be interested in doing so, and failing to do so – thus forcing a penalty on the seller – will generally not be accepted in most jurisdictions, as there is generally no recovery for loss which should (could) have been avoided.[48] Thus, if the buyer – for some reason – have excess EUAs they would have to surrender these in order to avoid the penalty and claim damages from the reneging seller.

However, the buyer will not be obligated to default on its own contracts.[49] If the buyer has an excess amount of EUAs which are intended to be sold under a different contract, which could be used to surrender to the authorities, the buyer will generally not, in its duty towards the seller, be obligated to surrender EUAs that would put the buyer at risk of defaulting under another contract.

Moreover, the further away from the deadline for surrendering the EUAs the seller fails to perform, the more difficult it will be for the buyer to prove that despite bona fide efforts, it could not obtain a sufficient amount of EUAs.

However, including provisions in the contract regulating how to deal with potential excess emissions penalties will eliminate many uncertainties when calculating damages following a breach of contract.

The parties could avoid the uncertainty with respect to payment of the excess emissions penalty by simply – and where legally feasible – opting for agreed penalties instead. Agreed penalties will take away the unpredictability – and potential disputes – of dealing with potential excess emissions penalties.

VI. Other Contractual Provisions

As previously mentioned, the contract for transferring EUAs is in itself simple. However, a few more issues should be considered before entering into a contract for trading EUAs.

A. Jurisdiction and Choice of Law Clauses

The ETS is overall subject to uniform EU law. The excess emissions penalties, as well as the auctioning rules and rules for the Union Registry, are all governed by the ETS Directive and affiliated directives. However, the rules will be enforced and interpreted by the local authorities to a great extent. Rules on contract interpretation and calculation of damages also differ from jurisdiction to jurisdiction. The parties should, therefore, closely consider choosing the law and venue governing the contract and dispute resolution mechanisms before entering into a contract for transferring EUAs, as well as a venue for the dispute and enforcement options.

[48] *Benjamin on Sale of Goods* (n 36) para 16-054.

[49] ibid. The buyer will not be obligated to do anything excess of the ordinary course of business, which entails he will not be obligated to take any excess risk of his own money or jeopardise other business relations.

B. Assignment of Rights

The parties should strongly consider to what extent they may assign their rights and obligations under the contract to any third parties. EUAs are a scarce resource, and it is not possible for everyone to obtain EUAs through the EEX. Further, EUAs represent a significant value and will likely be traded in larger quantities and thus also will be expected to represent large transaction sums.

The buyer will want to ensure that the seller can deliver the EUAs in time and can pay damages should they fail to deliver. The buyer will, therefore, want to make sure that the seller cannot transfer the contract to another entity. Similarly, the seller will want to ensure that the buyer does not transfer the payment obligations to another entity without the seller's prior approval.[50]

C. Force Majeure, Theft and Hacking

In 2013, Interpol reported that the Union Registry in several member states suffered from being 'pervasively lax',[51] which made them prone to hacking and theft. Equally, entities with large numbers of EUAs could also be victims of phishing attempts and other sorts of cyber-attacks or crimes. While cyber security has improved significantly over the last decade, cybercriminals have also become more refined and globally, cyber-attacks are on the rise.[52]

Online registries are at risk of major cyber-attack events that make it impossible to undertake a promised transfer – either for reasons in the seller's or buyer's registry (or both) as well as other IT-break downs, thus causing either of the parties to default on the contract involuntarily.

Theft is not normally considered a force majeure event,[53] and there may be many reasons for not qualifying it as such. Cyber risks and cyber theft are significant risks, and the parties will do well in implementing a mechanism in their contracts dealing with impossibility, either due to hacking, theft, fraud or other cyber-attacks.

The buyer (or seller) will need to be able to rescind the contract fairly quickly after the other party's non-performance, as it might be paramount for the buyer to meet its compliance requirements.

VII. The Envisioned Parties to Carbon Contracts

Although the rules regarding the ETS have been agreed, we do not yet have an idea how the market will eventually evolve. What follows is an assessment of what parties and

[50] As a general rule it is not possible to assign liabilities (ie payment obligations) under a contract to another party without the contractual party's consent: E McKendrick, *Contract Law: Text, Cases and Materials*, 10th edn (Oxford, Oxford University Press, 2022).

[51] *Guide to Carbon Trading Crime* (Interpol, 2013) 26, www.interpol.int/en/Resources/Documents.

[52] A report by Check Point Software Technologies on 5 January 2023 suggests a global surge in cyber-attacks of 38% from 2021 to 2022, blog.checkpoint.com/2023/01/05/38-increase-in-2022-global-cyberattacks/.

[53] Force Majeure events were traditionally categorised as 'Acts of God' (see *Chitty on Contracts* (n 40) para 27-064), but now concern events where non-performance was due to circumstances beyond the party's

contracts might be part of the market for EUAs following the inclusion of the maritime sector in the ETS.

A. The Current Market for EUAs

In February 2022 the United Kingdom-based consultancy firm, Oxera, analysed the carbon market within the European Union in a report made publicly available.[54] According to the report, the EUA market has moved from bilateral transactions, meaning over-the-counter transactions, to mainly having transactions being administered by the exchanges.[55] In 2007 EUA transactions conducted through an exchange amounted to approximately 30 per cent of all transactions, whereas in 2022, the number was 70 per cent.[56] The report lists transparent pricing, accessibility and a broader range of participants as reasons for market actors to move towards the exchanges. The current and previous market for EUAs is centred around entities in heavy industry, aviation and other heavy emitters, who likely have the capacity to set up an administration to handle transactions on the EEX. Further, and especially in the earlier years of the ETS, emitters were granted large amounts of free EUAs[57] that they could freely trade, creating a potential market for bilateral trade. As fewer and fewer EUAs are allocated for free, Compliance Entities have to obtain their EUAs through exchanges such as the EEX or from other industry Compliance Entities.

The sectors covered by the ETS are, aside from the maritime sector, the aviation industry and energy-intensive industry sectors such as oil refineries, steel works and production of metal, and glass. Compared to the one-vessel shipowner, these industries will likely be better equipped for setting up a compliance function that meets the requirements for emitters acquiring EUAs through the exchanges.

B. The Envisioned Market for Shipping

All shipowners trading in the European Union will be subject to submitting EUAs every year and will thus have to acquire EUAs. EUAs are not allocated to compliance entities in the maritime sector for free, and thus all entities will have to purchase EUAs themselves. As previously described, all EUAs will be auctioned by the national authorities through the EEX and shipowners and other compliance entities will thus have to acquire the EUAs by way of auction or on the secondary market.

control and that there were no reasonable steps that the party could have taken to avoid or mitigate the event or its consequences (*Chitty on Contracts* (n 40) para 27-066). Force Majeure events are normally pre-defined (and may thus include all kinds of events) but commonly concern events like natural disasters, war, general strikes, embargoes etc. (*Chitty on Contracts* (n 40) para 27-071). Theft will normally be excluded due to the third requirement; that the effects of the event could not have been mitigated.

[54] *Carbon Trading in the European Union: An Economic Assessment of Market Functioning in 2021* (February 2022), available at www.oxera.com/wp-content/uploads/2022/02/Oxera-EU-carbon-trading-report-2.pdf.

[55] ibid 26.

[56] ibid.

[57] In 2007, almost all allowances were given for free. It was only in 2013 that the system changed to central auctioning.

C. EUA Intermediaries

Large shipowners with a fleet of vessels will likely acquire the EUAs directly through the EEX, as they will likely have the staff and administration in place to meet the compliance requirements from the EEX. However, large shipowners might also trade EUAs in the secondary market either as a risk management tool or as an ancillary part of other transactions.

Smaller shipowners and one-vessel companies might find it cumbersome to engage with the compliance requirements, testing and documentation connected with trading through the EEX and will likely benefit more from trading OTC with a well-renowned intermediary who can manage risk and acquire EUAs from the EEX and resell to smaller shipowners. This also applies to non-EU entities that will be subject to surrendering EUAs arising from trade to or from the European Union.

Most shipowners do not acquire bunker fuel and lubricants directly from physical suppliers but through intermediaries – so-called bunker traders. Bunker traders not only procure fuel delivery to vessel owners and charterers from the physical suppliers but, to a greater extent, also provide credit lines and ongoing supply contracts with guaranteed prices and supply.

Similar intermediaries will likely be established following the inclusion of the maritime industry in the ETS. They will be able to take on the risk from shipowners – both in terms of prices and availability of EUAs. This will create certainty and foreseeability for the Compliance Entities. Further, the intermediaries will likely be the only practical way for non-EU Compliance Entities to obtain EUAs, as setting up an account with the EEX might not be practically possible for them.

The contracts with these Intermediaries will likely be very straightforward and similar to a standard OTC contract with amendments to reflect any long-term commitments or subsequent deliveries.

EUAs are qualified as a financial instrument under the MiFID II Directive.[58] While the MiFID II Directive excludes compliance operators under the ETS Directive from the MiFID II Directive,[59] this does not apply to intermediaries trading EUAs.[60] Entities considering entering the market as intermediaries should consider the compliance and reporting requirements under the MiFID II Directive before offering to act as an intermediary.

D. Sale and Purchase Transactions

It could also be expected that the transfer of EUAs will be seen in connection with the sale and purchase of vessels. Shipowners will, from time to time, need to either acquire

[58] As well as the EMIR Directive, Regulation (EU) No 648/2012 of the European Parliament and of the Council of 4 July 2012 on OTC derivatives, central counterparties and trade repositories [2010] OJ L302/1.

[59] Directive 2014/65/EU of the European Parliament and of the Council of 15 May 2014 on markets in financial instruments and amending Directive 2002/92/EC and Directive 2011/61/EU (recast) [2014] OJ L173/249, Art 2(1)(e).

[60] With few exceptions for entities who trade EUAs as an ancillary activity to their main business. *cf* Art 2(1)(j) of the MiFID II Directive.

new vessels or capitalise their assets in an adjustment of their business operation. In such situations, shipowners may find themselves in situations where they either have an excess amount of EUAs or require EUAs.

As well as bunkers, lubricants and sometimes excess spares are traded as part of a ship sale, we might see shipowners simply trading EUAs as part of the transactions. To begin with, they might take the form of a separate OTC transaction, but it might form part of the standard ship sale documents as an optional part of the transaction as it becomes more common.

E. Charterparty Agreements

In international shipping, there is often a discrepancy between the entity causing the emissions and the party liable under the ETS. Time charterers will normally undertake voyage planning and decide the utilisation of the vessel and will thus be the party ultimately deciding how much the vessel will emit within the jurisdiction of the ETS and thus, how many EUAs the vessel will need. The shipowner, on the other hand, will be the party having to surrender the EUAs as Compliance Entities.

To solve this problem, the ETS directive determines that member states must ensure that shipowners are entitled to be reimbursed for EUA costs when they are not the party responsible for purchasing fuel or deciding the route or cargo carried.[61] How this statutory right to reimbursement will be implemented is still uncertain, but shipowners and charterers will likely need to agree bilaterally on the costs for the EUAs.

BIMCO, which provides suggested clauses and contracts for the industry, has drafted a charterparty clause for charterers and shipowners to incorporate in their existing agreements.[62] The clause essentially works so that by the end of each month, the owner will inform the charterer of the greenhouse gas emitted, and the charterer will have to transfer the amount of EUAs needed for covering the previous month's emissions.

Such a clause might work in some commercial relationships but not all. Whether the clause is applicable between a charterer and a shipowner will rely heavily on the balance of commercial and economic power between the two. For large shipowners or those chartering vessels to non-EU entities, it might be more commercially feasible to simply acquire the EUAs themselves and collect the costs from the charterer.

VIII. Future Considerations

Including the maritime sector under the ETS is a first in the world. Being a regional measure in a global market, it remains to be seen how effective it will be and how Compliance Entities will adapt to the new set of rules. This chapter was written before

[61] ETS Directive, Art 3gc.

[62] www.bimco.org/contracts-and-clauses/bimco-clauses/current/etsa_clause.

the rules even came into effect, and it is still largely uncertain what the market for trading carbon allowances will look like.

Given that it is a regional measure and emissions only count in some parts of the world, we will likely see many disputes in the first years. Both between authorities and Compliance Entities, shipowners and charterers and between sellers and buyers of EUAs and the rules will likely evolve to accommodate this.

8

Carbon Clauses and Spill-over Effects on Bills of Lading and the Supply Chain

VIBE ULFBECK*

I. Introduction

As described in the previous chapters of this volume, new measures have been introduced at both the international level and the EU level to curb carbon emissions in the shipping industry. Most notably, the CII system introduces annual ratings of ships according to their energy efficiency during the past year, and the EU ETS requires shipowners to acquire allowances to cover their annual emissions.

These new regulatory initiatives need to be reflected in the contracts distributing obligations, risks and liabilities between the parties in the shipping sector. As described, standard clauses to regulate the relationship between shipowners and charterers with regard to both the CII system[1] and the EU ETS[2] (carbon clauses) have been developed.

However, quite clearly, the new regulation will affect not just the shipowner and charterer but the entire maritime supply chain and a wide range of contracts. For instance, the allocation of contractual obligations, risks and liabilities between the shipowner and charterer in the charterparty will have direct effects on the bill of lading. However, other contracts such as sub-charterparties, management contracts and sales contracts, will also be affected.

This chapter analyses the implications of CII and ETS regulation in charterparties for the bill of lading. Subsequently, it reflects on the implications of these regulations for other contracts in the maritime supply chain.[3]

* Professor, Head of Centre for Private Governance (CEPRI), Head of Shipping and Ocean Law Group (SHOC), Faculty of Law, University of Copenhagen.

[1] On this see Girvin (ch 3).

[2] On this see Eftestøl (ch 5) and Baughen(ch 6).

[3] On the related topic of social sustainability in the maritime supply chains, see V Ulfbeck, 'Maritime Value Chains and Liability for Work Injuries' in S Girvin and V Ulfbeck, *Maritime Organisation, Management and Liability. A Legal Analysis of New Challenges in the Maritime Industry* (Oxford, Hart Publishing, 2021).

II. The Bill of Lading and its Interaction with the Charterparty

A bill of lading that is issued or endorsed to a third party (the holder of the bill of lading) governs the relationship between the holder and the carrier.[4] If the vessel for the carriage of the goods under the bill of lading is chartered (tramp trade), there is an interaction between the terms of the bill of lading and the terms of the charterparty.

The bill of lading may be issued either by the shipowner or the charterer. Often, the charterer issues the bill of lading on behalf of the shipowner or 'to be signed' by the shipowner, and typically, the shipowner is the carrier under the bill of lading.[5] Whether it is the shipowner or the charterer who is identified as the carrier and bears liability as carrier under the bill of lading, alignment between the obligations in the bill of lading and the charterparty is important. Thus, distribution of risk and liability in the charterparty may become illusory, if one of the parties ends up incurring a wider liability on the basis of the bill of lading.[6] One way of achieving alignment is by adjusting specific terms and definitions in the bill of lading to fit the charterparty. Another way is to incorporate wholly or partly the terms of the charterparty into the bill of lading. This can be done either by making use of specific or general reference clauses in the bill of lading.[7]

The new carbon clauses for charterparties deal with new types of problems. They concern the carbon footprint of shipping and, thereby, externalities of the commercial activities of the parties. In this sense, they regulate matters that are detached from the (core) subject matter of commercial contracts. Not surprisingly, the clauses also make use of new techniques to regulate the relationship between the charterer and the owner, such as reliance on the concept of 'good faith' and collaborative obligations. The following analysis investigates the ways these characteristics affect the interplay between the charter party and the bill of lading.

III. The CII System and CII Clauses

Since the CII system focuses on the efficient running of the vessel and energy saving, rights to re-route and slow steaming play a central role in the formulated CII standard clauses.

Under a time charterparty, the charterer has commercial control over the ship.[8] This implies that the charterer bears the cost of the fuel.[9] Consequently, slow steaming

[4] The bill of lading may be regulated by the Hague or Hague-Visby Rules, either due to the mandatory nature of this regulatory framework, or because it is incorporated into the bill of lading by reference.

[5] See eg T Falkanger, HJ Bull and I Brautaset, *Scandinavian Maritime Law, The Norwegian Perspective*, 4th edn (Oslo, Universitetsforlaget, 2017) 536. For English law, see eg *Wehner v Dene Steam Shipping Co* [1905] 2 KB 92, 98; *SS Knutsford Ltd v Tillmanns & Co* [1908] AC 406 (HL), 410.

[6] See eg Falkanger et al (n 5) 496.

[7] On the general topic of incorporating charterparty provisions into the bill of lading, see M Özdel, *Bills of Lading Incorporating Charterparties* (London, Bloomsbury Publishing, 2017).

[8] See Girvin (ch 3) section V(B)(iii).

[9] This is often reinforced by express clauses in time charter parties. See eg Girvin (ch 3) section III(B)(iii).

will often be in the interest of the time charterers since slow steaming can save fuel.[10] Accordingly, under BIMCO's Slow Steaming Clause for Time Charter Parties,[11] the charterer has the right to instruct owners to slow steam.

Under the CII system, the situation is more complicated. Here, slow steaming may also be in the interest of the shipowner, but for different reasons. For the shipowner, slow steaming is important because it can reduce emissions. At the same time, as noted above, it is the charterer who has the commercial control over the ship. While slow steaming may also be in the interest of the charterer, the charterer will want to be able to make broader commercial considerations when deciding whether to slow steam or not. The same goes for questions of re-routing. This makes the task of formulating slow steaming rights and re-rerouting rights much more complicated. As described above in chapter three,[12] the BIMCO time charter CII clause contains a detailed system for collaboration in good faith between the parties.[13] In the end, however, provided certain conditions are fulfilled, the clause gives the owners the right to choose to slow steam in order to live up to the CII requirements for the vessel, even if this means disregarding instructions from the charterer.

Under voyage charterparties, the situation is less complicated because the voyage is planned in advance by both parties. Also under voyage charterparties, slow steaming clauses can be inserted, giving the owner the right to slow steam without being in breach of the obligations under the charterparty.[14] As also discussed in chapter three,[15] a CII voyage charter clause has now been developed.[16] To a very large degree, it builds on the general voyage charterparty slow steaming clause, leaving some details for the parties to settle.[17]

IV. Spill-over Effects on the Bill of Lading

A. The Problem

Whether it is the charterer or the owner who has the right to slow steam, and whether the contract is a time charterparty or a voyage charterparty, making use of this technique may cause problems with regard to third party rights under a bill of lading. Thus, a bill of lading will often contain due despatch requirements that could potentially conflict with slow steaming rights.[18] Consequently, slow steaming clauses often contain

[10] See eg Girvin (ch 3) section III(B)(iv).

[11] See www.bimco.org/contracts-and-clauses/bimco-clauses/current/slow_steaming_clause_for_time_charter_2011.

[12] Girvin (ch 3) section V(B).

[13] See www.bimco.org/contracts-and-clauses/bimco-clauses/current/cii-operations-clause-2022.

[14] See www.bimco.org/contracts-and-clauses/bimco-clauses/current/slow_steaming_clause_for_voyage_cp_2012. See also Girvin (ch 3) section VI.

[15] See Girvin (ch 3) section VI.

[16] www.bimco.org/news/priority-news/20231013-new-cii-clause-for-voyage-charter-parties.

[17] In particular, the Explanatory Notes point out that the parties will need to collaborate on the transfer of data and that there may be a need to negotiate demurrage conditions and rates.

[18] See the discussion on due despatch in Girvin (ch 3) section IV(B)(ii).

a requirement that if the charterer issues the bill of lading on behalf of the shipowner or presents the shipowner with a bill of lading to be signed, the charterer must ensure that the bill of lading does not trigger the liability of the owner for slow steaming and deviation. In addition, the charterer is obliged to indemnify the shipowner if such liability should arise.[19]

This model is also followed in both the CII clauses for time chartering and voyage chartering. The provision in both CII clauses reads:

> The Charterers shall ensure that the terms of the bill of lading waybills or of other documents evidencing contracts of carriage issued by or on behalf of the Owners provide that compliance by the Owners with this Clause does not constitute a breach of the contract of carriage. The charterers shall indemnify the Owners against all consequences and liabilities that may arise from the bills of lading, waybills or other documents evidencing contracts of carriage being issued as presented to the extent that the terms of such bills of lading, waybills or other documents evidencing contracts of carriage impose or result in breach of the Owners' obligation to proceed with due despatch or are to be held to be a deviation or the imposition or more onerous liabilities upon the Owners than those assumed by the Owners pursuant to this clause.

In the following, the consequences of this foreseen interplay between the bill of lading and the charterparty in the context of the CII system is analysed in more detail.

B. Consequences of Shipowner's Compliance with the Time Charter CII Clause

i. No Alignment in the Bill of Lading

If nothing has been done in the bill of lading to align with the CII requirements in the charterparty the question is whether complying with the CII clause in the charterparty could conflict with the shipowner's obligations under the bill of lading. A basic question is whether the shipowner's choice to slow steam could trigger liability for delay under the bill of lading. Liability for delay is not explicitly addressed in the Hague Rules or the Hague-Visby Rules. However, it is considered an implied term of a contract of carriage that the carrier must proceed 'with reasonable despatch'.[20] Often, the obligation or a similar one to proceed with 'due' despatch or 'utmost' despatch is also formulated as an express term of the bill of lading.[21] The remedy for breach of the obligation lies in damages.[22] It seems likely that a deliberate choice to slow steam, causing more than a minor delay, would easily conflict with the reasonable

[19] See BIMCO Slow Steaming Clause for Time Charter Parties 2011, cl (f) and the Slow Steaming Clause for Voyage Charter Parties 2012, cl (d). The model is also used more generally in charterparties. In Scandinavia, the shipowner's right to recourse against the charterer is codified in the maritime codes, see eg the Danish Maritime Code (act no. 1013 of 29 June 2023) section 338, subsection 3 (voyage charterparties) and section 383, subsection 2, 2nd sentence (time charterparties). See further on this Falkanger et al (n 5) 496–498.

[20] R Aikens et al, *Bills of Lading*, 3rd edn (London, Informa Law from Routledge, 2021) 453; S Girvin, *Carriage of Goods by Sea*, 3rd edn (Oxford, Oxford University Press, 2022) 545. See Girvin (ch 3) section IV(B)(ii).

[21] Aikens (n 20) 454.

[22] Girvin (n 20) 545.

despatch obligation. Likewise, it must be assumed that the shipowner's choice to re-route in order to live up to its obligations under the CII system could constitute a deviation and thereby a breach of the contract of carriage. Thus, in the absence of an express term, it is normally considered an implied term of the contract that the carrier will proceed without deviation.[23] The same basic principle is expressed in the Hague-Visby Rules Art IV, r 4, which is often incorporated into the bill of lading and which only allows for 'reasonable deviation'. The notions of reasonable despatch and reasonable deviation are closely linked. A deviation may constitute a breach of the reasonable despatch obligation, and a breach of the due despatch obligation may itself be regarded as a deviation.[24] The standard of 'reasonableness' is a flexible one, leaving room for interpretation in the concrete case. A basic test is what the merchant should expect.[25] Both concepts were relevant in *The Santa Isabella*,[26] where it was found that the choice of an alternative route had to be considered a 'reasonable' deviation inter alia because it avoided the fees associated with sailing through the Panama Canal. Although the CII system is not (yet) sanctioned with fines, the case could (perhaps) be used as a touchstone for arguing that re-routing in order to avoid not living up to the CII requirements should be considered a 'reasonable deviation' and not a breach of the obligations under the bill of lading. It could also be argued that following the introduction of the CII system, merchants must in general expect slow steaming and deviations to a much larger extent than was previously the case. At the moment however, if nothing is done in the bill of lading to address the implications of a CII clause in a charterparty, there is a risk that the shipowner's compliance with the CII clause could trigger liability under the bill of lading (and a consequential claim for indemnification towards the charterers).

ii. *Alignment in the Bill of Lading*

In order to avoid liability, the bill of lading should be aligned with the CII clause. There can be different ways of achieving such an alignment.

Inspiration could be found in the Conlinebill 2016, cl 5, designed to be used in liner trades and defining the 'scope' of the transport in the following way:

> The intended carriage shall not be limited to the direct route but shall be deemed to include any proceeding or returning to or slowing down off or at any ports or places for any reasonable purpose connected with the carriage including bunkering, loading, discharging or any cargo operations and maintenance of vessel and crew.

Including such a clause in the bill of lading could solve the problem in the sense that it opens the possibility of slow steaming and re-routing 'for any reasonable purpose' without being in breach of other requirements in the bill of lading.[27] To be on the safe side, it could be added in the clause that slow steaming and re-routing as means to comply with CII requirements should be regarded as a 'reasonable purpose'.

[23] Aikens (n 20), 447.
[24] S Baughen, *Shipping Law*, 7th edn (London, Routledge, 2019) 90; Aikens (n 20) 450.
[25] H Williams, *Chartering Documents*, 3rd edn (London, Lloyd's of London Press Ltd, 1996) 116.
[26] *Alianca Navegacao e Logistica Ltda v Ameropa SA (The Santa Isabella)* [2019] EWHC 3152 (Comm), [2020] 1 Lloyd's Rep 603.
[27] See Explanatory Notes to the BIMCO Slow Steaming Clause for Time Charter Parties (2011).

However, in the absence of such a specific clause, the question arises whether a general incorporation clause in the bill of lading would achieve the same result. Thus, in bulk trades, it is common that the bill of lading contains a reference clause which, according to its wording, incorporates the terms of the charterparty into the bill of lading (tramp bill of lading).[28] General reference clauses may be formulated in different ways.[29] One of the most far-reaching formulations incorporates 'All terms [whatsoever], conditions, clauses and exemptions' into the bill of lading.[30] Despite the broad wording of such clauses, it is the general rule that 'only those clauses of the charterparty which are 'applicable' to the contract contained in the bill of lading …' are incorporated.[31] In *Gullischen v Stewart*,[32] Bowen LJ explained: 'The bill of lading is a document regulating the rights and liabilities of the consignees; only those clauses of the charterparty, which are consistent with its character as a bill of lading are incorporated in it'.[33]

As an example, arbitration clauses in charterparties are *not* incorporated into bills of lading under general reference clauses.[34] This was the result in *The Portsmouth*, where Lord Atkinson observed that the arbitration clause was not 'germane' to the 'receipt, carriage and delivery of the cargo or the payment of freight – the proper subject-matters with which the bill of lading is conversant …'.[35] The term 'germane' has been used in subsequent authorities[36] to express the principle that a broad reference clause only incorporates terms of the charterparty which relate to the proper subject matter of a bill of lading and are necessary and relevant with regard to the issues of receipt, carriage, delivery and payment of freight. Exclusive jurisdiction clauses and choice of law clauses are also considered ancillary and not germane to the bill of lading.[37] In contrast, clauses concerning demurrage, war risks and general average are considered incorporated as germane clauses under a wide reference clause.[38]

The question is whether a CII clause in a charterparty would be considered 'germane' to a bill of lading. As a starting point, this might not be the case since a CII clause, whichever way it is formulated, basically concerns the obligations of the parties to the charterparty to bring down carbon emissions. On the face of it, this has nothing to do with the subject matter of the bill of lading concerning the receipt, carriage, and delivery of goods and the payment of freight. However, if it is assumed that a CII clause typically will involve the right of the shipowner to slow steam and re-route and thereby delay the shipment in order to comply with CII requirements, it would be possible to argue that the clause, in reality, concerns (timely) 'delivery'

[28] Girvin (n 20) 263; Falkanger et al (n 5) 495.

[29] On developments in practice, see P Todd, *Principles of the Carriage of Goods by Sea* (London, Routledge, 2016) 256–257.

[30] Girvin (n 20) 268, for other examples.

[31] *Gardner & Sons v Trechmann* (1884) 15 QBD 154 (CA), 157.

[32] *Gullischen v Stewart* (1884) 13 QBD 317.

[33] ibid 320.

[34] Girvin (n 20) 268, Aikens (n 20) 225.

[35] *TW Thomas & Co Ltd v Portsea Steamship Co Ltd (The Portsmouth)* [1912] AC 1 (HL), at 6. For arbitration clauses in Scandinavian law, see Falkanger et al (n5) 495.

[36] Aikens (n 20) 218 with references in fn 223.

[37] Girvin (n 20) 270–273. Özdel (n 7) 99.

[38] Girvin (n 20) 268.

and that it – or parts of it – are therefore 'germane' to the bill of lading and should be considered incorporated into it.[39]

However, even if a CII clause or parts of it are considered incorporated into the bill of lading by a general reference clause, the next question is how it should be understood in the context of the bill of lading. It is generally accepted that some amount of 'verbal manipulation' may be necessary in order to make sense of the terms of charterparty in the context of a bill of lading.[40] For instance, whereas the charterparty speaks about the obligations of the owner and the charterer, the bill of lading speaks about the obligations of the carrier and holder/consignee. If the terms of the charterparty are – to some extent – to be applicable in the context of the bill of lading it may be necessary to equate 'charterer' with 'holder'.[41] Returning to the BIMCO CII clause, it might be possible to argue that the right of the shipowner vis-à-vis the charterer to choose to slow steam should be construed to mean that this right of the shipowner (carrier) would also relieve it of liability vis-à-vis the holder of a bill of lading.

However, such an equation of 'charterer' with 'holder' is not always the right solution. For example, proper construction of the bill of lading, including the incorporated charterparty terms, may lead to the conclusion that when an obligation according to its wording is imposed on 'the charterer' it would be contrary to the intentions of the parties or make no sense to substitute this term with 'holder'. Returning to the BIMCO CII clause, it would clearly make no sense to impose the obligations of the charterer to collaborate and suggest a revised plan for the voyage in order to bring down CO_2 emissions on the holder of a bill of lading under the charterparty.[42] Re-routing is not within the role – or competence – of the holder and imposing such obligations on the holder would also be practically impossible since there will often be multiple holders in a particular shipment.

Likewise, it may be considered whether subclause (j) of the CII clause imposing liability on the charterer for 'any losses, damages, liabilities, claims, fines, costs, expenses, actions, proceedings, suits or demand suffered by the Vessel and/or the Owners which have been caused by any breach by Charterers or their obligations under this Clause' should be construed to mean that the holder of a bill of lading must bear any loss arising from such breach. Such losses could potentially be very burdensome. For example, a poor CII rating may affect the lending willingness of banks with regard to the vessel and increase interest rates. It could also lead to lower freight rates when operating the vessel under subsequent voyages. It seems highly doubtful whether such losses could be transferred to the holder of the bill of lading on the basis of a general incorporation clause.[43]

[39] Under the same line of reasoning, slow steaming clauses should in general be considered germane to the bill of lading under general reference clauses. There is no case law addressing this. According to Girvin (n 20) 274 wide reference clauses bring into the bill of lading 'most charter party clauses unless these are considered ancillary to the shipment, carriage or delivery of cargo'.

[40] On 'verbal manipulation' see Aikens (n 20) 220; Özdel (n 7) 121.

[41] See for instance *Adamastos Shipping Co Ltd v Anglo-Saxon Petroleum Co Ltd (The Saxon Star)* [1959] AC 133 (HL), where the expression 'this bill of lading' was equated with 'this charterparty'.

[42] It may be considered whether these terms – although they are closely linked to the right of the shipowner to slow steam – should even be regarded as 'germane' to the contract.

[43] See also further below section (V(B)(ii) on *The Miramar* (*Miramar Maritime Corp v Holborn Oil Trading Ltd (The Miramar)* [1984] 1 AC 676 (HL)), concerning the problem of allocating a big loss (demurrage) to one holder of a bill of lading rather than to all holders.

The incorporated terms must also be read in the context of the rest of the bill of lading. In general, terms incorporated by general reference clauses are considered ineffective if they are contrary to or inconsistent with an express term in a bill of lading.[44] Consequently, if a bill of lading contains an express 'due despatch' term, which as explained is often the case, it must be presumed that this term will take precedence over the CII terms in the charterparty that allow for slow steaming. In this case, the carrier (shipowner or charterer) could be met with a claim for damages from the holder of the bill of lading if the slow steaming causes delay according to the terms of the bill of lading. Presumably, the result is the same even if the charterparty clause – such as the BIMCO CII clause – specifies that slow steaming can be done without the shipowner being in breach of any other obligations in the charterparty,[45] including obligations to proceed with due dispatch.[46] Thus, the express term of the bill of lading must take precedence over the formulation of the term in the charterparty.[47]

C. Consequences of the Shipowner's Breach of the Time Charter CII Clause

If the CII clause is incorporated into the bill of lading by reference, the shipowner is relieved of liability under the bill of lading if it is in compliance with the CII clause. This means that if a holder of a bill of lading wants to pursue a claim against the shipowner arising out of slow steaming undertaken by the shipowner it must show that the slow steaming undertaken by the shipowner was *not* in compliance with the CII clause. Hereby, any possible uncertainties with regard to the rights and duties between the shipowner and the charterer under the CII clause will be 'imported' into the relationship between the holder of the bill of lading and the shipowner. In this respect, the CII clause operates a rather complicated system which only under certain circumstances, spelt out in the clause, gives the shipowner the right to slow steam. The intention is to also safeguard the interests of the charterer.[48]

According to the clause, the shipowner has the right to slow steam if, first, based on certain data, there is a 'reasonable likelihood' that the charterers may fail to meet their obligations (of meeting the CII goal at the end of the year). Second, if the charterer presents a new plan, the shipowner must 'reasonably show' that the written plan will result in the charterer not meeting its obligations and only if the parties do not succeed in creating a new plan together, collaborating in good faith, will the shipowner have the right to take the decision to slow steam. It is not specified who is to determine whether these conditions are fulfilled. It is not explicitly stated that the shipowner has

[44] *Gardner* (n 31).

[45] See BIMCO's CII cl (g)(iii)(1) specifying this.

[46] See BIMCO's Slow Steaming Clause for Time Charterparties 2011, subcl (e) and BIMCO's Slowsteaming Clause for Voyage Charterparties 2012, subcl (b).

[47] Aikens (n 20) 219.

[48] The ordinary slow steaming clause for time charter parties also tried to balance the interests of the charterer and the shipowner. However, it is much simpler as the objective is to allow the charterer to save fuel and money which is most often not contrary to the interests of the shipowner. Under the Time Charter Slow Steaming Clause (2011) it is stated that 'the charterers may at their discretion provide, in writing to the Masters, instructions to reduce speed … to meet a specified time of arrival at a particular port'.

the right to make this assessment. Consequently, it must be presumed that, in the end, it will be for the courts to decide whether the conditions were fulfilled when the shipowner took the decision to slow steam. Consequently, the charterer will also be able to challenge such decisions taken by the shipowner, arguing that the conditions were not fulfilled.[49]

However, if the charterer does not protest against the decision, the question is whether the holder of a bill of lading could challenge it in a claim for damages for delay against the owner. Likewise, one could ask whether the holder could argue that a new plan allowing for deviations and, thereby, delay has not been negotiated in good faith by the shipowner, even if the charterer has not raised this issue itself.

In other words, all of the uncertainties in the clause with regard to the international relationship between the shipowner and the charterer are 'imported' into the relationship between the holder and the shipowner. In addition, the question arises whether the holder will have to accept decisions taken by the charterer vis-à-vis the shipowner.

D. CII under Voyage Charter Parties

Challenges in living up to CII requirements may also arise under voyage charterparties. However, here the situation is different. Under voyage charterparties, the voyage is described in the charterparty from the outset, and energy efficiency aspects can be taken into account when the contract is negotiated, and the freight rate is fixed. However, also under a voyage charterparty, the owner may want to choose to slow steam or re-route to keep down emissions. As mentioned, a CII voyage charterparty clause has been developed by BIMCO to regulate the situation. Under this clause, the owner has the right to 'adjust course and/or to reduce speed or RPM' down to a certain minimum standard, 'with a view to reducing the carbon intensity of the Vessel'.

The exercise of these rights may contrast with the interests of the charterer. For example, the voyage charterer may want to give revised voyage orders that do not conform with slow steaming or re-routing (for example 'stop and wait' at interim ports, if the parties have agreed a range of ports in the charterparty). Slow steaming may also be contrary to the interests of the cargo owner, for example if the cargo consists in perishable goods sensitive to delays. In contrast to the CII clause for time charterparties, which spells out the conditions for slow steaming, the CII voyage charter clause (as slow steaming clauses in general) does not list conditions. The question is whether the right could be characterised as giving 'contractual discretion' to the shipowner as this concept has been defined in the case law. Whereas the precise definition of the concept has been discussed,[50] case law has categorised clauses which grant the right

[49] Since the clause does not give the owners an explicit 'determination discretion' to decide when the conditions are fulfilled and since the clause contains detailed 'procedural' requirements which take into account the interest of the charterer and only allows for slow steaming if the charterer is in breach of its obligations, the clause cannot be regarded as giving the owner 'contractual discretion': see eg D Foxton QC, *Controlling contractual discretions*, essexcourt.com/wp-content/uploads/2018/01/Controlling-contractual-discretions.pdf. See also further below, contrasting the voyage CII clause.

[50] Foxton (n 49). See also D Foxton 'A good faith goodbye? Good faith obligations and terminations rights' (2017) *LMCLQ* 339–456. For a recent discussion of the topic, see JNE Varuhas, 'Three Issues in the Law of

to vary a party's own performance as being clauses of contractual discretion.[51] The CII voyage charter clause gives the shipowner the right to vary its performance during the course of the contract even if this is contrary to the interests of the contractual partner and, consequently, it could be regarded as a contractual discretion clause. Interestingly, case law suggests that there may be limits to the right to exercise such contractual discretion. *The Product Star*,[52] which concerned the shipowner's right to choose a 'safe port', established that it is an implied term that 'a contractual discretion must be exercised in good faith and not arbitrarily or capriciously'. This will normally mean that it must be exercised 'consistently with its contractual purpose'.[53] Arguably, this could limit the right of the shipowner to choose to slow steam and reroute.[54] For example, since the 'contractual purpose' of the voyage CII clause is to enable the shipowner to comply with the CII system, the charterer might be able to argue that in the concrete situation, slow steaming was not necessary in order to comply with the CII system. Similarly, the charterer might be able to argue that slow steaming on a particular voyage was 'arbitrary' if it might as well have been done on a different voyage (with a different charterer) in the same year to achieve the desired CII result.

If the charterer does not object to a slow steaming decision taken by the shipowner, the question is whether the holder of the bill of lading could do so. Arguably, the holder would have this right if for instance a general reference clause in the bill of lading, incorporates the terms of the charter party into the bill of lading.[55] In liner trade, where there are typically multiple holders, each holders right will depend on the terms of the particular bill of lading.

V. The ETS System and the ETS Clause in Charterparties

In 2023, a revised version of the EU ETS directive was agreed (the revised ETS directive)[56] and the shipping industry included in the EU Emission Trading System

Contractual Discretion' (2022) 42 *OJLS* 787, 811, arguing that the distinction between 'discretionary rights' and 'absolute rights' seems to have been done away with in *Property Alliance Group Ltd v The Royal Bank of Scotland Plc* [2018] EWCA Civ 335, [2018] 1 WLR 3529.

[51] Foxton (n 49) 4 with reference to *JML Direct Ltd v Freesat UK Ltd* [2010] EWCA Civ 34, [14]; *McKay v Centurion Credit Resources* LLC [2012] EWCA Civ 1941, para 21. Foxton identifies four categories of contractual discretion: (1) rights to vary the other party's performance, (2) rights to vary own performance, (3) discretion conditional benefits, (4) determination discretion (where a party has the right to determine whether specific factual circumstances are present).

[52] *Abu Dhabi National Tanker Co v Product Star Shipping Ltd (The Product Star) (No 2)* [1993] 1 Lloyd's Rep 397 (CA).

[53] ibid 404.

[54] Moreover, in *Braganza*, Lady Hale held that 'The *contractual implied term* is drawing closer and closer to the principles applicable in judicial review': see *Braganza v BP Shipping Ltd* [2015] UKSC 17, [2015] 1 WLR 1661, paras 17–32. Subsequently, this view seems to have been followed in other cases applying the administrative law principles established in *Wednesbury* (*Associated Provincial Picture Houses Ltd v Wednesbury Corp* [1948] 1 KB 223 (CA)) to contractual discretion.

[55] It could also be considered whether the doctrine of discretion, which to some degree imports 'administrative law' principles into contract law, might also imply a duty for the shipowner to take into consideration third party interests, such as the interests on the holder of the bill of lading.

[56] Directive (EU) 2023/959 of the European Parliament and of the Council of 10 May 2023 amending Directive 2003/87/EC establishing a system for greenhouse gas emission allowance trading within the Union

(the ETS).[57] Under this system, the 'shipping company' is responsible for surrendering the required amount of greenhouse emission allowances on a regular basis. The shipping company can be fined if it does not live up to these requirements. In addition, according to the revised ETS directive, EU port states are obliged to reject or detain a ship if for two consecutive reporting periods, the necessary ETS allowances have not been surrendered.[58]

The problem with the system is that it imposes the obligation to surrender allowances on the 'shipping company', which according to the directive can be either the shipowner or the ISM responsible entity (the doc holder). At the same time, under a time charterparty it is the charterer which has the commercial control over the ship and can control the amount of emissions that a ship produces.

The BIMCO ETS clause for time charterparties attempts to solve this problem.[59] Thus, it imposes on both the shipowner and the charterer a duty to collaborate with regard to the transfer of the necessary data to estimate the needed allowances. In addition to this, it obliges the charterer to surrender the necessary amount of allowances to the shipowner's account on a monthly basis. Finally, it gives the shipowner the right to suspend the performance of its obligations under the charterparty, should the charterer not live up to its obligations. It is spelt out that 'the Owners shall have no responsibility whatsoever for any consequences arising out of the valid exercise of this right' and that 'The Owners' right to suspend performance under this Clause shall be without prejudice to any other rights or claims they may have against the Charterers under this Charter Party' (d).

Thus, the ETS clause for time charterparties basically transfers responsibility connected to the surrendering of the allowances to the time charterer. Since it is the obligation of the charterer to transfer the needed allowances to the shipowner, it must be assumed that the shipowner would be entitled to claim reimbursement of the costs of the allowances if the charterer does not live up to this obligation and the shipowner is forced to acquire the allowances itself. In contrast, the clause does not specify what happens if the shipowner does not do this and is fined for not having surrendered the required amount of allowances that should have been acquired by the charterers. The question is whether, in this situation, the shipowner would be entitled to claim reimbursement for the fine from the charterer. The clause only states that 'the Owners shall have no responsibility whatsoever for any consequences arising out of the valid exercise of this right'. The 'right' mentioned is the right to suspend performance under the charterparty, not a right not refrain from acquiring the necessary allowances. The shipowner will also be under a duty to mitigate the loss, which could involve paying and surrendering allowances in due time to avoid being fined. Consequently, it must be assumed that normally, a fine cannot be transferred to the charterer under the damages provision in the ETS clause for time charterparties. However, if the charterer does not fulfil its obligation to collaborate by transferring data and information on the planned commercial use of the vessel, it can be difficult for the shipowner to estimate the

and Decision (EU) 2015/1814 concerning the establishment and operation of a market stability reserve for the Union greenhouse gas emission trading system (Revised ETS directive).

[57] On this, see Eftestøl (ch 5), Baughen (ch 6).

[58] Article 11a in the Revised ETS directive.

[59] The ETS clause for time charter parties can be found here: www.bimco.org/contracts-and-clauses/bimco-clauses/current/etsa_clause.

needed amount of allowances. In this situation, the extent to which a fine can be passed on to the charterer will likely depend on the formulation of the damage clause or other clauses in the charterparty.[60]

BIMCO has also developed ETS clauses for voyage charterparties. Here, it is easier to estimate the amount of needed allowances in advance since the voyage(s) are fixed in the charterparty at the outset. BIMCO has developed three different clauses for voyage charter parties, building on three different models.[61] One is a 'freight clause' under which the costs of the needed allowances are included in the freight under the commercial agreement between the parties. The other is a surcharge clause in which the charterer is obliged to pay a sum (surcharge) equivalating the value of the estimated needed allowances in addition to the freight. Under both models, the charterer is released from responsibility, once payments have been made, save for breach of contract situations. The third model is more similar to the ETS clause for charterparties in that it obliges the charterer to transfer the necessary allowances into the shipowners nominated Emission Schemes account. However, here it is made clear that, save for cases of breach of contract, the shipowner has no recourse action against the charterer once the transfer has been made. As with the ETS clause for time charterparties, it must be assumed that the shipowner's duty to mitigate will normally prevent it from passing on a fine to the charterer, even if the charterer has breached its obligation of timely transfer of allowances.

VI. Spillover Effects on the Bill of Lading?

A. The Problem

The question is what spill-over effects this system will have on the bill of lading.

One basic problem is that the ETS may cause delays. For example, the vessel may be delayed either because the shipowner under a time charterparty suspends performance to force the charterer to surrender the necessary allowances or because a port state detains it due to non-compliance with the ETS. In either case, the holder of the bill of lading may want to claim damages for delay. Another problem is that not living up to the requirements under the ETS may trigger fines that the owner may want to pass on to the holder of the bill of lading. In the following, the main focus is on spill over effects from the ETS clause for time charterparties as an example.

B. Consequences

i. No Alignment in the Bill of Lading

Unlike the CII clause, the ETS clause for time charterparties does not contain an obligation for the charterer to ensure that the shipowner does not incur liability towards

[60] Sometimes fines are dealt with specifically in charterparties, for example in NYPE 93, cl 42, concerning fines for smuggling.

[61] The clauses can be found here: www.bimco.org/insights-and-information/contracts/20231208-ets-clauses.

the holder of the bill of lading when exercising its rights under the ETS clause. If there is no provision in the bill of lading addressing the issue, the ETS system may expose the shipowner to liability from the holder of the bill of lading in different ways. First, if the shipowner decides to suspend performance of the time charterparty because the charterer is not acquiring the needed allowances, the shipowner may be liable for delay on the basis of due despatch requirements (as described above). If the delay is due to port state detention of the vessel because the required allowances have not been surrendered for two consecutive years, it might be considered whether the shipowner could escape liability on the basis of the 'restraint of princes' exception which will normally be included in the bill of lading by incorporation or mandatory application of the Hague or Hague-Visby Rules.[62] This exempts the carrier from liability for breach of contract if the breach is due to acts of the 'prince', ie governmental interference, such as for example detention due to lack of payment of export duties in certain situations.[63] However, the exemption will probably not apply if the ship is detained due to lack of surrender of allowances for a longer period of time, since the shipowner will have been aware of this problem when embarking on the voyage.[64]

In addition, it is also possible that the mere fact that the vessel lacks documentation for having acquired the necessary allowances[65] and/or is at risk of detention due to lack of allowances would render the vessel unseaworthy under the bill of lading. In this case, the shipowner would not be protected by a restraint of the princes provision because the seaworthiness obligation is considered overriding under the Hague and Hague-Visby Rules, at least in common law countries.[66]

Consequently, if the ETS system is not reflected in the bill of lading, the shipowner may well face liability towards the holder of the bill of lading in a number of situations.

ii. Alignment in the Bill of Lading

As explained above, a general reference clause is often found in the bill of lading for the purpose of wholly or partly incorporating the terms of the charterparty into the bill of lading. However, as with the CII clause, it is necessary to consider whether the ETS clause could be considered 'germane' to the bill of lading in order for it to have implications in the relationship between the shipowner and the holder of the bill of lading. On the face of it, the clause does not concern any of the core elements of a bill of lading, such as delivery, carriage, freight and payment. However, as is the case with the CII clause, the ETS clause may also give rise to delays and thereby be related to (core) requirements on delivery. Furthermore, it is likely that the ETS system will have a direct impact on freight rates, in the sense that, in the end, the costs of the system will

[62] On the 'restraint of princes' exception, see inter alia, JF Wilson, *Carriage of Goods by Sea*, 7th edn (London, Pearson Education Ltd, 2010) 268. The rules are embedded in the Hague and Hague-Visby Rules, Art IV, r 2(g).

[63] Girvin (n 20) 611.

[64] Girvin (n 20) 611.

[65] On documentary unseaworthiness, see Girvin (n 20) 508 and on MARPOL requirements specifically, 511–512.

[66] In English law, see eg *Maxine Footwear Co Ltd v Canadian Government Merchant Marine Ltd* [1959] AC 589 (PC), 602–603. See the discussion in F Berlingieri, *Int'l Maritime Conventions* vol 1 (London, Informa, 2014) para 4.1.1.

be passed on to the cargo owners. On this basis, it must be assumed that an ETS clause incorporated by a general reference clause, could be regarded as germane to the bill of lading. However, this also gives rise to two questions.

First, if the charterer does not surrender the required allowances, does the clause then imply that the shipowner can pass on the costs to the holder of the bill of lading instead? Here, the clause must be read in the context of the rest of the obligations under the bill of lading. One such obligation is the obligation of the holder to pay the freight. It is likely that the holder has already wholly or partly paid for the costs of the ETS through an increased freight rate. This speaks against allowing the ETS allowance bill to be passed on to the holder of the bill of lading.[67]

Second, if a fine imposed on the shipowner for not surrendering the required allowances can be wholly or partly passed on to the charterer (see above), does incorporation of the ETS clause into the bill of lading then mean that the holder can be held liable for this cost? A (perhaps) comparable situation was presented in *The Miramar*.[68] Here, the terms of a voyage charterparty were considered incorporated into the bill of lading under a general reference clause in the bill of lading.[69] The question was whether an obligation imposed on the 'charterer' to pay demurrage should be construed to mean that this obligation fell on the holder of the bill of lading under the voyage charterparty following the insolvency of the charterer. The House of Lords found that on a proper construction of the contract, only the charterer was intended to be liable. One of the reasons for this was that equating 'charterer' with 'consignee' in this situation would mean imposing liability on the consignee of only one part of the cargo for the total demurrage claim. In the words of Lord Diplock: 'No business man who had not taken leave of is senses would intentionally enter into a contract which exposed him to a potential liability of this kind'.[70] Likewise, it may be argued that imposing liability for a fine under the ETS system on the holder of a bill of lading for only part of the cargo would imply holding this particular consignee liable for a loss that in reality relates to the general operation of the vessel and the carriage of multiple consignments over a longer period of time.

[67] If the holder of the bill of lading is only the consignee for part of the cargo that has been shipped, also this may speak against passing on the cost of acquiring the ETS allowances to the holder, see further below.

[68] Above (n 43).

[69] The clause in the bill of lading read: 'This shipment is carried under and pursuant to the terms of the charter dated … and all the terms whatsoever of the said charter except the rate and payment of freight specified therein apply to and govern the rights of the parties concerned in this shipment.'

[70] ibid 684–685. The problem has been addressed in the Conlinebill (1978), additional clause A, which reads: 'The Carrier shall be paid demurrage at the daily rate per ton of the vessel's gross register tonnage as indicated on Page 2 if the vessel is not loaded or discharged with the dispatch set out in clause 8, any delay in waiting for berth at or off port to count. Provided that if the delay is due to causes beyond the control of the Merchant, 24 hours shall be deducted from the time of demurrage. Each Merchant shall be liable towards the Carrier for a proportionate part of the total demurrage due, based upon the total freight on the goods to be loaded or discharged at the port in question. No Merchant shall be liable in demurrage for any delay arisen only in connection with goods belonging to other Merchants. The demurrage in respect of each parcel shall not exceed its freight …'. There is no equivalent of this clause in the Conlinebill (2000/2016).

VII. Other Contracts and Spillover Effects in the Supply Chain

A. Management Contracts

The carbon clauses will also affect other contracts in the maritime supply chain. For example, management companies will be directly affected by the ETS. Thus, according to the revised ETS directive, the obligation to acquire the necessary amount of allowances rests on the 'shipping company'. According to Article 3(w) in the revised ETS directive, not only the shipowner but also management companies fall within this definition. According to the wording, both the shipowner and the management company are responsible to the authorities. This is a complicated solution. However, clarification has been provided in a an Implementing Regulation,[71] according to which it is the shipowner which is responsible but responsibility can be delegated to the management company. Such delegation must be approved of by the relevant authority. A contractual delegation is not in itself sufficient.[72] The system leaves three options: (1) The shipowner retains responsibility for surrendering the allowances while delegating other tasks to the ship management company; (2) the administrative task of surrendering the allowances is delegated to the ship management company, but the shipowner remains responsible towards the public authority, and (3) the task of surrendering the allowances is entirely left to the ship management company with the shipowner being 'off the hook' vis-à-vis the authorities. The BIMCO ETS-Shipman Emission Trading Scheme Allowances Clause reflects these options.[73]

Already under existing ship management contracts, the ship manager will be dragged into handling the new carbon emission regulatory framework for the shipping industry, ie both the CII system and the ETS. Thus, under the Shipman contract (2009), a ship manager who is responsible for commercially managing the ship will need to take into consideration these new regimes when concluding new charter parties. Clause 20 of Shipman (2009) obliges both parties not to do anything or allow anything that would be a breach or infringement of the laws or regulations of the flag state or where the vessel trades. Presumably, this must mean that a ship manager who is in charge of the commercial management of the ship must ensure that new and possibly also existing charterparties comply with the carbon emission frameworks.

B. Other Contracts

Other contracts will also be affected. For example, if slow steaming and deviation rights of the shipowner are found under the head charterparty, these rights should also be in any sub-charterparties, whether on a time or voyage basis.

[71] Commission Implementing Regulation (EU) 2023/2599 of 22 November 2023 laying down rules for the application of Directive 2003/87/EC of the European Parliament and of the Council as regards the administration of shipping companies by administering authorities in respect of a shipping company (Implementing Regulation).

[72] Implementing Regulation Art 1(2).

[73] The clause can be found here: www.bimco.org/contracts-and-clauses/bimco-clauses/current/ets-shipman-allowances-clause.

Eventually, slow steaming and deviation rights could also raise liability issues in sales contracts further down the contractual chain. Thus, if the cargo is delayed due to the exercise of these rights by the shipowner, a seller may incur liability under its sales contract with a buyer. A shipowner's choice to slow steam will probably not normally qualify as a 'force majeure' event under a sales contract, relieving the seller of liability. If delays in the supply chain become more widespread due to the new carbon regulation, risks and liabilities for this will need to be allocated in the sales contracts in the supply chain. At the same time, the new carbon regime must be expected to generate higher freight rates, and the extra expenses will, in the end, be passed on to the buyers of the commodities being shipped via the sales contracts.

Some buyers may, for idealistic or commercial reasons (or both), want to have guarantees that the goods they are buying have been shipped with zero or low carbon emissions, and sellers can have a commercial interest in marketing their business as a 'low carbon business'. To accelerate this process, initiatives have been taken to develop 'book and claim' systems for the shipping sector.[74] Thus, in the future, the way a product has been shipped may become an important part of the description of the product itself, calling for new types of conformity provisions in sales contracts.

VIII. Conclusion

The new carbon emission regulatory framework will directly affect the contractual relationship between shipowner and charterer, but quite clearly, it will also have implications for the bill of lading and indirectly for the entire maritime supply chain. Basically, all the contracts in the maritime supply chain will need to be aligned with the new requirements.

The new charterparty carbon clauses have been developed to deal with matters that are not typical, commercial matters. Rather, the matters are 'external' to the party interests in the sense that they are concerned with the societal goal of bringing down carbon emissions. On this basis, one might think that the carbon clauses can only be considered 'accessory' and not 'germane' to the bill of lading when incorporated by use of a general reference clause. However, on a closer look, it is quite clear that addressing the issue of carbon emissions involves and affects the core commercial obligations of the contracting parties. Regulatory compliance with the CII system requires new slow steaming and de-routing rights and the ETS directly imposes costs on shipments which need to be allocated between the parties. Basically, the new regulatory regimes will demand contractual adaptations that go to the heart of commercial operations. Consequently, a general reference clause must normally be considered sufficient to incorporate the charterparty carbon clauses into the bill of lading and future cases may concern the question of how to understand the carbon clauses in the context of the bill of lading.

[74] See www.zerocarbonshipping.com/news/new-maritime-book-claim-system-strengthens-business-case-for-green-shipping/; www.globalmaritimeforum.org/press/major-maritime-companies-agree-to-develop-book-and-claim-approaches-in-order-to-accelerate-shippings-decarbonisation-transition.

Furthermore, dealing with these new matters on the contractual level requires close collaboration between the parties. For this reason, the clauses also bring in regulatory techniques that are new to charterparties, such as references to collaborative obligations and good faith duties. This type of obligation introduces some amount of uncertainty with regard to the exact obligations of the parties. A reference clause, to some extent, 'imports' these uncertainties into the bill of lading.

Not only the bill of lading but also all other contracts in the maritime supply chain will be affected by the demands to curb emissions. The management companies will be directly affected by the regulatory regime, but also contracting parties that are not directly included in the scope of the new regulatory frameworks will experience trickle-down effects of the rules through the chain of contracts.

The effect could be a general change of expectations in the market as to how shipments can and should be carried out. This, in turn, may affect the understanding of concepts such as 'reasonable despatch' and 'reasonable deviation'. Also, other general and open legal standards may be used to channel the new regulatory framework in the contracts and pave the way for new understandings of commercial obligations in a new reality.

PART III

Enforcement Issues

9

Port State Control as a Mechanism to Ensure Compliance with Carbon Intensity Regulations

VINCENZO BATTISTELLA MARINUCCI*

I. Introduction

The chapter is concerned with Port State Control (PSC),[1] which enables the competent authorities in port States to ensure compliance[2] with the International Maritime Organisation (IMO) carbon intensity regulations for the protection of the marine environment.[3]

* PhD Fellow, Centre for Private Governance (CEPRI) and Shipping and Ocean Law Group (SHOC), Faculty of Law, University of Copenhagen.

[1] On port State control, R Derrig, 'Inspecting Ships Autonomously under Port State Jurisdiction: Towards Sustainability and Biodiversity in the EU' (2022) 37 *Int'l J of Marine & Coastal Law* 529; A Graziano, MQ Mejia Jr and J Schröeder-Hinrichs, 'Achievements and Challenges on the Implementation of the European Directive on Port State Control' (2018) 72 Transport Policy 97; ET Bulgherini, 'Port State Control' in A del Vecchio (ed), *International Law of the Sea: Current Trends and Controversial Issues* (The Hague, Eleven International Publishing, 2014) 205; ZO Özçayır, 'Impact of Port State Control on Pollution at Sea?' in B Soyer and A Tettenborn (eds), *Pollution at Sea: Law and Liability* (London, Informa Law from Routledge, 2012) 271; ZO Özçayır, 'The Use of Port State Control in Maritime Industry and Application of the Paris MOU' (2008) 14 *Ocean & Coastal LJ* 201; Z Oya Özçayir, *Port State Control*, 2nd edn (London, Informa Professional, 2004); L Schiano di Pepe, 'Port State Control as an Instrument to Ensure Compliance with International Marine Environmental Obligations' in A Kirchner (ed), *International Marine Environmental Law* (The Hague, Kluwer Law International, 2003) 137; GC Kasoulides, *Port State Control and jurisdiction. Evolution of the Port State Regime* (Dordrecht, Martinus Nijhoff, 1993) 2.

[2] Compliance may be distinguished from implementation (which relates to the adoption by States of domestic laws and regulations pursuant to relevant international obligations), effectiveness (which indicates whether or not the final aim of a given international regulation has actually been achieved, either partially or in its entirety), and enforcement (which refers to the actual application of a given set of laws of regulations to a particular case), see Pepe (n 1) 146.

[3] On the role of port States with particular regard to the powers and duties ascribed to port State in order to ensure compliance with Annex VI of MARPOL 1973/78 see eg Y Tanaka, *The International Law of the Sea*, 4th edn (Cambridge, Cambridge University Press, 2023) 348; D Mantoju, 'Analysis of MARPOL Implementation Based on Port State Control Statistics' (2021) 5 *J of Int'l Maritime Safety, Environmental Affairs, and Shipping* 132; MQ Mejia Jr, 'Air Pollution, Climate Change, and Port State Control' in PK Mukherjee, MQ Mejia Jr and J Xu (eds), *Maritime Law in Motion* (Cham, Springer Law International, 2020) 525; A Fakhry and B Bulut, 'MARPOL Energy Efficiency: Verging on Legal Efficiency?' in AI Olcer et al (eds), *Trends and Challenges in Maritime Energy Management* (Cham, Springer Law International, 2018) 15; Y Tanaka, 'Regulation of Greenhouse Gas Emissions from International Shipping and Jurisdiction of States' (2016) 25 RECIEL 333, 341;

As part of their sovereignty, PSC entitles port States to inspect[4] foreign ships that enter national ports.

This chapter determines the conditions whereby a port State may enforce cooperation by shipowners through PSC. In particular, enforcement refers to the entitlement to detain and ban a foreign-flagged ship from entering a national port.[5] These enforcement measures enable port States, under specific conditions, to detain or to ban a foreign ship which does not comply with the new international carbon regulations such as the Energy Efficiency Existing Ship Index (EEXI), the Carbon Intensity Indicator (CII), and the EU Emissions Trading System (ETS).

Port States protect a community interest regarding the prevention of marine pollution and may play a vital role in creating a legal framework to regulate the carbon emissions from ships by adopting a collaborative PSC mechanism on a regional basis.

II. The Legal Framework of Port State Control

The international legal framework governing PSC is determined by the 1982 United Nations Convention on the Law of the Sea (UNCLOS), and the most critical IMO conventions on protecting the marine environment,[6] SOLAS 1974 as amended and MARPOL 1973/78. The European legislator regulated the PSC regime by introducing Directive 2009/16 EC of the European Parliament and of the Council of 23 April 2009 on PSC. Furthermore, the legal framework is subject to continuous updates due to IMO resolutions[7] in the context of PSC and to multiple agreements on the procedures of PSC signed by States at a regional level, such as PSC Memoranda of Understanding (MoUs).

H-S Bang, 'Recommendation for Policies on Port State Control and Port State Jurisdiction' (2013) 44 JMLC 115; H-S Bang, 'Is Port State Control an Effective Means to Combat Vessel-source Pollution? An Empirical Survey of the Practical Exercise by Port States of their Powers of Control' (2008) 23 *Int'l J of Marine and Coastal Law* 715.

[4] D Anderson, 'Port State and Environmental Protection' in A Boyle and D Freestone (eds), *International Law and Sustainable Development. Past Achievement and Future Challenges* (Oxford, Oxford University Press, 1999) 342.

[5] See *Military and Paramilitary Activities in and against Nicaragua (Nicaragua v United States of America* [1986] ICJ Rep 14. For a detailed analysis of access to ports and the right of innocent passage in the territorial sea, see Tanaka (n 3) 103; 111. On the role of PSC and access to ports, see G Brugmann, *Access to Maritime Ports* (Hamburg, Books on Demand, 2003) 69.

[6] With regard to the protection of the marine environment and the role of coastal and port States, see GM Farnelli, 'International Convention for the Prevention of Pollution from Ships, MARPOL 2012, (and Annexes I, II, III, IV, V, VI)' in M Faure (ed), *Multilateral Environmental Treaties: Elgar Encyclopedia of Environmental Law*, vol 5 (Cheltenham, Edward Elgar, 2016) 166–174; MS Karim, *Prevention of Pollution of the Marine Environment from Vessels: The Potential and Limits of the International Maritime Organization* (Cham, Springer, 2015); R Virzo, 'Coastal State Competence Regarding Safety of Maritime Navigation' in Del Vecchio (n 1) 221; Pepe (n 1) 137; D Anderson, 'Port State and Environmental Protection' in Boyle and Freestone (n 4) 297. See European Directive 2009/16/CE of the European Parliament and the Council of 23 April 2009 on Port State Control [2009] OJ L 131/57. Regarding monitoring emissions in shipping in the EU, see M Adamowicz, 'Decarbonization of Maritime Transport – European Union Measures as an Inspiration for Global Solutions?' (2022) 145 *Marine Policy* 105085.

[7] See Resolution MEPC.181(59), '2009 Guidelines for port state control under the revised MARPOL Annex VI' and Resolution A.1155(32), 'Procedure on Port State Control 2021'.

The present chapter examines the role of PSC as provided for by the revised MARPOL 1973/78, Annex VI, in force from 1 January 2023,[8] and Resolution A. 1155 (32) Procedure for Port State Control 2021,[9] paying particular attention to the 'Guidelines for Port State Control under MARPOL Annex VI' and the IMO Guidelines on Carbon Intensity Regulations.[10] Finally, reference is made to the role of PSC and the EU Emission Trading System (ETS).

PSC general provisions are laid down in MARPOL Article 5.[11] This clearly states that ships must carry on board relevant documentation and that ships are subject to inspection to verify whether the condition of the ship corresponds to the certificate. Pursuant to para (2):

> A ship required to hold a certificate in accordance with the provisions of the regulations is subject, while in the ports or off-shore terminals under the jurisdiction of a Party, to inspection by officers duly authorized by that Party. Any such inspection shall be limited to verifying that there is on board a valid certificate, unless there are clear grounds for believing that the condition of the ship or its equipment does not correspond substantially with the particulars of that certificate.

If a valid certificate is not provided, Article 5 prescribes that the party entitled to inspect the ship is responsible for ensuring that a ship can sail only if does not constitute a danger to the environment:

> In that case, or if the ship does not carry a valid certificate, the Party carrying out the inspection shall take such steps as will ensure that the ship shall not sail until it can proceed to sea without presenting an unreasonable threat of harm to the marine environment.

Article 5, para 3 requires that a party denying a foreign ship entry must inform the representative of the Party whose flag the ship is entitled to fly:

> If a Party denies a foreign ship entry to the ports or off-shore terminals under its jurisdiction or takes any action against such a ship for the reasons that the ship does not comply with the provisions of the present Convention, the Party shall immediately inform the consul or diplomatic representative of the Party whose flag the ship is entitled to fly, or if this is not possible, the Administration of the ship concerned.

MARPOL, Article 5, recognises the denial of entry to a ship but:

> before denying entry or taking such action the Party may request consultation with the Administration of the ship concerned. Information shall also be given to the Administration

[8] Resolution MEPC 328 (76): 'Amendments to the annex of the protocol of 1997 to amend the international convention for the prevention of pollution from ships, as modified by the protocol of 1978 relating thereto'.

[9] In 1997 the IMO adopted Annex VI to the MARPOL Convention to address air pollution from shipping. This entered into force on 19 May 2005. The IMO adopted the first document on PSC in 1995 pursuant to the Resolution A.787 (19) Procedures for Port State Control of 23 November 1995. This Resolution has been amended several times. The latest version is Resolution A. 1155 (32), 'Procedure on Port State Control 2021', adopted 15 December 2021.

[10] Resolution MEPC.350(78), 2022, Guidelines on the Methods of Calculation of the Attained Energy Efficiency Existing Ship Index (EEXI); Resolution MEPC.351(78), 2022, Guidelines on Survey and Certification of the Attained Energy Efficiency Existing Ship Index, EEXI; Resolution MEPC.354(78), 2022 Guidelines on the Operational Carbon Intensity Rating of ships (CII Rating Guidelines, G4). CII and the EU regulations regarding the Emissions Trading System ETS were most recently introduced in the maritime sector. For EEXI, see Kløft and Cai (ch 4); for CII, see Girvin (ch 3).

[11] 'Certificates and special rules on inspection of ships'.

> when a ship does not carry a valid certificate in accordance with the provisions of the regulations.

In addition, Article 6 states:

> Parties to the Convention shall co-operate in the detection of violations and the enforcement of the provisions of the present Convention, using all appropriate and practicable measures of detection and environmental monitoring adequate procedures for reporting and accumulation of evidence.

Resolution A. 1155 (32)[12] gives essential guidance on the conduct of port State control inspections performed by port State Control Officers (PSCO) supporting the recognition of deficiencies in a ship and the application of control procedures. The introductory section[13] provides a set of general control procedures to be followed when foreign ships visit their ports. This states that 'the authorities of port States should make effective use of these provisions for the purposes of identifying deficiencies, if any, in such ships which may render them substandard and ensuring that remedial measures are taken'.

In case of non-compliance with the requirements in the relevant Convention, this may be sufficient to establish a deficiency that renders a ship a substandard ship, namely 'a ship whose hull, machinery, equipment or operational safety is substantially below the standards required by the relevant convention or whose crew is not in conformity with the safe manning document'.[14] It is appropriate to provide a link between the concept of seaworthiness and the right to detain a ship when lacking the relevant certificates required by international conventions. The concept of seaworthiness requires that 'a ship must have that degree of fitness which an ordinary careful and prudent owner would require his vessel to have at the commencement of his voyage having regard to all the probable circumstances of it'.[15] In the case of a vessel approaching a port, this may extend to having adequate documentation attesting to the required carbon emissions standards. In the absence of adequate certification on carbon emissions, the ship may be declared unseaworthy and subject to detention. Detention is defined[16] as the

> intervention action taken by the port State when the condition of the ship or its crew does not correspond substantially with the relevant conventions to ensure that the ship will not sail until it can proceed to sea without presenting a danger to the ship or persons on board, or without presenting an unreasonable threat of harm to the marine environment, whether or not such action will affect the normal schedule of the departure of the ship.

Chapter 2 of the Procedures[17] points out that 'parties may conduct inspections by PSCOs of foreign ships in their ports'. Such inspection consists of an 'Initial Inspection'

[12] Procedures for Port State Control 2021 (hereafter 'Procedures').

[13] ibid ch 1, para 1.4.

[14] ibid para 1.7.11.

[15] See *McFadden v Blue Star Line* [1905] 1 KB 697, 706; *FC Bradley & Sons Ltd v Federal Steam Navigation Co Ltd* (1926) 24 Ll LR 446, 454. See S Girvin, 'The Obligation of Seaworthiness: Shipowner and Charterer' CML Working Paper 17/11, para 5.2.

[16] Procedures (n 12), para 1.7.4.

[17] 'Port state inspections'.

where, after the certificate and document check are completed, the PSCO should check the overall condition of the ship.[18] If, from general impressions or observations on board, there emerge clear grounds for believing that the ship, its equipment or its crew do not substantially meet the requirements, the PSCO should proceed to a more detailed inspection utilising the guidelines contained in the appendix of the Procedures specifically designed for each Annex of MARPOL.[19] The 'General Procedural Guidelines for PSCOs'[20] provides an exception to the general rule concerning the detention of a ship to the effect that 'where the grounds for detention are the result of accidental damage suffered to a ship, no detention order should be issued'.[21]

Further, the Procedures highlight the relevance of cooperation between the PSCO and the flag State's representatives to avoid possible arguments relating to the detention of a ship 'since detention of a ship is a serious matter involving many issues, it may be in the best interest of the PSCO to act together with other interested parties'.[22] For example, the officer may request the shipowner's representatives to provide proposals for correcting the situation.[23] The PSCO should also consider cooperating with the flag State Administration's representatives or the RO responsible for issuing the relevant certificates, and consulting them regarding their acceptance of the shipowner's proposals and their possible additional requirements. Without limiting the PSCO's discretion in any way, the involvement of other parties could result in a safer ship, avoiding subsequent arguments relating to the circumstances of the detention and prove advantageous in the case of litigation involving 'undue delay'.[24]

Appendix 2, on 'Guidelines for the detention of ships', offers a guide to the principles governing rectification of deficiencies or detention of a ship, stating that:[25]

> In taking a decision concerning the rectification of a deficiency or detention of a ship, the Port State Control Officer (PSCO) will have to take into consideration the results of the more detailed inspection carried out in accordance with paragraph 2.5 of the procedures and guidelines contained in this appendix.

This is further supported by a clear specification of the function of the PSCO:[26]

> The PSCO will exercise professional judgement in determining whether to detain the ship until the deficiencies are rectified or to allow the ship to sail with certain deficiencies without unreasonable danger to safety, health or the environment, having also considered the particular circumstances of the intended voyage.

The guidelines indicate a list of deficiencies that, if detected, may result in the detention of a ship under inspection. Pursuant to para 5, 'Detainable Deficiencies' includes a list of deficiencies which are considered to be of such a serious nature that they may warrant the detention of the ship involved. The list is not considered exhaustive but is intended

[18] ibid para 2.2.4.
[19] ibid para 2.2.7.
[20] ibid para 2.3.
[21] ibid para 2.3.7.
[22] ibid para 2.3.8. This also cross-refers to para 4.1.3.
[23] ibid.
[24] ibid.
[25] Pursuant to para 1.1.
[26] ibid para 1.2.

to give examples of relevant items. In the case of certificates under MARPOL Annex VI, some of the relevant documentation regarding carbon emissions are:

1. A valid International Air Pollution Prevention Certificate (IAPP Certificate) and, where relevant, Engine International Air Pollution Prevention Certificates (EIAPP Certificates) and Technical Files.
2. Valid IEEC (International Energy Efficiency Certificate).[27]

Where these are absent, the possibility of the port State to detain the ship will arise. The above Appendix must be read with Appendix 18 on the Guidelines for Port State Control under MARPOL Annex VI. According to Ch 1, para 1 of this Appendix:

> This document is intended to provide basic guidance on the conduct of port State control inspections for compliance with MARPOL Annex VI … and afford consistency in the conduct of these inspections, the recognition of deficiencies and the application of control procedures.

The PSCO should use their professional judgement to determine whether: (a) to detain the ship until any noted deficiencies are corrected, or (b) to allow the ship to sail with certain deficiencies that do not pose an unreasonable threat of harm according to para 2.3.5. However, para 7.2 provides a list of deficiencies of such a serious nature that they may warrant the detention of the ship involved, taking into account the provisions of MARPOL Annex VI, reg VI, 'International Air Pollution Prevention Certificate' on the Issue or endorsement of Certificates and Statements of Compliance related to fuel oil consumption reporting and operational carbon intensity rating. Pursuant to para 3 of this Regulation 'such certificate shall be issued or endorsed either by the Administration or by any person or organisation duly authorised by it. In every case, the Administration assumes full responsibility for the certificate'. Concerning carbon emissions, the relevant certifications are the IEE Certificate, EEDI Technical File or SEEMP.

PSC procedures can be found in multiple agreements[28] signed by States at a regional level in Memoranda of Understanding (MoU). These agreements are necessary to make PSC more effective because some States have difficulty ratifying international conventions in a short period.

The classic example of such an agreement is the Memorandum of Understanding signed in Paris in 1982 (the Paris MoU).[29] This represents a substantial step forward in establishing a port State regime, creating a system whereby participating maritime

[27] ibid para 5.

[28] Nine such agreements have been finalised.

[29] The agreement took the form of a memorandum because, generally, the implementation of an international Convention may be an extremely difficult process, something that the signatories could not afford. On Regional Memorandums of Understanding on PSC, see HS Bang & DJ Jang, 'Recent Developments in Regional Memorandums of Understanding on Port State Control' in (2012) *Ocean Dev & Int'l Law* 170; I Christodoulou-Varotsi, 'The Memoranda of Understanding (MOUs) on Port State Control' in I Christodoulou-Varotsi and DA Pentsov (eds), *Maritime Work Law Fundamentals. Responsible Ship-owners, Reliable Seafarers* (Berlin, Springer, 2008) 709; R Barston, 'Port State Control: Evolving Concepts' in HN Scheiber (ed), *Law of the Sea: The Common Heritage and Emerging Challenges* (The Hague, Martinus Nijhoff, 2000) 87; TL McDorman, 'Regional Port State Control Agreements: Some Issues of International Law' (2000) 5 *Ocean & Coastal LJ* 207; J Hare, 'Port State Control: Strong Medicine to Cure a Sick Industry' (1997) 26 *Georgia J Int'l & Comp L* 571; T Keselj, 'Port State Jurisdiction in Respect of Pollution from Ships: The 1982 United Nations Convention on the Law of the Sea and the Memoranda of Understanding' (1999) 30 *Ocean Dev & Int'l Law* 146.

administrations must inspect a certain number of ships visiting their ports. However, the Paris MOU does not provide new rules to the provisions already in force and contained in international Conventions. It requires that States respect determined standards when inspecting vessels calling at any ports of States that are part of it in the so-called 'relevant international instruments'.[30] Contrary to Procedures discussed earlier, the Paris MoU contains provisions on the possibility of refusing access to a ship when it has been subject to various detentions. Paragraph 4.1 (Banning) of the Paris MoU provides for the cases of the refusal of access of ships following multiple detentions:

> 1. Each Authority is recommended to ensure that a foreign merchant ship is refused access to its ports and anchorages if it: flies the flag of a State appearing in the grey list as published in the annual report of the MoU and has been detained more than twice in the course of the preceding 24 months in a port or anchorage within the region of the Memorandum, or; flies the flag of a State appearing in the black list as published in the annual report of the MoU and has been detained more than twice in the course of the preceding 36 months in a port or anchorage within the region of the Memorandum.
> 2. The refusal of access following multiple detentions will become applicable as soon as the ship leaves the port or anchorage.
> 3. The refusal of access order shall be lifted after a period of three months has passed from the date of issue of the order and when the conditions in a PSCC Instruction are met. If the ship is subject to a second refusal of access, the period shall be 12 months.
> 4. Any subsequent detention in a port or anchorage shall result in the ship being refused access to any port or anchorage. This third refusal of access order may be lifted after a period of 24 months has passed from the issue of the order and only if: (a) the ship flies the flag of a State whose detention rate falls neither into the black list nor the grey list, (b) the statutory and classification certificates of the ship are issued by an organisation or organisations which are recognised by one or more of the Paris MoU Member States as listed in Annex 7, (c) the ship is managed by a company with a high performance, and the conditions set in a PSCC Instruction are met. Any ship not meeting the criteria as specified above after a period of 24 months has passed from the issue of the order, shall be permanently refused access to any port and anchorage.
> 5. Any subsequent detention in a port or anchorage after the third refusal of access shall result in the ship being permanently refused access to any port or anchorage.
> 6. Before denying entry, the Authority may request consultations with the Administration of the ship concerned.[31]

The role and the function of port States has been reaffirmed by the Italian Regional Administrative Court of Sardinia in 2020 and is described as the power:[32]

> to inspect a ship, also a foreign ship, moored in port in order to verify that her structure, equipment and crew comply with international requirements, and, possibly, in case of reported irregularities, to adopt appropriate administrative measures ranging from simple correction

[30] For 'international relevant instrument', see the list of international conventions in section 2.1 of the Paris MOU.

[31] *cf* also para 4.2.

[32] Italian Regional Administrative Court of Sardinia (TAR Sardegna), Cagliari Section I, 21 March 2020, n 188 (author's translation). Concerning the power of the port State to detain a ship not in compliance with international standard on safety see Italian Regional Administrative Court of Friuli-V Giulia Trieste Section I, 13 April 2022, n 198.

of the identified deficiencies to requiring the ship to head to the nearest repair yard to be corrected or, in the most serious cases, involving the detention of the ship.

This has also been upheld by the European Court of Justice, *Sea Watch eV v Ministero delle Infrastrutture e dei Trasporti*,[33] where the court recalled the definition of PSC. The PSC mechanism, although having some limitations owing to its function as an 'administrative measure', is a valid tool for attempting to counter the phenomenon of flags of convenience and makes it possible to identify sub-standard vessels that can result in harmful environmental damage.[34]

III. The IMO Strategy on Carbon Intensity Regulations and Port State Control (PSC)

The international community is focused on fighting climate change to reduce carbon emissions across all transportation sectors. This challenge is evidenced by numerous measures undertaken at the IMO and the European level that aim to reach a successful outcome on sustainability in the mid-term.

Among the EU measures are the European Green Deal of 2019[35] and the Annex of the Action Plan COM/2020/789 final of 2020 – Sustainable Mobility Flag 1, on 'boosting the uptake of zero-emission vehicles, renewable & low-carbon fuels and related infrastructure'.[36] In the maritime sector, the impending necessity to regulate energy efficiency and reduce carbon intensity from ships may be considered a new pillar within the evolution of the traditional concept of safety in maritime navigation.

In the IMO, amendments were made in 2021 to Ch 4 of MARPOL Annex VI,[37] and represent the continuation of a developing process started in 2011.[38] The new measures regulate the energy efficiency and carbon intensity of ships[39] and were adopted at the 76th session of the MEPC.[40] They introduced the new mandatory goal-based technical and operational measures to reduce the carbon intensity from international shipping, namely the Energy Efficiency Existing Ship Index – EEXI[41] (which applies

[33] Judgment of 1 August 2022, Cases C-14/21 and C-15/2.

[34] S Sucharitkul, 'Liability and Responsibility of the State of Registration or the Flag State in Respect if Sea-going Vessels, Aircraft and Spacecraft Registered by National Registration Authorities' (2006) 54 *Am J Comp Law* 409.

[35] COM/2019/640 final of 11 September 2019, Communication of Commission 'The European Green Deal', para 2.1.5.

[36] See COM/2020/789 final – Annex to Communication from the Commission to the European Parliament, the Council, The European Economic and social Committee and the Committee of the Regions – Sustainable and Smart Mobility Strategy – putting European Transport on track for the future.

[37] Resolution MEPC 328/(76).

[38] Resolution MEPC.203(62) adopted on 15 July 2011 Amendments to the annex of the protocol of 1997 to amend the international Convention for the prevention of pollution from ships, 1973, as modified by the protocol of 1978 relating thereto (Inclusion of regulations on energy efficiency for ships In MARPOL Annex VI). See Y Shi, 'The challenge of Reducing Greenhouse Gas Emissions from International Shipping: Assessing the International Maritime Organization's Regulatory Response' (2012) 23(1) *Yearbook of Int'l Environmental Law* 131.

[39] ibid.

[40] Resolution MEPC.328(76).

[41] See Kløft and Cai (ch 4).

to ships falling outside the EEDI regulations – Energy Efficiency Design Index), the enhanced Ship Energy Efficiency Management Plan (SEEMP), and Carbon Intensity Indicator (CII) certifications.[42] These regulations aim to reduce carbon intensity from ships and provide obligations for the States to adopt relevant tools to reduce any harmful emissions from ships. It is common to define the measures introduced to regulate and reduce the carbon intensity from ships as 'energy efficiency measures', but there is no such definition of energy efficiency measures in any IMO Resolution so far. A further point to note is that the relevant amendments to Ch 4 of Annex VI must be read jointly with the revised Guidelines for Port State Control.[43]

In July 2023, the Marine Environment Protection Committee (MEPC 80) of the IMO adopted the IMO Strategy on Reduction of GHG Emissions from Ships, with enhanced targets to tackle harmful emissions.[44]

IV. Port State Control (PSC) and the Energy Efficiency Existing Ship Index (EEXI)

The EEXI measure in Ch 4 is provided for by Reg 23,'Attained Energy Existing Ship Index (attained EEXI)'. According to this, the attained EEXI must be calculated for each ship and for each ship which has undergone a major conversion recalling the categories described in different Regulations of Annex VI.[45] Regulation 23.2 refers to the 'Guidelines on the method of calculation of the attained Energy Efficiency Existing Ship Index (EEXI)'[46] and is supplemented by the 'Guidelines on Survey and Certification of the Attained Energy Efficiency Ship Index' (EEXI).[47] Paragraph 3 states that these Guidelines '[…] should be applied to ships for which the application for a survey for verification of the ship's EEXI specified in Regulation 5 of MARPOL Annex VI has been submitted to a verifier'[48] and para 4.1.1 of the Guidelines states that: 'The attained EEXI should be calculated in accordance with regulation 23 of MARPOL Annex VI and the 2022 Guidelines on the method of calculation of the attained Energy Efficiency Existing Ship Index (EEXI) (resolution MEPC.350(78)) (EEXI Calculation Guidelines)'.

That PSC also plays a role in EEXI is highlighted in reg 10,[49] which provides that:

> In relation to Chapter 4 Regulation 10 of this Annex, any port State inspection may verify, when appropriate, that there is a valid Statement of Compliance related to fuel oil consumption reporting and operational carbon intensity rating, an International Energy

[42] See Girvin (ch 3).

[43] In particular, Appendix 18 of Resolution A 1153 (31).

[44] Resolution MEPC.377(80) (adopted 7 July 2023) 'IMO Strategy on Reduction of GHG Emissions from Ships, with enhanced targets to tackle harmful emissions' which revised Resolution MEPC.304(72), 'Initial IMO Strategy on reduction of GHG emissions from ships' (adopted 13 April 2018).

[45] See Reg 23, para 1 of Resolution MEPC.328 (76). It describes the EEXI characteristics regarding the information required for the calculation of the attained EEXI and the verification of the information by the Administration or the organisation authorised by it.

[46] Resolution MEPC.350(78).

[47] Resolution MEPC.350(78).

[48] See Ch 2, Reg 5.

[49] Reg 10.5.

> Efficiency Certificate and a Ship Energy Management Plan on board, in accordance with article 5 of the present Convention.

Regulation 10 states that, 'notwithstanding the requirements in paragraph 5 of this regulation, any port State inspection may inspect whether the Ship Energy Efficiency Management Plan is duly implemented by the ship in accordance with Regulation 28 of this Annex'.[50] A ship failing to comply with EEXI, and which does not meet the targets set out in the EEXI, will not receive an International Energy Efficiency Certificate and accordingly may be technically considered 'unseaworthy' and potentially subject to detention as provided for the general principle in Article 5.2 of MARPOL 1973/78. If the ship does not carry adequate documentation on board, the Party carrying out the inspection 'shall take such steps' to ensure that the ship will continue the navigation only if it does not constitute a threat of harm to the marine environment. The expression 'such steps' must be understood as the possibility for the port State to make a detention order against the ship not in compliance with international standards.

V. Port State Control (PSC) and the Carbon Intensity Indicator Rating (CII)

Regulation 28,[51] on 'Operational Carbon Intensity', provides that each ship of 5,000 gross tonnage and above will have to:

> Calculate the attained annual operational carbon intensity indicator – (CII) over a 12-month period from 1 January to 31 December for the preceding calendar year, using the data collected in accordance with regulation 27 of this Annex,[52] taking into account the guidelines to be developed by the organisation.

On 17 June 2021, IMO developed 'Guidelines on the operational Carbon Intensity Rating of Ships' (CII Rating Guidelines)[53] which aim at providing the methods for assigning operational energy efficiency performance ratings to ships as indicated in Reg 28. The 'introduction' of the Guidelines indicates that there are boundaries for determining a ship's annual operational carbon intensity performance from 2023 to 2030. The guidelines in the 'definition' provide an explanation of 'operational carbon intensity rating' and intended to be the assignment of 'a ranking label from among five grades (A, B, C, D, E) to the ship based on the attained annual operational carbon intensity indicator, indicating a major superior, minor superior, moderate, minor inferior performance level'.[54] Regulation 28.4 describes how to determine and calculate the

[50] Reg 10.6.

[51] MEPC. 328 (76).

[52] Reg 27 must be read jointly with Reg 6. Para 8 states that: '... a ship rated D for three consecutive years or rated E in accordance with regulation 28 of this Annex shall not be issued a Statement of Compliance unless a plan of corrective actions is duly developed and reflected in the SEEMP and verified by the Administration or any organization duly authorised by it in accordance with regulations 28.7 and 28.8 of this Annex'.

[53] Resolution MEPC.339(79) revoked in 2022 by Resolution MEPC.354(78).

[54] The new mandatory goal-based technical and operational regime applies from 1 January 2023. It is mandatory for the ship to calculate the attained Energy Efficiency Existing Ship Index (EEXI) in order to

annual operational CII – 'Required annual operational carbon intensity indicator (required annual operational CII)'. Each year, as indicated by the IMO guidelines, each ship will be labelled from grade from A to E according to the ship's annual operational carbon intensity and the required annual operational CII.

Concerning PSC and CII, a relevant issue is whether a port State may detain or ban from its port a ship rated D or E. In the case of a ship rated D for three consecutive years or rated as E, the provision mentions 'a plan of corrective actions' including a review of the SEEMP.[55]

In 2022, the Intersessional Working Group on Reduction of GHG Emissions from Ships (ISWG-GHG 12)[56] drafted amendments to the 2021 Procedures for PSC to enforce short-term GHG reduction measures by port State control authorities. In particular, Sub-Committee III was requested to consider what could be regarded a 'detainable deficiency' concerning the Carbon Intensity Indicator (CII). A Correspondence Group of the Sub-committee on Implementation of IMO Instruments[57] evaluated the possibility of incorporating the various amendments supporting the enforcement of the short-term GHG reduction measure into the PSC procedures. In relation to CII, the Sub-Committee unfortunately agreed that:

> at that stage there was no support for the proposed amendment to regard as a detainable deficiency the absence of implementation by the ship as planned at the time of the inspection of the three-year implementation plan and/or the plan of corrective actions for a ship rated as D for three consecutive years, or rated as E.[58]

Eventually, the Sub-committee agreed to advise the MEPC 79 accordingly. The Sub-Committee noted reports presented by the regional port State control (PSC) regimes and the United States on PSC activities, Concentrated Inspection Campaign (CIC), inspection rates and detentions and invited them to continue submitting annual reports.[59] The Sub-Committee, which reports to the Maritime Safety Committee (MSC) and the MEPC, assessed and updated four key IMO Assembly resolutions on implementation. Concerning the key to harmonising port State control (PSC) activities and procedures worldwide, the Sub-Committee noted that information provided by all ten PSC regimes revealed that 63,761 inspections were carried out in 2020, 74,574 in 2021 and 81,346 in 2022.[60]

measure their energy efficiency and to initiate the collection of the data for the reporting of their annual operational carbon intensity indicator (CII) and CII rating.

[55] Reg 28.7.

[56] IMO Intersessional Working Group on Reduction of GHG Emissions from Ships (ISWG-GHG 12), 16 to 20 May 2022. The aim of the Working Group is to draft and finalise guidelines to support the implementation of the carbon intensity measures. With regard to the report of the Sub-committee on Implementation of IMO instruments (III 8), 25–28 July 2022 see www.imo.org/en/MediaCentre/MeetingSummaries/Pages/III-8th-session.aspx.

[57] (III 8), 25–28 July 2022.

[58] (III 8), 25–28 July 2022.

[59] The Sub-committee on Implementation of IMO instruments (III 9), 31 July–4 August 2023.

[60] With regard to the report of the IMO Sub-committee on Implementation of IMO instruments (III 9), 31 July–4 August 2023, see www.imo.org/en/MediaCentre/MeetingSummaries/Pages/III-9th-session.aspx. In 2020, 1,530 detentions were reported, 1,746 in 2021 and 2,160 in 2022. The overall detention rate increased from 2.34% in 2021 to 2.66% in 2022. The Sub-Committee considered the regulatory basis for port State

The issue concerning the interpretation of a 'detainable deficiency' may, it is submitted, establish to what extent port States may intervene in the process of reducing emissions with respect to the EEXI and CII. It is likely it would only be possible to delineate a preliminary overview based on previous experience related to environmental standards adopted in recent years. Accordingly, where certifications are not in compliance with international conventions, EU legislation and regional agreements have held that the ship is unseaworthy. It is likely that the same will happen if a vessel calling at a port fails to comply with the regulations on carbon intensity[61] drawing on existing authority covering the absence of documentation carried on board a vessel. In *Ciampa v British India Steam Navigation Co*, a ship lacked any document certifying a 'clean bill of health' after a call at Mombasa at the time when the port was in the grip of an outbreak of plague.[62] Adequate documentation such as carbon certification required by the law of ship's flag or by the law of the port State may be considered necessary for the ship to navigate and operate without impediment. Moreover, in *The Derby*, Kerr LJ affirmed, referring to 'adequate documentation', that:

> The nature of such certificates may vary according to the requirements of the law of the vessel's flag or the laws or regulations in force in the countries to which the vessel may be ordered, or which may lawfully be required by the authorities exercising administrative or other functions in the vessel's ports of call pursuant to the laws there in force. Documents falling within this category, which have been considered in the authorities, are certificates concerning the satisfactory state of the vessel which is in some respect related to her physical condition, and accordingly to her seaworthiness. Their purpose is to provide documentary evidence for the authorities at the vessel's ports of call on matters which would otherwise require some physical inspection of the vessel, and possibly remedial measures – such as fumigation – before the vessel will be accepted as seaworthy in the relevant respect. The nature of description of such certificates, which may accordingly be required to be carried on board to render the vessel seaworthy, must depend on the circumstances and would no doubt raise issues of fact in individual cases.[63]

More particularly, the question raised depends on the interpretation of 'detainable deficiency' and the possibility that a port State can detain a ship if it does not comply with Energy Efficiency Certification, such as the International Energy Efficiency Certificate(IEE)[64] and where a ship obtains a low carbon intensity indicator CII rating such as D or E under the Regulation on carbon intensity.

control, roles and responsibilities of Contracting Governments in their right to exercise port State control, and the supporting role of IMO. Additionally, the Sub-Committee considered the prospect of possible future developments, which include the potential development of an overarching database under the umbrella of IMO, the need for analysis of PSC data stored in GISIS to establish trends to support regulatory and policy developments, and the increasing number of PSC MoUs/Agreements working on the development of a port State control regime for fishing vessels.

[61] With regard to the relevant documentation and seaworthiness, see Girvin (n 15) para 4.6; V Piccolo, 'GHG Emissions from Shipping: How to Overcome Persistent Challenges', CML Working Paper 23/06, 34.

[62] [1915] 2 KB 77. For a case involving inadequate charts and navigational aids, see *Rey Banano del Pacifico CA v Transportes Navieros Ecuatorianos (The Isla Fernandina)* [2000] 2 Lloyd's Rep 15. See S Baughen, *Shipping Law*, 7th edn (London, Routledge, 2019) 83.

[63] *Alfred C Toepfer GmbH v Tossa Marine Co Ltd (The Derby)* [1985] 2 Lloyd's Rep 325, 333.

[64] See Resolution MEPC. 328(76), Reg 8.

The scope of application of the CII Regulations provided by Reg 19 is limited to 'all ships of 400 gross tonnage and above'. There are a series of exceptions where the provisions do not apply. These can be contrasted with Reg 20 which states that 'the goal of this chapter is to reduce the carbon intensity of international shipping, working towards the level of ambition set out in the Initial IMO Strategy on reduction of GHG emissions from ships' and aims at reaching the initial goal indicated by the 2018 IMO Strategy on reduction of GHG.[65]

Following a description in Reg 21,[66] a ship must comply with two functional requirements to reduce carbon intensity. The first requirement is a technical requirement namely the 'technical carbon intensity requirements' among which must be included the following: Reg 22, 'Attained Energy Efficiency Design Index – attained EEDI' (introduced in 2011); Reg 23 'Attained Energy Efficiency Existing Ship Index – attained EEXI'; Reg 24 'Required Energy Efficiency Design Index – EEDI' and Reg 25 'Required EEXI Energy Efficiency Existing Index'. Second, the provision foresees an operational requirement, the 'Operational carbon intensity requirements', which includes: (1) a management plan with the purpose of improving the energy efficiency of a ship, the 'Ship Energy Efficiency Management Plan (SEEMP)'.[67] The SEEMP, according to Reg 26.1, requires that: 'Each ship shall keep on board a ship a specific Ship Energy Efficiency Management Plan (SEEMP). This may form part of the Ship's Safety Management System (SMS). The SEEMP shall be developed and reviewed taking into account the guidelines adopted by the Organization;[68] (2) a mechanism aimed to collect and report the ship fuel oil consumption data, the 'Collection and reporting of ship fuel oil consumption data' pursuant to Reg 27; (3) An operational carbon intensity aimed at calculating the attained annual operational carbon intensity indicator followed by an Operational Carbon Intensity rating. In case of a low rating, it is possible to design a plan of corrective actions and incentives with the possibility of review under Reg 28. Finally, the last relevant provision, Reg 29 is concerned with the 'Promotion of technical cooperation and transfer of technology relating to the improvement of energy efficiency of ships.[69] This considers the importance of 'cooperation' and 'transfer of technology' for improving the reduction of carbon intensity. These are essential tools for equipping developing States with the necessary instruments to properly implement the measures provided in Annex VI.

As anticipated, the Sub-Committee agreed that there was no support for the proposed amendment concerning a detainable deficiency as the absence of implementation by the ship at the time of the inspection of the three-year implementation plan

[65] Resolution MEPC.304(72), Initial IMO Strategy on reduction of GHG emissions from ships, adopted on 13 April 2018.

[66] Resolution MEPC. 328(76), Reg 21.

[67] SEEMP is an operational measure which designs a mechanism to improve the energy efficiency of a ship in a cost-effective manner. It was first introduced by Reg 22 of Resolution MEPC.203(62). The SEEMP Guidelines were enacted in 2012 by Resolution MEPC.213(63) adopted on 2 March 2012, in 2016 by Resolution MEPC.282 (70) adopted on 28 October 2016, and in 2022 by Resolution MEPC.346(78) adopted on 10 June 2022.

[68] Resolution MEPC.346(78), 2022 Guidelines for the development of a ship energy efficiency management plan (SEEMP).

[69] Resolution MEPC. 328 (76), Reg 29. It refers to Resolution A.1067 (28), Framework and procedures for the IMO Member State Audit Scheme.

and/or the plan of corrective actions for a ship rated as D for three consecutive years, or rated as E. Although a port State has to detain (PSC procedures) and ban (Paris MOU) a ship that does not comply with the carbon intensity regulatory framework provided by Annex VI, the new provision does not urge or require Administrations and port authorities to intervene with strong action in the case of non-compliance. The purpose of the provision, in addition to the introduction of a rating scheme, 'Ships will get a rating of their energy efficiency (A, B, C, D, E – where A is the best)', seems to support the achievement of the highest energy efficiency rates by Administrations, port authorities and other stakeholders as appropriate. To this end, such entities 'are encouraged to provide incentives to ships rated as A or B also sending out a strong signal to the market and financial sector'.[70] Apart from these incentives directed to ships rated A or B, there is no specific reference to measures such as administrative detention, ban or rejection of ships from ports. It is also recommended to provide incentives to port States that inspect and detain ships lacking the required documentation, especially where there are complexities rating a large number of ships A or B. In addition, there are strong reasons to recommend the adoption of strong measures, such as the administrative detention of the vessel, especially for flag of convenience vessels that represent a threat to the marine environment and safety of navigation. Regional agreements on PSC constitute the most effective instrument to provide a uniform set of rules aimed at monitoring and inspecting ships not fulfilling international standards protecting the marine environment and air pollution from ships.

VI. Port State Control (PSC) and European Trading System (ETS)

The European Trading System (ETS)[71] establishing a system for greenhouse gas emission allowance trading within the Union was officially introduced by Directive (EU) 2023/959 of the European Parliament and of the Council of 10 May 2023.[72]

Initially, the EU Emissions Trading System (ETS) was part of a European Directive[73] designed to lower greenhouse gas (GHG) emissions. In line with the EU Green Deal, the Fit for 55 package aims to reduce the EU's emissions by 55 per cent in 2030 compared to a 1990 baseline. The 'Fit for 55' package extends the existing ETS to new sectors, including shipping. As a result, the shipping industry will need to mitigate its emissions. The emission trading system aims to reduce the total volume of GHG emitted over time. It is implemented through a 'cap and trade' mechanism, meaning that every registered emitter must buy allowances corresponding to their emissions through an auction system. Prices per ton of emissions will generate revenues to partially finance the decarbonisation of the maritime sector.

[70] (III 8), 25–28 July 2022.

[71] See Eftestøl (ch 5).

[72] This amends Directive 2003/87/EC establishing a system for greenhouse gas emission allowance trading within the Union and Decision (EU) 2015/1814 concerning the establishment and operation of a market stability reserve for the Union's greenhouse gas emission trading system. The European Parliament voted to incorporate the EU ETS in 2024 following approval by the European Council.

[73] 2003/87/EC.

Article 16 of Directive (EU) 2023/959 has been amended by inserting a new paragraph 11 a. Pursuant to the new provision, in the case of persistent non-compliance for two or more consecutive reporting periods, expulsion orders may be issued at the port of entry in case of non-compliance by the law of the flag of the vessel. A detention order is adopted until the shipping company fulfils its obligations (for ships under an EU Member State Flag within a port in that Member State).

In case of persistent non-compliance with the ETS Directive, the European legislator adopted more robust measures:

> As a result of the issuing of such an expulsion order, every Member State, with the exception of the Member State whose flag the ship is flying, shall refuse entry of the ships under the responsibility of the shipping company concerned into any of its ports until the shipping company fulfils its surrender obligations in accordance with Article 12.[74]

Further, if there is a failure in two consecutive years to surrender allowances, a vessel sailing to a port in the EU will likely be unseaworthy because the lack of documentation on board the ship means it is at risk of detention or exclusion from the port.

VII. Conclusion

Preventing air pollution from ships as part of the fight against climate change may be regarded as a 'common concern of mankind'.[75] For this reason, the IMO in the past few decades has provided a strategy to introduce mandatory measures to regulate energy efficiency and reduce carbon emissions intensity from ships, as the amendments to Annex VI of MARPOL Convention 1973/78 demonstrate.[76]

The legal framework on PSC as an instrument to ensure compliance with international obligations regarding the protection of the marine environment described in the present chapter has highlighted the increasing role of the port State as the advocate of the 'collective interests of the international community' when PSC is institutionalised in a Memorandum of Understanding.

It is said that PSC is a complementary instrument to flag State control, which enables States to abide by the Regulations stipulated at the international level to fight against the phenomenon of substandard ships and to limit the risk of the increasing occurrence of the 'port of convenience'. In this regard, although the institutionalisation of PSC in the Paris Memorandum may be a valid tool to ensure compliance with environmental obligations, at the same time, it limits the inspecting activity of the port state to the formal verification of the existence on board of the vessel of the certifications issued by the flag state. In case of discrepancies, port States must intervene against ships that potentially harm coastal state interests.

[74] Para 11a of the Directive (EU) 2023/959. With regard to the distinction between the refusal of access to EU Ports as a type of enforcement measure and the 'banning' of ships from EU ports as the result of a positive verification of non-compliance during an (in-port) inspection of a particular ship, see H Ringbom, *The EU Maritime and Safety Policy and International Law* (Leiden, Martinus Nijhoff, 2008) 310.

[75] Tanaka (n 3); Tanaka (2016) (n 3) 340.

[76] MQ Mejia Jr, 'Air Pollution, Climate Change, and Port State Control', in Mukherjee et al (n 3) 542.

The current scenario offers three different cases. First, the ETS Directive expressly introduced the possibility of detention of the ship and the expulsion of the vessel not in compliance with the ETS provisions. Second, there are the EEXI Regulations relating to the structure of the ships and which in the case of the lack of inadequate certification, may render the ship unseaworthy and therefore subject to detention. Third, contrary to the EXXI regulations, which pertain to the structural element of the craft, the CII Regulations relate to the ship's performance and the resulting rating. For this reason the CII Regulations contemplate two scenarios, including no rating at all. The absence of any rating is an example of inadequate documentation, and the ship is considered unseaworthy. The alternative scenario is where the ship is rated, but there is a poor rating, such as D or E. In this case, international standards create doubts whether the ship can be considered unseaworthy. At this stage, we do not know whether a ship with a poor CII rating and with adequate certification will be subject to administrative measures such as detention or banning of the ship from a port.

It is therefore recommended that shipowners have a 'protected period' from the entry into force of the amendment of Annex VI so as to prepare their ships and make them seaworthy in compliance with the new regulations. Indeed, Reg 28.7 provides for 'a plan of corrective actions' to achieve the annual operational CII in the case of a ship rated D for three consecutive years or rated as E. Pursuant to Reg 28, a review of the SEEMP must include the plan of corrective actions. It would be appropriate to provide an explicit interpretation of 'corrective actions' for ships rated D or E and 'incentives' to ships rated A or B, given that the provisions are still too generic pending the completion of review by 1 January 2026.

10

Environmental Targets as Mere 'Crowd-pleasers'? Enforcement of Green Targets through Ship Financing Contracts

ASLI ARDA*

I. Introduction

Many legislative frameworks concerning environmental law are fundamentally the products of the 'normative frenzy'[1] that took place from the 1970s to the 1990s, where the predominant concern was constructing a body of regulations targeting environmental protection.[2] However, problems concerning effective implementation and enforcement have gradually emerged, and many remain unresolved. The long-neglected enforcement of environmental protection is beyond the scope of this chapter. However, there are global environmental targets and legal tools to facilitate complying with trajectories designed to achieve these targets. In the context of shipping, polluters polluting less and financiers aiming to 'finance greenly' is now the rule of thumb. It has been commented that 'central banks and financial sector authorities are increasingly interested in understanding and quantifying climate and environmental risks.'[3] However, the ultimate problem is the lack of enforceability of target adherence. The finance sector is key to pushing these targets and creating a ripple effect concerning target-adherent commercial behaviour. Climate change concerns have contractual implications for the ship finance sector. This particular sector has contractual instruments that specifically accommodate the push of environmental target adherence and the incentive to push it so

* Assistant Professor, Centre for Private Governance (CEPRI) and Shipping and Ocean Law Group (SHOC), Faculty of Law, University of Copenhagen. I would like to thank Professor Vibe Ulfbeck of the University of Copenhagen and Dr Kyriaki Noussia of the University of Reading, for their comments on earlier drafts of this chapter. I would further like to thank Fanny Fabricius Bye of Export Finance Norway for taking the time to talk about the ship finance sector.

[1] S Maljean-Dubois, 'Introduction – The Effectiveness of Environmental Law: A Key Topic' in S Maljean-Dubois (ed), *The Effectiveness of Environmental Law* (Cambridge, Intersentia, 2018) 2.

[2] ibid.

[3] O Nie, M Regelnik and D Wang, 'Banking Sector Risks in the Aftermath of Climate Change and Environmental-related Disasters' (*World Bank Blogs*, 18 April 2023) blogs.worldbank.org/developmenttalk/banking-sector-risks-aftermath-climate-change-and-environmental-related-disasters.

due to the eventuality of their environmental liability to arise. Accordingly, this chapter concerns contractual instruments that enable the push of green-adherent commercial behaviour and the incentives to do so from the perspective of the ship finance sector. It, thus, investigates the enforcement of environmental targets through green financing contracts in light of environmental liability. It will argue that these targets are achievable if they are genuinely considered to go beyond being mere 'crowd-pleasers' and that there are applicable legal tools to ensure and effectuate such achievement.

II. Environmental Targets and their Pervasive Impact on Shipping Contracts

While steps in the right direction are being taken, the shipping industry is still far from its destination. The International Maritime Organization (IMO), the main regulatory body for the global shipping industry, has set ambitious carbon emission reduction goals that may only be achieved by pushing target-adherent commercial behaviour from the ship finance sector. As of October 2023, IMO's revised strategy targets to reach net-zero greenhouse gases (GHG) emission from international shipping by or around 2050, and a commitment to ensure an uptake of alternative zero and near-zero GHG fuels by 2030 with the indicative check-points for the international shipping industry to reach net-zero GHG emissions for 2030 (by at least 20 per cent, striving for 30) and 2040 (by at least 70 per cent, striving for 80 per cent).[4]

There are also amendments to the International Convention on the Prevention of Pollution from Ships (MARPOL) that aim to enable the achievement of the lined-up strategy targets.

The Efficiency Existing Ship Index (EEXI) is designed to improve the energy efficiency of a vessel's design, whereas the Carbon Intensity Indicator (CII) illustrates a vessel's carbon intensity. Whereas the former focuses on technical design improvements,[5] the latter requires operational changes.[6] Key considerations include responsibility, cost of compliance, exposure to third-party claims, and the impact of non-compliance on insurance coverage. Implementing these frameworks to reduce carbon emissions in international shipping will raise compliance responsibilities. Such implementation will necessitate contractual enhancements, especially with charterparties, and accordingly, the approach towards these new constraints will be a contractual matter.[7]

[4] IMO's work to cut GHG emissions from ships, IMO, www.imo.org/en/MediaCentre/HotTopics/Pages/Cutting-GHG-emissions.aspx.

[5] Perhaps by making technical modifications, such as engine/shaft power limitation, bow or propeller improvements, use of alternative fuels, and/or installation of energy efficiency technology: A Sbraga and J Malpas, 'Reducing International Shipping's Carbon Intensity Through the IMO's EEXI and CII: Charterparty Implications and Challenges' (HFW, April 2021) www.hfw.com/downloads/002941-HFW-Reducing-International-Shippings-Carbon-Intensity.pdf.

[6] ibid. These may include operating at a reduced speed and/or slow steaming; diverting from the shortest or quickest route on a voyage/increasing distance sailed; reducing cargo volume intake; and/or installing energy-efficient technology.

[7] 'EEXI and CIIs – Changes and implications post IMO MEPC 76' (*Lloyd's Register*, June 2021) Webinar Questions and Answers.

The Energy Efficiency Design Index (EEDI) focuses on improving energy efficiency in the building and design of new ships, and its requirements will be tightened: newly built ships will gradually have to meet higher standards. The Ship Energy Efficiency Management Plan (SEEMP) provides a practical tool for 'green management', whereas the Energy Efficiency Operational Indicator (EEOI) facilitates performance monitoring to improve fleet efficiency. The SEEMP facilitates ship efficiency through measures like speed optimisation, course change and hull cleaning, affecting ship management contracts.

There are also amendments to MARPOL made in 2018 on the Data Collection System (DCS) pertaining to the fuel consumption of ships.[8] The system specifies the data to be collected and reported for each calendar year for ships 5,000 Gross Tonnage (GT) and above. The required data to be disclosed concerns the amount of fuel consumption for each type of fuel in metric tonnes, distance travelled, hours underway, and technical characteristics of the ship.

The disclosure of data pertaining to carbon emissions constitutes one of the core elements of Poseidon Principles,[9] which are developed as a set of private governance tools that reflect the dedication of its signatory financial organisations to make business decisions by initially looking through a 'green lens'. It is a private initiative that aims to align ship finance portfolios with responsible environmental behaviour towards the IMO strategy through the commitment of its signatories to annually measure and report the carbon emission levels of their ship loan portfolio. As of October 2023, there are 35 signatories representing a bank loan portfolio of over 65 per cent of the global ship finance, which is approximately US$ 200 billion.[10] The magnitude of this private governance framework is as significant as the amendments made to MARPOL. From a contract law perspective, the Poseidon Principles (and, accordingly, the DCS of MARPOL) predominantly affect the ship financing agreements of its signatories.[11]

Last but not least, the position of the finance sector as an enabler of the achievement of green targets is also reflected in the 'Proposal for a Directive of European Parliament and the Council of Corporate Sustainability Due Diligence and amending Directive (EU) 2019/1937.' The Proposal emphasises that, in accordance with the green commitments of the European Union, 'changes in corporate governance rules and practices, including on sustainable finance, will make company owners and managers prioritise sustainability objectives in their actions and strategies.'[12] Accordingly, the important role of the finance sector in achieving green targets is also reflected in European legislative documents.

The desire to move towards a more sustainable future is gaining more momentum every day, and it is becoming more crucial to evaluate the repercussions of this on the

[8] MARPOL Annex VI, Chapter 4, Reg 19.

[9] Poseidon Principles: www.poseidonprinciples.org/finance/about.

[10] Poseidon Principles: www.poseidonprinciples.org/finance/about. In 2019, when 11 banks signed the framework agreement, this represented 20% of the global ship finance market.

[11] The Poseidon Principles are incorporated into the ship loan agreement through the Poseidon Principles Standard Covenant Clause (SCC), the inclusion of which is strongly recommended but not compulsory.

[12] Proposal for a Directive of European Parliament and the Council of Corporate Sustainability Due Diligence and amending Directive (EU) 2019/1937, 29.

ship finance sector. The reason for this is attributable to the fact that finance organisations hold the key to funding decarbonisation, and the business choices they make can potentially bring it into effect. Their green conduct could considerably accelerate the achievement of the IMO targets in shipping. This accordingly necessitates evaluating the contractual instruments that are at the disposal of the ship finance sector to 'push green' and the incentives within this sector to enforce green adherence.

III. Contractual Instruments: The Enforcement of Environmental Targets and Sustainable Ship Financing

Green targets need not only to be agreed upon and construed, but also implemented and enforced. The lender needs the means to supervise and monitor the activity it is funding to prevent any environmental damage from such activity. Accordingly, loan agreements usually contain environmental covenants 'to control and monitor such risk.'[13] Such covenants often require the borrower/shipowner to execute the project diligently and emphasise the requirement of 'due regard to be paid to environmental and ecological factors.'[14] Furthermore, the Poseidon Principles include a Standard Covenant Clause (SCC), incorporation of which is strongly recommended. This elaborates on how the data on the carbon emission of vessels is to be provided by shipowners to lender banks. Environmental, Social and Governance (ESG) Based Performance Clauses are also inserted in these contracts as environmental provisions. Among the contractual tools that may potentially enable the enforcement of green targets through legal arrangements, there is also the possible market enforcement of green compatibility. 'Green enforcement' may also reflect in the financial and commercial decisions made by the lender banks.

A. Loan Agreements, Poseidon Principles and Covenants

Loan agreements usually contain 'the terms of the loan or credit, the repayment obligations, provisions for use of the proceeds of the loan and for procurement financed by it'[15] as well as the 'obligations with respect to carrying out the project.'[16] Some legal tools are available in loan agreements that enable the promotion of compliance with particular terms of the agreement, and the most specific of these is covenants.[17]

Covenants may fundamentally be positive or negative. Positive covenants generally require specific performance to be performed, whereas negative covenants consist of promises not to do something.[18] Under a covenant, the loanee commits not to carry

[13] P Rebelo, 'Poseidon Principles: Legal Directions for Implementation & Enforcement' (2020) 26 *JIML* 9.
[14] IFI Shihata, 'The World Bank and the Enforcement: A Legal Perspective' (1992) 16 *Maryland J of Int'l L & Trade*, 1, 14–15.
[15] ibid 14.
[16] ibid.
[17] ibid.
[18] A Kramer, *The Law of Contract Damages* (Oxford, Hart Publishing, 2017) para 10.01.

out acts that may potentially be detrimental to the bank's rights or otherwise increase the risk of default, whereas the bank may be granted the right to renegotiate or terminate the loan if the relevant covenant is breached.[19] Should the loanee comply with the covenants, this may lead to some improvements to be made pertaining to the terms of the loan. In contrast, should they fail to comply, this would create the potential for the imposition of more stringent financial terms because, in this case, the creditworthiness of the loanee may have deteriorated.[20] In the ship loan context, positive covenants usually necessitate compliance with the terms and conditions of financial and other obligations

> to register the vessel in a ship register reasonably acceptable to the lender and to fly a flag, which has been approved by the lender, to provide all necessary information required by the lender and to promptly disclose to the lender any event of default.[21]

Negative/restrictive covenants, on the other hand, usually necessitate an undertaking not to encumber the asset with liens, selling or transferring the vessel, or entering into any agreement on the operation or chartering of the vessel without the prior consent of the lender.[22]

An important issue concerns the legal classification of covenants in contract law. It is true that in the context of ship loan agreements, covenants indicate the undertakings of the loanee/shipowner. However, enforcing such covenants is subject to assessing whether such undertakings fall into the category of 'enforceable contractual provisions.' In his very well-known statement, Diplock LJ distinguishes contractual undertakings and provides a categorisation of conditions, warranties, and innominate terms.[23] There may be some contractual provisions that arguably fall into a 'limbo' category that may not be considered as conditions or warranties. Rebelo furthermore argues particularly in the context of covenants that, although there are conditions that go to the root of the contract and warranties that are more superficial, there is also a third category that consists of intermediate or innominate terms that covenants may fall under, and the legal outcome of breaching such provisions is quite ambiguous.[24]

It follows that the effect of the breach of an innominate provision is generally decisive concerning its contractual taxonomy. If the breach of a particular term deprives the innocent party substantially of the whole of the benefit of the contract, then this may be categorised as a fundamental breach, and the remedy is equivalent to the remedy for breach of a condition. In such a case, the contract may be terminated. If this would

[19] G Morri and A Mazza, *Property Finance: An International Approach* (Chichester, Wiley, 2015) 56.

[20] ibid 56–57.

[21] S Otto and T Scholl, 'Legal Treatment of Ship Finance Loans: Analysis of the Ship Loan Contract' in O Schinas, C Grau and M Johns (eds), *HSBA Handbook on Ship Finance* (Heidelberg, Springer, 2015) 64.

[22] ibid.

[23] *Hong Kong Fir Shipping Co Ltd v Kawasaki Kisen Kaisha Ltd* [1962] 2 QB 26 (CA). Also, for a detailed evaluation of the classification of contractual categories in light of *Hong Kong Fir*, see: JW Carter and C Hodgekiss, 'Conditions and Warranties: Forebears and Descendants' (1977) 8 *Sydney LR* 31; D Nolan, 'Hongkong Fir Shipping Co. Ltd. v. Kawasaki Kisen Kaisha Ltd., the Hongkong Fir (1961)' in C Mitchell and P Mitchell (eds), *Landmark Cases in the Law of Contract* (Oxford, Hart Publishing, 2008).

[24] Rebelo (n 13).

not be the case, then the remedy would be similar to the breach of a warranty, and the aggrieved party is entitled to damages. The clarification of what remedies are potentially available in case of the breach of a covenant remains with the parties and depends on their willingness to spell these out.

Because covenants are private contractual undertakings, they usually do not come in any standard form as they reflect the preferences and terms on which the finance has been offered.[25] However, the Poseidon Principles strongly recommend the incorporation of its Standard Covenant Clause (SCC). The clause elaborates how the data pertaining to the carbon emission of vessels is to be reported. It should be emphasised at this point that this is not a provision delimiting carbon intensity but is concerned with the disclosure of the data regarding its emission. Such disclosure is in line with Reg 22A of Annex VI of the Protocol of 1997 to amend the MARPOL Convention.[26] Accordingly, the 'Poseidon Covenant' (SCC) in a standard form is a big step towards the wider implementation of the Poseidon Principles. Such a standard clause is clear, convenient, and easy to incorporate.

The SCC of the Poseidon Principles reads as follows:

> The Owner] shall, upon the request of [any Lender] and at the cost of the Owner], on or before [31st July] in each calendar year, supply or procure the supply to [the Facility Agent] [such Lender] of all information necessary in order for [any Lender] to comply with its obligations under the Poseidon Principles in respect of the preceding year, including, without limitation, all ship fuel oil consumption data required to be collected and reported in accordance with Regulation 22A of Annex VI and any Statement of Compliance, in each case relating to the [Vessel] for the preceding calendar year 3 [provided always that [no Lender] shall publicly disclose such information with the identity of the [Vessel] without the prior written consent of the Owner]/[.For the avoidance of doubt, such information shall be ['Confidential Information']['Information'] for the purposes of [Clause [•] (Confidential Information)][Section [•] (Treatment of Certain Information; Confidentiality)]] but the Owner] acknowledges that, in accordance with the Poseidon Principles, such information will form part of the information published regarding the [relevant] [Lender's] portfolio climate alignment.

The provision stipulates that the loanee/shipowner promises 'to supply all information necessary in order for the lender to comply with their obligations under the Principles in respect of the previous year.'[27] There are a few fundamental issues concerning the implementation and enforceability of the SCC.

First, incorporation is 'strongly recommended' and not 'compulsory.' This is quite clear from the wording of the supplementary resources of the Poseidon Principles pertaining to the SCC.[28] It is true that signing the Poseidon Principles is the voluntary

[25] S Girvin, 'Aspects of Ship Finance: The Market, Ship Mortgages, and their Enforcement' (30 August 2019) *CML Working Paper Series* No 19/05 papers.ssrn.com/sol3/papers.cfm?abstract_id=3445340.

[26] Ie, the International Convention for the Prevention of Pollution from Ships 1973.

[27] MA Moussalli and I Tsekoura, 'The Poseidon Principles – Part I – Overview' (Clyde & Co, 26 February 2020) www.mondaq.com/uk/marine-shipping/897514/the-poseidon-principles-part-1--overview..

[28] The supplementary document pertaining to Standard Covenant Clause (SCC), updated on January 2020 is available at www.poseidonprinciples.org/finance/wp-content/uploads/2020/01/PP-Standard-Covenant-Clause.17.1.20.pdf. The document suggests that the relevant covenant wording 'to be inserted' is subject to appropriate drafting adjustments to consider each specific set of definitions in the relevant ship financing documents.

act of its signatories. However, the core element that ensures the effective implementation and enforcement of the Principles being their SCC, its lack of incorporation would inevitably signal underlying intentions of greenwashing. However, it is safe to say[29] this is not the way the Principles operate in practice, and signatories are generally more than willing to insert the SCC into their ship loan agreements in order to comply with the Principles as a matter of contract law.

Second, the data that is disclosed on carbon emissions is confidential information. This means that 'in its standard form, the covenant only allows the lender to publicly disclose information with the identity of the vessel if the borrower/shipowner have given consent for them to do so.'[30] Consent is supposed to be given through the SCC,[31] and unless given, the shipowner is not publicly identifiable concerning their disclosure of carbon emissions data. The lender finance organisation accordingly appraises and monitors the general environmental behaviour and carbon emission trajectory of their shipping portfolio in bulk based on the relevant data received.[32] The individual data disclosed to the lender only impacts this overall pattern and the trajectory such a lender entity reveals. The SCC indeed imposes an obligation upon the borrower/shipowner to provide the relevant information. However, this is not intended to be more onerous than any of their other obligations on the provision of periodic information to lenders under its facility agreements, such as the International Safety Management (ISM) documentation[33] or copies of class.[34] This may arguably impair the 'detrimental effect' of the Poseidon Principles because, for the time being, they merely encourage shipowners and finance organisations to make business decisions by looking through a green lens as a starting point. However, it is also arguable whether we have already not passed the 'starting point' and whether climate change requires immediate action.

The third issue concerns the enforceability of the SCC. Baughen rightly argues that it is not clear what remedies exist in the event of a breach of the Poseidon Principles SCC.[35] This takes us back to the general assessment of the enforceability of covenants in loan agreements. As already indicated, the effect of the breach is a decisive element in determining what possible remedies may exist in the context of a ship finance agreement that incorporates the SCC of the Poseidon Principles. The effect of any breach has much to do with the type of the covenant. The next part of this chapter investigates the concept of environmental conditionality of bank loans. In particular, it considers whether the Poseidon Principles SCC fall within this category, and if they do so, what are the possible outcomes concerning their enforceability in contract law.

[29] Based on multiple interviews the author conducted in 2023 with some of the representatives of the signatories of the Poseidon Principles.

[30] Moussalli and Tsekoura (n 27).

[31] Technical Guidance Version 4.1. of the Poseidon Principles, 27 June 2019, www.poseidonprinciples.org/finance/wp-content/uploads/2019/07/Poseidon_Principles.pdf.

[32] A Arda, 'Rush of Green: The Poseidon Principles' (2023) 1 *Lloyd's Shipping and Trade Law.*

[33] Document of Compliance (DOC) and Safety Management Certificate (SMC).

[34] Standard Covenant Clause (n 28).

[35] S Baughen, 'Shipping and Climate Change' in B Soyer and A Tettenborn (eds), *Disruptive Technologies, Climate Change and Shipping* (London, Informa Law from Routledge, 2022) 139.

Concerning the legal status of the SCC, it may be argued that it is an environmental covenant concerning the disclosure of relevant carbon emission data. It is fundamentally a promise to take relevant environmental action, essentially concerned with disclosing information and reporting. From a contract law perspective, 'the mechanism to enforce that promise is the suspension of a right already vested.'[36] It is true that 'conditionality offers an incentive for action by providing for financing only if the agreed action is implemented.'[37] However, not all environmental covenants are conditionalities, and the safest way to make them more effective is perhaps to include the element of conditionality into covenants.[38] Furthermore, because the SCC merely concerns the reporting and disclosure requirements from the borrower/shipowner, the direct impact of the breach of the covenant on the environmental risk avoidance of the lender bank may be difficult to assess. Rebelo argues that failure to comply 'with the requisite periodic reporting would not deprive the lender "substantially of the whole benefit" of the contract'[39] as outlined in *Hong Kong Fir Shipping v Kawasaki Kisen Kaisha*.[40] However, every financial decision may have a different underlying reason. We can take the hypothetical example of a brand-new 'green bank', 'Neptune Bank', committed to only financing green shipping companies and establishing their whole brand based on green financing. If Neptune Bank signs the Poseidon Principles intending to be 100 per cent green and motivated to make green financing its fundamental business policy, it would hypothetically be possible to argue that a possible environmental covenant contained in the loan agreement goes to the core of the contract. Accordingly, a failure to comply with such an environmental covenant may have a hugely detrimental impact on the bank's 'green branding' and reputation as its shipping portfolio would not be transparent concerning its carbon emission trajectories as initially promised as a substantial business policy. However, even in such a case, it would be safest to draft the loan agreement (including its covenants) to reflect the bank's focus on green financing.

Accordingly, the SCC may be re-drafted to give it a degree of effectiveness. It would perhaps be possible for this covenant to be restructured in a way that sets out how it may be enforced and what the available remedies are in the case of breach. As noted earlier, covenants may be in limbo as they are neither conditions nor warranties unless the impact of their breach indicates such. Thus, the safest contractual tool available is 'clear drafting.' It is true that the SCC provides a starting point. However, it is broad and ambiguous concerning the remedies available concerning its breach. An environmental covenant may be designed to enable more efficient enforcement of green policies, in particular, the Poseidon Principles in the future. Furthermore, this would also eliminate some of the concerns regarding 'whether Signatories really are committed to environmental governance standards'[41] or if they just want to be seen as 'greener'.[42]

[36] MA Bekhechi, 'Some Observations Regarding Environmental Covenants and Conditionalities in World Bank Lending Activities' (1999) 3 *Max Planck Yearbook of UN Law* 287, 296.

[37] ibid.

[38] ibid.

[39] Rebelo (n 13) 18.

[40] *Hong Kong Fir Shipping Co Ltd* (n 23).

[41] Rebelo (n 13) 7.

[42] Moussalli and Tsekoura (n 27).

B. Environmental, Social and Governance (ESG) Clauses and Market Enforcement

ESG performance has become more important in the shipping industry. Perhaps the most fundamental of these is the increasing number of regulations that shipping companies have to comply with at different stages of their ships' lifecycle.[43] Market trends and policies in international initiatives also indicate the importance of ESG. IMO targets concerning the reduction of carbon emissions are perhaps achievable but are missing the element of enforceability. The ship finance sector attaches importance to the ESG performance of potential borrowers. Consequently, shipowners are now developing relevant 'strategy plans to improve their ESG performance, which may, in turn, increase their chances to access financing and investments.'[44]

Financial enterprises and banks have started inserting various ESG clauses into their loan agreements, which evidently also include the ones concerning ship finance. These clauses generally reflect the considerations of the entities pertaining to environmental, social, and governance-related issues and their ESG targets. In this context, social considerations usually concern inequality, inclusiveness, labour relations, and human rights, whereas governance clauses generally reflect the policy aspects of the management structure, the commitment of the entity to diversity and inclusion, employee relations and so on.[45] The environmental clauses, on the other hand, usually concern 'the mitigation of climate change and adoption, the preservation of biodiversity and the prevention of pollution.'[46]

A crucial element affecting ESG clauses is the reporting requirement. Accordingly, pursuant to ESG reporting requirements, companies are expected to be transparent about the impact of their activities on the environment, commit to reducing that impact, and be accountable for the way in which they conduct their operations.[47] Furthermore, the lending entity may also insert a Corrective Action Plan (CAP) provision following an environmental incident. In this regard, it may be stipulated that the borrower is to develop a CAP in the precontracted amount of time following an environmental incident and that this be diligently pursued. Furthermore, the agreement may also contain a provision stipulating that should the CAP not be provided in the agreed time or if it be unsatisfactory because it is not diligently and timely pursued, then the lender can cancel its commitment and declare an interest/damage/penalty due and payable within the period agreed in the contract. It is particularly crucial to insert suspension and termination rights when negotiating with a counterparty unable or unwilling to commit to transparency.[48] Other clauses that potentially enforce environmental targets such as provisions 'covering remedies for breach such as climate remediation fees in which an

[43] 'Green and Sustainable Ship Finance' (Stephenson Harwood, 2022) www.esglegalhub.com/sites/default/files/pdf/Green%20and%20sustainable%20ship%20finance%20brochure.pdf.

[44] ibid.

[45] S Gunton, 'ESG Contract Clauses: Helping your business meet its ESG goals' (Harper James, 1 September 2022) harperjames.co.uk/article/esg-contract-clauses/.

[46] ibid.

[47] ibid. Also see: Proposal for a Directive of European Parliament and the Council of Corporate Sustainability Due Diligence and amending Directive (EU) 2019/1937.

[48] ibid.

agreed sum can be paid to a climate charity for breaches of the ESG commitments in the agreement'[49] should also be included. ESG clauses generally contain generic indications such as 'the company recognises the importance of environmental, social and governance factors in conducting its business operations' or 'the company is committed to integrating sustainable practices and principles into its decision-making processes and to promote environmental responsibility.' This wording attempts to make these clauses as inclusive as possible. However, enforceability is mainly a matter of contract drafting and, especially with environmental and social commitments, it may be difficult to assess and quantify damage suffered from breaches of the ESG clause. It may be said that the insertion of the CAP requirement effectuates the enforceability of the ESG clause because these clauses generally have generic indications, and the CAP necessitates the provision of a clear and corrective roadmap.

Furthermore, sustainability-linked financing has lately been an important tool for 'enforcing' green implementation to achieve the abovementioned IMO targets concerning the reduction of GHG emissions. Under this system, interest is linked to achieving sustainability goals. Accordingly, it is possible for the bank to encourage the borrower by offering improved financing provided the disclosed data concerning carbon emission is in line with the IMO's strategy. On the other hand, if the shipowner fails to comply with the predetermined trajectories, this may have repercussions for the interest rates for the loan. Accordingly, banks have some financial tools to 'enforce' environmental targets. Recently a US$ 154 million sustainability-linked secured term loan for DNB Bank ASA was made available, where the finance documentation for a fleet of ten vessels contained a number of bespoke green finance provisions, including a margin ratchet linked to sustainability key performance indicators as determined by the Poseidon Principles.[50]

From a contract law point of view, it should also be noted that the Chancery Lane Project, a collaborative initiative that creates contract clauses to incorporate into commercial agreements to meet climate goals, has developed Noah's clause, which governs green or sustainability-linked lending requirements. The clause stipulates that 'Borrowers should set sustainability-linked lending thresholds for Lenders to meet to: (i) participate in the loan; and (ii) receive the full Margin payment (or other pre-selected consequences)'.[51] Accordingly, borrowers are expected to set sustainability-linked lending thresholds under this clause to ensure lenders are aligned with the borrower's net zero values and thus it promotes greater transparency within the banking sector.'[52] Accordingly, the clause goes both ways. The 'Essential Notes and Guidance' of Noah's Clause indicates that

> The banking industry has seen an exponential increase in 'green' or sustainability-linked loans as well as bonds. These products usually focus exclusively on the climate credentials of the Borrower. Whilst these products incentivise the Borrower to improve its own eco-footprint,

[49] ibid.

[50] G Di Palma, 'DNB Bank ASA's US$154 Million Sustainability Linked Secured Term Loan' (Global Legal Chronicle, 31 January 2022) globallegalchronicle.com/dnb-bank-asas-us154-million-sustainability-linked-secured-term-loan/. The Chancery Lane Project – Noah's Clause available at chancerylaneproject.org/climate-clauses/green-or-sustainability-linked-lending-requirement/.

[51] ibid: the Chancery Lane Project.

[52] ibid.

> there is no transparency on Lender sources of funding. For example, a Lender's main source of funds might derive from the profit it makes financing the oil and gas industry. Promoting sustainable activities whilst continuing to lend to businesses with unsustainable practices and products undermines efforts to curb the effects of climate change and decrease exposure to climate-related risks in the banking industry.[53]

This clause fundamentally promotes transparency and alignment in the banking sector. It is significant because it strikes a balance between the environmental liability of the borrower as well as of the lender because it also places some burden on lenders too rather than only on borrowers concerning the achievement of decarbonisation. Noah's clause underscores that the financial sector's pivotal role in advancing decarbonisation extends beyond promoting it as a concept; it necessitates active participation of the sector in achieving environmental goals. The sector must play its part in decarbonisation and not only 'push' it.

In the context of sustainability-linked financing, the market makes it attractive to become greener by making the opposite option financially unattractive. Moreover, this affects how lenders assess the credit risk of the potential companies they are considering lending to.[54] Contemporary market practices suggest that decarbonisation necessitates the pervasive adoption of the concept of environmental liability throughout relevant sectors. One of the fundamental incentives of the ship finance sector to contractually push green-adherent commercial behaviour is the eventuality of their own environmental liability to arise. The potential for exposure to environmental liability functions is a substantial triggering mechanism to 'push green.'

IV. Incentives to Push Green Targets: Environmental Liability and Risks for Financial Institutions

Although banks do not directly contribute to practices that may degrade the natural environment, their lending practices may be linked to activities that potentially create such results, so they could be considered enablers of environmental degradation.[55] In light of their involvement in such practices, evaluating the potential risks that could affect their operation becomes necessary. It is commonplace for projects to have environmental impact and this may expose financial institutions to environmental risks that are 'direct, indirect and reputational.'[56] These risks may affect the lender's liability or may be credit-related as well as reputational.[57] The potential environmental

[53] ibid: Noah's Clause – Essential Notes and Guidance.

[54] *Green and Sustainable Ship Finance* (n 43).

[55] D Sarokin and J Schulkin, 'Environmental Concerns and the Business of Banking' (1991) 74 *Journal of Commercial Bank Lending* 6; P Thompson and CJ Cowton, 'Bringing the Environment into Bank Lending: Implications for Environmental Reporting' (2004) 36 *The British Accounting Review* 197, 199.

[56] P Thompson, 'Assessing the Environmental Risk Exposure of UK Banks' (1998) 16 *The Int'l J of Bank Marketing* 129. Also see D Campbell and R Slack, 'Environmental Disclosure and Environmental Risk: Sceptical Attitudes of UK Sell-side Bank Analysts' (2011) 43 *The British Accounting Review* 54.

[57] Y Xu, Q Liu and J Cotter, 'The Impacts of Environmental Risks on Bank Loan Covenants and the Cost of Bank Loans: An Australian Case Study and the Implications for China' (2018) *International Conference on E-Business and Applications* 3636.

liability that may be faced by financial institutions acts as a green incentive for the finance sector to push green targets.

A. Direct Risk and Lender Liability

Financial institutions may be held liable for environmental damage that occurs by virtue of activities pertaining to projects or the conduct of companies they finance. Such liability may also arise due to non-compliance with international or domestic environmental regulations. Many governments have introduced laws 'to recover from the liable parties the clean-up costs caused by pollution damages.'[58] Accordingly, the liability of banks as lenders may arise under environmental legislation in case of non-compliance, and this can take different forms. Banks may be at risk of 'direct lender liability for clean-up costs or claims for damages if they have actually taken possession of contaminated or pollution-causing property as a result of releasing security.'[59] It may even be the case in some jurisdictions that the sole act of lending funds to a project that eventually causes environmental damage leads the lender bank to incur liability for clean-up costs.[60]

The United States provides some good examples of the environmental liability of the lender. In the United States, the Comprehensive Environmental Response, Compensation and Liability Act (CERCLA) 1980 (or Superfund) establishes that parties responsible for clean-up costs that may arise from an environmental accident may include the current and former owners and operators[61] of the facility. An exemption from liability is included for secured creditors in order to avoid the possible detrimental impact of the phrase 'owners and operators' on the lending industry.[62] The exemption essentially 'precludes from liability those who hold indicia of ownership primarily to protect their security interests in a facility.'[63] The courts have generally not held a party liable for environmental damage unless that party had been involved in the day-to-day management of the relevant facility, as occurred in *United States v Mirabile*.[64] It follows that 'when a bank has been relatively closely involved in the supervision or monitoring of a firm's activities, it may be considered by the courts as an operator and therefore liable for cleaning up the damages.'[65] Accordingly, the assessment of liability may directly be influenced by the involvement of banks in supervisory monitoring activities. In *United States v Maryland Bank and Trust*,[66] the US District Court found that the bank, which held a mortgage on the property, was liable for clean-up.

[58] M Boyer and JJ Laffont, 'Environmental Risks and Bank Liability' (1997) 41 *European Economic Review* 1427.

[59] Keynote Speech by Mr D Carse, Deputy Chief Executive of the Hong Kong Monetary Authority, at the Conference on Environmental Risk Management for Hong Kong Financial Institutions, held in Hong Kong on 29 November 2000, BIS Review 108/2000. See also ibid.

[60] ibid.

[61] 42 USC § 9607(a)(1)–(4) (1988).

[62] BA Margolin, 'United States v Fleet Factors Corp: Expanding the Scope of Lender Liability' (1991) 22 *Loyola University Chicago LJ* 1139.

[63] ibid.

[64] *United States v Mirabile* 15 Envtl L Rep (Envtl. L. Inst.) 20994 (ED Pa 1985).

[65] Also see: Boyer and Laffont (n 58) 1428.

[66] *United States v Maryland Bank & Trust Co* 632 F Supp 573 (D Md 1986).

At the time pollution was discovered, the bank was the owner of the facility that it had purchased at the foreclosure sale. Accordingly, one may argue that 'courts were reluctant to hold a party liable for environmental response costs unless that party had participated in the day-to-day management of the facility or had foreclosed on the property'.[67] However, eventually, the provisions of CERCLA started to be interpreted much more broadly to impose widespread liability for the costs of cleaning up.[68] In *United States v Fleet Factors Corp*[69] the bank was found liable for clean-up costs because its participation in the firm's financial management gave it the ability to influence the overall management regardless of the bank not being involved in the operations of the firm. Accordingly, the secured creditor could be held liable for decontamination costs if they 'participated in the management of the facility to a degree indicating a "capacity to influence" waste management decisions regardless of whether the creditor actually exercised this capacity'.[70] The court rejected the argument that a creditor must have been involved in the day-to-day management of the facility.[71]

Banks play a crucial role in financing economic activity that is environmentally accountable. Therefore, the interpretation of the courts' decisions concerning the liability of banks in assessing the overall liability for environmental damage in the light of *Fleet Factors* is unlikely to be a very restricted one. This decision 'greatly expanded potential lender liability'.[72] Although what the 'potential of influencing' truly consists of may be considered ambiguous[73] and 'not all courts agreed to follow this',[74] the consideration of the court was that the involvement of the lender in the financial management of the facility was 'pervasive, if not complete'.[75] To put it differently, the elements that trigger environmental liability may realistically be assessed quite broadly. In response to the potential for such a broad assessment, the attitude of the banks has moved significantly towards a cautious approach. Following *Fleet Factors*, US bank surveys have illustrated

> that banks had changed their lending policies in an attempt to avoid environmental lending liability and commercial loan transactions were undergoing environmental assessment. As a result of such changes some banks have rejected loan applications and discontinued financing 'dirty' industrial sectors such as chemicals processors.[76]

Moreover, the decision has sent 'shock waves through the banking community',[77] and its impact was reflected in a worldwide survey on banks conducted in 1995.[78]

[67] Margolin (n 62) 1139.

[68] C Rashby, 'United States v Maryland Bank & Trust Co: Lender Liability under CIRCLA' (1987) 14 *Ecology Law Quarterly* 569.

[69] ('Fleet Factors') 901 F2d 1550 (11th Cir 1990).

[70] Margolin (n 62) 1140.

[71] ibid.

[72] R Plato-Shinar and M Gelpe, 'Lender's Liability for Environmental Damages in the Absence of Statutory Regulation – Lessons from the Israeli Model: Part I' (2011) 5 *Law and Financial Markets Review* 367, 369.

[73] ibid 370. Even though there is some inconsistency regarding how this decision is interpreted by the courts, it is generally expected to be evaluated from a broader perspective rather than a restricted one.

[74] See the discussion in *In re Cuyahoga Equip Corp* 980 F2d 110, 118–19 (2nd Cir 1992).

[75] *Fleet Factors* (n 69) 1559.

[76] AB Coulson and V Monks, 'Corporate Environmental Performance Considerations within Bank Lending Decisions' (1999) 6 *Eco-Management and Auditing* 1, 4.

[77] R Gray and J Bebbington, *Accounting for the Environment* (London, Sage Publications, 2001).

[78] United Nations Environment Programme (UNEP) 1995 Survey of Environmental Policies and Practices of the Financial Services Sector.

It revealed that most banks considered environmental issues as influential in their businesses and accordingly were increasingly taking environmental risks into consideration.[79] Although the decision itself was considered ambiguous by some and thus the application of CERCLA has eventually been slightly clarified,[80] especially in light of the impact it created at an international level, *Fleet Factors* is one of the touchstones for wider interpretation and allocation of environmental liability.

At first, environmental liability was limited to the self-protection of financial institutions concerning their lending practices and business conduct. A study in 2004 illustrated the banks' interest in environmental information released by companies that are seeking loans.[81] Another study in 2002 indicated that only alternative or environmentally oriented banks integrated sustainability goals into their business policy and conduct.[82] Because banks have generally not been interested in becoming 'the environmental police',[83] the impact of environmental protection on their business conduct was limited to procuring the information that could either potentially trigger their environmental liability or release them from such. In the past, financial institutions were mainly interested in circumnavigating environmental liability rather than internalising the concept. However, we are now in an era where the internalisation of environmental concerns is ineluctable, and the interpretation of environmental liability is inevitably broader. Accordingly, financial institutions are increasingly leaning towards becoming more environmentally oriented and including environmental targets in their business strategies.

The broader interpretation of environmental liability illustrated in *Fleet Factors* should pave the way for a broader evaluation of what triggers such liability. Does pollution solely trigger it or could we consider it inclusive of conduct creating pollution-like results? From the shipping perspective, we may perhaps link the environmental liability of the lender for direct risk that potentially arises as a result of pollution with the position of the ship financer concerning carbon emissions. Although carbon dioxide is not considered an air pollutant, its concentration in the atmosphere has increased alarmingly due to human activity. Accordingly, regardless of whether or not it is a pollutant, the impact of carbon dioxide released in abnormal quantities creates results that may be perceived as much more devastating than environmental pollution itself. In line with this, it may not be very difficult to re-evaluate why accountability for environmental protection and liability is needed in the first place and why their contemporary evaluation should not be restricted to environmental pollution.

[79] O Elsakit and A Worthington, 'Using Environmental and Social Information in Lending Decisions' (2013) 5 *International J of Economics and Finance* 112, 114.

[80] Coulson and Monks (n 76) 4: 'Today the US situation has been clarified considerably by the CERCLA reform bills and the Asset Conservation, Lender Liability, and Deposit of Insurance Protection Act 1996. Under the new Act lenders may take specified actions concerning contaminated property on which they hold security interest without triggering CERCLA liability. It has been noted that the new law is not perfect but is a considerable step forward.'

[81] Thompson and Cowton (n 55).

[82] O Weber, R Reiland and B Weber, 'Sustainability Benchmarking of European Banks and Financial Service Organizations' (2002) ETH Zurich Working Paper/UNS 34.

[83] Carse (n 59).

B. Indirect Risk and Credit

The economic and environmental risks of the debtor regarding the sustainability aspect of its conduct may affect the lender's environmental or sustainability practices.[84] In other words, the environmental risks may also create a domino effect on the credit risk and may eventually lead to loan defaults. Such 'counterparty credit risks'[85] constitute an element of banks' environmental (or sustainability-related) risks. The potential for the impairment of loans because of the polluting activity of borrowers ultimately constitutes the 'indirect risk' of financial institutions.

The borrower's ability to repay a loan may be restricted due to a decline in the borrower's capital stock or its earning as well as liquidity and these factors may influence the credit risk of the bank.[86] For instance, the restriction (or disability) may be due to the 'increased costs of prescribed investments into environmental technologies.'[87] Putting it differently, environmental regulations may rightfully impose green investments on entities that happen to be the borrowers of banks and may 'decrease the debtor's liquidity and therefore the ability to repay the loan.'[88] The credit risk is impacted

> by the growing body of restrictive environmental regulations imposed on borrowing companies which weakens their position to repay loans, whilst security offered in the form of real property can mean impaired value of collateral and salability if non-compliance occurs.[89]

In other words, if the property held as collateral is 'environmentally contaminated, banks will suffer lower security from the impaired value and salability of the collateral'[90] because this would impair the ability of the borrower to repay loans. Furthermore, 'the costs of meeting new requirements on emission levels may be sufficient to put some companies out of business'[91] if they fail to comply with some contemporary environmental regulations.

In the past, a substantial amount of research on environmental credit risks was linked to real estate collateral, and predominantly concerned the rating phase of the credit risk management process.[92] Where the lender fails to calculate the potential risk accurately (perhaps due to not checking the property properly or not taking all necessary factors into account), the calculated value may not reflect the market value in case of environmental contamination. The assessed interest rate should ideally reflect the different sources of risk for the lender and borrower's financial leverage position.[93] Evaluation of the borrower's operations for environmental concerns may produce the following results:

[84] O Weber, RW Scholz and G Michalik, 'Incorporating Sustainability Criteria into Credit Risk Management' (2010) *Business Strategy and the Environment* 19, 39–50, 39.

[85] S Scandizzo, 'Counterparty Credit Risk Models' in S Scandizzo (ed), *The Validation of Risk Models: A Handbook for Practitioners* (London, Palgrave Macmillan, 2016).

[86] Weber et al (n 84) 40.

[87] ibid 41.

[88] ibid.

[89] Rebelo (n 13) 9.

[90] Xu et al (n 57) 36.

[91] Carse (n 59), Boyer and Laffont (n 58).

[92] MJ Billiot and ZW Daughtrey, 'Evaluating Environmental Liability through Risk Premiums Charged on Loans' (2001) 17(2) *Agribusiness* 177.

[93] ibid 276.

> The lender may choose to terminate the transaction; environmental problems (current or potential) that can be remedied may be corrected and the loan transaction continues; and/or potential environmental risks that are low-level and controllable may be incorporated into the terms of the loan.[94]

It is safe to say that contemporary environmental factors, as well as the types of properties pertaining to the evaluation of credit risk assessment, are now very varied. In the modern context, the common factors that can influence the assessment of credit risk are predominantly:

- Greenhouse gas (GHG) emissions: Gases released by burning fossil fuels and clearcutting forests as part of a business activity.
- Pollution and waste: Plastics, radioactive waste, and other contaminants produced.
- Biodiversity, water, and land use: The variety of lives and resources impacted by a business activity in a particular habitat or ecosystem.
- Natural conditions: Exposure to floods, hurricanes, earthquakes, and other adverse weather conditions.[95]

It may also be said that, in light of the IMO's recent shipping targets and the increasing interest of the financial authorities in understanding and quantifying environmental risks, research on the evaluation of the credit risk assessment of properties may not be limited to real estate.

It is possible to categorise environmental risk as 'sustainability risk.' The sustainability risk as defined by Weber et al is:

> the uncertainty about the future outcome of loans for a lender emerging from environmental, economic and social sustainability risks of a firm being a borrower, could influence its economic performance, i.e. its solvency or future earnings. This risk is transferred to the lender who has to rate and manage the risk. Thus if the lender does not identify these sustainability risks, or rates these risks incorrectly, his credit decision possibly does not reflect the real risk of the credit.[96]

Accordingly, environmental risk may also substantially impact economic performance and the allocation of risks. Furthermore, these risks should be carefully identified by the banks because when not necessarily scrutinised or understood, the increased risk that may potentially arise could have a pervasive effect and create a credit crisis.[97]

Another significant issue concerning the indirect/credit risk of the lender is the potential lack of confidence and reputational damage that may arise. If credit impairment occurs due to insufficient planning of risk allocation and management on the part of the financial institution, this would inevitably reflect negatively on the confidence of the debtors in the bank and consequently harm the institution's reputation.

[94] ibid.

[95] M Sindaco, 'The Evolution of ESG Factors in Credit Risk Assessment Environmental Issues' (S&P Global Market Intelligence, 19 February 2021) www.spglobal.com/marketintelligence/en/news-insights/blog/the-evolution-of-esg-factors-in-credit-risk-assessment-environmental-issues..

[96] Weber et al (n 84) 41.

[97] A Saunders and L Allen, *Credit Risk Measurement In and Out of the Financial Crisis: New Approaches to Value at Risk and Other Paradigms*, 3rd edn (Hoboken, John Wiley & Sons, 2010).

C. Reputational Risk and Social Capital

The overall capital that companies rely on consists of 'social capital' alongside economic capital, which is obtained through financial institutions and investors.[98] Woolcock defines social capital as '... a broad term encompassing the norms and networks facilitating collective action for mutual benefit.'[99] In the business context, social capital may have as important a value as economic capital.[100] However, the method of its procurement is less tangible than that of economic capital. The former fundamentally consists of how the company is perceived by society, its brand value, and the strength of its relationship with the community.[101] Thus, 'it is forged slowly over time through positive interactions with stakeholders, but maybe quickly lost when it is broken.'[102]

The reputation of financial institutions is usually directly correlated with the putative precondition of 'green abidance' in contemporary business practice. Environmental concerns produce their own reputational and hence, financial risks, because such a public requirement of green abidance is not merely relevant to 'those involved in fossil fuel production or deforestation' but 'any business with a public profile should now expect to be held accountable for its impact on the environment.'[103] Thus, the environmental risk may affect the public image of the bank and its long-term viability.[104] This is particularly important nowadays as establishing a green image for companies is becoming more crucial for stakeholders, in view of the visible detrimental impacts of climate change. The public is increasingly interested in corporate accountability for climate change. Financial entities generally do not want to be associated with polluters and attract public criticism.

Reputational risk can arise rapidly, and financial institutions may face problems where they finance projects perceived as controversial by stakeholders or companies widely known to be associated with polluting activities. Thus, 'institutions may wish to adopt policies related to engagement with clients and response to controversies, as and when they arise. Institutions may consider periodically screening counterparties for controversial activities, conducting environmental footprinting and/or damage cost exercises to identify potential pockets of risk. They should reflect the outcomes of such screening exercises in the relevant risk reports.'[105] Furthermore, the reputational risk concerning the environment also evidently exists for entities involved in 'environmental controversies' in which they 'are perceived not to take due consideration

[98] P Hohnen, 'Corporate Social Responsibility – An Implementation Guide for Business' in Jason Potts (ed) (International Institute for Sustainable Development, 2007) 77.

[99] M Woolcock, 'Social Capital and Economic Development: Toward a Theoretical Synthesis and Policy Framework' (1998) 27 *Theory and Society* 151, 155.

[100] Hohnen (n 98) 77.

[101] ibid.

[102] ibid.

[103] T Rudkin, 'When Things get Heated: Managing Climate Change Risk and Reputation for Business' (Ferrer & Co, 19 September 2019) www.farrer.co.uk/news-and-insights/when-things-get-heated-managing-climate-change-risk-and-reputation-for-businesses/..

[104] K Smith, M Smith and K Wang, 'Does Brand Management of Corporate Reputation Translate Into Higher Market Value?' (2010) 18 *J of Strategic Marketing* 201.

[105] Guide on Climate-related and Environmental Risks – Supervisory Expectations Relating to Risk Management and Disclosure (European Central Bank, November 2020) 40, www.bankingsupervision.europa.eu/ecb/pub/pdf/ssm.202011finalguideonclimate-relatedandenvironmentalrisks~58213f6564.en.pdf.

of environmental aspects in their business activities.'[106] Thus, as indicated above, the risk does not merely derive from being directly involved in polluting activities such as fossil fuel production or deforestation anymore,[107] but may simply arise due to not taking 'reasonable and expectable green steps' if the environmental impact of their business conduct could have been minimised. Therefore, reputational risk now has an even stronger correlation with environmental risk and liability and the concept should be evaluated more broadly.

This brings us back to the evaluation of the public role of the banks in achieving mutual environmental targets. Despite possibly not being directly associated with activities that potentially create environmental damage, banks may be seen as enablers of such damage because they finance the polluter who caused the damage. The commercial decisions that banks make will play an essential role in ensuring the shipping sector meets the recently revised IMO targets. Accordingly, financial institutions have both the incentive to include a substantial amount of green conditionality in their lending decisions and the potential to contractually push environmental targets.

V. Conclusions

The preceding discussion has demonstrated the legal tools that may effectuate the achievement of environmental targets in the shipping sector. These are reflected in the relevant contracts that govern shipping and ship finance. The IMO has established indexes and plans to abide by in order to achieve its targets. These fundamentally affect the drafting of ship management and ship design contracts and charterparties and other relevant contracts. The fundamental considerations in drafting these contracts mainly concern the allocation of responsibility, risk, and cost of compliance with the requirement for achieving green targets. Furthermore, there are international requirements regarding the collection of data concerning the fuel consumption of ships. This is directly correlated with the Poseidon Principles, which are produced as a set of private governance tools to be implemented by its signatory financial organisations when funding shipping. The Poseidon Principles stipulate that financial organisations must look through a 'green lens' when making business decisions and align their ship finance portfolios with responsible environmental behaviour to achieve green targets.

The ship finance sector holds the key to 'funding decarbonisation' as this sector has the power to assess the level of how vigorously decarbonisation targets may be imposed. The sector also has a great interest in imposing green targets because financial institutions may themselves be exposed to environmental liability in different forms. Despite not directly contributing to practices that may potentially create environmental damage, they may be perceived as facilitators of such damage if they fund the project or the debtor that gives rise to environmental contamination and pollution. Accordingly, financial institutions may be subject to environmental risks that are direct, indirect, or reputational. In certain jurisdictions, the liability of financial

[106] ibid 39.
[107] Rudkin (n 103).

organisations may arise directly by virtue of being lenders for the project or the party causing environmental damage. They may be liable for clean-up costs. The risk may also be about credit as environmental damage may create a domino effect affecting credit rating and may eventually cause loan defaults. Another risk financial institutions may be subject to pertains to the social capital of the institution and its reputation. The slowly forged reputation and public approval of not only financial organisations but of any entity in the contemporary context directly correlates with the putative precondition of 'green abidance' in business practice and conduct. Thus, banks have a major public role in funding decarbonisation, and they also have a great interest in facilitating the achievement of green targets as they are subject to environmental risks that they need to assess and manage effectively. However, the pervasiveness of the achievement of green targets majorly depends on how the financial institutions perceive the substance and the fundamental reasons for their establishment. If these are truly perceived as solid targets that are not just 'crowd-pleasers', then there are contractual instruments to actually enforce their achievement. The key here is the 'willingness to push green.'

Where there is a will, there is a way. Fortunately, legal tools are available to push green targets, and these may easily be implemented. As indicated, financial institutions hold the key to funding decarbonisation, and they may reflect green concerns in their contracts. In the ship finance sector, loan agreements usually include covenants that promote compliance with particular provisions of the agreement. Furthermore, the Poseidon Principles also include a Standard Covenant Clause (SCC). However, there are some problems with the effectiveness of this clause. The incorporation of the SCC is 'strongly recommended' and, thus, not compulsory. The confidentiality of the data on fuel consumption of vessels also impairs its effective implementation.

Moreover, it is unclear what remedies exist if the SCC is breached. Thus, at the end of the day, the financial institution decides how environmentally impactful their contracts will be, and this may be achieved by enhancing and clarifying the remedies that may be available following the possible breach of the SCC. Furthermore, for a better implementation of the clause, the issue regarding the confidentiality of data could also be clarified, and it could be drafted in a more demanding way than it currently is. Ultimately, it will be the decision of the parties to get into this contract or not. Besides the potential enhancement of the SCC, there are also Environmental, Social, and Governance (ESG) Clauses that substantially reflect environmental concerns. ESG performance has become increasingly significant in the shipping sector, especially in light of the established IMO decarbonisation targets. Accordingly, a well-drafted ESG clause that clearly indicates the reporting and corrective action plan requirements as well as the available remedies that may be resorted to, would give the desired 'greenisation' a boost that fundamentally derives from its 'enforceability'. Consequently, if environmental targets really go beyond being mere 'crowd-pleasers', it is irrefutable that the inclusion of enforceability into the equation is vital and financial institutions hold the key to decarbonisation as they have the power to push green targets through their contracts and business decisions.

11

Climate Change Litigation in the Maritime Sector as Enforcement Mechanism?

VIBE ULFBECK* AND MAXIM USYNIN**

I. Setting the Scene

Climate change litigation originated in the US but over the past years several suits have been brought in Europe, in particular against European governments.[1] The cases take many shapes and some of them have the direct goal of forcing governments to make more ambitious carbon reduction strategies.[2] In this regard, the big breakthrough in Europe came with the Dutch Urgenda ruling from December 2019.[3] In this case, brought by the NGO, Urgenda, against the Dutch state, the Dutch Supreme Court found the basis for such claim in human rights law. More precisely, it found that Articles 2 and 8 ECHR should be interpreted in such a way that these provisions oblige the contracting states to do 'their part' to counter the danger of climate change[4] and that the Dutch

* Professor, Head of Centre for Private Governance (CEPRI), Head of Shipping and Ocean Law Group (SHOC), Faculty of Law, University of Copenhagen.

** Tenure Track Assistant Professor, CEPRI, Faculty of Law, University of Copenhagen.

[1] Parts of this chapter are based on V Ulfbeck, 'Climate Change in Tort Law? – the New Regulatory and External Effects of Suits Against Private Actors' in A Beckers et al, *The Foundations of European Transnational Private Law* (Oxford, Hart Publishing, 2024). An updated overview of various types of climate change litigation in different jurisdictions can be found in F Sindico and MM Mbengue (eds), *Comparative Climate Change Litigation: Beyond the Usual Suspects* (Cham, Springer, 2021). For an overview of European climate change suits against states, see also Cleary Gottlieb, Alert Memorandum – Climate Claims against governments in Europe (2021), www.clearygottlieb.com/-/media/files/alert-memos-2021/climate-change-litigation-in-europe-increasing-judicial-scrutiny-over-state-climate-policies.pdf.

[2] Other cases have concerned the public authority duty to take into consideration climate aspects when granting permissions and licences, see for instance the UK case *R (on the application of Friends of the Earth Ltd) v Secretary of State for Transport (Heathrow Airport Ltd)* [2021] UKSC 52, [2021] 2 All ER 967, and in general M Spitzer and B Burtscher, 'Liability for Climate Change: Cases, Challenges and Concepts' (2017) 8 *J of European Tort L* 137, 141–142, categorising these cases as more 'ordinary', 'bread and butter' cases. In a recent Norwegian case, the Supreme Court found that granting an oil exploitation licence did not violate the Norwegian Constitution: see E Columbo, 'Climate Change and the Individual: a Norwegian Perspective' in Sindico, ibid 91; 97.

[3] Hohe Raad 20 December 2019, ECLI:NLHR:2019:2006, unofficial English translation ECLI:NL:HR 2019:2007.

[4] *Urgenda* (n 3) legal ground 5.8.

state was obliged to achieve a reduction of at least 25 per cent of its carbon emissions by 2020.[5] The court furthermore combined the duty found in human rights law with an injunction and ordered the state to adjust its legislation to achieve this goal.[6] The case is regarded a breakthrough in establishing the link between climate change and human rights[7] and as an example of a case that, from a public law perspective, demonstrates that courts can play a role in this area without acting as a legislator in disguise that oversteps the boundaries of the judiciary.[8] As such, the case has been a source of inspiration for a number of parallel suits in Europe over the past years.[9]

Whereas the ultimate goal of a suit against a state is to make it enact legislation that will change the behaviour of its subjects, including companies, one might also ask whether suits could simply be brought – more efficiently – directly against these companies forcing them to reduce carbon emissions. With 90 major private carbon emitters being responsible for over 30 per cent of global industrial greenhouse emissions,[10] one might think they should be an obvious target.

Whereas international treaties and human rights obligations can form the basis of claims against states, these frameworks are not binding on private parties. This brings tort law into play. And in fact, tort lawsuits against private actors have also emerged in Europe, to some extent inspired by *Urgenda*, which at District court level *did* rely on tort law in establishing the basis for the imposition of reduction requirements.[11]

So far, climate change suits against private parties have primarily been targeting big oil companies, the so called 'carbon majors'. However, recently, also other types of companies have been sued.[12] It has been estimated that the top four dominant European shipping companies are responsible for 1–2 per cent of the global GHGs[13] and it is

[5] ibid legal ground 8.3.5.

[6] ibid legal ground 8.2.1: 'If the government is obliged to do something, it may be ordered to do so by the courts, as anyone may be, at the request of the entitled party' (Art 3:296 DCC).

[7] For an early analysis of this relation, see A Gouritin, 'Potential liability of European States under the ECHR for failure to take appropriate measures with a view to adaptation to climate change' in M Faure and M Peeters (eds), *Climate Change Liability* (Cheltenham, Edward Elgar, 2011) 134.

[8] The court itself found that it had not overstepped its boundaries because it had not decided on the specific content of the legislation to be enacted: *Urgenda* (n 3) legal ground 8.2.6. See further, J Spier, 'The "Strongest" Climate Ruling Yet': The Dutch Supreme Court's *Urgenda* Judgment (2020) 67 *Netherlands Int'l LR* (2020) 319, 334.

[9] For instance, in Belgium, the Brussels Court of First Instance has ruled that based on the general tort law duty of care principle in the Belgium Civil Code Arts 1382 and 1383 as well as human rights obligations, the Belgian Government is obliged to take measures to meet more ambitious reduction targets in 2025, 2030 and 2050: see *VZW Klimaatzaak v Kingdom of Belgium* no. 2015/4585/A (June 17, 2021). The German Constitutional Court has found that the German constitution obliges the State to protect the climate and aim at climate neutrality: see *BVerfG, Beschluss des Ersten Senats vom* 24. März 2021–1 BvR 2656/18 – Rn. 1-270, see www.bundesverfassungsgericht.de/e/rs20210324_1bvr265618.html.

[10] R Heede, 'Tracing Anthropogenic Carbon Dioxide and Methane Emissions to Fossil Fuel and Cement Producers, 1854–2010' (2014) 12 *Climatic Change* 229.

[11] The District Court had originally found that the Dutch state breached its tort law duty of care under Art 6:162 towards the Dutch people by not having a sufficiently ambitious carbon reduction policy when measured against the scientific IPCC reports: *Urgenda* (n 3) legal ground 2.3.1.

[12] See Study from June 2023: www.lse.ac.uk/granthaminstitute/wp-content/uploads/2023/05/working-paper-397_-Sato-Gostlow-Higham-Setzer-Venmans.pdf.

[13] E McGaughey, 'Liability for Climate Damage and Shipping' in S Baughen, 'Shipping and Climate Change' in B Soyer, A Tettenborn and S Baughen (eds), *Disruptive Technologies, Climate Change and Shipping* (London, Informa Law from Routledge, 2022) 194, 199.

foreseen that suits in the shipping sector might also occur.[14] Shipping companies involved in the oil trade may be particularly vulnerable because of the ties to the fossil industry.[15] Such suits might function as a form of private enforcement of the regulatory carbon measures that lack (strong) public enforcement mechanisms.

This chapter starts out by giving an overview of the reasoning behind the climate change litigation brought against private actors and reflects on the extent to which the reasoning could be transferred to shipping companies. In section II, the classical tort law suits are described. In section III, the focus is on a new type of preventive tort law claims. In section IV, another new 'regulatory' type of tort law claim is described. Section V focuses on climate change litigation in the context of shipping companies as forming parts of value chains, and finally section VI reflects on the role of the IMO in the context of climate change litigation. Section VII concludes.

II. First Stage Strategy: Traditional Backward-looking Claims for Compensation for Damage

Some of the first tort law climate change claims brought against private parties were classical tort law claims for damages for loss allegedly suffered by climate change phenomena partially caused by private actors.

In *Comer v Murphy Oil*,[16] it was claimed that emitting activities of the energy companies had reinforced the consequences of the Katrina hurricane eventually leading to the loss of the home of the plaintiff. In *Kavalina v ExxonMobil Corporation*,[17] peoples from Alaska claimed that energy companies were responsible for transboundary GHG emissions leading to coastal erosion and melting Arctic ice and eventually displacement and relocation since the village was threatened. Both cases were basic tort law cases in which the plaintiffs claimed compensation for property loss and economic loss.[18]

From a tort law perspective, such suits face several challenges. In the concrete cases, the claims were dismissed by the district US courts on the basis of the 'political question doctrine', namely that the cases raised political questions which it was not for the courts but rather for the legislator to deal with.[19] In a European context, the political question doctrine may also pose barriers albeit perhaps to a somewhat lesser degree.[20] However, there are other problems.

A basis of liability must be established. Strict liability may to some extent be available, notably under the tort of nuisance in Anglo-American law[21] but the most general

[14] See eg shippingwatch.com/regulation/article13011039.ece.

[15] See www.ics-shipping.org/news-item/climate-law-poses-new-emerging-challenge-for-ship-owners/.

[16] *Comer v Murphy Oil USA Inc* 607 F.3d 1049 (5th Cir 2010).

[17] *Kavalina v ExxonMobil Corporation* 696 F.3d 849 (9th Cir 2012).

[18] The claims very brought in the areas of nuisance, civil conspiracy and negligence.

[19] At the appellate level, *Comer* was eventually dismissed. In *Kivalina*, it was held that federal legislation pre-empted the plaintiff's federal common law claims. See in general, G Ganguly, J Setzer and V Heyvaert, 'If at First You Don't Succeed: Suing Corporations for Climate Change' (2018) 38 *OJLS* 841, 849.

[20] See further below, section VII.

[21] See further below, section IV. Also the EU Environmental Liability Directive, Directive 2004/35/CE of the European Parliament and of the Council of 21 April 2004 on environmental liability with regard to the

and universally recognised principle of liability is the tort of negligence or 'fault based' liability.[22] Moreover, with regard to professionals, it is widely accepted that liability is 'objectivised'.[23] This means that with regard to large GHG emitters the basic question is whether the company by its activity has infringed any generally accepted standards of behaviour. Here, it can be noted that throughout the years, no laws have prohibited carbon major activity. On the contrary, carbon majors often provide products of crucial importance to society, such as energy and transport. Moreover, in identifying the generally accepted standards of behaviour, it is the general view that public law rules and standards may to some extent play a role.[24] With regard to carbon emissions, one of the main points of discussion has been the question of the possible impact of the European Emissions Trading Systems (ETS)[25] in which the shipping sector is now included. In the literature, opinions differ on the implications of the ETS for the liability assessment. Some argue that a company that does not exceed the allowed amount of emissions under this scheme cannot be held liable.[26] Others find that observing the level of the ETS system is no guarantee against liability and that likewise the fact that a company stays within the carbon emissions limits in a licence cannot by definition rule out tort liability.[27] Similarly, it has recently been argued that complying with the new IMO energy efficiency measures is not necessarily a protection against climate change liability, in particular if the IMO strategy is considered insufficient, as is often pointed out.[28] In general, however, it must be assumed that a company which does not comply with the new regulations will be more exposed to suits than one which does.

Since an objectified approach to the establishing of a basis of liability for big corporations must be assumed, it must also be assumed that courts will focus on the question of when it could *generally* be expected that such companies would have knowledge about the climate change effects of their activities. Consequently, one might need to

prevention and remedying of environmental damage, could be considered as a basis of liability. However, it is generally thought not to be a suitable basis for claims concerning carbon emissions for which it was not designed: see eg M Hinteregger, 'Civil Liability and the Challenges of Climate Change: A Functional Analysis' (2017) *J of European Tort L* 238, 251.

[22] Reflected in Principles of European Tort Law (PETL), Art 4.101. In some jurisdictions, the notion of fault is explicitly split into two parts, an objective one, requiring unlawfulness or wrongfulness of the act, and a subjective one, requiring blameworthiness of the concrete actor. Even if these two parts of the notion of fault are not explicit, they are generally understood to frame the concept of 'fault', see Hinteregger (n 21) 251, referring to France and Spain as examples of the latter model. For the comparable Scandinavian model, see eg B von Eyben and H Isager, *Lærebog i Erstatningsret* (DJOEF, 2019) 96.

[23] See eg Hinteregger (n 21) 251.

[24] Reflected in PETL, Art 4.102(3): Rules which prescribe or forbid a certain conduct have to be considered when establishing the required standard of conduct.

[25] The carbon trading system allows companies to emit a certain amount of carbon per year and trade unused amounts. The system is regulated in Directive 2003/87/EC of the European Parliament and of the Council of 13 October 2003 establishing a system for greenhouse gas emission allowance trading within the Union and amending Council Directive 96/61/EC, with further amendments to include the shipping sector.

[26] Spitzer and Burtscher (n 2) 162–164; C van Dijk, 'Civil liability for Global Warming in the Netherlands' in Faure and Peeters (n 7) 206, 215; Phon van den Biesen, 'Will Civil Society Take Climate Changers to Court?' in Faure and Peeters (n 7) 227, 234.

[27] Hinteregger (n 21) 254; Ulrich Magnus, 'Injunctions against Climate Change?' in OC Ruppel, C Roschmann and K Ruppel-Schlichting (eds), *Climate change: International Law and Global Governance*, vol 1 (Baden-Baden, Nomos Verlagsgesellsschaft mbH, 2013) 851.

[28] See www.ics-shipping.org/news-item/climate-law-poses-new-emerging-challenge-for-ship-owners/.

distinguish between 'innocent' emissions, predating (general awareness of) the climate crisis and 'guilty' emissions.[29]

Furthermore, in a classical tort law case, the plaintiff also has to document a loss. Here, climate change litigants face the challenge that whereas it is entirely foreseeable that climate change will cause losses in the future, as a starting point, only losses already suffered can be the object of a tort law claim.

Finally, one of the most basic challenges faced by tort law climate change litigation, is the requirement of proof of a causal link between the suffered loss and the negligent act. The general test for causation is the *conditio sine qua non* test, also called the 'but for' test. According to this test, the tortfeasor's act or omission is only the cause of a certain loss, if the loss would not have happened had it not been for the act or omission of the tortfeasor. This test has posed a basic challenge to climate change tort claims. Representative of these challenges is the formulation by the court in *Kivalina*, that there was 'no realistic possibility of tracing any particular alleged effect of global warming to any particular emissions by any specific person, entity, [or] group at any particular point in time'. Although some exceptions to the 'but-for' test have been developed, these are not widely used. In climate change tort cases, the principle that would be most helpful for plaintiffs is the principle of proportional liability.[30] The principle comes in different versions[31] and has been designed inter alia for situations in which a large number of actors each have delivered a small contribution to causing the damage (minimal causation). In this situation, it would be unjust to apply the principle of joint and several liability and hold each contributor liable for the entire loss. Rather each contributor should be held liable for a part of the loss proportionate to its contribution.[32] Although this legal principle has some support in doctrine, there has been a limited amount of case law to support it.[33]

Despite the legal hurdles to overcome, this type of litigation with its focus on damages and its expected deterrent effect was originally praised as a potential 'magic bullet' in climate change litigation.[34] However, the backward looking perspective in the classical tort law suit and the need to prove causation between a specific act and a specific loss, in reality makes this type of tort law suit less effective as a tool for achieving behavioural change.[35] This would also apply should such suits be attempted in the maritime sector.

[29] Spitzer and Burtscher (n 2) 167.

[30] See I Gilead, M Green and B Koch (eds), *Proportional Liability: Analytical and Comparative Perspectives* (Berlin, De Gruyter, 2013).

[31] Gilead et al (n 30), PETL Arts 3:103, 3:105, 3:106. For English law, see also *Barker v Corus UK Ltd* [2006] UKHL 20, [2006] 2 AC 572. On its potential application in maritime climate change suits, MacGaughey (n 13) 203.

[32] Hinteregger (n 21) 256.

[33] B Koch, 'Minimal Causation – Comparative Report' in B Winiger, H Koziol, B Koch and R Zimmermann, *Essential Cases on Natural Causation* (Wien, Springer, 2007) 541–543.

[34] Shi-Ling Hsu, 'A Realistic Evaluation of Climate Change litigation through the lens of a Hypothetical Lawsuit' (2008) 79(3) *Columbia LR* 701, 714.

[35] For this view, see also Spier (n 8) 48.

III. Second Stage Strategy: Forward Looking, Preventive Claims

In Europe, climate change litigation against private actors took off following the Heede study in 2014.[36] The study provided a better scientific basis for claiming that emissions to a very large extent originate from large carbon emitters (the so-called 'Major Carbons) and pinpointing when these emissions have taken place.[37] The study also calculates which percentage of the emissions has been emitted into the atmosphere by concrete private actors.[38]

It is characteristic for the cases in this category that they are not concerned with damage that has already been caused. Rather, the cases are forward looking, giving tort law a stronger regulatory role. The goal is to achieve monetary compensation for costs to cover foreseen necessary preventive measures against the consequences of climate change. As explained above, the forward-looking aspect poses a basic challenge for tort law. Although liability for preventive costs has been suggested in PETL,[39] it is not the general rule in most legal systems.[40] Thus, normally, tort law only comes into play as a compensatory mechanism when actual loss has been suffered. This is articulated clearly by Pieter Gillaerts: 'Tort law remains compensatory. With no loss, no claim'.[41] In the maritime sector an exception to this rule has long been recognised. Thus, in the case of oil pollution, the Civil Liability Convention (1992) provides for compensation for preventive measures.[42] However, this rule only applies where oil pollution has already happened and would not be relevant for climate change suits. Yet, as will be explained below, tort law does manage to play a role in climate cases concerning preventive measures, in some legal systems more indirectly, and in others more directly.

The most spectacular case in this category is the German case *Lliuya v RWE*,[43] initiated in 2015 and still pending. In this case, a Peruvian farmer sued RWE, Germany's largest electricity producer, claiming payment of US$ 21,000 dollars to partly cover expenses in securing his house against the risk of flooding. The risk stemmed from the glacial lake, Lake Palcacocha, located above the city in which the plaintiff's house was located, and which was threatening to overflow due to rising water levels or glacial ice avalanches. It was argued that RWE was partly responsible for this situation through the greenhouse gas emissions produced by itself and its subsidiaries over which RWE,

[36] Heede (n 10) 229.

[37] More specifically it is said to document that 90 Carbon Majors released more than half of their total contribution after 1988, Ganguly et al (n 19) 853.

[38] ibid 854.

[39] See Principles of European Tort Law (PETL) Art 2:104: 'Expenses incurred to prevent threatened damage amount to recoverable damage insofar as reasonably incurred'.

[40] In French law, the new Art 1251 in the Code Civil takes preventive costs into account as an item of loss. It states that the expenses made to prevent the imminent realisation of damage, in order to avoid the aggravation of damage or in order to reduce the effects, constitute an item of loss for which compensation can be claimed). Art 1251 reads (in French): 'Les dépenses exposées pour prévenir la réalisation imminente d'un dommage, pour éviter son aggravation ou pour en réduire les conséquences constituent un préjudice réparable'. For Norwegian law, see B Askeland, 'Erstatning for preventive utgifter' (2010) *Tidsskrift for Rettsvitenskap* 1.

[41] P Gillaerts, 'Instrumentalisation of Tort Law: Widespread yet Fundamentally Limited' (2019) 15(3) *Utrecht LR* 27, 41 with references.

[42] Civil Liability Convention 1992, Art 1(6)(b).

[43] See climatecasechart.com/non-us-case/lliuya-v-rwe-ag/.

as parent company, had control. Since RWE was responsible for 0.47 per cent of the CO_2 that had been emitted into the atmosphere in the industrial era, it was argued that RWE was obliged to pay compensation equivalent to 0.47 per cent of the sum that it was necessary to spend on preventive measures.[44]

The case is often described as a tort law case,[45] although technically, it is not. It is not a claim for damages, and it is not argued that RWE has acted unlawfully or negligently. Rather, the claim is based on property law principles. More specifically, the claim is based on § 1004 (1) of the German Civil Code (Bürgerliches Gesetzbuch, BGB).[46] The provision protects the owner of property from interference with his property, which he is not obliged to tolerate. Causing damage to the property is clearly an 'interference'. However, it is claimed in the case that a *risk* of damage may also qualify as 'interference' if it is inevitable that the condition will lead to interference.[47] According to § 1004 (1) sent. 1, the owner can demand that the disturber eliminates the interference. The interference, which in this case is the risk of the flooding of the house, can only be eliminated by taking costly precautionary measures. Under BGB article 1004 (1) sent 1, the costs of eliminating an interference rest on the disturber.[48] It is on this basis that the plaintiff argues he has a monetary claim against the German power plant station.[49]

Although the claim is not technically a tort law claim, it resembles a tort law claim in that the plaintiff seeks monetary compensation. Also, in other ways, tort law principles seep into the case. This is particularly relevant to the issue of causation. BGB § 1004 does not specify what kind of causal link there must be between the disturbance (activities of the power plant) and the interference (risk of flooding). Here, it seems that, to some extent, the tort law criteria are relied upon.[50] This was clear in the first instance decision where the Court in Essen dismissed the claim on the basis that the classical tort law 'but

[44] V Kumar and W Frank, 'Holding Private Emitters to Account for the Effects of Climate Change: Could a Case Like Lliuya Succeed under English Nuisance Laws?' (2018) 2 *Carbon & Climate LR*, 110, 114–115.

[45] See eg W Frank, C Bals and J Grimm, 'The Case of Huaraz: First Climate Lawsuit on Loss and Damage Against an Energy Company Before German Courts' in R Mechler et al (eds), *Loss and Damage from Climate Change, Climate Risk Management, Policy and Governance* (Cham, Springer, 2019) 475, also A Hösli, '*Milieudefense et al v. Shell*: A Tipping Point in Climate Change Litigation against Corporations?' (2021) 11 *Climate Law* 195–209, 205.

[46] In German: '(1) Wird das Eigentum in anderer Weise als durch Entziehung oder Vorenthaltung des Besitzes beeinträchtigt, so kann der Eigentümer von dem Störer die Beseitigung der Beeinträchtigung verlangen. Sind weitere Beeinträchtigungen zu besorgen, so kann der Eigentümer auf Unterlassung klagen'. (2) Der Anspruch ist ausgeschlossen, wenn der Eigentümer zur Duldung verpflichtet ist'. English translation: '(1) If the ownership is interfered with by means other than removal or retention of possession, the owner may require the disturber to eliminate the interference. If further interferences are to be feared, the owner may seek a prohibitory injunction. (2) The claim is excluded if the owner is obliged to tolerate the interference'.

[47] Claimant's writ, p 29 with reference to Münchener Kommentar zum Bürgerlichen Gesetzbuch (MüKoBGB). See also A Kling, 'Die Klimaklage gegen RWE – Die Geltendmachung von Klimafolgeschäden auf dem Privatrechtsweg' Kritische Justiz (2018) 1, 4–5.

[48] MüKoBGB (n 47) § 1004 (1) Rn 288: 'Die Kosten der Beseitigung fallen privatrechtlich nach allgM dem Störer zur Last'.

[49] As an exception to § 1004 (1), it follows from § 1004 (2) that a claim for the cessation of the disturbing activity is excluded if the owner is 'obliged to tolerate the impairment'. This means that if the general interest prevents the cessation of an activity that causes the disturbance, the disturbance must be tolerated. However, in the German case, it is not the cessation of the activity of the power plant that is claimed but only the cessation of the risk of the flooding of the house.

[50] MüKoBGB (n 47) § 1004 Rn 71: 'Die Rspr.selbst tendiert hier zu schadensersatzrechtlichen Kategorien: adäquate Kausalität …'. See also Magnus (n 27) 850, assuming that tort law criteria on causation apply with regard to § 1004 (1) sent 2.

for' causation test was not satisfied.[51] The court did not discuss the appropriateness of this test in a property law-based action.

The appellate court of Hamm seems to have taken a different perspective altogether. It did not dismiss the case but ordered it to move to the evidentiary phase. In its decision in November 2017,[52] it stated that the case concerned 'the role of the energy companies' operations as active (contributory) causes of the flood risk'.[53] More specifically, the court required expert opinion to be obtained on five aspects concerning causation: (1) a flood resulting from an expansion of Lake Palacacocha poses a serious threat to the plaintiff's property, (2) the carbon emissions by the defendant rise into the atmosphere and lead to a higher concentration of greenhouse gases throughout the Earth's atmosphere, (3) the result is an increase in global temperature, (4) the increase in average local temperatures accelerates the melting of the Palcaraju Glacier and the volume of water will rise to a level that can no longer be contained by natural moraine, and (5) the defendant's share in the contributory causation is measurable and calculable and the expert should quantify the correct proportion.[54]

As will be seen, these demands do not correspond to the demands under the classical but-for test. The court seems to be willing to be satisfied with a proof of causation at the more general level.[55] In its decision of 1 February 2018,[56] the court confirmed its 2017 decision and further noted that with regard to § 1004 (1) sent 1: '… the established interpretation is that, in the case of multiple "disturbers" each participant must eliminate its own contribution …'[57]

This plaintiff hereby has a basis for claiming a proportionate sum of the total preventive cost from the defendant. Commentators have found the decision confirms the principle that 'each person must do his or her share' as expressed in *Urgenda*, whether or not this share constitutes a necessary condition for climate change.[58] However, it is

[51] Court of Essen decision of 15 December 2016. First, the court found that the RWE emissions were not necessary for the flood risk to exist. It would have existed anyway, due to other emissions and other factors. On a similar line of thinking, see Spitzer and Burtscher (n 2) 167 concerning the situation where a certain threshold (tipping point) has been reached after which every emission no longer contributes. Second, the court found that it would not be possible to trace the specific emissions of the RWE to the specific flood risk in Peru. More precisely, the court found that it would be impossible to 'identify anything resembling a linear line of causation from one particular source of emissions to one particular damage', see Court decision, p 5. Here, the court referenced the German Forest Damage case (Waldschadenurteil, Federal Court, III ZR 220/86, 10 December 1987). In sum, the court's reasoning was clearly based on a traditional *conditio sine qua non* test resembling the reasoning in the *Kavalina* case described above.

[52] Hamm Court decision of November 30, 2017: see germanwatch.org/sites/germanwatch.org/files/static/20732.pdf.

[53] ibid section I(3).

[54] ibid section III.

[55] It has been noted that the most demanding requirement is probably obtaining evidence of (4), ie, that there is a link between global warming and the melting of the particular glacier, since local conditions may also play a role: Kumar and Frank (n 44) 119. Here, new attribution science studies may help: see eg B Ekwurzel et al, 'The Rise in Global Atmospheric Co2, Surface Temperature, and Sea level from Emissions Traced to Major Carbon Producers' 2017 (144) *Climatic Change* 579. See also S Marjanac and L Patton, 'Extreme Weather Event Attribution Science and Climate Change Litigation: An Essential Step in the Causal Chain? (2018) 36 *J of Energy and Natural Resources L* 265.

[56] Hamm Court decision of 1 February 2018: germanwatch.org/sites/germanwatch.org/files/static/21158.pdf.

[57] Hamm Court decision of 1 February 2018, section 4.

[58] See for instance Ganguly et al (n 19) 855, who with reference to Germanwatch states that the court declared 'it is enough that its emissions are partially responsible for the actual, present risk'. In line with this, it

unclear whether the view on causation in the case is also influenced by the fact that the case technically is not a tort law case but a property law case, providing a clearer basis for reaching the conclusion that each disturber must eliminate its own interference with the property ('do its part').

Relying on basic property law principles, combined to some extent with tort law principles, one may ask whether the case could be replicated in other jurisdictions. Historically, in Scandinavian law, which has often taken inspiration from German private law, basic property law principles are uncodified, and their reach is also uncertain. Basing a claim on neighbouring law might restrict the cases to concern (more) local nuisances.[59] In contrast, in English law, it has been suggested that the tort of nuisance (private or public) might provide the basis.[60] Whereas private nuisance law may be limited to disputes between private land owners,[61] the tort of public nuisance covers more broadly.[62] Since the claim under English law would be a tort law claim, it would be necessary to document harm and loss as a starting point. However, it has been suggested that a compensatory claim for expenses to preventive measures may be possible also under what was formerly known in English law as a *quia timet* mandatory injunction, and now known as a 'precautionary injunction', which is an order to do something to prevent damage that will otherwise occur, such as preventing flooding of private property by investing in protective measures.[63] However, the requirement of causation may pose problems under English law, which also proceeds from the 'but for' test as the general starting point.[64] The asbestos case, *Bonnington Castings Ltd v Wardlaw*,[65] could support the view that, in the case of concurrent (cumulative) causes that all add to the problem without each of them being neither a necessary nor a

has also been suggested that the court either finds that the *conditio sine qua non* test is satisfied since 'without RWE's contribution, the degree and extent of the flood risk would be lowered' or that the *conditio sine qua non* test does not apply in case of 'cumulative causation': see Kumar and Frank (n 44) 118. The term 'cumulative causation' is used by the parties in the case, although it is not a generally established category in tort law. It seems to cover the situation in which several actors contribute to the same harm without any single actor being necessary for the causing of the harm. The term seems also to be used in English tort law: see Kumar and Frank (n 44) 118. In other legal systems, the term 'concurrent causes' would be used to cover this situation, see Hinteregger (n 21) 255–256.

[59] See eg for Norwegian law, Columbo (n 2) 103–104. For Danish law, see P Pagh and T Haugsted, *Fast ejendom, regulering og køb*, 4th edn (Copenhagen, Karnov Group, 2022) 263 og 265.

[60] A very interesting and in-depth analysis of this question is found in Kumar and Frank (n 44), on which the following relies. For a recent view of public nuisance in English law, see also JW Neyers, 'Reconceptualising the tort of public nuisance' [2017] *Camb LJ* 87–115.

[61] Kumar and Frank (n 44) 112.

[62] In English law, it is defined as 'acts and omissions of the defendant that materially affect the reasonable comfort and convenience of a class of her Majesty's subjects', see Kumar and Frank (n 44) 112 with reference to Lord Denning LJ in *Southport Corp v Esso Petroleum Co Ltd* [1954] 2 QB 182 (CA), 196–197. Public nuisance claims may be brought either as tort law claims or as criminal law offences, Kumar and Frank (n 44) 112. It is noted that in English law, a public nuisance claim may be restricted to the subsidiaries as the direct source of the emissions rather than the parent company: Kumar and Frank (n 44) 115. On the tort of public nuisance, see also A Tettenborn (gen ed), *Clerk & Lindsell on Torts*, 24th edn (London, Sweet & Maxwell, 2023) para 19.03ff.

[63] For the details in this argument, see Kumar and Frank (n 44) 116, 122, G Kaminskaitė-Salters, 'Climate Change Litigation in the UK: Its Feasibility and Prospects' in Faure and Peeters (n 7) 165, 175. For the use of the term 'precautionary injunction' see *Barking and Dagenham London Borough Council v Persons Unknown* [2022] EWCA Civ 13, [2023] QB 295, para 8.

[64] Clerk & Lindsell (n 62) para 2-09ff.

[65] [1956] AC 613 (HL).

sufficient cause, each contributor could still be held liable.[66] However, a separate argument is needed to reach the conclusion that a claim for a proportionate amount of the costs should not be rejected on the basis that awarding such sum will not prevent the risk from materialising.[67] English law scholars conclude that it may be more difficult but still possible to bring suits similar to the German one also under English law.[68] In line with this, suits of this kind have already been brought under both private and public nuisance law in the US.[69]

The above might indicate that the 'German model' could to some extent be 'exportable' also to jurisdictions outside the EU, that have roots either in the German or common law traditions. The model has some advantages. By basing the claim on property law principles or in Anglo-American nuisance law, the plaintiff is relieved from proving negligence on the part of the plaintiff. In addition, by not claiming full compensation for a specific loss or injury but only a proportional sum to prevent a risk from materialising, the plaintiff's burden of proof concerning causation is reduced to concern *contribution* by the defendant, rather than the defendant being the necessary cause of the risk. In addition, as compared to the classical, backwards-looking tort law case, which can only be initiated once the damage has actually been suffered, this type of claim holds somewhat more potential as a regulatory mechanism as suits can be initiated in an earlier phase, that is as soon as a risk of damage can be identified.[70] However, the regulatory effect of this type of claim still consists mainly of a possible deterrent effect.

IV. Third Stage Strategy: Forward Looking Claims for Change of Policies ('Regulatory Claims')

The biggest potential in tort-based climate change litigation lies in using tort law as a truly regulatory mechanism that directly claims a change of behaviour with regard to carbon emissions. As explained, typically, tort law is used as a basis for claiming damages for loss that has already been suffered. Only by some stretch and partly reshaping of the claims into proprietary claims may it be possible to cover compensation for preventive measures.[71] However, in a ground-breaking decision in 2021, the Hague District Court used tort law as a basis for ordering Dutch Shell (RDS) to change policy, more specifically to reduce the carbon emissions from the entire Shell Group, over which RDS was

[66] Kumar and Frank (n 44) 118.

[67] ibid 122.

[68] ibid 123.

[69] Several of these cases have concerned procedural issues regarding preemption by federal law, see eg *County of San Mateo v Chevron Corp* 32 F.4th 733 where three local governments in California had filed separate lawsuits in the California Superior Court making compensatory claims on the basis that the carbon emissions by the defendants caused more severe flooding and sea level rise that jeopardise infrastructure, beaches, schools and communities. The claim was inter alia based on private and public nuisance. The Ninth Circuit ruled that the case should be remanded to state court. See also *City of New York v Chevron Corp* 993 F.3d 81 (preemption by the Clean Air Act); *City of Oakland v BP PLC* 969 F.3d 895 (9th Cir. 2020) (public nuisance claim for compensation for protective measures needed but no complete pre-emption).

[70] *cf* Spier (n 8) 49 found it 'not so very easy to explain why claims for damages should be dismissed, while adaptation costs could be recovered'.

[71] But compare the tort of nuisance which can give rise to both compensatory liability claims and criminal law claims.

found to have control, by 45 per cent below 2019 levels by 2030.[72] The court took a value chain perspective and found that the parent company could be held accountable – in its role as a 'private regulator' – not only for its own emissions (scope 1) but, under certain conditions, also for the emissions from subsidiaries and contractual partners (scope 2) and from end users (scope 3). The court briefly rejected the view that in reaching this conclusion, it was acting as a legislator and outside the function of a court.[73] However, the ruling gives tort law a clear regulatory role that is not only indirect but also 'directly' forward-looking. The court found that continuing greenhouse gas emissions according to the company policy would be negligent and consequently unlawful. On this basis, the court imposed an injunction on the company, ordering it to change its policies. Thus, the court uses the part of tort law that concerns the basis of liability and combines it with the law of injunctions to reach the result.

Concerning the basis of liability, the court took as its starting point the unwritten standard of care, proper social conduct,[74] laid down in Book 6, section 162 of the Dutch Civil Code. The standard is a broad and open-ended standard similar to those found in many other tort law systems. The standard must be interpreted in order to be applied in a concrete case. In interpreting the standard, the court used a wide range of criteria.[75] Noticeably, the court used human rights principles, specifically ECHR Articles 2 and 8.[76] Whereas, in *Urgenda*, the court found a basis for imposing reduction requirements on the state in human rights law, such rights are not directly binding on companies. Instead, the court used tort law as 'the missing link'. Thus, by referring to human rights to determine the standard of care, the court indirectly gives horizontal effect to these rights. However, as a general rule, human rights only apply vertically between states and individuals[77] and the court is 'taking in' standards that might ordinarily be thought of as belonging to public law.[78] In addition, the court also relied on the UNGPs[79] to interpret the tort law standard of care. Combined with scientific reports, therefore, the court has developed the value chain perspective and the notion of scope 1, 2 and 3 emissions.[80] Hereby, the court gives legal effect to principles that ordinarily are only thought of as soft law principles.[81] Finally, with regard to the argument that observance of the relevant public regulation ought to shield the company form liability, the court stated: 'The reduction target of the ETS system is not identical to the RDS's reduction obligation …

[72] ECLI:NL:RBDHA:2021:5339. The decision immediately generated several case comments, see eg C Macchi and J van Zeben, 'Business and Human Rights Implications of Climate Change Litigation: Millieudefensie et al v. Royal Dutch Shell' (2021) 30 *RECIEL* 409; O Spijkers, 'Friends of the Earth Netherlands (Milieudefensie) v Royal Dutch Shell' (2021) 5 *Chinese J of Environmental L* 237; C Vittorio Ciabardo, 'Climate Change Litigation & Corporate Responsibility. A comment on "Milieudefensie and Others v. Shell"' (2021), www.glawcal.org.uk/stories/climate-change-litigation-corporate-responsibility-a-comment-on-milieudefensie-and-others-vs-shell-2021; Hösli (n 45).

[73] Legal grounds, 4.1.2 and 4.1.3.

[74] Hösli (n 45) 198.

[75] Summarised in legal grounds 4.4.2.

[76] Legal grounds 4.4.9–4.4.10.

[77] For an explanation of this basic starting point, see eg, V Jentsch, 'Etappensieg bei Klimaklage zur Reduktion von CO2-Emissionen gegen Rohstoffunternehmen' (2021) 3 *GesKR* 321, 327–329.

[78] For a very clear analysis of the case in this regard, see Jentsch ibid.

[79] United Nations Guiding Principles on Business and Human Rights, www.ohchr.org/sites/default/files/documents/publications/guidingprinciplesbusinesshr_en.pdf.

[80] Legal grounds, 4.4.11–4.4.21 with reference to the UNGPs and 'the Oxford Report'.

[81] Jentsch (n 77) 332–333.

RDS cannot rely on the indemnifying effect of the ETS system …'.[82] Having established a basis of liability in tort law, and thereby unlawfulness, the court moved on to combine this with the law of injunctions and ordered the company to change its company policy to reduce its emissions.[83]

The linking of tort law and the law of injunctions is a technique also known in other jurisdictions. Injunctions are sometimes described as an 'in kind' tort law remedy.[84] In Scandinavian law, for example, it is also assumed that injunctions can be used against acts that general tort law would deem 'negligent' (and thereby unlawful).[85] German law uses the general tort law provision in BGB Article 823(1) to identify the 'interests' which an injunction can protect[86] and further requires the serious risk of a 'wrongful' infringement of these rights. However, what is considered wrongful in a liability context need not necessarily also be wrongful in the context of injunctions.[87] Likewise, one might ask whether the tort law criterion of causation can be transferred to the injunction context. The fact that the case concerns injunctions and not compensation for personal injury or property damage slightly transforms the theme of causation. It turns on the relationship between the alleged wrongful act and 'the threat of future damage' to property that the plaintiff wants to address, which is arguably a more general causation theme.[88] In German legal scholarship, it has been observed that 'the defendant's activity must be the cause of the actual or threatened infringement'[89] and further that:

> In a rather general sense, there is a causal link between any activity contributing to climate change and the threatened loss of land … On a concrete level it is very problematic to state that, for instance, the emissions of a German energy plant cause the rise of the level of the Pacific Ocean (to which extent)?[90]

Moreover, injunction cases may contain an extra layer of causal questions. Thus, in addition to showing that the infringement caused the threat of a loss, it may also be necessary to show that an injunction is both necessary and sufficient to protect the plaintiff against the risk.[91] In the *Millieudefensie* case, the Dutch court addressed this

[82] Legal grounds, 4.4.46.

[83] The basis for the order is found in Art 3:296(1) in the Dutch Civil Code which (in translation) reads: 'Where a person is legally obliged towards another person to give, to do or not to do something, the court shall order him, upon a request or claim of the entitled person, to carry out this specific performance, unless something else results from law, the nature of the obligation or a juridical act'.

[84] For a general analysis on injunctions as a tort law remedy, see J Murphy, 'Rethinking Injunctions in Tort Law' (2007) 37 *OJLS* 509.

[85] See C Salung Petersen, P Møgelvang-Hansen and T Riis, *Judicielle forbud/påbud og immaterialretsproces* (Copenhagen, Karnov Group, 2015) 42.

[86] Magnus (n 27) 850. Under BGB Art 823(1), the protected interests are, for instance, life, bodily integrity and property.

[87] Notably, compliance with licence requirements, although not necessarily a barrier to liability may in German law prevent an injunction, Magnus (n 27) 851. This can be contrasted with the view of the Dutch court, rejecting that compliance with the ETS system could shield the company against an injunction.

[88] See also van Dijk (n 26) 221–222.

[89] Magnus (n 27) 852.

[90] ibid.

[91] Thus, there could be many ways to protect oneself against a risk. In English law, the causal requirement is clearly expressed in relation to the *quia timet* mandatory injunction which as a starting point requires that 'it must be impossible for the plaintiff to defend himself without the relief granted via a quia timet action': Kumar and Frank (n 45) 122.

aspect of causation when it noted that the order (to adopt a more ambitious climate policy) could only be rejected if the order could 'not *contribute* to preventing the alleged imminent infringement of interests'.[92] RDS had argued that a court order would have no effect since the place of the Shell group 'would just be taken by competitors'.[93] The court took a different view on this, finding that:

> Due to the compelling interests which are served with the reduction obligation, this argument cannot justify assuming beforehand, there is no need for RDS to not meet this obligation. It is also important here that each reduction of greenhouse gas emissions has a positive effect on countering dangerous climate change. After all, each reduction means that there is more room in the carbon budget. The court acknowledges that RDS cannot solve this global problem on its own. However, this does not absolve RDS of its individual partial responsibility to do its part regarding the emissions of the Shell Group, which it can control and influence.[94]

Here, the court seems to do away entirely with the traditional tort law principle on causation embedded in the 'but for' test, not only regarding the question whether an injunction will protect against the risk, but also more generally. Thus, having regard to 'the compelling interests served with the reduction obligation', the fact that Shell's activities were not a necessary condition for the threat was not decisive. For the court, the causation 'in a more general sense' seemed to suffice, that is that it is scientifically established that part of the global warming is manmade, that Shell partly contributes to this and that global warming will threaten the Dutch people and specifically the people of Wadden. This simplified reasoning on causation is in line with the *Urgenda* reasoning.[95] The emphasis on the view that RDS must 'do its part' can be seen as a version of 'proportional liability' only in the context of injunctions.[96]

The regulatory role played by tort law here becomes clear in several different respects. By including both human rights and UNGPs in the interpretation of the standard of care, the decision very clearly uses tort law as a regulatory tool. Human rights are 'imported' into tort law and used not only in support of the result but to create a standard of care. In this way, tort law becomes an enforcer of human rights and the public policy behind them. The regulatory character of tort law even seeps into the test of causation where the simplified test seems to be legitimised at least in part by the 'compelling interests which are served with the reduction obligation', that is strong societal needs. Also, the use of the injunction as a remedy gives the tort law basis for the claim a clear regulatory effect. RDS is held accountable in its capacity as 'the policy setting entity'[97] and the RDS is not just asked to pay compensation to a concrete plaintiff but to alter its company policy, that is the private regulatory basis for the company's activities, which will have effect not only for a specific plaintiff but for a larger number of future potential victims of climate change.

[92] Legal ground, 4.5.5. Our emphasis.

[93] Legal ground, 4.4.49.

[94] ibid.

[95] See above in section I on the reasoning in this case.

[96] Perhaps in line with this, Spier suggests a more lenient standard for proof of causation with regard to injunctions: see J Spier, 'Injunctive relief: Opportunities and Challenges. Thoughts About a Potentially Promising Legal vehicle to Stem the tide' in J Spier and U Magnus (eds), *Climate Change Remedies* (The Hague, Eleven International Publishing, 2013) 54.

[97] Legal ground, 4.4.4.

The ruling will also have external effects. Concretely, *Millieudefensie* represents the Dutch residents and the inhabitants of the Wadden region who are particularly vulnerable to flooding. However, the ruling will also benefit potential climate change victims in parts of the world other than the Netherlands and – due to the value chain approach in the decision – the subsidiaries and business relations worldwide who will also have to adjust to the policies of the parent company.

The concept embedded in *Millieudefensie* of suing the carbon majors on the basis of what is a combination of tort law and the law of injunctions has also already been used in other legal systems besides the Dutch legal system.[98] In Germany, Greenpeace sued Volkswagen, one of the greatest car manufacturers in the world, claiming that the company be ordered to phase out the highly polluting internal combustion engine and to adapt its business strategy to the Paris Agreement.[99] The basis for the claim was a combination of BGB Article 823 (tort law) and Article 1004 (injunctions).[100] In France, a coalition of NGOs initiated a suit against Total before the Nanterre judicial court.[101] On the basis of the above, it can hardly be ruled out that large shipping companies could also be targeted in this type of suit.

V. Climate Change Litigation and Value Chain Perspectives

All of the cases mentioned above revolve around the same general idea of obliging companies to create self-regulation for the purpose of meeting the global challenge from climate change. This obligation to self-regulate with the goal of keeping the rise in temperatures below the 1.5 degrees target of the Paris Agreement may in the future be codified in EU legislation. Thus, the new proposal for a directive on corporate due diligence obligations with regard to human rights and the environment (the Proposal),[102] also imposes a regulatory duty on companies of a certain size to create self-regulation in the shape of company plans and strategies for this purpose.[103] Article 15(1) and (2) in the Proposal, reads as follows:

[98] An early US case failed for procedural reasons, see *American Electric Power Co Inc v Connecticut* 131 S. Ct. 2527 (2011). The case was dismissed on the basis that the Clean Air Act displaced federal common law public nuisance claim seeking to reduce CO_2 emissions from fossil-fuel power plant.

[99] The claim was rejected in February 2023, see www.business-humanrights.org/en/latest-news/klimaklage-gegen-vw-scheitert/.

[100] For the writ in German, see: www.greenpeace.de/publikationen/vw_klage_final_small_0.pdf. There is a summary in English at www.greenpeace.de/publikationen/greenpeace_vs_vw_english.pdf.

[101] The claim was recently dismissed, partly due to lack of standing of the NGO, see climatecasechart.com/non-us-case/notre-affaire-a-tous-and-others-v-total/.

[102] Proposal for a Directive of the European Parliament and of the Council on Corporate Sustainability Due Diligence and amending Directive (EU) 2019/1937, COM(2022) 71 final, 2022/0051 (COD).

[103] See the proposal, Art 15(1): Combating climate change: 1. Member States shall ensure that companies referred to in Article 2(1), point (a), and Article 2(2), point (a), shall adopt a plan to ensure that the business model and strategy of the company are compatible with the transition to a sustainable economy and with the limiting of global warming to 1.5 °C in line with the Paris Agreement. This plan shall, in particular, identify, on the basis of information reasonably available to the company, the extent to which climate change is a risk for, or an impact of, the company's operations. On the development of a concept of 'Climate Change Due Diligence' see further C Macchi, 'The Climate Change Dimension of Business and Human Rights: the gradual Consolidation of a concept of 'Climate Due Diligence' (2021) 6 *Business and Human Rights J* 93.

(1) Member States shall ensure that companies referred to in Article 2(1), point (a), and Article 2(2), point (a), shall adopt a plan to ensure that the business model and strategy of the company are compatible with the transition to a sustainable economy and with the limiting of global warming to 1.5 °C in line with the Paris Agreement. This plan shall, in particular, identify, on the basis of information reasonably available to the company, the extent to which climate change is a risk for, or an impact of, the company's operations.

(2) Member States shall ensure that, in case climate change is or should have been identified as a principal risk for, or a principal impact of, the company's operations, the company includes emissions reduction plans in its plan.

Shipping companies will also be covered by the regulation, provided they are the required size. According to Article 2(1) point (a), companies with more than 500 employees and a net worldwide turnover of more than €150 million are covered. Several shipping companies would live up to this requirement. In addition, according to Article 2(2) point (a), the directive also purports to have extraterritorial effect in that it applies also to companies 'which are formed in accordance with the legislation of a third country, and generate a net turnover of more than EUR 150 million in the Union I the financial year preceding the last financial year'. Thus, according to the wording of this provision, several shipping companies outside of the EU could also be covered by the provision.[104] Moreover, even if a company is not directly covered by the provision, the rule may still in reality have trickle down effects in the rest of the value chain, as the company which is 'in scope' is obliged to consider its 'business model' which will include thinking about business partners. For a shipping company, a plan in accordance with Article 15 could naturally include a business strategy with regard to both the EEXI and CII requirements introduced at international level, and the European allowance trading system (ETS).

Given that a duty to create self-regulation in the shape of plans and strategies exist at company level, either on the basis of tort law or on the basis of Article 15 in the coming directive or both, one might ask what the legal effect is of this type of regulation.

First, the question arises whether a company that lives up to such self-regulation would be protected against further climate claims.[105] If the line of reasoning in *Millieudefense* is followed, it would be possible for an NGO to challenge an internal company policy in a tort law suit to test whether the level of ambition in the policy is sufficient.

Likewise, one might ask to what extent such self-regulation would be legally enforceable. Normally, corporate policies do not have self-binding effect.[106] Internal policies created by the company can always be changed by the company.[107] However, it has been argued that such internal policies can influence the standard of care and specify the individual standard of care for a particular company.[108] If the internal policies are a

[104] It is an open question how EU Member States can 'ensure' the observance of these rules regarding foreign companies.

[105] The proposed directive on corporate accountability contains a 'safe harbour' clause to this effect (Article 22) but it does not apply to climate obligations.

[106] See eg A Beckers, *Enforcing Corporate Social Responsibility Codes* (Oxford, Hart Publishing, 2015) 82, noting about self-commitments in general that 'such self-commitments are from the orthodox perspective treated as voluntary in nature that cannot be enforced as a legally binding contract'.

[107] Perhaps for this reason, the view has been expressed that an injunctive relief is 'just another form of regulation': Hsu (n 40) 714.

[108] Beckers (n 106) 178; C Glinski, 'Bridging the Gap: The Legal Potential of Private Regulation' in O Dilling, M Herberg and G Winther (eds), *Responsible Business, Self-governance and Law in Transnational Economic*

result of a court decision, and hence not entirely voluntary, this argument must gain in force. On this basis it might be possible to argue that not living up to such internal rules created as a response to an injunction should be regarded as constituting a violation of the general duty of care and consequently also as providing the basis for imposing a (new) injunction to live up to company self-regulation.

Moreover, the duty to create such regulation, the existence of it and the general awareness of companies' climate obligations that the duty to self-regulate creates may have other indirect effects.

Thus, as has been pointed out in the legal literature, we are already beginning to see a new wave of climate change litigation cases concerning the 'financial infrastructure' surrounding companies.[109] Cases concern duties of directors and board members to handle climate change risk at the managerial level and duties of investors and financial actors to take climate change risk into consideration when deciding which market players to support.[110] In this way, market developments may also force companies to take their climate policies seriously.

VI. Suing the International Maritime Organization (IMO)?

As shown above, the growing political demand for climate action will lead to a broad range of legal claims against public and private actors. Within the maritime sector, the adjustment to climate change goals is coordinated by a specialised UN agency, the International Maritime Organization (IMO) and its Marine Environment Protection Committee (MEPC). The last decade has witnessed several IMO initiatives dealing with energy efficient design and operation of ships, reporting on fuel consumption and provision of onshore power supply, to name a few.[111] A matter of tedious political negotiation seeking an acceptable solution among states with different needs, these measures may fall short of the ones required by climate emergency. Hence comes a hypothetical question whether IMO can be subject to legal demands about its role in climate change adjustment, meaning, unrealised potential of regulation and the eventual delays in its adoption, to which critics have often pointed. Considerations relating to the jurisdiction of a potential forum for the settlement of such legal claims deserve a brief analysis here.

The Convention on the International Maritime Organization stipulates its relationship with the United Nations as a Specialised Agency in the field of shipping.[112] Annex II to the Convention declares the principle of functional immunity, according to which IMO 'shall enjoy in the territory at each of its Members such privileges and immunities

Transactions (Oxford, Hart Publishing, 2008) 41, 47ff; V Ulfbeck and O Hansen, 'Interplay between contract and tort' in V Ulfbeck, A Andhov and K Mitkidis (eds), *Law and Responsible Supply Chain Management* (London, Routledge, 2019) 133, 137.

[109] Ganguly et al (n 19) 858–861.

[110] RH Weber and A Hösli, 'Corporate Climate Responsibility – The rise of a New Governance Issue' [2021] *Sui Generis* 83. See also Expert Group on Climate Obligations of Enterprise in J Spier (ed), *Principles on Climate Obligations of Enterprises* (The Hague, Eleven Publishing, 2018) 198.

[111] See an overview in Baughen (n 13) 129.

[112] Convention on the International Maritime Organization (1948), Art 45.

as are necessary for the fulfilment of its purposes and the exercise of its functions'.[113] As noted by Kristen Boon, in practice, domestic courts interpret this status broadly as absolute immunity from claims.[114] Moreover, IMO enjoys unqualified and broad domestic immunity in the UK.[115]

The rationale lies in the mitigation of drainage of organisational resources for participating in legal battles and prevention of the state's ability to assert control over the organisation.[116] Limited exceptions are possible when the charter of an international organisation allows legal claims (such as in the case of the International Monetary Fund – for satisfying potential creditors) and when the organisation decides to waive its immunity.[117] For instance, in *Jam v International Finance Corp*, the US Supreme Court allowed tort action for environmental damage against an international organisation, drawing specifically on the absence of an immunity clause in its charter.[118] However, the IMO Convention contains a functional immunity clause, suggesting that none of these exceptions seems to be apparent in the case of climate change claims against IMO.

However, an argument can be made that certain third-party claims, including tort claims, are not precluded against IMO. As a Specialised Agency, the legal capacity, privileges and immunities of IMO fall under the governing regime of a separate Convention common to all Specialised Agencies.[119] Article IX Section 31 of the Special Agency Convention expressly mentions '[d]isputes arising out of contracts or other disputes of private character to which the specialized agency is a party'. Examples typically include disputes from sale of goods and services and employment-related disputes.[120]

The 'private disputes' clause is virtually identical to Article VIII, Section 29 of the Convention on the Privileges and Immunities of the United Nations (1946), a predecessor of the Special Agency Convention.[121] The 1995 Report of the UN Secretary-General provides authoritative interpretation of the clause.[122] A summary of cases against the UN reveals the following types of non-contractual disputes:

(a) third-party claims for personal injuries (arising outside the peace-keeping context),
(b) claims related to United Nations peace-keeping operations,
(c) claims related to operational activities for development, and

[113] ibid Annex II, s 2(a).

[114] KE Boon, 'Immunities of the United Nations and Specialised Agencies' in L Ferro, N Angelet and T Ruys (eds), *The Cambridge Handbook of Immunities and International Law* (Cambridge, Cambridge University Press, 2019) 202.

[115] *cf* The International Maritime Organisation (Immunities and Privileges) Order 2002, SI 2002/1826, reg 5: 'The Organisation shall have the legal capacities of a body corporate and, except in so far as in any particular case it has expressly waived its immunity, immunity from suit and legal process. No waiver of immunity shall be deemed to extend to any measure of execution.'

[116] Boon (n 114).

[117] ibid 203–205; 208–210.

[118] *Jam v International Finance Corp* 139 S.Ct. 759.

[119] Convention on the Privileges and Immunities of the Specialized Agencies (1947).

[120] Boon (n 114) 206.

[121] *cf* Convention on the Privileges and Immunities of the United Nations (1946), Article VIII, s 29: 'The United Nations shall make provisions for appropriate modes of settlement of: (a) disputes arising out of contracts or other disputes of a private law character to which the United Nations is a party (…).'

[122] Procedures in Place for Implementation of Article 8, Section 29, of the Convention on the Privileges and Immunities of the United Nations, Adopted by the General Assembly on 13 February 1946 (UN, 1995) Report of the UN Secretary-General A/C.5/49/65, digitallibrary.un.org/record/179596.

(d) other claims [related either to grievances about the UN policy or unsuccessful job applications].[123]

It seems likely that the substance of a claim at hand, failure to adopt an efficient climate mitigation policy, lacks on its face private character and thereby falls under the last category. According to the UN Secretary General, their public nature and controversial cause of action should prevent litigation attempts:

> The Organization does not agree to engage in litigation or arbitration with the numerous third parties that submit claims (often seeking substantial monetary compensation) based on political or policy-related grievances against the United Nations, usually related to actions or decisions taken by the Security Council or the General Assembly in respect of certain matters. Such claims, in many instances, consist of rambling statements denouncing the policies of the Organization and alleging that specific actions of the General Assembly or the Security Council have caused the claimant to sustain financial losses. The Secretary-General considers that it would be inappropriate to utilize public funds to submit to any form of litigation with the claimants to address such issues.[124]

While the Report refers to UN, the substance is equally relatable to IMO, providing strong impetus against admission of such claims.

The unconvinced reader may nevertheless accept that the tort claims in question are of private character, despite their forward-looking aim for change of policies, as explained above. This presumption is further strengthened by the lack of clear distinction between private and public law claims against international organisations.[125]

In such a case, the question of potential legal forum becomes relevant. The availability of the forum secures the right of access to court, which creates tension in cases, where the immunity precludes potential liability of an international organisation.[126] A natural view can be taken of domestic courts, which are rather uniformly considered unsuitable for cases against international organisations due to the risks of undue influence.[127] Here, a difference can be drawn between contractual disputes, which often have arbitration as an available neutral forum, and non-contractual disputes, which often lack one.[128] This is the case with IMO, which lacks a third party dispute settlement clause in its Headquarters agreement with the UK.[129] As Okeke concludes, '[a]n alternative

[123] ibid.

[124] ibid.

[125] Boon (n 114) 206.

[126] EC Okeke, 'The Tension between the Jurisdictional Immunity of International Organisations and the Right of Access to Court' in P Quayle (ed), *The Role of International Administrative Law at International Organisations: AIIB Yearbook of International Law* (Leiden, Brill Nijhoff, 2020) ch 2.

[127] ibid 27–28.

[128] For example, for adjudication of contractual (procurement) disputes IMO prefers UNCITRAL arbitration seated in London. See General Conditions of Contract: Contracts for the Provision of Services (IMO, February 2021) wwwcdn.imo.org/localresources/en/About/Procurement/Documents/IMO%20General%20condition%20Services.pdf, cl 16.2.

[129] Agreement between the Government of the United Kingdom of Great Britain and Northern Ireland and the Inter-Governmental Maritime Consultative Organization regarding the Headquarters of the Organization, 677 UNTS 3. Cf K Schmalenbach, 'Dispute settlement (Article IX Sections 31–32 Specialized Agencies Convention' in A Reinisch and P Bachmayer, *The Conventions on the Privileges and Immunities of the United Nations and its Specialized Agencies: A Commentary* (Oxford, Oxford University Press, 2016) 592 fn 16: 'No third party dispute settlement clause can be found in [the Headquarters Agreement].'

dispute resolution mechanism for disputes of a tortious nature involving third parties is still lacking'.[130]

Summing up, a potential tort law claim against the IMO would need to overcome the obstacles of its functional immunity, the narrow exceptions to it and the difficult choice of any potential forum for such claims.

VII. Conclusions

Today, climate change litigation targets not only states but also private companies. Whereas large oil companies have been the primary targets so far, companies in other sectors have also been sued, and there is no inherent reason why shipping companies could not also become the objects of such suits. New regulatory initiatives aim at pushing the industry towards a green transition. While these initiatives are not all backed by clear enforcement mechanisms, it cannot be ruled out that poor performance under the measures could inspire climate change litigation in the sector. Climate change litigation could hereby become an enforcement mechanism.

Moreover, seen in the light of the criticism of the regulator in this area, the IMO, and seen in the light of the 'creativity' behind many climate change suits, one could also pose the question of whether litigation could be directed at the IMO. Here, the principle of functional immunity implies that a climate change claim would only stand a chance if it could be seen as falling under the 'private disputes' clause. This, in turn, would raise complicated issues of drawing the line between private law and public law disputes in climate change litigation cases, where tort law today is used as a basis for generating private regulatory efforts as a supplement to public regulation.

[130] Okeke (n 126) 51.

12

The Future is General Average: General Average as Facilitator for Maritime Decarbonisation

JOLIEN KRUIT*

I. Introduction

Time is running out to take action against global warming.[1] The current plans to reduce the effects of global warming are insufficient to meet the Paris Climate Goals to hold 'the increase in the global average temperature to well below 2°C above pre-industrial levels'.[2] The world is on a trajectory of a temperature increase of 2.2° to 2.7° degrees.[3]

The transport sector has a bad track record and a substantial share in global warming. Not only do its emissions count for approximately 28 per cent of the total EU Green House Gas emissions, the same – with an ephemeral COVID-19-dip – are also increasing rather than decreasing.[4] In terms of numbers, shipping's international CO_2 emissions count for approximately 3 per cent of global CO_2 emissions,[5] whereas shipping is also

* Partner, Van Traa Advocaten NV, guest lecturer, Erasmus School of Law, and guest lecturer, Leiden University. Member of the CMI IWG on Maritime Decarbonisation. This chapter is based on a presentation given at the Inland Shipping Conference 2022, jointly organised by the IVR and the Erasmus School of Law, www.ivr-eu.com/wp-content/uploads/2022/11/Presentation-Dr.-Jolien-Kruit-ISLC.pdf.

[1] Synthesis Report of the IPCC Sixth Assessment Report (Ar6), Longer report (IPCC 2023) 23–24: 'Global GHG emissions in 2030 associated with the implementation of NDCs announced prior to COP26 would make it likely that warming will exceed 1.5°C during the 21st century and would make it harder to limit warming below 2°C – if no additional commitments are made or actions taken.'

[2] unfccc.int/process-and-meetings/the-paris-agreement.

[3] 'United Science: We are Heading in the Wrong Direction' (World Meteorological Organization, 13 September 2022) public.wmo.int/en/media/press-release/united-science-we-are-heading-wrong-direction, Emissions Gap Report 2022(UNEP, 27 October 2022) www.unep.org/resources/emissions-gap-report-2022.

[4] V Masterson, 'The European Union has Cut Greenhouse Gas Emissions in Every Sector – Except this One' (World Economic Forum, 29 September 2022) www.weforum.org/agenda/2022/09/eu-greenhouse-gas-emissions-transport/.

[5] Or, more tellingly, if shipping were a country, the emissions would be equal to those of Germany, the country that is the sixth biggest emitter worldwide: J Brown et al, 'Carbon Revenues from Shipping: A Game Changer for the Energy Transition' (*World Bank Blogs*, 12 May 2022) blogs.worldbank.org/transport/carbon-revenues-shipping-game-changer-energy-transition.

a significant methane emitter.[6] Moreover, such emissions contribute to ocean acidification and chemical pollution.[7]

Shipping does not directly fall under the Paris Climate Agreement but is regulated internationally by the IMO.[8] In its initial strategy published in 2018 and revised in July 2023, the IMO has set out a roadmap for greenhouse gas reduction.[9] Many interested parties consider IMO's 2018 initial target 'to cut annual greenhouse gas emissions from international shipping by at least half by 2050 and work towards phasing out GHG emissions from shipping entirely as soon as possible this century' relatively unambitious, or clearly insufficient.[10] Research by the University of Manchester has shown that in order to meet the targets set in the Paris Climate Agreement, shipping emissions will need to have been reduced by 34 per cent compared to 2010 in 2030 and will need to operate CO_2-neutral in 2050.[11] Various parties have urgently requested the IMO to announce a net zero strategy soonest.[12] Given IMO's involvement and shipping's global character, the EU has adopted a wait-and-see attitude for some time, taking small steps only.[13] However, it indicated that the IMO had to take sufficient action.[14] As the IMO appeared to be slow to respond, the EU has taken separate reduction measures for the shipping industry, also to encourage the IMO to take responsibility.[15] In July 2023, IMO revised

[6] According to the Fourth IMO Greenhouse Gas Study, between 2012 and 2018 methane emissions from ships grew 150%: *Fourth IMO GHG Study 2020* (London, IMO, 2020) 110.

[7] V Tarakanov, 'How Carbon Emissions Acidify Our Ocean' (2022) 63-4 *IAEA Bulletin* (International Atomic Energy Agency, December 2022) www.iaea.org/bulletin/how-carbon-emissions-acidify-our-ocean.

[8] The exception has not expressly been included in the Paris Climate Agreement but is generally accepted. Shipping and aviation emissions are not included in the calculation of the national contributions. The Kyoto Protocol (in Art 2.2) expressly made IMO responsible for reducing shipping emissions. See eg E Røsaeg, 'The Aviation and Shipping Exemptions in the Paris Agreement on Climate Change' (2021) 27 *JIML* 55.

[9] Resolution MEPC.304(72) adopted on 13 April 2018, 'Initial IMO Strategy on Reduction of GHG Emissions from Ships'. See for further background TH Joung et al, 'The IMO Initial Strategy for Reducing Greenhouse Gas (GHG) Emissions, and its Follow-up Actions Towards 2050' (2020) 4 *J of Int'l Maritime Safety, Environmental Affairs and Shipping* 1.

[10] In the last few years, measures have been adopted by IMO to increase the energy efficiency levels of vessels and their operation.

[11] S Bullock et al, 'The Urgent Case for Stronger Climate Targets for International Shipping' (2022) 22 *Climate Policy* 301.

[12] See inter alia A Adamopoulos, 'Call for Market-based Measures by 2025 to Ensure Shipping Hits 2050 Green Target' (21 September 2021) *Lloyd's List*. See also Global Maritime Forum, 'The Call to Action for Shipping Decarbonization' www.globalmaritimeforum.org/getting-to-zero-coalition/call-to-action.

[13] European Commission, 'Reducing Emissions from the Shipping Sector' available at: climate.ec.europa.eu/eu-action/transport-emissions/reducing-emissions-shipping-sector_en.

[14] Communication from the Commission to the European Parliament, the European Council, the Council, the European Economic and Social Committee, the Committee of the Regions and the European Investment Bank, 'A Clean Planet for all: A European strategic long-term vision for a prosperous, modern, competitive and climate neutral economy', COM(2018) 773 final, 12; 23.

[15] Proposal for a Regulation of the European Parliament and of the Council on the use of renewable and low-carbon fuels in maritime transport and amending Directive 2009/16/EC, COM (201) 562 final, 5, it is indicated that EU action stimulates responses from IMO. See also Proposal for establishing a system for greenhouse gas emission allowance trading within the Union, COM(2021)551 final, Explanatory memorandum, 8: 'EU action can also inspire and pave the way for broader action, e.g. as regards maritime transport within the International Maritime Organization IMO) and by third countries.' The EU is aware that a global regime is preferred and leaves room to adjust thereto. See inter alia Proposal for a Directive of the European Parliament and of the Council amending Directive 2003/87/EC establishing a system for greenhouse gas emission allowance trading within the Union, Decision (EU) 2015/1814 concerning the establishment and operation of a market stability reserve for the Union greenhouse gas emission trading scheme and Regulation (EU) 2015/757 (2021/0211 (COD)), Art 3ge(1): 'The Commission shall consider possible amendments in

its initial strategy and adopted enhanced targets.[16] The new level of ambition is to peak GHG emissions from international shipping as soon as possible and to reach net-zero GHG emissions by or around 2050. In addition, indicative checkpoints have been set for 2030 on a well to wake basis (at least 20 per cent striving for 30 per cent reduction compared to 2008) and 2040 (at least 70 per cent striving for 80 per cent reduction compared to 2008).

Even though the IMO's emission reduction agenda has not shown much urgency, the shipping industry is aware that action is required. Decarbonisation is regarded as the major challenge for the maritime industry going forward.[17] Emissions reduction – also in shipping – is no longer a question of when, but of how. In the meantime, it has also become clear that there is no silver bullet for maritime decarbonisation.[18] It is generally accepted that a combination of measures will need to be taken in order to get to net zero soonest.[19] This transition will be comprehensive and painful. It is clear that decarbonisation will require substantial changes at a technical level. The good news is that the technology is available (or will be in the not-too-distant future), just as various roadmaps on how to reduce emissions sufficiently in a timely manner.[20] But the same can only be successfully implemented and rolled out throughout the shipping business if the underlying legal and commercial infrastructure is substantively amended as well and when arrangements have been made regarding the costs of the transition. As noted in an opinion in *Lloyd's List*: 'Technology has an important part to play, and there are realistic prospects of getting carbon neutral vessels on the water by the end of the decade. But this is ultimately a climate finance battle, not an engineering problem.'[21]

The magic word seems to be 'collaboration'.[22] At a time of peril, that decision needs to be taken which is in the best interests of all the parties involved or affected. And this

relation to the adoption by the International Maritime Organization of a global market-based measure to reduce greenhouse gas emissions from maritime transport.'

[16] Resolution MEPC.377(80), adopted on 7 July 2023, 2023 IMO Strategy on Reduction of GHG emissions from Ships.

[17] 'Global Maritime Issues Monitor 2022' www.marsh.com/bg/en/industries/marine/insights/global-maritime-issues-monitor-2022.html.

[18] www.tradewindsnews.com/technology/bhp-says-no-silver-bullet-to-decarbonising-the-maritime-sector/2-1-997590; www.europort.nl/news-and-media/news-europort/no-silver-bullet-for-sustainable-shipping-; www.spglobal.com/commodityinsights/en/market-insights/latest-news/energy-transition/013122-shipping-should-not-wait-for-a-silver-bullet-to-meet-decarbonization-goals-panel.

[19] Some research has shown that the emission reduction goals cannot be met, unless a transition to a circular economy takes place: see 'Beyond Energy: Incentivizing Decarbonization through the Circular Economy' (Oxford Institute for Energy Studies, 2021). See also Communication from the Commission to the European Parliament, the Council, the European Economic and Social Committee and the Committee of the Regions – A New Circular Economy Action Plan for a Cleaner and More Competitive Europe COM/2020/98 Final, 18.

[20] See inter alia the Industry Roadmap developed by the Getting to Zero Coalition of the Global Maritime Forum (www.globalmaritimeforum.org/getting-to-zero-coalition); 'A Pathway to Decarbonise the Shipping Sector by 2050' (International Renewable Energy Agency, 2021); and the DNV Pathway to Net Zero Emissions (www.dnv.com/news/new-report-pathway-to-net-zero-emissions-210507). See also AS Grzelakowski et al, 'Maritime Shipping Decarbonization: Roadmap to Meet Zero-Emission Target in Shipping as a Link in the Global Supply Chains' (2022) 15 *Energies* 6150.

[21] 'Targets Matter, and that's why IMO Must Adopt Net Zero by 2050' (*Lloyd's List*, 8 October 2021).

[22] As indicated in the Houlder Navigation Whitepaper, 'Clean technology and the decarbonisation challenge' 3: 'Collaboration has become a decarbonisation buzzword'. See also MP Zacho, 'Why Collaboration is Key to Decarbonising the Maritime Sector' (*Euractiv*, 29 March 2022) www.euractiv.com/section/energy-environment/opinion/why-collaboration-is-key-to-decarbonising-the-maritime-sector/; M Lind, W Lehmacher et al, 'Decarbonizing the maritime sector: Mobilizing coordinated action in the industry using an ecosystems approach'

is counterintuitive; people are not always willing to work together when it is not in their direct, short-term (financial) interest to do so. Parties, especially in the commercial field, tend to work towards the deal that best suits their interests, which solution may not be the best for all the stakeholders involved. However, in shipping, it is standard practice that when sacrifices are made or costs are incurred to protect property involved in a common maritime adventure from peril, these costs are to be shared by the parties' interested in these properties. This is what the concept of general average (GA) has been doing for thousands of years. It is apportioning costs and losses incurred for the benefit of the common stakeholders to the common stakeholders pro rata with their financial share in the adventure. This chapter discusses how this ancient maritime burden-sharing mechanism of GA, in refurbished fashion,[23] can be and is already applied to fight the climate crisis and can assist in shipping's decarbonisation transition. First, the traditional concept of GA is discussed. Then some potential options for the application of the concept in the decarbonisation transition are considered. It will be concluded that GA can provide both the sharing mechanism and the narrative to fuel the maritime decarbonisation transition.

II. General Average

A. Background

Once upon a time, let's say the time before telex, telephone, internet and AIS, international shipping was a true adventure. Vessels set sail with their crew and cargo, and it was quite uncertain if, when and how they would make it back home safely. The voyage was full of perils, whereas contact with the shore was somewhat limited, at least with the interested parties back home. If, during a sea voyage, problems occurred, the solution had to be found by those on board, the master and the crew. Such a solution could consist of throwing overboard cargo to lighten the vessel to refloat her and selling cargo to pay port of refuge expenses or ransoms to pirates. If such sacrifices were made or costs incurred to safeguard the vessel and cargo in a common maritime adventure from a common peril, the financial consequences were shared by the parties interested in the ship and other property on board. This ancient maritime burden-sharing mechanism, originally known in Roman law as the *Lex Rhodia de iactu* is nowadays referred to as 'general average' (GA).[24] It entails that certain costs and losses incurred or suffered under particular circumstances to protect the property involved in a common maritime adventure from peril are shared between the parties interested in these properties.

(*UNCTAD*, 8 June 2022) *Transport and Trade Facilitation Newsletter* N°94: unctad.org/news/decarbonizing-maritime-sector-mobilizing-coordinated-action-industry-using-ecosystems-approach; S McLaughlin, 'Opinion: Collaboration is Fundamental to Decarbonization of Shipping' (*The Maritime Executive*, 11 January 2023) maritime-executive.com/editorials/opinion-collaboration-is-fundamental-to-decarbonization-of-shipping.

[23] One of the pillars of circularity is the refurbishment of materials. But why stop there and why not also refurbish techniques and principles?

[24] See on the Lex Rhodia de Iactu D Penna, 'General Average in Byzantium' in M Fusaro, A Addobbati and L Piccinno (eds), *General Average and Risk Management in Medieval and Early Modern Maritime Business* (London, Palgrave Macmillan, 2023) 95–119.

The underlying principle is cooperation in a time of danger for the benefit of all.[25] The burden-sharing mechanism provides the financial incentive to the parties to the maritime adventure to cooperate and take measures that keep the average overall exposure as low as possible for all parties involved. It provides for an equitable division of costs.[26]

The GA concept has survived the test of time. Nowadays, jettison of cargo and cutting of masts have been replaced as the main general average disbursements by salvage expenses and port of refuge costs. In the case of bigger and smaller shipping accidents, GA is still frequently declared.[27] Recent examples that have triggered general average declarations are the fire extinguishing operations after the fire on board the *mv Maersk Honam* and the salvage expenses incurred following the stranding of the *mv Ever Given* in the Suez Canal in March 2021.[28]

In the nineteenth and twentieth centuries, it was regularly argued that the concept of GA should be abolished.[29] Such voices, however, have never been in the majority. It was generally appreciated that the burden-sharing mechanism played an essential role in the maritime industry. In preparing for the 2016 version of the York-Antwerp Rules, CMI members were asked to complete an extensive CMI questionnaire.[30] The first question was whether GA should be abolished. Remarkably, none of the respondents supported abolition.[31] The view that GA should be maintained was substantiated by reference to principles of equity and fairness but also to the practical importance at the time of and

[25] Interestingly, the application in inland shipping is not. In the Netherlands, the principles were only incorporated in the Dutch Code in 1954.

[26] The concept is said to derive from equity (see eg *Strang, Steel & Co v A Scott & Co* (1889) 14 App Cas 601 (HL), 608) and supportable on public policy grounds: see eg FD Rose, *General Average: Law and Practice*, 3rd edn (London, Informa Law from Routledge, 2018) 6. Reasonableness is still one of the overall principles set out in the YAR's Rule Paramount.

[27] On the basis of market investigations, it was estimated in 2020 that only in the Netherlands there were roughly 60 general average case in inland shipping per year. See JA Kruit, 'The Future of General Average n Inland Waterway Shipping – Where are we Now and Where are we Going?' in F Smeele, K Haak, M Fisher, W Sprenger and F Stevens (eds), *Festschrift Resi Hacksteiner* (The Hague, Eleven International Publishing, 2020) 153.

[28] See eg E Wong et al, 'The Suez Canal Blockage: A Legal Analysis of Impacts, Liabilities and Risks for the Global Supply Chain' (2022) 28 *JIML* 252; F Stevens et al, 'Ever Given: potentiële aansprakelijkheden en verzekeringsdekking' (2021) 23 *AV&S* 23.

[29] It was argued that GA was expensive, sensitive to fraud and shipowner friendly. G Gilmore and CL Black Jr, *The Law of Admiralty*, 2nd edn (Mineola, Foundation Press Inc, 1975) 270: 'General average … is by no means self-evidently a necessary or useful institution on the whole. Its abolition would be thinkable, whether or not desirable. If it were abolished, no gap would be left that must indispensably be filled'. For a discussion of the various arguments see inter alia GR Rudolf, *The York-Antwerp Rules, their History and Development, with Comments on the Rules of 1924* (London, Stevens and Sons Ltd, 1926) 32–37; KS Selmer, *The Survival of General Average – A necessity or an Anachronism?* (Oslo, Oslo University Press, 1958) 136–295; W Tetley, 'General Average Now and in the Future' in *Liber Amicorum R Roland* (Brussels, Larcier, 2003) 419, 444; R Cornah, 'The Road to Vancouver – The Development of the York-Antwerp Rules' (2004) 10 *JIML* 155; RR Cornah, RCG Sarll, and JB Shead, *Lowndes and Rudolf – The Law of General Average and The York-Antwerp Rules* (London, Thomson Reuters, 2018) 15. See also *General Average a Preliminary Review*, TD/B/C.4/ISL/58 (UNCTAD, 19 August 1991) and *The Place of General Average in Marine Insurance Today*, UNCTAD/SDD/LEG/1 (UNCTAD, 6 March 1994).

[30] Substantive replies were received from 21 countries as well and from AAA, AMD, ICS/BIMCO and IUMI. The replies to the questionnaire, as well as the consolidating report (September 2013), are published at www.comitemaritime.org/Review-of-the-Rules-on-General-Average/0,27140,114032,00.html. The fact that the number of replies set an all-time record shows that the general average is still very much alive indeed.

[31] In response to the questionnaire, only the European Shippers Council has argued that general average should be abolished ('ESC Calls for an Open Debate on the Abolition of 'General Average', 26 July 2013) at the time published on its website. This position, however, was only advocated in the press and no official reply to the questionnaire was submitted to CMI.

after an incident. It was also correctly indicated that a substantial number of general average allowances would probably be recoverable under the equitable principles of unjust enrichment.[32] Moreover, given the widespread GA provisions in practically all national maritime legislation, a convention with worldwide acceptance would probably be necessary to do away with the system. In more recent times, GA has become much more efficient. Due to the inclusion of absorption clauses in the vessel's hull insurance policies, the number of (smaller value) cases in which general average was apportioned has decreased substantially,[33] whereas low-value cargoes under the YAR 2016 at the adjuster's discretion no longer have to be included.[34]

Interestingly, GA has stayed around, despite the absence of a sound legal basis for its application, as will be further explained below.

B. Legal Basis

Although GA is internationally accepted and applied, its legal basis is often uncertain. A general average convention does not exist. Most legal systems provide for some GA provisions. An analysis of the various systems shows that these provisions are similar but not the same and often very limited in scope.[35] In addition, mandatory GA provisions are scarce.[36] The main GA framework is contractual in nature.

The background to GA can be explained historically. At the end of the nineteenth century, domestic practices deviated to such an extent that some form of international uniformity was vital. Practitioners arranged an international conference and prepared a set of rules, which over time would develop into the York-Antwerp Rules (YAR). The initial idea was that the agreed rules were to be incorporated into the national legislation of the main maritime nations. The intention was that if all legislations included the rules, it would be irrelevant which law would be applicable. Until international uniform legislation was in place, contractual incorporation served as a bridging mechanism. The incorporation in legislation proved a bridge too far, but the intended temporary bridging solution was a survivor. A version of the YAR is still invariably incorporated into most – if not all – contracts for the carriage of goods by sea worldwide. The YAR are regarded as one of the most universally applied uniform rules.[37] And again, their application is entirely voluntary, as they are not stipulated by any mandatory law.

[32] IUMI's reply included in CMI IWG Report (n 30) 9.

[33] The use of absorption clauses has considerably reduced the number of general average cases, in 2013 by as much as 50%: *Lowndes and Rudolf* (n 29)15.

[34] YAR 2016, Rule XVII(a)(ii): 'Any cargo may be excluded from contributing to general average should the adjuster consider that the cost of including it in the adjustment would be likely to be disproportionate to its eventual contribution.' See *Lowndes and Rudolf* (n 29) para 17.13.

[35] For an analysis of the ancient regimes, see JA Kruit, 'General Average – General Principle Plus Varying Practical Application Equals Uniformity?' (2015) 21 *JIML* 190. For the recent rules, see JA Kruit, *General Average, Legal basis and Applicable Law* (Zutphen, Paris Legal Publishers, 2017) 90–189; *Lowndes and Rudolf* (n 29) section 4.

[36] The CMNI refers back to contractual provisions or national law: 'Nothing in this Convention shall prevent the application of provisions in the contract of carriage or national law regarding the calculation of the amount of damages and contributions payable in the event of general average.' (Art 26).

[37] General average is regarded as the 'field of maritime law where the international unification effort has succeeded to the greatest degree': see KS Selmer, *The Survival of General Average: A Necessity or an*

Rule A YAR, the wording of which has not changed since 1924, contains the criteria most frequently applied to define a general average act. It provides:

> There is a general average act when, and only when, any extraordinary sacrifice or expenditure is intentionally and reasonably made or incurred for the common safety for the purpose of preserving from peril the property involved in a common maritime adventure.

It is regarded as *the* general average definition. It should be noted, however, that the YAR themselves immediately downplay this role. They provide that this definition only applies when a situation does not fall within one of the specific GA examples set out in the YAR's numbered rules.[38] The 'unofficial definition', however, provides good insight into what the concept entails. It shows the sharing mechanism based on equity.

C. Flexible Application

Throughout the centuries, the GA principles have not been applied in a static manner. Historical research shows that there was a high level of flexibility: regarding the general average disbursements, ie the costs and sacrifices that were to be shared, as well as the establishment of contributory values, ie the value based on which the financial contribution was calculated.[39] The contributing parties and the claimants varied and still vary. If we look, for example, at the parties interested in the cargo, the interested parties include the cargo owners, the parties at risk, the legal holder of a bill of lading and (potentially several) cargo underwriters.[40] Looking at the development of the concept before the creation and successful contractual implementation of the YAR, there were many national regulations with their own specifics. Even though they all derived from the *Lex Rhodia de iactu*, and were all based on equity, the actual application varied. There has been and still is a level of flexibility that allowed the concept to be applied throughout the ages and to accommodate new developments.

III. General Average and the Climate Crisis

A. The Different Applications of General Average

It needs no explanation that shipping has changed completely in the last centuries. But the need for cooperation between the parties involved in the maritime adventure in times of peril has remained. At present, the world, including the maritime field, is facing the most significant peril, probably in its whole existence, ie the climate crisis. If there ever has been a need for common solutions, for collaboration against peril, it is now and in the years to come. First, this is so because the climate crisis and the required

Anachronism? (Oslo, Oslo University Press, 1958) 58, cited with approval in NG Hudson and MD Harvey, *The York-Antwerp Rules*, 3rd edn (London, Lloyd's List, 2010) 9.

[38] Rule of Interpretation, YAR 1950 and later versions. See *Lowndes and Rudolf* (n 29) para RI.01.

[39] See Kruit (n 35).

[40] Kruit (n 35) 134–157.

transition will increase the risks for shipping. The number of accidents is expected to rise and, as a result, the general average cases will increase in its slipstream. In addition, and more importantly, the climate crisis requires creating a new narrative. It is increasingly clear that collaboration is vital in order to successfully make the transition, both for each player in the maritime industry individually and for the industry as a whole. Research has shown that transformative narratives can be helpful, especially when they include near-term economic benefits.[41] GA principles can provide that narrative if we extend their scope. Its burden-sharing mechanism can inspire other burden-sharing mechanisms to bear the pains and gains of the decarbonisation transition jointly. These applications of the general average principles are discussed below.

B. More Accidents and More General Average Disbursements

Climate scientists have advised that the climate crisis has already led to more extreme weather events and that this pattern will increase – the events will be even more extreme and the same will happen more frequently.[42] The impacts will also become increasingly complex and more difficult to manage.[43] Extreme weather events will result in accidents, which will require measures to safeguard ships and cargo, resulting in more general average situations. Ships will need to deviate, whether or not to ports of refuge, to prevent the impacts of increasingly severe weather events. When the water level decreases, groundings will happen more frequently when ships are to service their inland ports of destination. At the same time, flooding may result in greater need for salvage assistance. Incidents are also expected to take place as a result of the fuel transition. Decarbonisation will require a transition to sustainable fuel, including methanol, ammonia and hydrogen. These alternative fuels are more flammable than gas oil and especially at the beginning of the transition may cause incidents, which will need actions to save the maritime adventure, which will give rise to GA.[44]

In addition, new disbursements will arise that will be considered as general average disbursements. From 2024, shipping has been included in the European Emission Trading System (ETS), ie a legislative scheme by which the EU caps the overall volume of greenhouse gas emissions emitted by certain industries.[45] Within the cap, which decreases every year, emission allowances will need to be obtained. This will result in additional costs, which may also be apportioned in GA. In his annual address to the Association of Average Adjusters in May 2022, the then president of the Association

[41] D Mangalagiu et al, 'Transformative Narratives for Climate Action' (2020) 160 *Climatic Change* 495.

[42] IPCC Report (n 1) 12: 'Human-caused climate change is already affecting many weather and climate extremes in every region across the globe.'

[43] ibid 37.

[44] WA Reinsch and W O'Neil, 'Hydrogen: The key to Decarbonizing the Global Shipping Industry?' (Centre for Strategic International Studies, 13 April 2021) www.csis.org/analysis/hydrogen-key-decarbonizing-global-shipping-industry.

[45] See eg 'Emissions cap and allowances' (European Commission, 14 July 2021), climate.ec.europa.eu/eu-action/eu-emissions-trading-system-eu-ets/emissions-cap-and-allowances_en; Directive (EU) 2023/959 of the European Parliament and of the Council of 10 May 2023 amending Directive 2003/87/EC establishing a system for greenhouse gas emission allowance trading within the Union and Decision (EU) 2015/1814 concerning the establishment and operation of a market stability reserve for the Union greenhouse gas emission trading system adopted on 16 May 2023 and entered into force on 5 June 2023. See, above, Eftestøl (ch 5).

of Average Adjusters, Michiel Starmans, argued that new carbon levies on bunkers subsequent to a general average act were allowable in GA and therefore will need to be included in the apportionment and hence shared by the interested parties.[46]

C. The General Average Sharing Mechanism

i. Common Peril?

GA *principles* can also assist with the financial burdens of the decarbonisation transition.[47] In exceptional situations and times of peril, collaboration is key. In shipping, the master and crew experience this during their voyages. Against that background, it is not uncommon that shipping legislation still reflects aspects of a 'community idea'. Classic shipping law concepts of salvage, global limitation of liability and GA are all based on sharing the financial burdens of maritime adventures. Most notably, GA principles provide that at a time of danger, the financial burdens of solutions to save all are to be shared and that the parties involved accept this, at least when the accident that necessitated the GA disbursement was not caused by a breach of contract of one of the parties involved in the maritime adventure.[48]

GA principles provide a solution, ie a tried and tested system for accommodating the transition to more sustainable shipping. Saving the planet could well be regarded as a common peril. We only have one earth on which we live, and there is a common interest to keep it habitable. The measures to be taken to decarbonise the shipping industry, and hence safeguard its existence, can be regarded as extraordinary. Changes are required at a technical and operational level. GA principles can provide an equitable solution,[49] that is also most efficient from an economic point of view.[50] Application of GA principles could result in a solution that would not be possible by the individual interests and provides that all interested parties are interested in creating the best overall outcome. As set out above, the principles allow for the required flexibility to be generalised[51] and adjusted to modern times.

[46] 'Shipowners have Strong Case to Recover Emission Levies in a General Average Deviation to a Port of Refuge, Contends Association of Average Adjusters Chairman' *American J of Transportation* (Plymouth, 23 May 2022) ajot.com/news/article/shipowners-have-strong-case-to-recover-emission-levies-in-a-general-average-deviation-to-a-port-of-refuge-contends-association-of-average-adjusters-chairman.

[47] See also: C Demonsant et al (eds), *Le changement climatique – un péril commun* (Paris, Presses des Mines, collection Économie et gestion, 2023); M Fusaro in *The Borders of Risk: Jurisdictional Boundaries and Risk Management in Early Modern Europe* (forthcoming, 2023).

[48] In general, most legal systems provide that there is no liability to contribute in general average, if the incident was caused by the actionable fault of one of the parties. See eg Kruit (n 35) 168–182. See also Rule D YAR 1924–2016. In more detail: *Lowndes and Rudolf* (n 29) para D.03.

[49] As set out in the joint Report on the State of Climate Action, 'the benefits and opportunities reaped from the transition must be shared equitably': see *State of Climate Action* 2022 (New Climate Institute, 2022). Berlin and Cologne, Germany, San Francisco, CA, and Washington, DC: Bezos Earth Fund, Climate Action Tracker, Climate Analytics, ClimateWorks Foundation, NewClimate Institute, the United Nations Climate Change High-Level Champions, and World Resources Institute doi.org/10.46830/wrirpt.22.00028.

[50] C Demonsant et al, 'De la ressource commune au péril commun: Repenser nos modèles de l'action climatique', *Revue de l'Organisation responsible* (ESKA, 2021) ffhal-03630940f.

[51] B Zalewski, 'Creative Interpretation of Lex Rhodia de iactu in the Legal Doctrine of Ius Commune' (2016) 8 *Krytyka Prawa* 173. Zalewski shows that medieval lawyers applied a new meaning to the principle. Its purpose was regarded as to provide compensation for any damage incurred in a joint interest or in other people's interest. For the extended application of the principle see also Kruit (n 35) 29–30.

At present, the YAR excludes environmental damage as general average disbursement[52] but costs to prevent such measures are to be allowed as general average after all if the same are incurred as a condition of a general average measure.[53] In years to come, this provision or at least its scope, may need to be reconsidered.[54]

ii. Inclusion of Gains?

GA traditionally relates to losses and costs only, ie so to shared pains. The transition to greener transport also provides opportunities to generate financial benefits only if parties cooperate. And the benefits may even outweigh the costs.[55] When benefits are derived jointly, the fruits should be divided as well. GA solves the split incentives problem and could be extended to include apportionment of benefits. Given that the financial implications are such an important factor for human action, this should incentivise parties to cooperate. We have to increase the cake and share it. This could make the transition less a problem for the ship's interested parties but would make it a common, more inclusive challenge, which is more in line with reality. Maritime voyages take place because users need the goods. Reduced pollution will benefit everybody. GA principles are capable of providing both a common frame of reference and valuable inspiration for the extension of the principle.

GA principles could be applied in various ways – and are flexible enough to be adapted to the specific purpose. If the use of battery containers results in a longer trip, the costs thereof may be compensated by higher freight. However, they may also, at least partially, be compensated by the energy generated by solar panels on the top row of containers. Obviously, only the top row can generate energy, but the energy could be used to cover part of the total voyage costs rather than just benefit the few 'top rowers'. Common gains could also exist in the form of carbon credits generated by forfeiting emissions.[56] McKinsey research has shown that front-running shippers are willing to pay a premium for sustainable transport offerings of 5–10 per cent.[57] This is a significant first step that, although probably insufficient, should not be ignored and included in the equation. Speed reductions will immediately lead to emissions reductions. Some shipowners and charterers with long-lasting relationships have agreed to share these

[52] Rule C (2) YAR 1994, YAR 2004 and YAR 2016; *Lowndes and Rudolf* (n 29) para C.36.

[53] Rule XI YAR 1994, YAR 2004 and YAR 2016; *Lowndes and Rudolf*, ibid para 11.01.

[54] In the German text of the IVR Rules, which are applied in inland waterway general averages, 'Wasserhaushaltschäden' (damages to waterways and water economy) are already mentioned separately. General Average Rules IVR and commentary Edition 2006, Rule IV, 9.

[55] Clinsh has calculated that the costs of the transition to a greener inland transport would amount to around €2 billion, whereas the social benefits would be €4.9 billion (*Clinsh Layman's Report* www.clinsh.eu/project-results.html). However, research performed at the instruction of the Central Commission for the Navigation on the Rhine (CCNR), which supports full decarbonisation of Inland Water Transports by 2050, finds that an additional €10 billion is needed to finance the European sector's energy transition: 'Study on Financing the energy transition to a zero-emission European IWT Sector' (CCNR, Rotterdam, July 2021). See also Briefing European Parliament, 'Inland waterway transport in the EU', European Union, 2022.

[56] Since September 2022, Marsh clients are allowed to pay fees by way of carbon credits and renewable energy certificates, www.marsh.com/us/about/media/marsh-clients-can-now-pay-fees-using-carbon-credits-and-renewable-energy-certificates.html.

[57] M van Gogh et al, 'Driving Decarbonisation: Accelerating Zero-emission Freight Transport (*WEF and McKinsey*, 28 July 2022) www.mckinsey.com/industries/travel-logistics-and-infrastructure/our-insights/driving-decarbonization-accelerating-zero-emission-freight-transport#/.

pains and gains in the market. Both parties accept the speed reduction and the financial savings on the bunker fuels are distributed between the two parties. Although their agreement does not bear the GA name, it is a perfect example of the refurbished ancient sharing mechanism. In addition, it is investigated whether the sharing mechanism could be applied more broadly in the supply chain in the Blue Visby Solution project, ie a multilateral platform for reducing shipping GHG emissions by about 15 per cent through eradicating the practice of 'Sail Fast, Then Wait'.[58]

iii. Extension of the Term 'Maritime Adventure'?

But why restrict the application of the GA concept to a particular voyage only? The application of GA principles could be extended from a single voyage to the wider shipping business. Wider cooperation is not uncommon in maritime practice. Shipowners and charterers generally insure their liability with mutual insurance companies, the P&I Clubs. The main P&I Clubs reinsure each other via the International Group of P&I Clubs.[59] Why not extend cooperation for decarbonisation purposes? Also, without decarbonisation, additional damage as a result of additional general average and other events and litigation caused by the climate crisis[60] will most likely be suffered by the underwriters of the maritime parties and hence by the parties themselves due to increased premiums.[61] It is quite clear that these costs may better be spent on preventing damage and hence in the transition.

And why only look at the parties directly involved in the maritime adventure? A maritime voyage is hardly a separate island. It has become inextricably linked with the whole supply chain because 90 per cent of trade is carried by sea.[62] So almost the whole world uses and depends on the maritime industry and is interconnected with and influenced by maritime trade as the stranding of the 'Ever Given' in the Suez Canal made abundantly clear.[63] At the same time, everyone suffers the consequences of the pollution caused by the maritime industry. The Intergovernmental Panel on Climate Change (IPCC) Report April 2022 mentions several health benefits that may also need to be included in the bigger picture.[64] The costs of climate inaction for shipping have been calculated to be very substantial:

[58] bluevisby.com.

[59] The 12 P&I Clubs comprising the International Group (the 'Group') between them provide marine liability cover (protection and indemnity) for approximately 90% of the world's ocean-going tonnage: www.igpandi.org/about/.

[60] JA Kruit, 'Sterke toename klimaatrechtspraak (verwacht)' (*Van Traa*, February 2022) www.vantraa.nl/nl/kennis/sterke-toename-klimaatrechtspraak-verwacht/#_ftn22.

[61] In 2020, the (then) Standard P&I Club advised that there has been a 46% rise in weather-related disasters since 2000; I Walia, 'Marine Insurance Sector Faces Turbulence from Climate Change' (*Lloyd's List*, 26 October 2020) lloydslist.maritimeintelligence.informa.com/LL1134406/Marine-insurance-sector-faces-turbulence-from-climate-change; E Roston, 'The World's Cargo Ships Are Sailing Into Worse Climate Risks' (*Bloomberg*, 14 March 2022) www.bloomberg.com/news/articles/2022-03-14/the-world-s-cargo-ships-are-sailing-into-worse-climate-risks#xj4y7vzkg; 'Climate Challenges in the Shipping Industry' (*Allianz*, 15 July 2020) www.agcs.allianz.com/news-and-insights/expert-risk-articles/shipping-2020-climate-change.html.

[62] www.oecd.org/ocean/topics/ocean-shipping/.

[63] Wong (n 28).

[64] IPCC Report April 2022, summary C-8, 42 – with reference to paras 10.2, 10.4–10.7: 'Many mitigation strategies in the transport sector would have various co-benefits, including air quality improvements, health benefits, equitable access to transportation services, reduced congestion and reduced material demand'.

> Without further action to reduce emissions, climate change impacts could cost the shipping industry an additional US$25 billion every year by 2100. To put these estimates into context, total operating profits for the global container shipping industry averaged less than US$ 20 billion per year during 2018–2020.[65]

If we zoom in on inland shipping, the CLean INland SHipping consortium (Clinsh) has calculated that the health and social benefits of greening inland transport would amount to €4,9 billion.[66] In other words, if the industry does not change, society as a whole rather than the individual company or specific players in the supply chain will have to suffer the consequences. Damage will have to be paid for without any gain. It seems obvious that it would be better for everybody if that damage could be prevented. The money that would need to be paid for damage caused without decarbonisation could be used to decarbonise the industry and prevent such damage from occurring. Research has shown that the actual costs of decarbonising at an earlier stage are expected to be lower than the damage caused by additional pollution.[67]

iv. Implementation of a Maritime Decarbonisation Fund?

Practical implementation could take place in the form of the creation of a fund to support the transition.

In the maritime decarbonisation discussions, the idea of a fund is not new.[68] On 25 October 2022, the International Chamber of Shipping (ICS) proposed a global shipping CO_2 reduction fund to reward 'first movers' using low-emission fuels.[69] Another example is the fund launched by CMA CGM to invest in French maritime decarbonisation projects.[70] The Central Commission for the Navigation on the Rhine also investigated options to establish a green fund[71] and the EU created an innovation fund, a funding programme for the demonstration of innovative low-carbon technologies, for which revenues have partially been earmarked for shipping specifically.[72]

These and other funding ideas could be extended to include not only the front-runners or parties of a specific country or region but all parties.[73]

[65] 'Act Now or Pay Later: The Costs of Climate Inaction for Ports and Shipping' (RTI International, March 2022) 4.

[66] Clinsh Layman's Report www.clinsh.eu/project-results.html.

[67] P Howard and D Sylvan, 'Gauging Economic Consensus on Climate Change', Institute for Policy Integrity, New York University School of Law (New York, 30 March 2021).

[68] In the general decarbonisation discussions, the use of a fund is well accepted. See eg the COP 27 Loss and Damage Fund (22 November 2022): 'COP27 ends with announcement of historic loss and damage fund' www.unep.org/news-and-stories/story/cop27-ends-announcement-historic-loss-and-damage-fund. See also EU's Just Transition Fund, ec.europa.eu/regional_policy/funding/just-transition-fund_en.

[69] www.ics-shipping.org/press-release/international-chamber-of-shipping-proposes-global-co2-reduction-fund-to-reward-first-movers-using-low-emission-fuels/.

[70] 'The CMA CGM Group launches a call for projects worth for €200 million to step up the pace of decarbonization of the French shipping industry' (CMA CGM, 30 January 2023) www.cma-cgm.com/news/4281/the-cma-cgm-group-launches-a-call-for-projects-worth-for-200-million-to-step-up-the-pace-of-decarbonization-of-the-french-shipping-industry.

[71] CCNR, 'Study on Financing the Energy Transition to a Zero-emission European IWT Sector' (Rotterdam, July 2021).

[72] European Commission, 'What is the Innovation Fund?' climate.ec.europa.eu/eu-action/funding-climate-action/innovation-fund/what-innovation-fund_en.

[73] It is important to note in this respect that research shows that historically the general average concept was mainly used by the middle section of the industry. S Go, 'Governance of General Average in the Netherlands

Funds are not uncommon in the shipping business. Under the Convention on Limitation of Liability for Maritime Claims, 1976/1996 (LLMC), persons alleged to be liable for shipping accidents may inter alia limit their liability by setting up a fund.[74] Regarding oil pollution caused by shipping incidents, a compromise was reached, also including a fund. Under the Civil Liability Convention (CLC), liability is channelled to the shipowner, who is strictly liable up to an amount based on the vessel's tonnage, in respect of which compulsory insurance has to be taken out.[75] The CLC is backed by the 1992 Fund Convention and the 2003 Supplementary Fund Protocol,[76] financed by contributions levied by receivers of substantial amounts of crude oil or heavy fuel oil in 1992 Fund Member States.[77] The contributions made by the receivers recognise that there is no single polluter in shipping, but multiple actors together are responsible for the pollution. Despite the added complexity, the Fund Convention is well established in practice.

However, the supply chain is not the only value chain that plays a role in shipping. In fact, the maritime industry can be regarded as 'a complex ecosystem composed of various value chains',[78] which in addition to the supply chain, includes the fuel chain, shipbuilding chain and operations chain.

As these examples show, various mechanisms exist to finance and distribute a maritime decarbonisation fund. Options may include premiums on pollution to reflect the actual costs, including the damage to the environment; revenues of an Emission Trading Scheme; revenues created by energy efficiency measures like reduced bunker consumption or carbon credits (regardless of whether they are obtained); penalties for non-compliance; and, possibly most interestingly, the financial equivalent of the damage to the environment that an earlier decarbonisation will prevent. It is generally accepted that the costs of taking action now are considerably lower than the damage that will be suffered if actions are postponed or not taken.[79]

It goes without saying that any plan should be implemented transnationally in order to level the playing field. To have the widest possible scope, a worldwide regime would be preferable. In seagoing shipping, this may not be easy to realise but initiatives are being rolled out. An example directly inspired by GA, is the above mentioned Blue Visby Solution,[80] a consortium that has developed an algorithm for the most sustainable route planning. As the costs and losses of the algorithm's application do not fall equally, a new contractual framework has been created for participants to share the pains and

in the Nineteenth Century: A Backward Development?' in P Hellwege and G Rossi (eds), *Maritime Risk Management* (Berlin, Duncker & Humblot GmbH, 2021) 248.

[74] LLMC, Art 11.

[75] International Convention on Civil Liability for Oil Pollution Convention (CLC) 1969, replaced by 1992 Protocol.

[76] iopcfunds.org/about-us/legal-framework/#.

[77] The Hazardous and Noxious Substances Convention (HNS) has not yet entered into force.

[78] M Lind et al, 'Decarbonizing the maritime sector: Mobilizing coordinated action in the industry using an ecosystems approach' (UNCTAD, 8 June 2022) unctad.org/news/decarbonizing-maritime-sector-mobilizing-coordinated-action-industry-using-ecosystems-approach.

[79] B Carton and JM Natal, 'Further Delaying Climate Policies Will Hurt Economic Growth' (IMF, 5 October 2022) www.imf.org/en/Blogs/Articles/2022/10/05/further-delaying-climate-policies-will-hurt-economic-growth; Howard and Sylvan (n 67). See also KI van der Wijst, et al, 'New Damage Curves and Multimodel Analysis Suggest Lower Optimal Temperature' (2023) 13 *National Climate Change* 434.

[80] bluevisby.com.

the gains created by the use of the algorithm, known as the Blue GA Rules, or the Blue General Apportionment Rules.[81]

In inland waterway shipping, implementation may be easier to realise, at least on the European continent. Both the Budapest Convention on the Contract for the Carriage of Goods by Inland Waterway (CMNI) and the Strasbourg Convention on the Limitation of Liability in Inland Navigation (CLNI), have entered into force relatively soon after their adoption and the number of member states that have ratified and implemented the conventions is high. Implementing a green premium would require a revision of the Mannheim Convention,[82] but there does not appear to be a reason why this could not be achieved. Another option would be to arrange a fund contractually.

The history of GA has shown that uniformity can be created contractually. Technology, including further digitalisation, opens up possibilities, also for GA, to make the system more efficient.[83]

D. The General Average Narrative

The technology to take the required decarbonisation steps exists. The spectrum of measures is wide and varies from different fuel to changes in design to a change of operations. Various road maps have been suggested.[84] Some actions are problematic from a technological perspective. Alternative fuel options require ships to be refitted, an alternative infrastructure, and licences. However, there are also those measures that, from a technological perspective, do not require any amendment and should already have become standard practice long ago, like slow steaming and further route optimisation. This 'low hanging fruit', which can reduce current emissions considerably, is not widely or sufficiently used yet and clearly shows that technology is not the only or even the main hurdle. Research from the Global Maritime Forum shows that short-term action opportunities could save US$50 billion annually.[85] But still, this is not yet happening on a wide scale. We all know that it is better for everybody when a vessel sails on green electricity,

[81] H Zagrofakis et al, 'The Contractual Architecture of the "Blue Visby Solution"' (2022) 22(6) *Lloyd's Shipping & Trade Law.*

[82] MAW van Maanen and JA Kruit, 'Sustainable Transport' in: *Koninklijke Vereeniging Handelsrecht, Preadviezen* (Zutphen, Paris Legal Publishers, 2021) 228.

[83] Digitalisation will make the application of GA principles much easier. It is a truism, but calculations can be made much more efficiently by computers than by humans. Digitally offered security forms prevent an overload of mail and subsequent administration. Payment of premiums into a fund can be better registered and distributed.

[84] Insight brief, 'Short-Term Action Opportunities' (*Global Maritime Forum*, 27 March 2023) www.globalmaritimeforum.org/news/short-term-action-opportunities.

[85] See eg Industry Roadmap developed by the Getting to Zero Coalition of the Global Maritime Forum www.globalmaritimeforum.org/getting-to-zero-coalition; 'A Pathway to Decarbonise the Shipping Sector by 2050' (International Renewable Energy Agency, 2021); and the DNV Pathway to Net Zero Emissions www.dnv.com/news/new-report-pathway-to-net-zero-emissions-210507. See also: A Grzelakowski et al, 'Maritime Shipping Decarbonization: Roadmap to Meet Zero-Emission Target in Shipping as a Link in the Global Supply Chains' (2022) *Energies* 15, 6150 and E Morante, 'Roadmap to decarbonize the shipping sector: Technology development, consistent policies and investment in research, development and innovation' (UNCTAD, 2022) *Transport and Trade Facilitation Newsletter N°96* unctad.org/news/transport-newsletter-article-no-99-fourth-quarter-2022.

hydrogen or at least biofuel.[86] The green premium – whether monetary or in time – is not happily paid by all.

Regulation can and should lead parties to choose the green(er) option.[87] Legislators could and should set strong decarbonisation targets as regulatory pressure is one of the most prevailing driver(s) of sustainability practices.[88] However, it is not as simple as waving a magic wand. The debates are strenuous and leave much open for the maritime parties to be discussed inter se.

Research shows that decarbonisation requires a mental shift or a new mindset;[89] 'what drives our machines won't change until we change what drives our ideas'.[90] We need to change our behaviour and shipping needs to move to new business models.[91] And, this is extremely difficult because changes are generally not made voluntarily. Letting go of old ideas is not something we voluntarily do. We do not need psychologists and spiritual teachers to tell us that any true transformation generally needs an external push. If there ever was such push, it is the climate disaster that we are running into. But mere information is insufficient. It is widely acknowledged that narratives can motivate or demotivate climate action much more than mere climate information:[92]

> Narratives – stories about how the world works, what the future will look like, and our own role in this process – can extend cognition, creating shared knowledge across space and time, and shape our beliefs, values and actions in the face of tremendous uncertainty. Narratives thus have political and psychological agency and can reinforce or challenge existing power relations and trajectories.[93]

[86] State of Climate Action 2022, 84 'Scenarios aligned with a 1.5°C pathway suggest that 5–17 percent of fuel used in maritime shipping will need to be zero-emission fuel by 2030 and 84–93 percent of fuel by 2050' (IEA 2021h; UMAS 2021).

[87] The Global Impact Assessment of Regulations and Policies for Sustainable Aviation by 2050-project (GLIMPSE2050) shows that the right regulation can reduce emissions considerably; 'GLIMPSE2050: How regulation can reduce aviation's environmental footprint', cleansky.eu, 5 July 2021; 'Global Impact Assessment of Regulations and Policies for Sustainable Aviation by 2050', GLIMPSE2050: How regulation can reduce aviation's environmental footprint (www.clean-aviation.eu/glimpse2050-how-regulation-can-reduce-aviations-environmental-footprint).

[88] See eg Industry Transition Outlook, *Maersk Mc-Kinney Moller Center for Zero Carbon Shipping* (25 October 2021), ch 3 www.zerocarbonshipping.com; MA Saeed and W Kersten, 'Drivers of Sustainable Supply Chain Management: Identification and Classification', (2019) 11 *Sustainability* 1137.

[89] *ESG Playbook for Shipping* (Maersk McKinney Møller Center for Zero Carbon Shipping and Boston Consulting Group, February 2023) 11-17 www.zerocarbonshipping.com/publications/the-esg-playbook-for-shipping/.

[90] R Solnit, '"If you Win the Popular Imagination, You Change the Game": Why we Need New Stories on Climate' (*The Guardian*, 12 January 2023) www.theguardian.com/news/2023/jan/12/rebecca-solnit-climate-crisis-popular-imagination-why-we-need-new-stories.

[91] Insight brief, 'Short-Term Action Opportunities (*Global Maritime Forum*, 27 March 2023) www.globalmaritimeforum.org/news/short-term-action-opportunities.

[92] See eg D Mangalagiu and A Bisaro, 'Transformative Narratives for Climate Action' (June 2020) *Climatic Change*; M Böhringer, 'The World's Biggest Problem Solvers Need to Craft Better Narratives', (*World Economic Forum*, 2 January 2023) www.weforum.org/agenda/2023/01/narratives-leaders-climate-change-wef23/; R Lejano and S Nero, *The Power of Narrative: Climate Skepticism and the Deconstruction of Science* (Oxford, Oxford University Press, 2020); S Veland et al, 'Narrative Matters for Sustainability: The Transformative Role of Storytelling in Realizing 1.5°C' (April 2018) *Environmental Sustainability* 41; K Fløttum and Ø Gjerstad, 'Narratives in Climate Change Discourse' (September 2016) *WIREs Climate Change*,; L Westerhoff and J Robinson, 'The Meaning(s) of Climate Change: Exploring Narrative and Social Practice in the Quest for Transformation' (Institute for Resources, Environment and Sustainability, 2013).

[93] SM Constantino and EU Weber, 'Decision-making Under the Deep Uncertainty of Climate Change: The Psychological and Political Agency of Narratives' (2021) *Current Opinion in Psychology*, 151.

Doom and gloom scenarios, even when supported by factual evidence, might even be counterproductive in motivating parties to take the necessary climate action. Narratives that seem more productive provide a positive story, include a vision going forward, set out solutions, highlight opportunities, and include near-term economic benefits.[94]

Therefore, a new narrative is (also) required for the shipping business going forward, including the maritime decarbonisation challenge. This narrative should address the shipping community as a whole and include all its players, invoking maritime history and the particularisms of the shipping industry. It should build on the danger that the industry is facing (whether defined as the climate crisis or anticipated very stringent decarbonisation targets) rather than the predominant business model of the last decades and show the possibilities of the change to the shipping business. The narrative should include the fact that people will not buy a story if they feel that its consequences are unjust, that they are the only ones that are required to do something and that others are left off the hook or burdened considerably more. In a nutshell, a just and equitable transition is required,[95] that steers away from 'I' to 'we' if we are to fight the worldwide climate crisis at all levels. For shipping decarbonisation, we are in the fortunate position that such a narrative already exists and has been in place for thousands of years in the form of the maritime burden sharing mechanism of GA. The new narrative must also be supported from an economic perspective. Researchers at the Paris Centre de Gestion Scientifique (the scientific management centre) plead for using GA principles to combat climate change. They argue that GA would be the better alternative as basis for action compared to the 'polluter pays' principle,[96] which provides that the polluter is to be responsible for the costs of the pollution caused.[97] The 'polluter pays' principle is based on the prevention of damage. GA principles – by contrast – are based on mutually created wealth and would make it a common effort to reduce climate change, unlike the individual approach of the 'polluter pays' principle. Moreover, if the application of GA is extended to include benefits, it seems difficult to resist.[98]

[94] Mangalagiu and Bisaro (n 92).

See also the report of J Hinkel, 'Transformative Narratives for Climate Action: Win-win Strategies Linking Climate and Sustainable Development Goals' (2018), Global Climate Forum (GCF), Germany: 'Transformative narratives have been found to be effective in crystallising action when they meet three requirements i) support and resonate with aspirations, ideals and desires; ii) are engaging and empowering, so that individuals feel that participation is voluntary and constructive; iii) resonate with moral authority e.g., fairness, responsibility, or inclusiveness (Pahl-Wostl et al, 2007).'

[95] A Shaw and C De Beukelaer, 'Why Should we Talk About a "Just and Equitable" Transition for Shipping?' (UNCTAD, 15 September 2022) unctad.org/news/why-should-we-talk-about-just-and-equitable-transition-shipping. Also: C Demonsant, 'Overcoming the Tragedy of Climate Change: An Examination of a Managerial Rule of Solidarity' (*Ideas*, 2021) ideas.repec.org/p/hal/journl/hal-03063693.html.

[96] C Demonsant, et al, 'De la ressource commune au péril commun: Repenser nos modèles de l'action climatique. Revue de l'Organisation Responsible', ESKA, 2021. ffhal-03630940f.

[97] The polluter pays principle has developed from an economic to a legal principle (Paper OESO, 'The Polluter-Pays Principle OECD, Analyses and Recommendations', 1992, 9). It is one of the pillars of the European environmental policy and is included, inter alia, in Art 192(2) of the Treaty on the Functioning of the European Union. It is also expressly mentioned inter alia in the Whitebook Roadmap to a Single European Transport Area – Towards a competitive and resource efficient transport system (COM (2011)144 final); the 'Fit for 55' proposal (COM(2021)550 final, Fit for 55, 2) and the European Parliament resolution of 27 April 2021 on technical and operational measures for more efficient and cleaner maritime transport (2019/2193(INI)).

[98] Mangalagiu and Bisaro (n 92). Research shows that climate action is still to a considerable extent by economic and social opportunities.

IV. Way Forward

In case of peril, measures need to be taken to safeguard the parties involved in the maritime adventure from that peril. When the classic shipping sector faces an existential threat, either as a result of a climate disaster or as a result of such stringent measures that the sector is to change completely, it seems logical to turn to the ancient burden-sharing mechanism of GA and investigate whether it can play its role as equitable game changer once more. The use of GA principles in a more extended manner is not a far-fetched, mere theoretical scenario. During the COVID-19 pandemic, pains and gains were shared in various ways.[99] More specifically for GA, its underlying principles are investigated as a risk management mechanism for the new economy,[100] whereas GA principles directly inspire the Blue Visby Solution sharing mechanism. At COP 26 in Glasgow, it was emphasised that it is not a question of regulation or market initiatives, but rather a situation of regulation and market initiatives.[101] Various actions are being taken commercially, such as the Sea Cargo Charter, CoZEV (Cargo Owners for Zero Emission Vessels)[102] and the Poseidon Principles for Financial Institutions and Marine Insurance respectively.[103] Even though such initiatives are critical, they are also insufficient. Time is running out, as is the time to initiate one-sided initiatives. Indeed, it is now time to create a plan that directly supports the sector and which may prevent other plans being imposed where revenues need to be shared with other sectors.[104] Further research, much more thought and collaboration with parties in and outside the maritime community will be necessary, but there is undoubtedly much potential.

Where we have to go is clear; a net-zero future. GA principles can show us *how* from a non-technical perspective. The road to net zero should not be paved with good intentions but with GA.

[99] In the Netherlands, the burdens were shared inter alia between lessors and lessees of commercial floor space. The practice developed in case law was confirmed by the Dutch Supreme Court: Dutch Supreme Court 24 December 2021, ECLI:NL:HR:2021:1974.

[100] M Fusaro et al (eds), *General Average and Risk Management in Medieval and Early Modern Maritime Business* (Cham, Springer International Publishing AG, 2023).

[101] Glasgow Climate Pact, inter alia para. 19, 47–48, 55 and 64.

[102] www.cozev.org.

[103] www.poseidonprinciples.org/finance, respectively, www.poseidonprinciples.org/insurance.

[104] See eg the proposal for the EU-ETS as accepted by the European Parliament. Only part of the revenues is dedicated to the maritime sector (draft 8 February 2023, 2021/0211(COD), preamble Art 28a *cf* 33). See also N Walker et al, 'A Greener Voyage: The EU Emissions Trading Scheme Finally Given the All Clear to Set Sail for Maritime' (*Watson Farley & Williams*, 21 April 2023) www.wfw.com/articles/a-greener-voyage-the-eu-emissions-trading-scheme-finally-given-the-all-clear-to-set-sail-for-maritime/.

PART IV

Shipping Carbon for Carbon Storage

13

Shipping Carbon Dioxide as Dangerous Goods: Questions of Liability

MAXIM USYNIN*

I. Introduction

Carbon capture and storage (CCS) is a technological process aimed at curbing carbon dioxide at the emission sites and converting it for long-term storage in the subsoil. The process involves three principal stages: capture, delivery and storage. If one concentrates on the middle stage, the two most likely ways of delivery are via pipeline or shipping by sea. The present contribution looks closely at one particular aspect of shipping: how carbon dioxide could fall under the legal regime of dangerous goods and how risks and liability can be distributed between the contracting parties.

CCS is a rapidly developing field of industrial activity. The North Sea area arguably presents the most relevant carbon shipping case study.[1] This aligns with the policy ambitions of its coastal states, which encourage investment in innovative technology. Norway is actively advertising its storage capacity on the continental shelf.[2] Germany and Denmark have expressed interest in cooperation, including producing biofuels (grey hydrogen and ammonia) and mitigating the impact of the cement industry.[3] Denmark

* Assistant Professor, Centre for Private Governance (CEPRI) and Shipping and Ocean Law Group (SHOC), Faculty of Law, University of Copenhagen.

[1] North Sea identified as a prospective case study in A O'Brien, 'The Liability Framework for the Shipping Phase of Carbon Capture and Storage' (2019) 512 *MarIus* 7, 19–20; V Weber, 'Are We Ready for the Ship Transport of CO2 for CCS? Crude Solutions from International and European Law' (2021) 30(3) *Review of European, Comparative & International Environmental Law* 387–95. A more recent empirical study of Danish maritime transport reached similar conclusions: '[T]he storage capacity in the North Sea is large enough to accommodate the planned volume from carbon capture installations from the leading countries.' See 'Maritim transport af CO_2' (Teknologisk Institut & Maersk Broker Advisory Services, 2022) 28 maerskbroker.com/wp-content/uploads/2022/10/Maritim-transport-af-CO2-final.pdf (adjusted automatic translation from the Danish).

[2] 'Utlysning av område knyttet til CO_2-lagring' (*Regjeringen.no*, 11 January 2023) www.regjeringen.no/no/aktuelt/utlysning-av-omrade-knyttet-til-co2-lagring/id2958814/; NA Røkke and M Mølnvik, 'Debatt: Må gjøre butikk av karbonlagring – snarest' (*Dagens Næringsliv*, 10 January 2023) www.dn.no/innlegg/klima/energi/ccs/ma-gjore-butikk-av-karbonlagring-snarest/2-1-1385219.

[3] 'Germany and Norway Announce Plans to Strengthen Collaboration on CCS' (*NCCS – Norwegian Centre for Environment-friendly Energy Research*, 9 January 2023) nccs.no/news/germany-and-norway-announce-plans-to-strengthen-collaboration-on-ccs/; 'Danish Ambassador to Norway Visits SINTEF to

has similar ambitions of developing its CCS industry, which has received the green light from the EU.[4] In 2023, the Danish project Greensand entered a pilot phase of shipping and deposition carbon dioxide from the Belgian chemical factory in the North Sea.[5]

As a nascent industry, CCS is accompanied by much scientific uncertainty.[6] The chapter relies on the relevant studies relating to the technological process of carbon dioxide shipping and its potential environmental impact. Furthermore, the chapter analyses existing available scholarship. In contrast, it is also possible that some studies are subject to commercial secrecy concerns.[7] Within these limitations the chapter focuses primarily on legal matters.

The focus on the shipping should not preclude references to studies from the two other stages (capture and injection/storage) and beyond. For instance, an accidental release of carbon dioxide may happen at any moment other than its loading, delivery or discharge from the ship. It may happen at the capture site and, hypothetically,[8] from the storage location (in case of seismic activities in the area of injection[9]). In case of pipeline transfer, it may slip away from the damaged or otherwise loose installations. All these accidents have common issues, such as the character and length of exposure, whether instantaneous or continuous and its impact on human health and the environment. Hence, the nascent character of carbon dioxide in shipping calls for greater acceptance of indirectly applicable examples.

The chapter proceeds in the following way. The first section summarises the potential dangers arising from the shipping of carbon dioxide. The next section introduces

Discuss Hydrogen and CCS Activities' (*SINTEF*, 27 January 2023) www.sintef.no/en/latest-news/2023/danish-ambassador-to-norway-visits-sintef-to-discuss-hydrogen-and-ccs-activities/.

[4] 'State Aid: Commission Approves €1.1 Billion Danish Scheme' (*European Commission – European Commission*, 12 January 2023) ec.europa.eu/commission/presscorner/detail/en/IP_23_128.

[5] M Sæhl, 'Fra kontrolrummet i Nordsøen: Deres Kongelige Højhed, vi har nu begyndt nedpumpningen af CO2' (*DR*, 8 March 2023) www.dr.dk/nyheder/viden/klima/fra-kontrolrummet-i-nordsoeen-deres-kongelige-hoejhed-vi-har-nu-begyndt.

[6] On the Danish government plan for CCS, the National Climate Council comments as follows: 'Carbon capture, transport and storage is still a relatively untested technology and depends on several technological, regulatory and market elements and infrastructure being in place by 2030. It is also unclear how the economics and market design of carbon capture and storage will work.' See 'Statusrapport 2022: Danmarks nationale klimamål og internationale forpligtelser [Status update report 2021 – Denmark's national and international climate efforts]' (Klimarådet [The Danish Council on Climate Change (DCCC)] 2022) 115 klimaraadet.dk/sites/default/files/node/field_file/statusrapport_2022_webpdf_final.pdf.

[7] As testified by a recent study of Danish maritime actors engaged in carbon dioxide shipping: 'The industry is also characterised by fierce competition to become a *First Mover*, so there are significant trade secrets at stake. Therefore, respondents are not always in a position to comment specifically on prices and costs, as this is competitively sensitive information.' See 'Maritim transport af CO_2' (n 1) 9 (automatic translation from the Danish; italics original).

[8] 'Safe Geologic Storage of Captured Carbon Dioxide – DOE's Carbon Storage R&D Program: Two Decades in Review' (National Energy Technology Laboratory (NETL), US Department of Energy 2020) www.netl.doe.gov/sites/default/files/Safe%20Geologic%20Storage%20of%20Captured%20Carbon%20Dioxide_April%2015%202020_FINAL.pdf. The study stipulates that 'no DOE supported project has observed migration of CO_2 outside of the intended storage reservoir or confining cap rock' (Executive summary, 1). *cf* Amy Brunsvold et al, 'The Safety of CO_2 Storage' (*#SINTEFblog*, 28 May 2020) blog.sintef.com/sintefenergy/ccs/the-safety-of-co2-storage. The authors conclude that '[w]ith rigorous procedures for the selection, operation and monitoring of selected storage sites, the safety bar for Norwegian CO_2 storage sites is extremely high.'

[9] See the discussion about containment risks in 'CO2 Storage Safety in the North Sea: Implications of the CO_2 Storage Directive: TWG Collaboration across the CCS Chain Workstream 1 Report' (Advisory Council of the European Zero Emission Technology and Innovation Platform (ETIP ZEP), 2019) 18–22 zeroemissionsplatform.eu/wp-content/uploads/ZEP-report-CO2-Storage-Safety-in-the-North-Sea-Nov-2019-3.pdf.

the regime of dangerous goods as accepted in commercial shipping and looks closely at contractual mechanisms of risk distribution. The third section discusses the potential impact on the environment seen through the legal lens. The concluding section summarises the findings and the identified uncertainties of regulation.

II. Background: Studies of CCS-related Hazards

As with any new technology, CCS poses legitimate questions about its safety and environmental soundness. An accidental carbon dioxide emission may significantly impact the ship and its surroundings. It is, therefore, helpful to sketch out different objects which the regulatory framework should cover in such an event:

- the humans, who, in addition to the carrier's crew, may include the crew on the colliding vessel or object, as well as the coastal population;
- the machinery of the ships involved in the accident;
- local animals and plants, whether marine or coastal;
- the environment, which carbon dioxide will affect as a greenhouse gas.[10]

Different studies have looked into potential dangers from accidents involving carbon dioxide. The present section looks at some studies as a prelude to discussing its legal dimensions.

A. Risks to Humans

A 2011 study produced by the UK Health and Safety Executive suggested that a combination of two factors, the inherent dangers of carbon dioxide and its scale in CCS operations, would create the potential for a Major Accident Hazard (MAH).[11] The dangers primarily concern human life and health, as the gas can have a toxicological impact (at concentrations above 15 per cent). Furthermore, the gas becomes immediately dangerous to life when inhaled in excess of 50 per cent concentration in the air.[12] While the gas has relatively mild toxicity at low concentrations, after reaching seven per cent concentration (above 70,000 parts per million by volume in air [ppm]), humans become increasingly sensitive to further increases.[13] A review of accidents involving inhalation of carbon dioxide provided some relevant comparisons to CCS operations: large-scale releases were followed by intoxication and hospitalisation. Release in confined spaces could result in death and injury.[14] Recently, an accident happened

[10] *cf* the preamble to the International Gas Carrier Code, stating its purpose 'to minimise the risk to the ship, its crew and the environment.' This declared goal may be too narrow as compared to the number of other objects, which may be potentially affected by a gas emission.

[11] P Harper, J Wilday and M Bilio, 'Assessment of the Major Hazard Potential of Carbon Dioxide' (UK Health and Safety Executive, 2011) 2 www.hse.gov.uk/carboncapture/assets/docs/major-hazard-potential-carbon-dioxide.pdf.

[12] ibid.

[13] ibid 3.

[14] ibid 4.

during dock maintenance of a Chinese bulk tanker, when a failure of fire extinguishing systems and the resulting carbon dioxide intoxication led to the death of ten people and injury to another 19.[15]

The study mentions other dangers which may result from an accidental release of the pressurised gas, such as:

> cryogenic burns, embrittlement of pipework, toxic contamination and possibly 'grit blasting' of neighbouring plant (although information suggests that CO_2 snow also needs to be compressed in order to give a grit blasting effect).[16]

The study further engaged in several models of a catastrophic release of carbon dioxide, concluding that its lower temperature presents more significant hazards due to increased release distances.[17] A model of 50 mm diameter release from a storage vessel was said to endanger safety within a 100 meter range.[18]

Furthermore, the study added that potential impurities of the carbon dioxide stream (such as more toxic SO_2 and H_2S) could increase the overall toxicity of the gas. Other studies routinely reiterate this danger:

> Inclusion of toxic impurities is equally important [for assessing the toxicity of CO_2 operations], though it depends on the expected concentration. H2S is one that is known to be highly toxic. Even at 100 ppmv, it has the potential to be lethal and should be included in the risk assessment if expected to be present. H2S concentration of up to 3% have been reported for CCS related CO_2 compositions. SO2 is also highly toxic but generally its quantity is low (<100 ppmv) for the expected CO_2 composition for CCS applications.[19]

The 2011 HSE study concluded that their proportion in the stream was expected to be negligible, adding that no studies of their impact have been made.[20] The point is relevant to the legal assessment, as different exposure limits and precautions could apply depending on the type of liquefied gas, whether pure or rectified.

A presentation on the major accident potential of CCS operations from 2021 mentions similar risks.[21] Notably, this mentions potential complications arising from the placement of gas architecture close to populated areas.[22]

[15] K Si, '10 Dead in Chinese Ship Repair Accident' (*Seatrade Maritime*, 27 May 2019) www.seatrade-maritime.com/asia/10-dead-chinese-ship-repair-accident; '3rd Officer Detained as Suspect after 10 Dead Due to CO_2 Leak' (*SAFETY4SEA*, 6 June 2019) safety4sea.com/3rd-officer-detained-as-suspect-after-10-dead-due-to-co2-leak/; M Chawla, 'Carbon Dioxide: Risk Assessment, Environmental, and Health Hazard' in J Singh, RD Kaushik and M Chawla (eds), *Hazardous Gases* (Cambridge, Academic Press, 2021) 78. *TradeWinds* reports poisoning by carbon *monoxide* (see A Pierce, 'Ten Die Following Carbon Monoxide Leak on Fujian Shipping Bulker' *TradeWinds* (London, 27 May 2019)), while other sources agree that it was *dioxide*. *cf* also C Shen, 'Third Officer Blamed for China Bulker Deaths' *Lloyd's List* (London, 31 May 2019).

[16] Harper et al (n 11) 3.

[17] ibid 7. There are other hazard models, see, for example, 'CO_2 Hazard Assessment – Gexcon Blog' (*Gexcon AS – Fire & Explosion Consultants*, 2 October 2020) www.gexcon.com/blog/co2-hazard-assessment/; Chawla (n 15) 70–73.

[18] Harper et al (n 11) 9.

[19] N Curson, 'Assessing Safety Risks for CO2 Pipelines' (*Penspen*, 28 July 2021) www.penspen.com/insights/assessing-safety-risks-for-co2-pipelines/.

[20] Harper et al (n 11) 9.

[21] H Holt and M Simms, 'Managing the Major Accident Potential of Carbon Capture and Storage CO2' (Institution of Chemical Engineers (IChemE) Hazards 31 Conference, Virtual, 18 November 2021) www.icheme.org/media/17367/haz31_098_holt.pdf.

[22] ibid 3.

In turn, the variation of impurities between different sources of carbon dioxide complicates the prognosis of the speed of saturation of the gas and its toxicity.[23] The presentation particularly stressed the low temperatures accompanying an accidental release of liquid carbon dioxide.[24] According to its conclusions, 'CCS CO_2 systems with large CO_2 inventories will have major accident potential,' which could be mitigated by appropriate regulatory oversight and hazard management processes.[25]

B. Risks to Machinery

Another study, performed similarly in 2011, provided more details about the dangers that CCS may present to the machinery.[26] Among these were potential corrosion due to the humidity of the gas (which necessitates dehydration systems) and its solvent properties, which may add to the toxicity of the liquid carbon dioxide due to the absorption of heavy metals and radioactive contaminants.[27]

C. Risks to the Local Environment

Potential danger to the marine environment also deserves a mention. There is strong evidence that a potential gas leakage would have both minimal and temporary consequences on aquatic life due to its resilience to the natural fluctuations of carbon dioxide concentrations.[28] The hypothetical risks of local character may be seen in a broader perspective: 'The minor risks to the local marine environment presented by CO_2 storage have to be balanced against the serious impacts that climate change and related ocean acidification are having today on the marine environment.'[29]

Despite the limited local impact, it seems appropriate to treat a leak of carbon dioxide as an accident subject to further investigative inquiry.

D. Risks to the Global Environment: Elevated Greenhouse Gas Emissions

An accidental emission of carbon dioxide during the shipping stage would run against the purpose of this enterprise: 'For climate stabilisation, CO_2 must be captured and permanently prevented from reaching the atmosphere.'[30] Due to the difference in scale,

[23] ibid: 'Impurities vary considerably between sources and they can change the properties and behaviour of CO_2 stream significantly.' See also the graph on p 236.

[24] ibid 17–18.

[25] ibid 20.

[26] J Wilday et al, 'Hazards from Carbon Dioxide Capture, Transport and Storage' (2011) 89 *Process Safety and Environmental Protection* 482.

[27] ibid 485.

[28] 'CO_2 Storage Safety in the North Sea: Implications of the CO_2 Storage Directive: TWG Collaboration across the CCS Chain Workstream 1 Report' (n 9) 15–16.

[29] ibid 3.

[30] ibid.

it may be unreasonable to compare an accidental emitter with significant emitters ('climate majors'), such as big oil and gas companies, cement production enterprises and others. Nevertheless, even an accidental release may draw attention to questions of prevention, mitigation, and potential liability for climate change.

To conclude, the abovementioned risks suggest that shipping carbon dioxide may involve different sets of rules depending on the object of protection. The following sections will look closely at the contractual distribution between shipowners and cargo interests concerning potential liability claims. However, questions of work safety and prevention of damage to machinery will not be investigated further.

III. Dangerous Goods in Shipping Contracts

Ships can experience external perils of the sea and internal perils coming from their cargo. Therefore, from a commercial shipping perspective, the ship and its crew would act as a primary object of protection, which the law should accord concerning carbon dioxide as a cargo. The nature and character of the goods transported may impact the safety of shipping, necessitating the distribution of liability between the shipper and the carrier. In the case of damage to third parties, this distribution of liability would also be applicable. The carrier would incur primary liability for third-party claims for which it may be indemnified in a recourse action against the shipper.[31] It is, therefore, useful to flag some of the issues that may arise around shipping contracts with a concrete cargo in bulk, namely liquid carbon dioxide.

According to Article 4(6) of the Hague Rules and Article IV, r 6, of the Hague-Visby Rules, the carrier must consent to their carriage with knowledge of the nature and character of the dangerous goods.[32] Without such consent, the carrier can land or destroy the goods and hold the shipper liable for all damages and expenses. Even if consent is given, the provision allows the carrier to dispose of the dangerous goods without incurring liability to the shipper.

The Hamburg Rules have an even more elaborate regime. In particular, they oblige the shipper to mark the dangerous goods and inform the carrier of their character. They provide a defence against liability claims whenever the carrier or subcarrier had knowledge of the dangerous goods and consented to their transport.[33] The Hamburg Rules are particularly interesting due to their role as a guide in the modernisation of the Nordic Maritime Codes.[34] While not having ratified the Hamburg Rules and therefore still

[31] MD Güner-Özbek, *The Carriage of Dangerous Goods by Sea* (Berlin, Springer 2008) 137.

[32] For an overview of the legal regime, see eg R Gay, 'Dangerous Cargo and "Legally Dangerous" Cargo' in D Rhidian Thomas (ed), *The Evolving Law and Practice of Voyage Charterparties* (London, Informa Law, 2009) 97–136; FD Rose and FMB Reynolds, *Carver on Bills of Lading*, 5th edn (London, Sweet & Maxwell, 2022) 9-301ff.

[33] Hamburg Rules, Art 13(1–2).

[34] Due to the traditional Nordic cooperation, the Maritime Codes of Norway, Denmark, Sweden and Finland resemble each other, although to a varying extent. See L Gorton, 'Regional Harmonization of Maritime Law in Scandinavia' in J Basedow, U Magnus and R Wolfrum (eds), *The Hamburg Lectures on Maritime Affairs 2009 & 2010* (Springer, Berlin, Heidelberg, 2012) 35–36; T Falkanger, HJ Bull and L Brautaset, *Scandinavian Maritime Law: The Norwegian Perspective*, 4th edn (Oslo, Universitetsforlaget, 2017) 28–30.

bound by the Hague-Visby Rules, the Norwegian and Danish legislators 'also decided to take into consideration and to some extent use certain solutions adopted in the Hamburg Rules'.[35] This is related, in particular, to the regime of dangerous goods in the Nordic countries, as observed in greater detail below.[36]

Separate mention should be made concerning the scope of the comparative legal inquiry in what follows. Despite their brevity, the provisions of international conventions named above hide a rather complicated legal regime of dangerous goods, explained in more detail elsewhere.[37] The brevity also testifies to the regulatory gaps that national legal systems fill with varying degrees of uniformity.[38] The present study continues the scholarly tradition of drawing comparative parallels between the common law and Nordic law,[39] focusing primarily on English and Norwegian law and occasionally mentioning other legal systems.

The argument advanced here can be summarised as follows:

(a) Qualification of liquid carbon dioxide as 'dangerous goods' should not be taken for granted but may depend
  (i) on its legal status, meaning inclusion in the International Gas Carrier (IGC) Code and various national work safety guidelines;
  (ii) on its factual state, meaning the presence of impurities, which can significantly aggravate the danger.
(b) If qualified as 'dangerous goods,' the application of the Hague or Hague-Visby Rules further depends on communication between the shipper and the carrier.
(c) Carriage of CO_2 in bulk differs from regular cargo, typically addressed as 'dangerous goods' (in packaged form). Liquid carbon dioxide requires special equipment onboard, which signifies that both shipper and carrier are professional actors and the ship equipped for this particular cargo.
(e) Thus, the carrier will have actual and constructive knowledge of liquid carbon dioxide as 'dangerous cargo.'
(f) However, there remains the question of impurities and communication about them:
  (i) Whether the shipper was aware of the impurities;
  (ii) Whether the shipper has actively communicated the impurities;
  (iii) Alternatively, whether the carrier could have had constructive knowledge of the impurities, providing grounds to presume the carrier's consent.

[35] Gorton (n 34) 40.

[36] Below, section II(B)(iii).

[37] See, generally, C Grue, 'Transport Av Farlig Gods: Ansvar Og Saerregler Ved Stykkgodstransport Av Farlig Gods i Sjøloven 1994' (1998) 238 *MarIus* 5 heinonline.org/HOL/P?h=hein.intyb/scdinsmly1998&i=1. For summary in English, see C Grue, 'Liability for Damage Caused to and by Dangerous Goods under the Maritime Code of 1994' in HJ Bull (ed), *MarIus, Scandinavian Institute of Maritime Law Yearbook 1997, 240* (1998) 3–15. The references in this chapter concern only the first article. See also Güner-Özbek (n 31).

[38] H Tiberg, 'Legal Survey' in K Grönfors (ed), *Damage from goods* (Akademiförlaget, Gothenburg, 1978) 11–12.

[39] ibid.

Figure 1 CO_2 as dangerous cargo

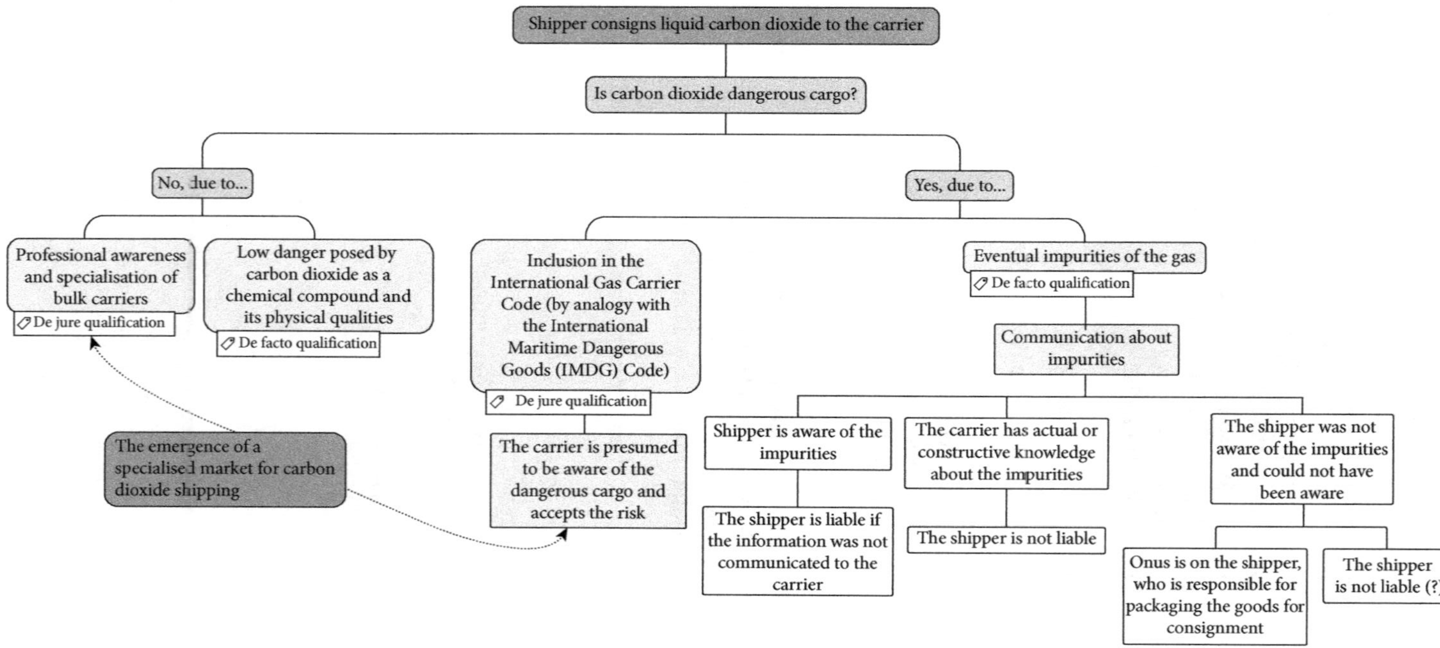

IV. Whether Liquid Carbon Dioxide is 'Dangerous Cargo'

As a starting point, one may question whether this new type of cargo falls under the legal regime for 'dangerous goods'. The historical mention of dangerous goods in the Hague Rules did not seek to cover all possible hazards (as many things can be dangerous under certain conditions) but exclusively exceptionally dangerous cargo.[40] Being not flammable or explosive and having comparably little corrosive activity, liquid carbon dioxide presents almost no chemical hazards and may, therefore, fall outside their characterisation as 'dangerous goods.'

The packaging also matters. Previous studies focused on dangerous goods in *packaged* form, arguing that the industry actors were well aware of the dangers of bulk cargo due to its limited variety.[41] However, as Güner-Özbek notes, this does not mean that chemically hazardous substances fall outside the scope of the dangerous goods regime simply because they are carried in bulk.[42] In her view, such substances 'should be deemed dangerous for the purpose of carriage contracts.'[43] The preparatory work leading to the Norwegian Maritime Code also confirmed that the dangerous nature of the goods for the purpose of their transport should not be determined by their regulation by public law.[44]

So characterised, liquefied carbon dioxide may fall within the same category of dangerous goods. The suggested solution of treating any liquefied gas named in the International Gas Carrier (IGC) Code as 'dangerous goods' seems to be rather straightforward. A similar conclusion has been drawn in the EU and international regulations, which, by reference to IGC Code, add carbon dioxide to the list of dangerous goods.[45]

Upon a closer look, the proposed solution may be oversimplified, however, as it does not account for different types of the liquefied gas in question, the parties' knowledge and the ability to supervise the packing and handling of the cargo. There is an age-long debate in legal doctrine about the origins of the danger presented either as an inherent quality of the goods ('inherent vice') or the combination of circumstances creating danger.[46] Shipping explosive or inflammable substances is an example of the former. In contrast, the shipping of wool capable of accumulating heat with excess moisture and thus prone to self-ignition is an example of the latter.[47] A comparison can be made between the risks of asphyxiation from high concentrations of pure carbon dioxide or toxicity risks from much lower concentrations of rectified gas with impurities.

Assistance may be obtained from de Pontavice, who draws on the French judicial distinction between the shipper's 'supervision of structure' and the carrier's 'supervision

[40] See F Berlingieri (ed), *The Travaux Préparatoires of the Hague Rules and of the Hague-Visby Rules* (Antwerp, CMI, 1997) 592, downloadable from comitemaritime.org/publications-documents/travaux-preparatoires/.

[41] Güner-Özbek (n 31) 86.

[42] ibid.

[43] ibid.

[44] 'Godsbefordring Til Sjøs: Utredning XV Fra Utvalget Til Revisjon Av Sjøfartslovgivningen' (Sjølovkomiteen, 1993) Norges offentlige utredninger (NOU) 1993:36 25.

[45] See the sections concerning the EU Environmental Liability Directive and the HNS Convention, below sections III(A)(i) and III(B)(i).

[46] Güner-Özbek (n 31) 72–74.

[47] ibid 39–40.

of comportment'.[48] The distinction arose from the provision of the French Civil Code imposing liability on the tortfeasor 'not only for the damage he causes by his fault, but also for that which is caused by the action of things under his supervision'.[49] Pontavice further questions who would be a tortfeasor in the situation where the damage is caused by dangerous cargo.

In a decision of Court of Cassation from 1941, the owner of the car left it to his minor son, after which the car was stolen and ended up in an accident. The court concluded that the owner was 'deprived of the use, direction and control of his car, no longer had custody of it and was therefore no longer subject to the presumption of liability laid down [in the Civil Code]'.[50] According to Pontavice, a carrier has control and custody over the goods and, therefore is considered liable for the damage while the goods are in the carrier's custody.[51] This is equivalent to the earlier presumption that any cargo of liquid carbon dioxide is dangerous goods for which the carrier is responsible.

Building upon this presumption, one starts noticing gradations of responsibility. The case the Court of Cassation decided in 1956 involved a set of facts directly relevant to the present discussion.[52] The claim concerned the carriage of liquid oxygen in metal bottles by rail, where one of the bottles exploded upon delivery. The court criticised the narrow understanding of the term 'custody' as only material possession: the carrier, who ended up with the defective cargo on its hands, could not supervise or control how the bottles were produced and packed. In the words of Pontavice:

> To the extent that the supervisor of the comportment (i.e. the carrier) lacks power over the structure of the thing, he could not be held liable for damage caused by the vice of the goods. Only the supervisor of the structure (i.e. here, the producer), who retains a power over the inner anatomy of the thing, should be liable.[53]

In the case of liquified carbon dioxide, the carrier would receive the gas with different levels of impurity, which will be of crucial importance to its performance in transit. The shipper is in a better position to know what type of gas is in the container. Thus it is better for the shipper to be liable for the cargo's eventual 'vices'. In turn, the carrier will be liable only if the damage results from the handling of the liquefied gas during carriage.[54] However, the liability of the parties further depends on the performance of their duties, as discussed further in the chapter.

A. General Distribution of Duties for Dangerous Cargo

Both the shipper and the carrier have duties under the contract of carriage. In the case of dangerous goods, this has certain unique features. The shipper is obliged to inform

[48] E de Pontavice, 'The Victims of Damage Caused by the Ship's Cargo' in Grönfors (n 38) 38–40.
[49] ibid 37.
[50] *Cour de Cassation, Chambres réunies, du 2 décembre 1941, Publié au bulletin* (automatic translation from the French).
[51] Pontavice (n 48) 38.
[52] *Cour de Cassation, Chambre civile 2, du 5 janvier 1956, 56-02126 56-02138, Publié au bulletin.*
[53] Pontavice (n 48) 38.
[54] See further discussion of this division of responsibilities, ibid 39–40.

the carrier about the nature and character of the goods.[55] A failure to do so, which may also come as incomplete or incorrect information, would affect the carrier's knowledge of the potential dangers accompanying the cargo. Depending on the applicable law, the carrier is entitled to refuse to accept the non-conforming cargo or even obliged to do so under the public law regulations.[56]

In turn, the carrier would have a duty to provide a seaworthy ship and exercise due care of the cargo, whether at common law or under the Hague and Hague-Visby Rules.[57] The carrier is liable for the damage to the cargo while in its custody. The seaworthiness standard at common law[58] and under Nordic law is the 'relative fitness' of the cargo.[59]

Similarly to the discussion of 'dangerous goods' above, the duties of the parties present more challenges for packaged goods due to their great variety, particularly when transported in containers which, being sealed, have limited capacity for inspection.[60] In turn, shipping carbon dioxide in bulk would require a new type of gas carrier tailored for this specific industry.[61] This is in line with the legal requirement requiring the provision of a seaworthy ship, which requires that the ship is constructed and equipped and the crew trained to deal with a particular (dangerous) cargo.[62] Thus, shippers and carriers would gain expert knowledge about the potential dangers and the appropriate carriage regime.[63]

B. Inquiry and Communication about the Impurities

As noted earlier, the impurities of gas depend on its source and vary between the sources. More importantly, the source would likely affect gas performance and toxicity.

Many questions may arise. Depending on the peculiarities of the supply chain, the shipper may be aware of the impurities or lack such information. Correspondingly, carriers who are integrated with the same supply chains, could also have constructive knowledge of the impurities. At least in the industry's early years, the limited participation and variety within supply chains would provide better knowledge about the gas than trading with packaged goods on the spot market. In other words, the owner of a specially-equipped ship calling at port A would know that gas supply comes from a cement facility, while in port B from a refinery, with predictable distribution of the impurities.

[55] Güner-Özbek (n 31) 98–103.

[56] ibid 129–131.

[57] For the Hague and Hague-Visby Rules, see Art III, r 1 (seaworthiness); Art III, r 2 (due care). See the discussion in S Girvin, 'The Obligation of Seaworthiness: Shipowner and Charterer,' CML Working Paper Series 17/11, December 2017, law.nus.edu.sg/cml/publications/.

[58] *Northern Shipping Co v Deutsche Seereederei GmbH (The Kapitan Sakharov)* [2000] 2 Lloyd's Rep 40. See also *Carver on Bills of Lading* (n 32) 9.134, 9.137.

[59] Grue (n 37) 13; Falkanger and Bull (n 34) 357–359 (referring to ND 1975.85 SUNNY LADY [HR]). More recently, the principle was affirmed in *ND-2020-8 (MV Cheshire)* (Oslo tingrett) para 66.

[60] *cf* Güner-Özbek (n 31) 91.

[61] O'Brien (n 1) 21. See also 'Maritim transport af CO_2' (n 1) 6 (automatic translation from the Danish): 'Reference to maritime transport in this report will refer to the transport of CO_2 carried by ships specially designed for this purpose.'

[62] *Empresa Cubana Importadora de Alimentos Alimport v Iasmos Shipping Co SA (The Good Friend)* [1984] 2 Lloyd's Rep 586 (concerning cargoworthiness under common law and the Hague Rules). See further *Papera Traders Co Ltd v Hyundai Merchant Marine Co Ltd (The Eurasian Dream) (No.1)* [2002] 1 Lloyd's Rep 719, [128]ff (the crew lacked training in dealing with a particular cargo).

[63] Güner-Özbek (n 31) 124.

i. *The Shipper's Duty to Inquire*

It is interesting to question whether the shipper should inquire about potential impurities from the producer of the gas within the supply chain. As summarised by Rose, the common law holds the shipper absolutely liable for the act of 'shipment'. Thus, even in the absence of fault, the shipper would be liable for the damage resulting from preparing the cargo for consignment, even if exercised by third parties.[64] As a result, the shipper is better off finding out the exact characteristics of the gas.

Similarly, Article 291 of the Norwegian Maritime Code maintains that the shipper will be objectively liable for damage, provided it failed to give notice about the dangerous character of the cargo.[65] The duty is nevertheless relieved to the extent of the shipper's actual or constructive knowledge.[66] However, the statutory provisions do not expressly mention the latter, and there is some debate whether the shipper can be expected to know about the dangerous character.[67] In the absence of such knowledge, there can be no fault and no liability of the shipper.

ii. *The Carrier's Duty to Inquire*

There is a corresponding duty on the carrier to inquire about the cargo under suspicion. In other words, the carrier cannot ignore such facts as the gas coming from a different emitter or having otherwise changed or unusual content. In case of an accident resulting from improper cargo treatment, the carrier would be liable for its omission to obtain the necessary information.[68] Grue stresses the duty to inquire and investigate the state and treatment of the cargo is a positive duty; failure to perform that duty signifies negligence on the carrier's part.[69] A similar expectation exists at common law, as negating the carrier's responsibility for risks resulting from the lack of inquiry constitutes a 'premium on ignorance'.[70]

The case *M/V Cheshire* is an example.[71] The ship carried Nitrogen-Phosphor-Kalium (NPK) fertiliser in bulk from Norway to Spain. During carriage, fumes and poisonous gases started spreading from the cargo hold, resulting in the evacuation of the crew and the destruction of the ship. Following investigation, the immediate cause of the damage was found to be a lamp in the cargo hold, which was left working and eventually heated the fertiliser. The court underlined the importance of the carrier's duty to inquire about the cargo and its handling procedures:

> [T]he carrier has a strict duty of care and is considered the professional in sea transport. He has an independent responsibility to have sufficient information about the cargo he is to carry

[64] FD Rose, 'Cargo Risks: "Dangerous" Goods' (1996) 55 CLJ 601, 606–607. See *Brass v Maitland* (1856) 6 E & B 470; *Effort Shipping Co Ltd v Linden Management SA (The Giannis NK)* [1998] AC 605 (HL), 619.

[65] 'Godsbefordring til sjøs: utredning XV fra utvalget til revisjon av sjøfartslovgivningen' (n 44) 43.

[66] Below, section II(B)(iii)–(iv).

[67] Grue (n 37) 48–49.

[68] ibid 11.

[69] ibid 19.

[70] Rose (n 64) 608 referring to *The Athanasia Comninos and Georges Chr Lemos* [1990] 1 Lloyd's Rep 277, 283, per Mustill J.

[71] *ND-2020-8 (MV Cheshire)* (n 59).

> so that the sea transport can be carried out safely, and he has a duty to familiarise himself with the available information about the cargo if the knowledge he already has about the type of cargo in question is not good enough.[72]

The court found a clear breach of the carrier's obligations to take due care of the cargo.[73]

It follows that the carrier's duty to inquire was firmly underlined by the court, despite its absence from the text of the conventions. In relation to liquid carbon dioxide shipping, that would mean that the carrier would be under a separate and independent obligation to inquire about the type of the gas, its impurities and any additional procedures which could affect the degree of its liability in case of an accident.

iii. The Shipper's Duty to Give Notice

The shipper is obligated to communicate its knowledge about the impurities in every case ('the particular state of the bulk cargo'[74]), as a failure to do so would undermine the carrier's consent to perform under the contract.[75] As noted by Tetley, '[a] shipper should give the carrier instructions for cargo requiring special care.'[76] The carrier's ability to transport the cargo could diminish as well, if the ship equipment cannot be adjusted to the changed physical qualities of the gas.

An English case *Micada Compania Naviera SA v Texim*[77] illustrates this problem. The charterparty was for the transport of iron ore, typically not considered dangerous. However, the iron ore in question had a high moisture content, and the shipper misled the master about the extent of the problem. If this special characteristic had been communicated to the carrier, it could have adopted measures to ensure better care of the cargo. As this was not the case, the cargo shifted and the ship had to seek refuge in a port, causing delay. The shipper could have avoided the accident – and its own liability – and the non-disclosure rendered the cargo 'dangerous goods'. There was nothing to put the carrier 'on notice that the cargo was something radically and fundamentally different from that which it appeared to be [and] … the cargo was dangerous beyond all argument'.[78]

Another example follows from the Nordic law, where Article 257 of the Norwegian Maritime Code (1993) imposes several duties on the sender: to mark the dangerous goods, to notify the sender about their nature and state the required precautions, and to give notice if the goods 'are of such a nature that their carriage may entail danger or significant inconvenience to persons, the ship or the cargo'.[79] The provision combines the duties under Article IV, r 6, of the Hague-Visby Rules and Article 13 of

[72] ibid 77 (automated translation from the Norwegian).

[73] ibid 162.

[74] Güner-Özbek (n 31) 158.

[75] *The Giannis NK* (n 64) per Lord Lloyd of Berwick: 'Since the carriers did not consent to the shipment of the groundnut cargo with knowledge of its dangerous character, the shippers are prima facie liable for all damages and expenses suffered by the carriers.'

[76] W Tetley, *Marine Cargo Claims*, 4th edn (Cowansville, Lés Édition Blais, 1998) vol 1, 1300; Grue (n 37) 14.

[77] [1968] 2 Lloyd's Rep 57.

[78] ibid 62 (Donaldson J).

[79] P Bilton, T Solvang and E Røsæg, 'The Norwegian Maritime Code of 24 June, 1994, No. 39 with Later Amendments up to and Including Act of 2 August, 1996, No. 2' (University of Oslo) www.uio.no/studier/emner/jus/jus/JUR5401/h08/undervisningsmateriale/Norwegian%20Maritime%20Code.pdf.

the Hamburg Rules and has an imperative character, meaning that the parties cannot derogate from them.[80] These considerations are equally valid to Article 257 of the Danish Maritime Code.[81]

Nevertheless, whenever the carrier could have actual or constructive knowledge of the cargo, the shipper could escape liability for not communicating this information to the carrier.[82] This primarily concerns the transport of special cargo when the shipper could rely on the carrier's prior knowledge.[83]

iv. Genuinely Unknown Characteristics of the Cargo

A more challenging situation arises if the dangers of the cargo are genuinely unknown. As noted earlier, CCS is only a nascent technology, which leaves many operational questions unanswered. The legal rules need to apportion any potential liability between the shipper and the carrier, where the foreseeability of the danger plays a central role.

The discussion in the literature on the absence of actual or constructive knowledge of the shipper seems to be a profound one, showing certain regional differences. The US case *Sucrest v M/V Jennifer*[84] concerned the apportionment of liability for the previously unknown quality of the cargo. The dispute resulted from a maritime accident resulting from a deliberate ship stranding, which became unstable due to the sudden liquefying of raw sugar.[85] Neither the scientific nor the maritime community were aware of this. The court stipulated that while the onus of informing the carrier was on the shipper, it did not form part of its actual or constructive knowledge. As a result, the shipper was relieved from liability.[86]

The decision was not based on the provisions of US Carriage of Goods by Sea Act 1936 (COSGA), which incorporates the Hague Rules, as the parties struck out the clause paramount from their contract. The court concluded in passing that COSGA was not applicable to the relationship between the parties, yet suggested that this question made no material difference in its reasoning.[87]

Similarly, interpreting Article 257 of the Norwegian Maritime Code, mentioned above, Grue stipulates that it only covers the sender's actual knowledge, in the absence of which the sender cannot be held liable.[88] Conversely, in a commentary to the identical Article 257 of the Danish Maritime Code, Appel maintains that a failure to give notice leads to the objective liability of the shipper.[89] The failure is a matter of fact, and no excuse is given for the situation when the shipper is genuinely unaware, thereby potentially contesting Grue's interpretation.

[80] 'Godsbefordring til sjøs: utredning XV fra utvalget til revisjon av sjøfartslovgivningen' (n 44) 24.

[81] P Appel et al, *Søloven Med Kommentarer*, 5th edn (Copenhagen, Djøf Forlag, 2020) 539–540.

[82] Norwegian Maritime Code, Art 291(2). See also 'Godsbefordring til sjøs: utredning XV fra utvalget til revisjon av sjøfartslovgivningen' (n 44) 43; Grue (n 37) 20.

[83] Grue (n 37) 20.

[84] (1978) 455 F Supp 371 (D Me ND).

[85] The sugar was moist due to the prior exposure to salt water and underwent bacterial degradation, which was further exacerbated by the pressure in the cargo hold and the movements of the ship.

[86] *Sucrest* (n 84) 384–385.

[87] ibid 380 fn 16.

[88] Grue (n 37) 49.

[89] Appel and others (n 81) 539–540.

There is a solid line of authorities affirming the shipper's liability. The UK House of Lords reached the opposite conclusion in the *Giannis NK* case.[90] The case concerned a shipment of groundnut extractions from Senegal to the Dominican Republic under a charterparty, which incorporated the Hague Rules. Unknown to the shipper or the carrier, the cargo became infested with Khapra beetles, resulting in a quarantine and eventual dumping of the whole cargo at sea. Interpreting Article IV, r 6, of the Hague Rules, Lord Lloyd of Berwick stated that '… the shippers' liability for shipping dangerous goods cannot be made to depend on the state of his knowledge'.[91] Moreover, in the words of Lord Steyn, his liability was not confined to cases where it is at fault' In his view, 'the inference must be that the framers of the Hague Rules proceeded on what was at that time an unsurprising assumption that shippers would be absolutely liable for the shipment of dangerous cargo'.[92]

The situation of divergent interpretation based – directly or not – on the same provisions of an international convention is unfortunate. The imposition of strict liability upon the shipper finds further support in the policy rationale that the carrier is 'in the best position to discover the nature of his goods'.[93]

One can also add that while the risk of similar disputes will be higher when carbon dioxide shipping is still a novelty, it will diminish with the growing awareness of its peculiarities. Nevertheless, it demonstrates the legal incentive for market actors to keep abreast of the latest scientific developments.

V. Protection of the Environment

An accidental release of carbon dioxide may present environmental consequences of different scales, from threats to the immediate environment around the ship (whether marine or coastal) to more general contributions to climate change. While the former falls naturally within the discussion of dangerous goods, the latter seems to be more specific for carbon dioxide and other greenhouse gases.

It is possible to be more precise about necessary or inevitable releases of the gas (for example, during equipment change) and accidental releases on a bigger scale. The distinction is constructed by analogy with other dangerous goods. According to Grue, the danger resulting solely and exclusively from the cargo property cannot be ascribed to the carrier's failure in handling the cargo and will not lead to the carrier being liable.[94] Indeed, the possibility of such situation – or liability claims arising from small-scale releases – seems to be rather low.

The present section looks at the legal mechanisms covering environmental impact from both the regional and global perspectives, focusing on questions of liability of shippers and carriers.

[90] *The Giannis NK* (n 64).
[91] ibid 614.
[92] ibid 625.
[93] Güner-Özbek (n 31) 157.
[94] Grue (n 37) 8.

A. Regional Mechanisms of Protection: The North Sea Example

In the event of an accident involving dangerous goods, the local environment will bear the most serious consequences. Depending on the exact location of the accident and its effects, different domestic environmental laws may apply. One may reduce the scope of inquiry by specifying the geographical region and further concentrating on the regional (as compared to domestic[95]) international regulatory instruments dealing with the protection of environment. Further limitations can be made to mechanisms dealing expressly with liability claims applicable to shipping carbon dioxide.

i. EU Environmental Liability Directive (ELD)

The EU Environmental Liability Directive (ELD) sought to establish a harmonised system of preventive and remedial action for environmental damage among the EU Member States.[96] The Directive prescribes both fault-based and strict liability for different activities, raising the question of the qualification of carbon dioxide shipping among them.

According to O'Brien, the solution is relatively straightforward.[97] Annex III refers to '[t]ransport by … sea … of dangerous goods or polluting goods' as defined in Directive 93/75/EEC.[98] The latter Directive defines 'dangerous goods' by reference to, among others, Ch 19 of the International Gas Carrier Code.[99] Chapter 19 of the IGC Code summarises the minimum requirements for gas carriers and allocates their types according to a particular gas cargo. Thus, the transport of liquefied carbon dioxide falls under the strict liability regime of the ELD.

The varying degree of implementation of the Directive within the EU, the possibility of national exemptions from liability, the modest harmonisation effect and the exclusion of liability for damage to biodiversity from the EEA Agreement may undermine its legal effects.[100]

A potential caveat for the application of the ELD lies in the express exemption from its scope of matters regulated by other international conventions.[101] This includes the International Convention on Liability and Compensation for Damage in Connection with the Carriage of Hazardous and Noxious Substances by Sea (the HNS Convention).[102] However, as the HNS Convention has not yet entered into force, this confuses the application of the ELD to, among other things, shipping carbon dioxide as dangerous goods. The prevalent opinion suggests that the ELD must apply for environmental damage in the interim period before the NHS Convention enters into force, after which the latter

[95] *cf* an overview of different liability regimes of North Sea coastal states as applied to carbon dioxide shipping in O'Brien (n 1) 31–36.

[96] Directive 2004/35/CE of the European Parliament and of the Council of 21 April 2004 on environmental liability with regard to the prevention and remedying of environmental damage.

[97] O'Brien (n 1) 34.

[98] Directive 2004/35/CE (n 96) annex III (8).

[99] Council Directive 93/75/EEC of 13 September 1993 concerning minimum requirements for vessels bound for or leaving Community ports and carrying dangerous or polluting goods, Art 2(c).

[100] O'Brien (n 1) 35–36.

[101] Directive 2004/35/CE (n 96) Art 4(2).

[102] Below, section III(B)(i).

will be prioritised.[103] Thus, the Member States can rely on the Directive to bring their public liability claims against companies engaged in carbon dioxide shipping.

A question can be raised about the potential distribution of liability between the shipper and the carrier. The ELD defines 'operator' as

> any … person who operates or controls the occupational activity or, where this is provided for in national legislation, to whom decisive economic power over the technical functioning of such an activity has been delegated, including the holder of a permit or authorisation for such an activity or the person registering or notifying such an activity.[104]

The occupational activity in question is transport by sea, exercised by the carrier, which is the 'operator' under the Directive.

It follows that the liability claims against the carrier for environmental damage resulting from dangerous cargo are similar to other third-party claims falling under Article IV, r 6, of the Hague and Hague-Visby Rules. The carrier can limit them as other maritime claims[105] and recover for them in an indemnity action against the shipper, as mentioned above.[106]

ii. EU Emissions Trading Scheme

In another EU law development, carbon dioxide transport by sea was included in the EU Emissions Trading Scheme (ETS).[107] The ETS relies on remedies of a financial nature, so any increase in emissions must be backed by allowances.[108] The amended ETS directive includes the 'release of greenhouse gases … from ships performing a maritime transport activity listed in Annex I of the gases specified in respect of that activity.'[109] Annex I mentions '[t]ransport of greenhouse gases [*carbon dioxide*] for geological storage in a storage site' under the CCS directive.[110] It therefore follows that accidental emissions under transport count under the ETS scheme and will be covered by allowances.

[103] Commission Staff Working Document – REFIT Evaluation of the Environmental Liability Directive Accompanying the document Report from the Commission to the European Parliament and to the Council pursuant to Article 18(2) of Directive 2004/35/EC on environmental liability with regard to the prevention and remedying of environmental damage 2016 [SWD/2016/0121 final]: 'The ELD currently applies to environmental damage related to the carriage of HNS by sea in all Member States (…).'

See also E De Soomer, 'Liability for Environmental Damage from Shipping Incidents in the European Union: A Shipowner's Perspective' (Royal Belgian Shipowners' Association, 2022) safety4sea.com/wp-content/uploads/2022/03/Royal-Belgian-Shipowners-Association-Liability-for-Environmental-Damage-from-shipping-incidents-in-EU-2022_03.pdf. The author thanks Szilárd Gáspár-Szilágyi for the discussion of this matter.

[104] Directive 2004/35/CE (n 96) Art 2(6).

[105] ibid 4(3); O'Brien (n 1) 34.

[106] Above, section II.

[107] Directive (EU) 2023/959 of the European Parliament and of the Council of 10 May 2023 amending Directive 2003/87/EC establishing a system for greenhouse gas emission allowance trading within the Union and Decision (EU) 2015/1814 concerning the establishment and operation of a market stability reserve for the Union greenhouse gas emission trading system (Text with EEA relevance) Art 69 of the Preamble.

[108] O'Brien (n 1) 38.

[109] Directive 2003/87/EC of the European Parliament and of the Council of 13 October 2003 establishing a system for greenhouse gas emission allowance trading within the Union and amending Council Directive 96/61/EC Art 3(b). For an example of cost sharing arrangement before the amendment, see 'Regulatory Lessons Learned from Longship – The Public Sector's Involvement in Europe's First Industrial CCS Chain' (Gassnova SF 2022) 36–38. ccsnorway.com/publication/regulatory-lessons-learned/.

[110] Directive 2003/87/EC (n 109) annex I.

The amended ETS Directive also includes maritime transport in the list of activities eligible for ETS. The problem of potential double counting of emissions under the transport of carbon dioxide and maritime transport is resolved in favour of the latter so that accidental emissions are 'counted' only under maritime transport.[111]

The question arises whether the carrier can obtain an indemnity for the additional allowances caused by such accidental release in a recourse action from the shipper. It seems possible, referring to provisions regulating emissions from maritime transport. The amending Directive admits that emissions from ships may depend on persons other than shipowners and calls for the introduction of recourse actions in national laws:

> In line with the 'polluter pays' principle and to encourage the adoption of efficiency measures and the uptake of cleaner fuels, the shipping company should therefore be entitled, under national law, to claim reimbursement for the costs arising from the surrender of allowances from the entity that is directly responsible for the decisions affecting the greenhouse gas emissions of thc ship.
>
> While such a mechanism of reimbursement could be subject to a contractual arrangement, Member States should, to reduce administrative costs, not be obliged to ensure or check the existence of such contracts, but should instead provide for, in national law, a statutory entitlement for the shipping company to be reimbursed and the corresponding access to justice to enforce that entitlement.[112]

These provisions concern emissions from fuel combustion and were not designed to address accidental emissions from cargo on board a ship. However, on its face, the text can be applied by analogy: accidental carbon dioxide emissions are no different from any other greenhouse gas emissions, and the carrier must have a right to claim reimbursement from the shipper for its economic loss.

To conclude, the North Sea area combines geographic feasibility, growing political interest in carbon dioxide shipping and long-standing regional cooperation mechanisms in environmental matters, making it an attractive area for innovative development. The regulatory proposals by the EU are directly applicable to the maritime transfer of carbon dioxide.

B. The Global Regulation of Carbon Dioxide Emissions

The environmental consequences of carbon dioxide release in the environment can be further addressed from two perspectives: contamination and contribution to climate change. The first case concerns the prevention and mitigation of and mitigation of accidents involving hazardous and noxious substances. Such accidents result in the consequences of local and regional nature but form the object of a global convention, as discussed below. The second case involves the recent regulations adopted by the International Maritime Organization (IMO) for the limitation of greenhouse gas emissions. Both mechanisms may involve questions about the distribution of liability.

[111] Directive (EU) 2023/959 (n 107) Art 69 of the Preamble.
[112] ibid Art 32 of the Preamble.

i. The HNS Convention

The International Convention on Liability and Compensation for Damage in Connection with the Carriage of Hazardous and Noxious Substances by Sea (1996, as amended in 2010)[113] establishes mechanisms of compensation for accidents at sea resulting from pollution by chemicals and substances carried as cargo. The Convention recognises that the 'danger' may, in addition to shippers and carriers, also affect third parties, thereby serving the goal of compensating for damage brought to them and the environment.[114] Furthermore, in situations when it is not possible to separate the damage originating from hazardous and noxious substances from the damage caused by other factors, the damage would be 'deemed' to originate from the former category, so that the Convention would still apply.[115]

The Convention establishes a two-tier compensation system. First, the shipowner is strictly liable for any damage resulting from the cargo. That means that the injured party does not need to establish fault and can recover even the blame rests with another party.[116] The fact of carriage of goods would suffice for establishing liability.[117] As a second tier, claims can be brought to the HNS Fund, covering the outstanding claims.[118]

The HNS Convention provides the shipowner a 'unique defence'[119] against liability claims in cases where the shipper or any other person did not share the information about the dangerous nature of the cargo.[120]

The amended Convention includes liquefied gases, as listed in Ch 19 of the IGC Code, in the definition of hazardous and noxious substances.[121] Upon its entry into force, the Convention may harmonise different liability regimes for environmental accidents among its State Parties. O'Brien names several shortcomings of the Convention when applied to carbon dioxide shipping, such as:

- partial overlaps with the EU Environmental Liability Directive;
- potentially discouraging effects of the strict liability regime on the emerging industry;
- the lack of special treatment for carbon dioxide as a cargo type, as compared to the special place given to liquefied natural gas (LNG), again limiting the desired financial incentives;
- mischaracterisation of storage operators as 'receivers' of the goods, whereas their role is the permanent burial of carbon dioxide;

[113] Not in force. For negotiation history, see R Shaw, 'Hazardous and Noxious Substances: Is the End in Sight?' [2009] *LMCLQ* 279. See also C de la Rue, CB Anderson and J Hare, 'HNS Damage and the Hazardous and Noxious Substances Convention 2010' in *Shipping and the Environment*, 3rd edn (London, Informa Law from Routledge, 2022).

[114] Güner-Özbek (n 31) 27–28. However, the coverage depends on the territorial jurisdiction and the type of the damage, see Rue et al (n 113) 368.

[115] HNS Convention, Art 1(6).

[116] Rue et al (n 113) 377.

[117] Güner-Özbek (n 31) 266.

[118] HNS Convention, Art 13.

[119] Güner-Özbek (n 31) 267.

[120] HNS Convention, Art 7(2)(d).

[121] Protocol to the International Convention on Liability and Compensation for Damage in Connection with the Carriage of Hazardous and Noxious Substances by Sea (2010) Art 3.

- absent account of leakages during the injection stage;
- and, probably, most interestingly, the lack of account of leakages as climate change contributions.[122]

Further criticism is advanced by Weber and Mittler, who both consider the Convention ill-suited to regulate CO_2 emissions due to the different nature of CO_2 as compared to other polluting substances. Weber suggests that CO_2 should be exempted from the regulation to stimulate the investment in CCS. Mittler adds that the varying acceptance of the Convention may result is patchy regulatory framework, where some CCS activities will not be covered. Thus, both advocate for *sui generis* regulation covering CCS.[123]

Despite not being in force, the HNS Convention is a guide to other regulatory and recommendatory initiatives,[124] increasing the consistency of environmental protection.

ii. IMO Initiatives to Reduce the Carbon Intensity of Shipping

As is discussed elsewhere in this book, the impact of carbon dioxide on the environment has resulted in several regulatory initiatives, which for the shipping industry were spearheaded by the IMO Marine Environment Protection Committee (MEPC). The developments concerned the gradual amendment of the principal environmental convention of the law of the sea, the International Convention for the Prevention of Pollution from Ships (MARPOL 73/78), Annex VI of which seeks to prevent different types of air pollution, including the emission of greenhouse gases.[125]

The exemptions to Annex VI exclude 'any emission resulting from damage to a ship or its equipment' from its coverage.[126] However, the problem seems to be more hypothetical than real, as a leakage would likely involve some sort of failure of the ship's equipment. The exemptions do not apply when such an emission resulted from the intentional or reckless behaviour of the owner or master with knowledge of the probable damage and where the appropriate mitigating actions after the emission were absent.[127] On its face, the negligence standard seems rather high, meaning that an accidental emission of carbon dioxide in the atmosphere could 'slip away' from the carrier's responsibility.

Another potential exemption concerns the international character of the regulations, which do not apply to 'ships solely engaged in voyages within waters subject to the sovereignty or jurisdiction of the State the flag of which the ship is entitled to fly.'[128] Nevertheless, states are under a 'best efforts' obligation to ensure compliance with the carbon intensity requirements in the construction and operation of ships 'so far as is reasonable and practicable'.[129]

[122] O'Brien (n 1) 46–59. The next section of this chapter (section III(B)(ii)) explains this point in greater detail.

[123] Weber (n 1) 393; C Mittler, 'The Carbon Voyage – Emissions Liability in Transporting CO2 by Sea for CCS' CML Working Paper Series 23/05 (1 July 2023) 16–17, law.nus.edu.sg/cml/publications.

[124] L Alcaro et al, *MARINE HNS RESPONSE MANUAL: Multi-Regional Bonn Agreement, HELCOM, REMPEC* (Project West MOPoCo 2021) 2–3, 6.

[125] See eg Tsimplis (ch 2) section II.

[126] MARPOL Annex VI, Art 3(1)(2).

[127] ibid Art 3(1)(2)(1–2).

[128] ibid Art 19(2)(1).

[129] ibid.

However, the provisions of MARPOL concern emissions resulting from a ship's *performance*. Commenting on an earlier reform document, the IMO Initial strategy (2018),[130] O'Brien noticed that it did not cover emissions from cargo, leaving a significant regulatory gap on the shipping of carbon dioxide in bulk.[131] Several years later, the MEPC clarified the two main indicators concerning ships in transit. The Energy Efficiency Existing Ship Index (EEXI) concerns the ship's energy efficiency and ties together her fuel consumption and carbon dioxide emissions.[132] The Carbon Intensity Indicator (CII) seeks to determine the average CO_2 emissions per transport work,[133] again tying emissions to the efficiency of fuel consumption. Cargo emissions do not form part of energy efficiency calculations and are 'outside the scope' of Annex VI.

MARPOL Annex VI does not deal with liability claims. The enforcement of its provisions relies on control by classification societies so that non-compliant ships do not receive mandatory certificates or an appropriate CII rating. Enforcement of compliance falls on flag state and port state control. The exploitation of the ship by time charterers may influence its climate performance, posing questions about the contractual distribution of risks in charterparties. However, to the extent the current IMO initiatives concern only emissions resulting from the ship's operational (fuel-based) performance, the question is irrelevant here.

VI. Conclusions

The CCS industry is actively developing, and carbon dioxide will be shipped as cargo to hopefully permanent storage locations. While the development of CCS is accelerating, some of its critical aspects may end up being overshadowed by expectations of extensive growth. The chapter centred on one such aspect, the potential dangers of liquefied carbon dioxide, and mapped out the regulatory framework relevant for the shipping stage of CCS, focusing on the contractual distribution of potential liability between shippers and carriers.

Various studies have considered the major accident potential of carbon dioxide, which on the scale of CCS operations will present an actual risk. Most identified regulatory instruments are concerned with human safety in situations of potential exposure to carbon dioxide. As an asphyxiant, it can be of immediate danger to life in

[130] 'IMO Strategy on Reduction of GHG Emissions from Ships' (International Maritime Organization (IMO) 2018) unfccc.int/sites/default/files/resource/250_IMO%20submission_Talanoa%20Dialogue_April%202018.pdf.

[131] O'Brien (n 1) 57–59.

[132] '2021 Guidelines on the Method of Calculation of the Attained Energy Efficiency Existing Ship Index (EEXI)' (Marine Environment Protection Committee, International Maritime Organization (IMO) 2021) Resolution MEPC.333(76), wwwcdn.imo.org/localresources/en/OurWork/Environment/Documents/Air%20pollution/MEPC.333(76).pdf. See the discussion in Kløft and Cai (ch 4).

[133] '2022 Guidelines on Operational Carbon Intensity Indicators and the Calculation Methods (CII Guidelines, G1)' (Marine Environment Protection Committee, International Maritime Organization (IMO) 2022) Resolution MEPC.352(78), 3 wwwcdn.imo.org/localresources/en/OurWork/Environment/Documents/Air%20pollution/MEPC.352(78).pdf. See the discussion in Girvin (ch 3).

high concentrations, which necessitates limiting exposure and evacuation of personnel. Humans are also sensitive to its lower concentrations, which explains the inclusion of the gas in various national work exposure limits. Other effects, such as frostbite and 'grit blasting' from accidental release, receive only a brief mention.

The potential contamination of the gas with more toxic substances seems to be of major importance to its operational safety. The low toxicity of pure carbon dioxide, its standardised labelling and handling requirements and the expected variation of impurities coming from different sources suggest that industrial actors might risk downplaying the danger. However, the significant risks accompanying such impurities may affect the cargo status as 'dangerous goods.' As a rule, the shipper must communicate its knowledge to the carrier, which needs to secure an adequately trained crew and a properly equipped ship. The parties are further subject to certain obligations necessitated by the dangerous nature of the cargo, which include mutual duties to inquire and the shipper's duty to give notice of the cargo and the necessary precautions.

Studies have also looked at the potential liability for damage to other objects of protection. Taking the North Sea area as an example, the chapter looked closely at the EU Environmental Liability Directive and EU Emissions Trading Scheme. Both of these can potentially lead to the carrier's liability for accidental emissions. However, contractual mechanisms can provide grounds for the carrier's recourse action against the shipper.

Similarly, the global mechanisms could be approached from the perspective of the carrier's obligation to reduce greenhouse gas emissions. The existing regulation of carbon intensity of shipping excludes accidental emissions unless they are attributable to the carrier's actual or constructive knowledge or lack of appropriate mitigating action. However, this provision seems irrelevant to the present issue, as it concerns the ship's performance and excludes emissions from the carriage of cargo. Different mechanisms of enforcement of carbon performance also complicate questions of liability and its potential distribution between shippers and carriers.

To conclude, while the prospects of carbon dioxide shipping seem to be optimistic, the industry should not tempt fate by neglecting its safety, environmental and climate change concerns. The chapter has underlined the importance of contractual mechanisms for the distribution of risks between the parties, which can assist in mitigating these concerns and provide a more predictable legal framework for the industry.

14

Environmental Obligations Concerning Oceanic Carbon Capture and Storage in International Law: Toward the Long-term Sustainability of CO_2 Storage at Sea

YOSHIFUMI TANAKA*

I. Introduction

This chapter examines the environmental obligations of international law concerning oceanic carbon dioxide (CO_2) capture and storage (CCS) to secure the long-term sustainability of CO_2 storage at sea. According to the Intergovernmental Panel on Climate Change (IPCC), CCS refers to 'a process consisting of the separation of CO_2 from industrial and energy-related sources, transport to a storage location and long-term isolation from the atmosphere'.[1] The CCS Directive of the European Union (EU) regards CCS as 'a bridging technology that will contribute to mitigating climate change'.[2] Technically two types of CO_2 storage exist: geological storage and ocean storage.

As regards geological storage, there are multiple options.[3] Liquefied carbon dioxide can be injected into deep geological formations beneath the seabed, such as depleted

* Professor, Centre for Private Governance (CEPRI), and Shipping and Ocean Group (SHOC), Faculty of Law, University of Copenhagen.

[1] B Metz et al (eds), *IPCC Special Report on Carbon Capture and Storage* (2005) 3 (IPCC Special Report). Further, see International Energy Agency (IEA), *About CCUS* (Paris, IEA, 2021) www.iea.org/reports/about-ccus.

[2] Preambular para 4. Directive 2009/31/EC of the European Parliament and of the Council of 23 April 2009 on the geological storage of carbon dioxide and amending Council Directive 85/337/EEC, European Parliament and Council Directives 2000/60/EC, 2001/80/EC, 2004/35/EC, 2006/12/EC, 2008/1/EC and Regulation (EC) No 1013/2006 (Text with EEA relevance), available at: eur-lex.europa.eu/legal-content/EN/TXT/PDF/?uri=CELEX:32009L0031&from=EN. The resolution adopting the amendment to the London Protocol also stated that 'carbon dioxide capture and sequestration represents an important interim solution'. Resolution LP.1(1) on the Amendment to Include CO_2 Sequestration in Sub-Seabed Geological Formations in Annex 1 to the London Protocol. Adopted on 2 November 2006 (in force in 2007).

[3] IPCC Special Report (n 1) 6.

oil and gas reservoirs and saline aquifers, to store it there permanently.[4] This technology can be called offshore geological storage.[5] Among other things, oil fields, depleted gas fields, deep coal seams and saline formations can provide all possible formations for CO_2 storage.[6] In this regard, the IPCC stated that '[t]he technical geological CO_2 storage capacity is estimated to be on the order of 1000 Gt CO_2, which is more than the CO_2 storage requirements through 2100 to limit global warming to 1.5°C, although the regional availability of geological storage could be a limiting factor';[7] and that 'CCS is an option to reduce emissions from large-scale fossil-based energy and industry sources, provided geological storage is available'.[8]

As regards ocean storage, there are dissolution type and lake type. The dissolution type injects and dissolves CO_2 into the water column (typically below 1,000 meters) via a fixed pipeline or a moving ship. The lake type deposits CO_2 via a fixed pipeline or an offshore platform onto the sea floor at depths below 3,000 meters. As CO_2 is denser than water, it is expected to form a 'lake' that would delay the dissolution of CO_2 into the surrounding environment.[9] For the purpose of this chapter, offshore geological storage and ocean storage can be called oceanic CCS.

Given that climate change is 'a common concern of (hu)mankind',[10] oceanic CCS can be considered as a technology for protecting community interest respecting climate change.[11] Yet oceanic CCS is not without risks for the marine environment, such as ocean acidification and harm to marine organisms.[12] This holds particularly true of ocean storage.[13] Thus, an essential issue is how one can reconcile oceanic CCS with protecting the marine environment.[14]

[4] B Milligan, 'Planning for Offshore CO_2 Storage: Law and Policy in the United Kingdom' (2014) 48 *Marine Policy* 162.

[5] For a detailed analysis of offshore geological storage, see N Bankes, 'Carbon Capture and Storage and the Law of the Sea' in E Johansen, SV Bush, and IU Jacobsen (eds), *The Law of the Sea and Climate Change* (Cambridge, Cambridge University Press, 2021) 160–183.

[6] IPCC Special Report (n 1) 200.

[7] PR Shukla et al, *Climate Change 2022 Mitigation of Climate Change Working Group III Contribution to the Sixth Assessment Report of the Intergovernmental Panel on Climate Change Summary for Policymak*ers (IPCC, 2022) 32, available at www.ipcc.ch/report/ar6/wg3/downloads/report/IPCC_AR6_WGIII_SPM.pdf.

[8] ibid. However, CCS is not free from criticism. C Armeni, 'Carbon Dioxide Storage in the Sub-seabed and Sustainable Development: Please Mind the Gap' (2013) 27 *Ocean Yearbook* 1, 15–20.

[9] IPCC Special Report (n 1) 7.

[10] Preamble of the Paris Agreement (in force, 4 November 2016). The electronic text of the Paris Agreement is available at: unfccc.int/process-and-meetings/the-paris-agreement/the-paris-agreement. See also Preamble of the UN Framework Convention on Climate Change (UNFCCC) (in force 21 March 1994). Text in: 1771 *UNTS* 107.

[11] Community interests refer to common interests of the international community that transcend the individual interests of each State. Therefore, community interests cannot be divided into the interests of each State, and they are not merely a sum of individual interests. See S Thin, 'Community Interest and the International Public Legal Order' (2021) 68 *Netherlands International Law Review* 35–59, at 41; S Besson, 'Community Interests in International Law: Whose Interests Are They and How Should We Best Identify Them?' in E Benvenisti and G Nolte (eds), *Community Interests Across International Law* (Cambridge, Cambridge University Press, 2018) 36, 38.

[12] Offshore Storage Technologies Task Force, Technical Barriers and R&D Opportunities for Offshore, Sub-Seabed Geologic Storage of Carbon Dioxide (September 2015), 6 available at: www.cslforum.org/cslf/sites/default/files/documents/OffshoreStorageTaskForce_FinalCombinedReport.pdf; ICPP Special Report (n 1) 197; D Langlet, 'Safe Return to the Underground? The Role of International Law in Subsurface Storage of Carbon Dioxide' (2009) 18(3) *RECIEL* 286, 289–290; Armeni (n 8) 4.

[13] KN Scott, 'The Day After Tomorrow; Ocean CO_2 Sequestration and the Future of Climate Change' (2005) 18 *Georgetown Int'l Environmental LR* 57, 86.

[14] Milligan (n 4).

In international law, States are obligated to protect and preserve the marine environment.[15] As commentators suggest, this obligation can be considered as an obligation *erga omnes*,[16] that is, 'an obligation under general international law that a State owes in any given case to the international community, in view of its common values and its concern for compliance, so that a breach of that obligation enables all States to take action'.[17] Given that an obligation *erga omnes* reflects 'common values' of the international community, one can say that protecting the marine environment is also a community interest.[18] Hence oceanic CCS creates a crucial issue concerning the reconciliation of two community interests, climate change mitigation and the protection of the marine environment.

In considering this issue, the long-term sustainability of CO_2 storage in the oceans is key.[19] Technologies for climate change mitigation, including oceanic CCS, cannot be considered in isolation from a global goal of sustainable development.[20] The IPCC Special Report stated that 'CCS also poses issues relating to long-term liability for possible unintended releases or contamination which may have inter-generational and, in some cases, international consequences'.[21] Given that CCS may have implications for sustainable development and the well-being of future generations,[22] the regulation of oceanic CCS requires consideration over extensive timescales. Hence oceanic CCS must be considered from the viewpoint of inter-generational equity.[23] There, temporal elements are critically important for the long-term sustainability of CO_2 storage.[24] Thus this chapter focuses particularly on temporal elements in environmental obligations applicable to oceanic CCS operations in international law.[25]

[15] Art 192 of the UN Convention on the Law of the Sea. Adopted 10 December 1982 (in force 16 November 1994).

[16] Y Tanaka, 'Changing Paradigms in the Law of the Sea and the Marine Arctic' (2020) 35 *Int'l J of Marine and Coastal Law* 439, 441–443. See also J Harrison, *Saving the Oceans through Law: The International Legal Framework for the Protection of the Marine Environment* (Oxford, Oxford University Press, 2017) 24–25; P Chandrasekhara Rao and P Gautier, *The International Tribunal for the Law of the Sea: Law, Practice and Procedure* (Cheltenham, Edward Elgar, 2018) 327; International Tribunal for the Law of the Sea (ITLOS), *Responsibilities and Obligations of States Sponsoring Persons and Entities with Respect to Activities in the Area*, Advisory Opinion, ITLOS Case No. 17, [2011] ITLOS Reports, 59, para 180.

[17] Art 1(a). *Institut de droit international*, Resolution: Obligation *Erga Omnes* in International Law, Krakow Session 2005, available at: www.idi-iil.org/app/uploads/2017/06/2005_kra_01_en.pdf.

[18] M McCreath, 'Community Interests and the Protection of the Marine Environment within National Jurisdiction' (2021) 70 *ICLQ* 569–603.

[19] Langlet (n 12) 302.

[20] ICPP Special Report (n 1) 70; Armeni (n 8) 14ff.

[21] ICPP Special Report (n 1) 70.

[22] ibid 68.

[23] Weiss argued that: '[A]ll generations,– past, present and future – are partners in caring for an using the Earth. The present generation, which means everyone living today, must pass the Earth and our natural (and cultural) resources to future generations in at least as good condition as we received them so that future generations can meet their own needs' (footnote omitted). EB Weiss, *Establishing Norms in a Kaleidoscopic World* (Leiden, Brill/Nijhoff, 2020) 283. The concept of sustainable development can be seen as a reflection of 'intergenerational equity'. International Law Association, New Delhi Declaration of Principles of International Law Relating to Sustainable Development, available at: www2.ecolex.org/server2neu.php/libcat/docs/LI/MON-070850.pdf.

[24] Havercroft pointedly observed that '[a] further novel element, which is peculiar to CCS, are the temporal aspects to be addressed when contemplating geological storage'. See I Havercroft, 'Long-Term Liability and CCS' in I Havercroft, RM Hon, and R Steward (eds), *Carbon Capture and Storage: Emerging Legal and Regulatory Issues*, 2nd edn (Oxford, Hart Publishing, 2018) 307.

[25] Technically, CCS consists of three principal stages: (1) capturing the CO_2, (2) transportation of the CO_2 to a storage site, and (3) final storage of the CO_2. D Langlet, 'Safe Return to the Underground? The Role of

Following the introduction, as a preliminary consideration, section II reviews the jurisdiction of the coastal State to regulate oceanic CCS in maritime jurisdictional zones. Sections III and IV examine the legal frameworks for the regulation of oceanic CCS as dumping in global and regional treaties, respectively. Section V addresses environmental obligations to prevent transboundary pollution from offshore geological storage before offering a conclusion in section VI.

II. Regulation of Oceanic CCS in UNCLOS

The 1982 UN Convention on the Law of the Sea (hereinafter UNCLOS), sometimes called the 'constitution for the oceans',[26] provides a global legal framework for the regulations of all ocean activities, including CCS. Thus it is necessary to review the coastal State jurisdiction to regulate oceanic CCS under UNCLOS.

A. Regulation of Oceanic CCS in Marine Spaces under National Jurisdiction

Based on the national jurisdiction of the coastal State, marine spaces in the law of the sea are divided into two main categories: marine spaces under and beyond the national jurisdiction. Furthermore, the marine spaces under national jurisdiction are divided into two sub-categories: marine spaces governed by territorial sovereignty (ie internal waters, the territorial sea, and the archipelagic waters) and marine spaces beyond territorial sovereignty but under the national jurisdiction of the coastal State, that is, the exclusive economic zone (EEZ) and the continental shelf.[27]

Under Article 2(1) UNCLOS, 'The sovereignty of a coastal State extends, beyond its land territory and internal waters and, in the case of an archipelagic State, its archipelagic waters, to an adjacent belt of sea, described as the territorial sea'. As territorial sovereignty comprises comprehensive jurisdiction over all matters within its territory, the coastal State has jurisdiction to regulate oceanic CCS in internal waters, the territorial sea, and the archipelagic waters, subject to the relevant UNCLOS provisions and other rules of international law.[28]

In the EEZ, the coastal State has

> sovereign rights for the purpose of exploring and exploiting, conserving and managing the natural resources, whether living or non-living, of the waters superjacent to the seabed and of

International Law in Subsurface Storage of Carbon Dioxide' (2009) 18(3) *RECIEL* 286, 287. Among the three stages of CCS mentioned above, this article focuses on the issues that arise at the third stage of oceanic CCS only.

[26] TTB Koh, 'A Constitution for the Oceans', available at: www.un.org/Depts/los/convention_agreements/texts/koh_english.pdf.

[27] Y Tanaka, *The International Law of the Sea*, 4th edn (Cambridge, Cambridge University Press, 2023) 8–10. The contiguous zone becomes part of the EEZ where it is established. Where the EEZ is not claimed, however, the contiguous zone forms part of the high seas.

[28] Given that ocean storage requires the depths, it is unlikely that direct injection into the water column would take place in internal waters and the territorial sea less than twelve nautical miles. Scott (n 13) 87.

> the seabed and its subsoil, and with regard to other activities for the economic exploitation and exploration of the zone, such as the production of energy from the water, currents and winds.[29]

Sovereign rights over the EEZ are exclusive in that no one may undertake the exploration and exploitation of natural resources without the express consent of the coastal State. As the term 'natural resources' is generic, its meaning has evolved.[30] This point was confirmed by the Appellate Body of the World Trade Organization (WTO) in the *United States – Import Prohibition of Certain Shrimp and Shrimp Products*, stating that: '[T]he generic term "natural resources" in Article XX (g) [of the WTO Agreement] is not 'static' in its content or reference but is rather 'by definition, evolutionary'.[31]

In light of the development of technology, it may not be unreasonable to consider that the capacity of the ocean for CO_2 storage would fall within the scope of 'natural resources' for the purpose of Article 56(1)(a) UNCLOS. Thus there may be some scope to consider that the coastal State has sovereign rights to manage oceanic CCS in its EEZ. Furthermore, in the EEZ, the coastal State has jurisdiction concerning the protection and preservation of the marine environment under Article 56(1)(b)(iii). Accordingly, in the EEZ, the coastal State can exercise jurisdiction to protect the marine environment from oceanic CCS. It is clear that no other States may conduct oceanic CCS in the EEZ of a coastal State without that State's permission.[32]

The seabed of the EEZ constitutes the continental shelf of the coastal State. Under Article 77(1) UNCLOS, '[t]he coastal State exercises over the continental shelf sovereign rights for the purpose of exploring it and exploiting its natural resources'. As explained earlier, there appears to be some scope to argue that the concept of 'natural resources' can be interpreted to include geological storage capacity.[33] As sovereign rights over the continental shelf are exclusive, no States may conduct geological CO_2 storage on the continental shelf of a coastal State without that State's permission.[34] Furthermore, '[t]he coastal State shall have the exclusive right to authorise and regulate drilling on the continental shelf for *all purposes*' pursuant to Article 81.[35] This provision allows the coastal State to exercise the exclusive jurisdiction to regulate geological CO_2 storage on the continental shelf.[36] Moreover, under Articles 208 and 214 UNCLOS, the coastal State has legislative and enforcement jurisdiction regarding the prevention of pollution from seabed activities on the continental shelf.[37] Arguably such seabed activities include offshore geological storage. Thus, the coastal State has jurisdiction to regulate geological CO_2 storage on the continental shelf.

[29] UNCLOS, Art 56(1)(a).

[30] Scott (n 13) 66.

[31] United States – Import Prohibition of Certain Shrimp and Shrimp Products, Doc.WT/DS58/AB/R, 12.10.1998, 48, para 130. Further, see Y Tanaka, 'Reflections on Time Elements in the International Law of the Environment' (2013) 73 *ZaöRV (Heidelberg J of Int'l Law)* 150–154.

[32] Scott (n 13) 67.

[33] In this regard, Scott argued that 'geological storage capacity should be regarded as a "non-living resources" for the purpose of Art 77(4) of UNCLOS'. ibid.

[34] ibid.

[35] Emphasis added. See also Art 85 UNCLOS.

[36] Bankes (n 5) 168; A Proelss and K Güssow, 'Carbon Capture and Storage from the Perspective of International Law' (2011) 2 *European Yearbook of Int'l Economic Law* 151, 156.

[37] Bankes (n 5) 170.

B. Regulation of Oceanic CCS in Marine Spaces Beyond National Jurisdiction

The high seas are governed by the principle of freedom of the seas.[38] It seems arguable that oceanic CCS would fall within the scope of the freedom of the high seas. However, it must be stressed that oceanic CCS on the high seas is subject to rules of UNCLOS and customary international law regarding the protection of the marine environment.

The seabed of the high seas constitutes either the continental shelf beyond 200 nautical miles or the Area, which is 'the seabed and ocean floor and subsoil thereof, beyond the limits of national jurisdiction'.[39] Under Article 137 UNCLOS, '[a]ll rights in the resources of the Area are vested in mankind as a whole, on whose behalf the Authority [International Seabed Authority] shall act'. 'Resources' in the Area means 'all solid, liquid or gaseous mineral resources *in situ* in the Area at or beneath the seabed, including polymetallic nodules'. In light of a textual interpretation, geological CO_2 storage would not fall within the scope of 'resources' in the Area.[40] If so, at first sight, it would appear that the International Seabed Authority has no jurisdiction to regulate geological CO_2 storage in the Area because the primary role of the Authority is to control exploration for and exploitation of the 'resources' of the Area under Art 153(1) UNCLOS. However, it must be noted that the International Seabed Authority has jurisdiction to adopt appropriate rules concerning, inter alia, 'the prevention of damage to the flora and fauna of the marine environment' by virtue of Article 145. Given that geological CO_2 storage in the subsoil beneath the seabed affects the environment of the Area, it is debatable whether States can freely carry out CCS in the Area, without the involvement of the Authority.[41]

III. Global Legal Framework for the Regulation of Oceanic CCS as Dumping

A debatable issue is whether oceanic CCS should be regarded as dumping, a form of marine pollution. This section examines the treatment of oceanic CCS in global treaties concerning dumping: UNCLOS, the 1972 London Convention,[42] and the 1996 London Protocol as amended in 2006.[43]

[38] Art 87 UNCLOS.

[39] Art 1(1.1) UNCLOS.

[40] Further see, K Zou and L Zhang, 'Legal Challenges of Carbon Capture and Storage in the South China Sea Region' (2017) 84 *Marine Policy* 167, 170.

[41] See also Bankes (n 5) 169–170.

[42] The 1972 International Convention on the Prevention of Marine Pollution by Dumping of Wastes and Other Matter. Further, see KN Scott, 'From Ocean Dumping to Marine Geoengineering: The Evolution of the London Regime' in R Rayfuse, A Jaeckel, and N Klein (eds), *Research Handbook on International Marine Environmental Law* (Cheltenham, Edward Elgar, 2023) 240–263.

[43] Protocol to the Convention on the Prevention of Marine Pollution by Dumping of Wastes and Other Matter, IMO Doc. LC/SM 1/6 (1996), entered into force 24 March 2006. The London Protocol superseded the 1972 London Convention for those States that ratified the Protocol. As of March 2021, 53 States ratified the

A. UNCLOS and the 1972 London Convention

Both UNCLOS and the London Convention contain obligations to protect the marine environment from dumping. Under Article 210(5) UNCLOS,

> Dumping within the territorial sea and the exclusive economic zone or onto the continental shelf shall not be carried out without the express prior approval of the coastal State, which has the right to permit, regulate and control such dumping after due consideration of the matter with other States which by reason of their geographical situation may be adversely affected thereby.[44]

The phrase 'without the express prior approval of the coastal State' implies that dumping would be allowed, should there be the express prior approval of the coastal State. In this sense, UNCLOS does not prohibit dumping, while requiring States to regulate and control marine pollution by dumping at sea.

The question is whether oceanic CCS should be considered as dumping for the purposes of UNCLOS. Art 1(1)(5)(a) of the LOSC defines 'dumping' as:

> (i) any deliberate disposal of wastes or other matter from vessels, aircraft, platforms or other man-made structures at sea;
> (ii) any deliberate disposal of vessels, aircraft, platforms or other man-made structures at sea.

Under Article 1(1)(5)(b), however, 'dumping' does not include:

> (i) the disposal of wastes or other matter incidental to, or derived from the normal operations of vessels, aircraft, platforms or other man-made structures at sea and their equipment, other than wastes or other matter transported by or to vessels, aircraft, platforms or other man-made structures at sea, operating for the purpose of disposal of such matter or derived from the treatment of such wastes or other matter on such vessels, aircraft, platforms or structures;
> (ii) placement of matter for a purpose other than the mere disposal thereof, provided that such placement is not contrary to the aims of this Convention.

The definition under Article 1(1)(5) is virtually a replica of the definition provided in Article III(1) of the 1972 London Convention.[45] However, the definition is not wholly unambiguous. Three issues arise here.

The first issue is whether or not the term 'at sea' covers the subsoil beneath the seabed. In the law of the sea, the concept of the marine environment encompasses the seabed and its subsoil.[46] In fact, there is no doubt that the territorial sea encompasses

London Protocol. The full text of the Protocol, with its 2006 amendments, is available at: wwwcdn.imo.org/localresources/en/OurWork/Environment/Documents/PROTOCOLAmended2006.pdf.

[44] There is no reference to internal waters in this provision. However, it is clear that no dumping may be carried out in these waters without the consent of the coastal State.

[45] Scott (n 42) 244. Under Art III(1)(c) of the 1972 London Convention, however, '[t]he disposal of wastes or other matter directly arising from, or related to the exploration, exploitation and associated off-shore processing of sea-bed mineral resources will not be covered by the provisions of this Convention'. It follows that the London Convention does not apply to enhanced oil recovery using carbon dioxide. Bankes (n 5) 164. See also A Birchenough and F Haag, 'The London Convention and London Protocol and Their Expanding Mandate' (2020) 34 *Ocean Yearbook* 255, 267.

[46] Scott (n 13) 75.

the seabed. Furthermore, Article 76(1) makes it clear that the continental shelf comprises the seabed and subsoil. Accordingly, there may be room for the view that the term 'at sea' covers the subsoil beneath the seabed.[47]

The second issue concerns the meaning of 'waste'. While UNCLOS contains no definition of 'waste', Article III(4) of the London Convention defines 'wastes or other matter' as 'material and substance of any kind, form or description'. Furthermore, paragraph 11 of Annex I defines 'industrial wastes' as 'waste materials generated by manufacturing or processing operations'.[48] CO_2 is not covered by Annex I. An issue thus arises whether CO_2 would fall within the scope of 'industrial wastes'. While an answer may vary according to sources of CO_2 emissions, for instance, it may not be unreasonable to consider that captured CO_2 from large power plant would fall within the scope of 'waste'.[49] If CO_2 could be regarded as 'industrial wastes', any deliberate disposal of CO_2 from vessels, aircraft, platforms or other man-made structures in the oceans is to be regulated by the 1972 London Convention[50] and UNCLOS in accordance with Article 210.[51]

Third, under Article 1(1)(5)(ii) UNCLOS and Article III (1)(b)(ii) of the London Convention, 'placement of matter for a purpose other than the mere disposal thereof' does not constitute dumping, 'provided that such placement is not contrary to the aims of this Convention'. For instance, there may be some scope to argue that placement from a vessel for the purposes of scientific experiments could fall within the scope of 'a placement of matter for a purpose other than the mere disposal thereof'.[52] However, it is less clear whether offshore geological CO_2 storage for climate mitigation purposes could be considered as 'placement of matter for a purpose other than the mere disposal thereof' or whether it is not contrary to the aims of UNCLOS and the London Convention.

In contrast to offshore geological CO_2 storage, ocean CO_2 storage can entail greater risk of adverse impacts on the marine environment, including marine ecosystems.[53] Under Article 1(1)(4) of UNCLOS, 'pollution of the marine environment' is defined as:

> the introduction by man, directly or indirectly, of substances or energy into the marine environment, including estuaries, which results or is likely to result in such deleterious effects as harm to living resources and marine life, hazards to human health, hindrance to marine activities, including fishing and other legitimate uses of the sea, impairment of quality for use of sea water and reduction of amenities.

This is an open definition that may include both existing and new sources of marine pollution and thus, the scope of marine pollution may expand over time. Indeed, the phrase 'likely to result' suggests that the definition covers potentially harmful effects

[47] ibid 75–76; Harrison (n 16) 93.

[48] Since 1996, the dumping of industrial wastes so defined has been prohibited. Art IV(1)(a) of the 1972 London Convention. See also Annex I to the 1972 London Protocol, paras 9 and 11; Scott (n 13) 77.

[49] ibid 77. Langlet argued that 'it does seem reasonable to consider it [CO_2] to fall under the heading of "industrial waste"'. D Langlet, 'Exporting CO_2 for Sub-Seabed Storage: The Non-Effective Amendment to the London Dumping Protocol and Its Implications' (2015) 30 *Int'l J of Marine and Coastal Law* 395, 404.

[50] See, in particular, Art IV of the London Convention.

[51] Scott (n 13) 77.

[52] This interpretation was supported by: OSPAR Commission, Report from the Group of Jurists and Linguists on Placement of Carbon Dioxide in the OSPAR Maritime Area, Summary Record OSPAR 2004, OSPAR 04/23/1-E, Annex 12 (2004), para 21.

[53] Harrison (n 16) 268.

on the marine environment. The definition is broad enough to include CO_2. In light of this, there may be room for the view that direct injection of CO_2 into the ocean constitutes marine pollution under UNCLOS.[54] It follows that direct injection of CO_2 into the ocean may be contrary to the obligation to protect and preserve the marine environment.[55]

B. The 1996 London Protocol as Amended in 2006

On 2 November 2006, the 1996 London Protocol was amended to permit the storage of CO_2 under the seabed by the Resolution adopted by the First Meeting of Contracting Parties to the London Protocol.[56] There, the Preamble to Resolution LP.1(1) recognised that carbon dioxide capture and sequestration should not be considered as a substitute to other measures to reduce carbon dioxide emissions.

Under para 1(8), 'carbon dioxide streams from carbon dioxide capture processes for sequestration' may be considered for dumping, being mindful of the Objectives and General Obligations of the 1996 London Protocol set out in Articles 2 and 3. Under paragraph 4 of Annex I,

> Carbon dioxide streams referred to in paragraph 1.8 may only be considered for dumping, if:
>
> 1. disposal is into a sub-seabed geological formation; and
> 2. they consist overwhelmingly of carbon dioxide. They may contain incidental associated substances derived from the source material and the capture and sequestration processes used; and
> 3. no wastes or other matter are added for the purpose of disposing of those wastes or other matter.

The above paragraph permits the disposal of CO_2 into a sub-seabed geological formation only. It follows that direct ocean injection of CO_2 from vessels, platforms or other man-made structures at sea is not allowed under the London Protocol as amended in 2006.[57]

Regarding offshore geological CO_2 storage, issuance of permits and permit conditions must comply with provisions of Annex 2.[58] Annex 2 contains relatively detailed requirements for dumping, such as waste prevention audit, considerations of waste management options, action list, dump-site selection, assessment of potential effects and monitoring. The requirements for geological storage were further amplified by

[54] Scott (n 13) 90; Proelss and Güssow (n 36) 154.

[55] In this regard, Scott took the view that 'the direct injection of CO_2 into the water column or beneath the seabed from a vessel or platform is prohibited under UNCLOS and its associated instruments, unless such activities constitute scientific experimentation or take place as part of an enhanced oil and gas recovery procedure': (n 13) 106. See also ibid 92.

[56] Resolution LP.1(1) on the Amendment to Include CO_2 Sequestration in Sub-Seabed Geological Formations in Annex 1 to the London Protocol (n 43).

[57] Under Art 8(1), however, the prohibition of dumping shall not apply in the case of force majeure. Under Art 8(2), a Contracting Party may issue a permit as an exception to the above prohibition in emergencies posing an unacceptable threat to human health, safety or the marine environment and admitting of no other feasible solution.

[58] Art 4 (1.2) of the London Protocol.

the 2006 Risk Assessment and Management Framework for CO_2 Sequestration in Sub-seabed Geological Structure (CS-SSGS) (the London Protocol Risk Assessment Framework)[59] and the 2012 Specific Guidelines for the Assessment of Carbon Dioxide for Disposal into Sub-seabed Geological Formations (the London Protocol Specific Guidelines).[60]

It is particularly interesting to note that the three abovementioned instruments commonly refer to temporal elements. As regards the assessment of potential effects, for instance, para 13 of Annex 2 states that the assessment for dumping 'should define the nature, *temporal and spatial scales* and *duration* of expected impacts based on reasonably conservative assumptions'.[61] The London Protocol Risk Assessment and Management Framework also highlights the importance of defining 'the nature, *temporal and spatial scales* and *duration* of expected impacts'.[62] As regards a temporal scale, in particular, it states that '[o]ver the longer term, the risk assessment should also address any change in the integrity of the seal and of the plugs in the abandoned wells and might include the effects of CO_2 dissolution and mineralisation'.[63] Furthermore, the London Protocol Specific Guidelines states that 'in selecting a sub-seabed geological formation for the disposal of carbon dioxide streams', it is important to consider 'potential migration and leakage pathways *over time* (including transboundary movement) and potential effects to the marine environment of leakage of CO_2'.[64] Temporal considerations are further amplified by the Specific Guidelines, stating:

> Given the time-scales associated with carbon dioxide sequestration in sub-seabed geological formations, it may be necessary to consider characterisation of the risks at different stages of a project. The risks during injection and in the short-term may be different to the longer term risks depending upon site-specific considerations. *Consideration of risks over time will be important in the design of monitoring programmes.*[65]

In summary, one can say that consideration of temporal elements is crucial to secure the long-term sustainability of CO_2 storage at sea and inter-generational equity.

Another amendment of the London Protocol concerns Article 6, the export of wastes for dumping purposes. Article 6 of the Protocol prohibits the export of wastes or other matter to other countries for dumping or incineration at sea. However, it became apparent that there may be a need for parties which do not have suitable geological storage capacity to use CCS to reduce emissions.[66] In response, on 30 October 2009, Article 6 of the London Protocol was amended with a view to permitting the export of carbon

[59] Adopted at the joint session of the 28th Consultative Meeting of Contracting Parties under the London Convention and the 1st Meeting of Contracting Parties under the London Protocol (30 October-3 November 2006), available at: www.imo.org/en/OurWork/Environment/Pages/CCS-Default.aspx.

[60] Adopted 2 November 2012. The document is available at: www.imo.org/en/OurWork/Environment/Pages/CCS-Default.aspx.

[61] Emphasis added.

[62] The London Protocol Risk Assessment and Management Framework (n 59) para 5.2.

[63] ibid para 5.3.

[64] Emphasis added. The London Protocol Specific Guidelines (n 60) para 6.2.5.

[65] Emphasis added. ibid para 7.9. See also para 8.11.

[66] T Dixon, J Garrett, and E Kleverlaan, 'Update on the London Protocol: Developments on Transboundary CCS and on Geoengineering' (2014) 63 *Energy Procedia* 6623, 6624; Birchenough and Haag (n 45) 267.

dioxide streams for disposal under Annex 1.[67] As a consequence, a new paragraph 2 was added to Article 6 as follows:

> 2 Notwithstanding paragraph 1, the export of carbon dioxide streams for disposal in accordance with annex 1 may occur, provided that an agreement or arrangement has been entered into by the countries concerned. Such an agreement or arrangement shall include:
>
> 2.1 confirmation and allocation of permitting responsibilities between the exporting and receiving countries, consistent with the provisions of this Protocol and other applicable international law; and
>
> 2.2 in the case of export to non-Contracting Parties, provisions at a minimum equivalent to those contained in this Protocol, including those relating to the issuance of permits and permit conditions for complying with the provisions of annex 2, to ensure that the agreement or arrangement does not derogate from the obligations of Contracting Parties under this Protocol to protect and preserve the marine environment.
>
> A Contracting Party entering into such an agreement or arrangement shall notify it to the Organization [International Maritime Organization].

While the amendment is not in force, in 2019, the London Protocol Parties adopted a resolution to allow the provisional application of an amendment of Article 6 of the London Protocol.[68]

Preamble to Resolution LP.3(4) noted that 'the transboundary movement of carbon dioxide after injection (migration) is not export for dumping and therefore not prohibited by Article 6'. Related to this, the London Protocol Specific Guidelines stated that '[i]n the case of transboundary sub-seabed geological formations that could be used by more than one country or where sub-seabed geological formations are located in areas where there is the potential for transboundary movement of CO_2 streams after injection, the Contracting Party where the injection occurs should be responsible for the implementation of these Specific Guidelines'.[69] The Guidelines also stated:

> The Contracting Party where the injection occurs should cooperate with other relevant Contracting Parties, other States and other relevant entities, to ensure adequate sharing

[67] Resolution LP.3(4) on the Amendment to Art 6 of the London Protocol. This is not in force.

[68] Resolution LP.5(14) on the Provisional Application of the 2009 Amendment to Art 6 of the London Protocol. Adopted on 11 October 2019. Specifically, the Resolution decided 'to allow for the provisional application of the 2009 amendment pending its entry into force by those Contracting Parties which have deposited a declaration on provisional application of the 2009 amendment' (para 1). 41st Consultative Meeting of Contracting Parties to the London Convention and the 14th Meeting of Contracting Parties to the London Protocol (LC 41/LP 14), 7–11 October 2019. Reproduced in: N Bankes, 'Provisional Application of an Amendment to the London Protocol to Facilitate Collaborative CCS Projects' (10 December 2019), online: ablawg.ca/wp-content/uploads/2019/12/Blog_NB_Article6.pdf. Norway, Denmark and the Netherlands have deposited their declarations in accordance with the Resolution. I Havercroft and C Consoli, 'Perspective: Developments and Opportunities-A Review of National Responses to CCS under the London Protocol' www.globalccsinstitute.com/wp-content/uploads/2022/05/Perspective-A-review-of-national-responses-to-CCS-under-the-London-Protocol-Global-CCS-Institute.pdf. Further, see V Weber, 'Are We Ready for the Ship Transport of CO_2 for CCS? Crude Solutions from International and European Law' (2021) 30 *RECIEL* 387; IEAGHG, Exporting CO_2 for Offshore Storage – The London Protocol's Export Amendment and Associated Guidelines and Guidance, 2021-TR02, April 2021, available at: www.club-co2.fr/files/2021/04/IEAGHG-2021-TR02-Exporting-CO2-for-Offshore-Storage-The-London-Protocol-s-Export-Amendment-and-Associated-Guidelines-and-Guidance.pdf.

[69] The London Protocol Specific Guidelines (n 60) para 1.10.

> of information as needed and in accordance with international law, including by way of arrangement or agreement to ensure that these Specific Guidelines are implemented effectively.

Arguably, 'other relevant entities' would include the International Seabed Authority. It would seem to follow that Parties must cooperate with the Authority where sequestered CO_2 migrates from a geological formation under the national jurisdiction to the Area.[70]

IV. Regional Legal Framework for the Regulation of Oceanic CCS as Dumping

Next, the regional legal framework for the regulation of dumping must be examined. As no examination of each and every regional treaty can be made here because of limitations of space, by way of example, this section analyses two contrasting treaties: the OSPAR Convention,[71] and the Helsinki Convention.[72]

A. OSPAR Convention

At the regional level, amendments to the OSPAR Convention merit discussion.[73] Dumping is regulated by Article 4 of the OSPAR Convention. Under Article 1(f), 'dumping' means:

> (i) any deliberate disposal in the maritime area of wastes or other matter
>
> (1) from vessels or aircraft;
> (2) from offshore installations;
>
> (ii) any deliberate disposal in the maritime area of
>
> (1) vessels or aircraft;
> (2) offshore installations and offshore pipelines.

However, dumping under the OSPAR Convention does not include: (i) the disposal under the 1973 MARPOL Convention as modified by the Protocol of 1978 relating thereto, (ii) placement of matter for a purpose other than the mere disposal thereof, and (iii) for the purposes of Annex III, the leaving wholly or partly in place of a disused offshore installation or disused offshore pipeline.

'The maritime area' means 'the internal waters and the territorial seas of the Contracting Parties, the sea beyond and adjacent to the territorial sea under the

[70] Scott (n 42) 252.

[71] Convention for the Protection of the Marine Environment of the North-East Atlantic. Entered into force 25 March 1998. The text of the Convention is available at the home page of OSPAR: www.ospar.org.

[72] Convention on the Protection of the Marine Environment of the Baltic Sea. Opened for signature 9 April 1992. Entered into force 17 January 2000. The text of the agreement is available at: www.helcom.fi/.

[73] Amendments of Annex II and Annex III to the Convention in Relation to the Storage of Carbon Dioxide Streams in Geological Formations, available at: assets.publishing.service.gov.uk/government/uploads/system/uploads/attachment_data/file/238565/7696.pdf. See also www.ospar.org/work-areas/oic/carbon-capture-and-storage; Proelss and Güssow (n 36) 159–160.

jurisdiction of the coastal state to the extent recognised by international law, and the high seas, including the bed of all those waters and its sub-soil', situated within the limits described in Article 1(a). According to OSPAR's technical working group, the term 'sub-soil' 'seems to be intended to cover all underground strata below the sea-bed'.[74] Hence the OSPAR Convention covers the ocean floor and the subsoil beneath the seabed. There, the technical group took the following view:

> There seems no doubt that the placement of CO_2 in the maritime area for the purposes of mitigating its effects on climate change is a deliberate disposal. Shipment in a vessel for placement from the vessel would therefore be prohibited under Annex II, since none of the exclusions of specific materials from the definition of 'wastes or other matter' or from the ban on dumping seem relevant. The same would apply to any other placement for the purposes of mere disposal.[75]

In response, in 2007, the OSPAR Commission adopted amendments to the Annexes II and III of the OSPAR Convention to allow CO_2 storage in geological formations under the seabed.[76] In this regard, OSPAR Decision 2007/02 states:

> The storage in geological formations of carbon dioxide streams from carbon dioxide capture processes shall not be permitted by Contracting Parties without authorisation or regulation by their competent authorities. Any authorisation or regulation shall be in accordance with the OSPAR Guidelines for Risk Assessment and Management of Storage of CO2 Streams in Geological Formations, *as updated from time to time*.[77]

The phrase 'as updated from time to time' suggests that the OSPAR Guidelines evolve over time. Furthermore, '[t]he provisions of the permit or approval shall ensure the avoidance of significant adverse effects on the marine environment'.[78] In addition, the Preamble of OSPAR Decision recalled that CCS 'is not a mandatory obligation for the Contracting Parties to the Convention but an option which the individual Contracting Parties can choose to allow the use of'.[79]

In this connection, the OSPAR Commission adopted the OSPAR Guidelines for Risk Assessment and Management of Storage of CO_2 Streams in Geological Formations.[80] These Guidelines provide 'generic guidance for Contracting Parties, when considering applications for permits for the storage of CO_2 streams in geological formations'.[81] In light of uncertainties regarding the resilience of marine ecosystems,[82] the Guidelines stress the importance of a thorough site characterisation for 'defining the nature and *temporal and spatial scales* of potential impacts'.[83] In particular, the Guidelines stressed

[74] Report from the Group of Jurists and Linguists on Placement of Carbon Dioxide in the OSPAR Maritime Area (n 52) 2, fn 7.

[75] ibid 4, para 20.

[76] Amendments of Annex II and Annex III to the Convention in Relation to the Storage of Carbon Dioxide Streams in Geological Formations (n 73). See also Art 3(3) and (4) of Annex III to the OSPAR Convention.

[77] Emphasis added. OSPAR Decision 2007/02 on the Storage of Carbon Dioxide Streams in Geological Formations, OSPAR 07/24/01, Annex 6, para 3.1.

[78] ibid para 3.2.

[79] ibid.

[80] Reference number 07-12, available at: www.ospar.org/work-areas/oic/carbon-capture-and-storage.

[81] ibid para 6.

[82] ibid para 4.9.

[83] Emphasis added. ibid para 5.2.

that '[i]t is important to update the risk characterisation periodically, as part of the risk management process, based on new field data and/or performance assessment data and/or new/improved scientific knowledge'.[84] It follows that the risk characterisation may vary over time according to the development of data and scientific knowledge. By contrast, OSPAR Decision 2007/1 prohibited the placement of CO_2 streams in the water column or on the seabed 'unless it results from normal operations as described in Art 1(g)(i) of the Convention or is for a purpose other than the mere disposal thereof as described in Art 1(g)(ii) of the Convention and is in accordance with the relevant provisions of the Convention'.[85]

B. The Helsinki Convention

Should regional treaties not have made relevant amendments, an issue arises concerning the relationship between regional and global treaties. This issue may be raised in relation to the Helsinki Convention. Under Article 11(1) of the Convention, dumping (with exemptions) is prohibited in the Baltic Sea Area.[86] The exemptions concern dredged materials and force majeure under Article 11(2) and (4) of the Convention.

As explained earlier, ocean CO_2 storage is arguably contrary to the obligation to protect and preserve the marine environment. Hence it may be reasonable to consider that ocean storage is also not permitted in the Helsinki Convention.

However, the CO_2 storage in geological formations may need careful consideration. Under Article 29 of the Helsinki Convention

> The provisions of this Convention shall be without prejudice to the rights and obligations of the Contracting Parties under existing and future treaties which further and develop the general principles of the Law of the Sea underlying this Convention and, in particular, provisions concerning the prevention of pollution of the marine environment.

It seems possible to consider that the London Protocol as amended could be considered as 'future treaties which further and develop provisions concerning the prevention of pollution of the marine environment'. If so, to harmonise the interpretation of the London Protocol and the Helsinki Convention, the better interpretation seems to be that as between Parties to both treaties, the CO_2 storage in geological formations is permissible subject to regulations. Arguably this interpretation could also be supported by Article 30(4)(a) of the Vienna Convention on the Law of Treaties[87] and a *lex posterior* or *lex specialis* principle. In any case, like the OSPAR Convention, it is desirable to amend the relevant provisions of the Helsinki Convention to clarify the legality of offshore geological CO_2 storage.

[84] ibid para 5.3.

[85] OSPAR Commission, OSPAR Decision 2007/01 to Prohibit the Storage of Carbon Dioxide Streams in the Water Column or on the Sea-bed, OSPAR 07/25/1, Annex 5, available at: www.ospar.org/documents?v=32641. Entered into force on 15 January 2008.

[86] For a definition of the Baltic Sea Area, see Art 1. For a definition of dumping, see Art 2(4).

[87] Adopted 22 May 1969 (in force 27 January 1980).

V. Obligations to Prevent Transboundary Pollution from Offshore Geological Storage

A. Due Diligence as an Evolutionary Obligation

Offshore geological CO_2 storage can cause transboundary pollution because the plume may migrate across the boundary.[88] Prevention of transboundary pollution constitutes a crucial element of the long-term sustainability of CO_2 storage at sea. In this regard, there is a need to specify environmental obligations concerning preventing transboundary pollution from CO_2 storage in geological formations.

Article 194(2) UNCLOS places an obligation upon States to

> take all measures necessary to ensure that activities under their jurisdiction or control are so conducted as not to cause damage by pollution to other States and their environment, and that pollution arising from incidents or activities under their jurisdiction or control does not spread beyond the areas where they exercise sovereign rights in accordance with this Convention.

This provision reflects the principle of *sic utere tuo ut alienum non laedas* or the no-harm principle. This provision requires States to protect the environment beyond the limits of sovereign rights, that is, the high seas and the Area. Accordingly, the no-harm principle is no longer bilateral but operates *erga omnes* concerning areas beyond the limits of national jurisdiction.[89]

In this regard, the International Court of Justice (ICJ), in its Advisory Opinion concerning the *Legality of the Threat or Use of Nuclear Weapons*, stated:

> [T]he existence of the general obligation of States to ensure that activities within their jurisdiction and control respect the environment of other States or of areas beyond national control is now part of the corpus of international law relating to the environment.[90]

Hence, under customary international law, all States are under the obligation to ensure that the CO_2 storage in geological formations within their jurisdiction does not cause damage by pollution to other States and the areas where they exercise sovereign rights, that is, the high seas and the Area.

It is generally understood that the no-harm principle provides an obligation to exercise due diligence to avoid causing transboundary damage.[91] To invoke State responsibility, an injured State must prove a lack of diligent efforts on the part of the

[88] N Bankes, 'The Use of Sub-Seabed Transboundary Geological Formations for the Disposal of Carbon Dioxide' in C Banet (ed), *The Law of Seabed: Access, Uses, and Protection of Seabed Resources* (Leiden, Brill, 2020) 405.

[89] A Boyle and C Redgwell, *Birnie, Boyle and Redgwell's International Law and the Environment*, 4th edn (Oxford, Oxford University Press, 2021) 162.

[90] *Legality of the Threat or Use of Nuclear Weapons* (Advisory Opinion) [1996] ICJ Rep 226, 241–42, para 29.

[91] *Pulp Mills on the River Uruguay (Argentina v Uruguay)* (Merits) (2010) ICJ Rep 14, 55, para 101 (*Pulp Mills*, Merits). See also Boyle and Redgwell (n 89) 163; R Pisillo-Mazzeschi, 'The Due Diligence Rule and the Nature of the International Responsibility of States' (1992) 35 *German Yearbook of Int'l Law* 9, 38–41.

origin State.[92] As 'due diligence' is an elusive concept, the application of due diligence is context-specific.[93] In light of the vagueness of the standard of due diligence, an international court or tribunal may encounter challenges when deciding an alleged breach of a State's obligation of due diligence.

In this regard, it is of particular interest to note that the Annex VII arbitral tribunal specified two components of the obligation of due diligence in the *South China Sea* arbitration (merits). The first concerned an obligation to *adopt* rules and measures to prevent harmful acts, and the second element related to an obligation to *maintain* a level of vigilance in enforcing those rules and measures.[94] Given that the obligation to maintain is continuous, a temporal element is crucial in applying the obligation of due diligence. The temporal element of due diligence was highlighted by the Seabed Disputes Chamber of ITLOS:

> It [due diligence] may change *over time* as measures considered sufficiently diligent at a certain moment may become not diligent enough in light, for instance, of new scientific or technological knowledge.[95]

It would seem to follow that States are required to regulate offshore geological storage in light of the development of scientific knowledge and technology.

As the obligation of due diligence is evolutionary,[96] there is a need to explore an evolving standard of due diligence that can take account of changes in technology and environmental knowledge over time.[97] In this regard, it is notable that the ITLOS Seabed Dispute Chamber highlighted the inter-link between the obligation of due diligence and the obligation to apply best environmental practices and/or best available techniques, stating:

> The adoption of higher standards in the more recent Sulphides Regulations would seem to indicate that, in light of the advancement in scientific knowledge, member States of the Authority have become convinced of the need for sponsoring States to apply 'best environmental practices' in general terms so that they may be seen to have become enshrined in the sponsoring States' obligation of due diligence.[98]

Admittedly, the ITLOS Seabed Disputes Chamber did not clearly define the concept of best environmental practice. By way of example, the OSPAR Convention defines this concept as 'the application of the most appropriate combination of environmental control measures and strategies'.[99] Appendix 1, para 8 of the OSPAR Convention highlights the evolutionary nature of best environmental practices, providing that 'best

[92] ibid para 30.

[93] S Besson, *La* due diligence *en droit international* (Leiden, Brill/Nijhoff, 2021) 165–180.

[94] PCA Case No 2013-19. The *South China Sea Arbitration (Philippines v China)* (Merits), Award of 12 July 2016, (2020) 33 *Reports of International Arbitral Awards*, 521, para 944.

[95] Emphasis added. *Responsibilities and Obligations of States Sponsoring Persons and Entities with Respect to Activities in the Area*, [2011] ITLOS Reports 43, para 117. See also ILC, *Draft Articles on Prevention of Transboundary Harm from Hazardous Activities with Commentaries, Commentary to Article 3*, (2001) 2 *Yearbook of Int'l Law Commission*, Part 2, 154, para 11.

[96] Besson (n 93) 138.

[97] See also Tanaka (n 31) 161–165.

[98] *Responsibilities and Obligations of States Sponsoring Persons and Entities with Respect to Activities in the Area* [2011] ITLOS Reports 42, para 136.

[99] Emphasis added. OSPAR Convention, Appendix 1, para 6.

environmental practice for a particular source will *change with time* in the light of technological advances, economic and social factors, as well as changes in scientific knowledge and understanding'. Likewise, since 'best available technique' means the technique at the latest stage of development, it also develops over time.[100] The evolutionary nature of best environmental practice and best available technique is also confirmed in the 1992 Helsinki Convention[101] and the Syracuse Protocol.[102] Where States are obligated to apply best environmental practices and best available techniques, they are required to review and update their technology and practice concerning environmental protection in light of technological and scientific advances.[103]

B. Inter-link between the Due Diligence Obligation, an EIA, Monitoring, and the Precautionary Approach

To enhance the normative strength of the due diligence obligation, the link between the obligation of due diligence and the obligation to conduct an EIA must be considered.[104] An EIA is a procedure to detect environmental risks and likely impacts of a proposed project and integrate environmental concerns into the decision-making process before authorising or funding the project.[105] As discussed elsewhere, an EIA can be considered a legal device to address inter-temporality in protecting the environment.[106] The due diligence obligation and the obligation to perform an EIA are intimately intertwined in the sense that the due diligence obligation cannot be considered fulfilled if an EIA was not carried out.[107] In this regard, the ICJ, in the *Pulp Mills* judgment, held:

> [D]ue diligence, and the duty of vigilance and prevention which it implies, would not be considered to have been exercised, if a party planning works liable to affect the regime of the river or the quality of its waters did not undertake an environmental impact assessment on the potential effects of such works.[108]

Thus, the obligation to conduct an EIA provides a legal procedure for effectuating a due diligence obligation in the context of environmental protection.[109] The obligation to

[100] OSPAR Convention, Appendix 1, para 2.

[101] Reg 4 of Annex II to the Helsinki Convention.

[102] Annex IV, paras 3 and 8.

[103] Boyle and Redgwell (n 89) 165. Care should be taken in noting that the best environmental practices and best available techniques may differ according to the technological capabilities of States. ibid 166.

[104] Y Tanaka, 'Obligation to Conduct an Environmental Impact Assessment (EIA) in International Adjudication: Interaction between Law and Time' (2021) 90(1) *Nordic J of Int'l Law* 86, 89–94.

[105] Boyle and Redgwell (n 89) 184; Tanaka, ibid 87. For a definition of EIA, see also Convention on Environmental Impact Assessment in a Transboundary Context (opened for signature 25 February 1991, entered into force 10 September 1997), Art 1, para vi (Espoo Convention).

[106] Tanaka (n 31) 168.

[107] Tanaka (n 104) 93.

[108] *Pulp Mills on the River Uruguay (Argentina v Uruguay)* (Merits) [2010] ICJ Reports 83, para 204. See also *Certain Activities Carried Out by Nicaragua in the Border Area (Costa Rica v Nicaragua) and Construction of a Road in Costa Rica along the San Juan River (Nicaragua v Costa Rica)* (Merits) [2015] ICJ Rep 707, para 104 (*Construction of a Road*).

[109] Tanaka (n 104) 89–94.

conduct a transboundary EIA is generally regarded as a rule of customary international law.[110]

Currently the obligation to conduct an EIA is increasingly provided by treaties, such as UNCLOS,[111] OSPAR Convention,[112] and Helsinki Convention.[113] In a particular context of the conservation of marine biological diversity of areas beyond national jurisdiction, the obligation to conduct an EIA was further amplified by the new BBNJ Agreement.[114] Under Article 28(1) of the Agreement, Parties are obliged to ensure that 'the potential impacts on the marine environment of planned activities under their jurisdiction or control, which take place in areas beyond national jurisdiction, are assessed as set out in this Part [IV] before they are authorized.' Furthermore, Article 28(2) provides an obligation to conduct an EIA '[w]hen a Party with jurisdiction or control over a planned activity that is to be conducted in marine areas within national jurisdiction determines that the activity may cause substantial pollution of or significant and harmful changes to the marine environment in areas beyond national jurisdiction' in accordance with Part IV of the BBNJ Agreement or under the Party's national process. Moreover, Article 39(1) obliges Parties to 'consider conducting strategic environmental assessments for plans and programmes relating to activities under their jurisdiction or control, to be conducted in areas beyond national jurisdiction, to assess the potential effects of that plan or programme, as well as alternatives, on the marine environment.' The EIA obligations set out in the BBNJ Agreement are to be applied to oceanic CCS, once that Agreement enters into force.

As environmental conditions may change with time, there is a need to continue monitoring the ongoing environmental risks and impacts after a project has begun. Accordingly, environmental impact assessment must be complemented by a monitoring system.[115] As monitoring is a continuous assessment of the environment, it can be regarded as a temporal procedure. The London Protocol Risk Assessment and Management Framework clearly states:

> Long-term monitoring and mitigation of any leakage of CO_2 will be important activities in the context of the London Convention and Protocol, due to the long time-scales of CS-SSGS, the potential for much larger sites than those used for conventional dumping operations and the nature of CO_2.[116]

Indeed, the need for monitoring is referred to in multiple instruments concerning the regulation of offshore geological storage.[117] Monitoring is of particular importance with

[110] This view was echoed by the ICJ and ITLOS. *Pulp Mills on the River Uruguay (Argentina v Uruguay)* (Merits), [2010] ICJ Reports 83, para 204; *Construction of a Road* [2015] ICJ Rep 706–707, para 104. See also *Responsibilities and Obligations of States Sponsoring Persons and Entities with Respect to Activities in the Area* [2011] ITLOS Reports 50, para 145.

[111] Art 206.

[112] Art 6.

[113] Art 7.

[114] Agreement under the UN Convention on the Law of the Sea on the Conservation and Sustainable Use of Marine Biological Diversity of Areas Beyond National Jurisdiction. Adopted 19 June 2023. Not entered into force. The text is available at: www.un.org/Depts/los/XXI10CTC%28EN%29.pdf.

[115] *Pulp Mills on the River Uruguay (Argentina v Uruguay)* (Merits) [2010] ICJ Reports 83–84, para 205.

[116] The London Protocol Risk Assessment and Management Framework (n 59) para 7.5.

[117] See, for instance, the London Protocol Specific Guidelines (n 60) para 8ff; Art 2(a) of Annex IV to the OSPAR Convention; OSPAR Decision 2007/02, para 3.2.6 and para 3.3; OSPAR Guidelines for Risk

a view to checking any leakage of CO_2 from geological formations and the existence of adverse effects on marine ecosystems. It can be said that monitoring is one of the key elements of the long-term sustainability of CO_2 storage in geological formations. If a State fails to conduct monitoring and environmental harm is caused, arguably, that State cannot deny the breach of due diligence obligation because it failed to maintain vigilance. In light of this, one can say that the obligation of monitoring is also linked to the due diligence obligation.

Finally, the inter-link between the due diligence obligation and the precautionary approach merits discussion. As noted earlier, there are still some uncertainties regarding the environmental risks of offshore geological storage. Here the precautionary approach comes into play. Whilst the definition of the precautionary approach or principle varies,[118] Principle 15 of the 1992 Rio Declaration on Environmental and Development formulates this approach as follows:

> In order to protect the environment, the precautionary approach shall be widely applied by states according to their capabilities. Where there are threats of serious or irreversible damage, lack of full scientific certainty shall not be used as a reason for postponing cost-effective measures to prevent environmental degradation.

Even though the precautionary approach is not explicitly included in UNCLOS, many writers have expressed the view that the Convention's provisions must be interpreted in accordance with this principle.[119]

Regarding dumping, Article 3(1) of the London Protocol explicitly obliges the Contracting Parties to apply 'a precautionary approach to environmental protection from dumping of wastes or other matter …'. It follows that the Contracting Parties to the Protocol must apply a precautionary approach to CO_2 storage in geological formations. By the same token, the OSPAR Convention also provides the obligation to apply the 'precautionary principle'.[120]

Of particular note in this regard is the interlink between the obligation to apply the precautionary approach/principle and the obligation to conduct an EIA. The precautionary approach is inter-temporal in that it aims to take protective measures to respond to probable or potential risks, including risks arising from ongoing activities that cannot be fully identified through present-day science but might create environmental damage *in the future*.[121] To apply the precautionary approach, there is a need to identify potential risks that may arise in the future, even though such risks may not be well known or it may not be possible to discover them through present-day science.[122] By identifying potential risks, an EIA can assist decision-makers in judging whether precautionary action needs to be taken. Where an obligation to apply the precautionary approach is

Assessment and Management of Storage of CO_2 Streams in Geological Formations para 18(b)(vi); Art 13 of EU CCS Directive.

[118] The terminology of 'the precautionary approach' or 'the precautionary principle' is not unified. In this chapter, the terms 'the precautionary approach' or 'the precautionary principle' are used interchangeably.

[119] AL Jaeckel, *The International Seabed Authority and the Precautionary Principle: Balancing Deep Seabed Mineral Mining and Marine Environmental Protection* (Leiden, Nijhoff, 2017) 135.

[120] Art 2(2)(a).

[121] Tanaka (n 31) 165–167.

[122] P Martin-Bidou, 'Le Principe de Précaution en Droit International de l'Environnement' (1999) 103 *Revue Générale de Droit International Public* 631, 647.

set out in a treaty, a State party to the treaty whose activities cause serious environmental damage could not deny the breach of the obligation if it has not conducted an EIA effectively. In this sense, it can be argued that an EIA and the precautionary approach are intimately intertwined.[123]

VI. Conclusion

The application of technologies for climate change mitigation in the oceans creates a sharp tension between climate change mitigation and marine environmental protection. By way of illustration, this chapter examined environmental obligations concerning oceanic CCS focusing particularly on temporal elements. The principal points considered can be summarised as follows.

First, direct ocean injection of CO_2 from vessels, platforms or other man-made structures at sea is not allowed under the London Protocol as amended in 2006 and the OSPAR Convention. Direct ocean injection of CO_2 also constitutes marine pollution under UNCLOS. Hence there may be room for the view that oceanic storage is prohibited under UNCLOS and its associated instruments.

Second, in light of amendments to the London Protocol, CO_2 storage in geological formations under the seabed is now allowed for those States that are Contracting Parties to the Protocol. Likewise, Annexes II and III of the OSPAR Convention were amended to allow CO_2 storage in geological formations under the seabed. However, the Parties to the London Protocol and the OSPAR Convention stressed that CCS should not be considered as a substitute for other measures to reduce CO_2 emissions.[124]

Third, environmental harm from unintended releases of CO_2 storage from geological formations into the oceans may affect marine species and ecosystems for a long period of time. Accordingly, the long-term sustainability of CO_2 storage in the oceans is of critical importance. The sustainability of CO_2 storage must be considered over a long timescale. In this regard, Annex 2 to the London Protocol and its Risk Assessment Framework commonly highlight the importance of defining 'temporal and spatial scales' and 'duration of expected impacts' when assessing the potential effects of CO_2 storage in geological formations and the assessment for dumping. The London Protocol Specific Guidelines further amplify temporal considerations.

Fourth, States are obligated to prevent transboundary pollution from offshore geological storage. In this regard, four obligations that are closely interlinked are important: (1) a due diligence obligation, (2) the obligation to perform an EIA, (3) the obligation of monitoring, and (4) the obligation to apply the precautionary approach. The obligations commonly include temporal elements. Thus, ensuring compliance with the obligations should be crucial in achieving the long-term sustainability of CO_2 storage in the geological formations and inter-generational equity.

[123] Tanaka (n 104) 102 and 120; Separate Opinion of Judge Cançando Trindade in the *Pulp Mills* case, [2010] ICJ Reports 171, para 96.

[124] Resolution LP.1(1) on the Amendment to Include CO2 Sequestration in Sub-Seabed Geological Formations in Annex 1 to the London Protocol (n 57); Amendments of Annex II and Annex III to the Convention in Relation to the Storage of Carbon Dioxide Streams in Geological Formations (n 73).

15

Carbon Storage and Waste Law

CAROLA GLINSKI*

I. Introduction

This chapter analyses the relationship of carbon storage with European and international waste law and the requirements for carbon storage arising from European law as compared to international law. In principle, CO_2 that is captured and stored must be regarded as waste according to European and international definitions, which refer to 'substances or objects which are disposed of, intended to be disposed of or required to be disposed of', including gaseous and liquid substances. Thus, exemptions from the (general) waste law requirements in the respective regimes depend on the exceptions defined or specific codified requirements.

In this regard, the EU has set up a specific regime for CO_2 storage with Directive 2009/31/EC on the geological storage of carbon dioxide.[1] The Directive applies specific requirements that differ from those of Directive 1999/31/EC on the landfill of waste.[2]

However, storage in sub-seabed geological formations must also comply with international agreements on the protection of the seas, such as the London Convention,[3] the OSPAR Convention[4] and the Helsinki Convention,[5] which have all prohibited the 'dumping of wastes and other matter'. While the London Convention and the OSPAR Convention have explicitly excluded CO_2 for storage in sub-soil geological formations from this prohibition, the Helsinki Convention, dealing with the protection of the marine

* Professor in FB Umweltwirtschaft/-recht – FR Umweltrecht, Hochschule Trier and Associate Professor, Centre for Private Governance (CEPRI) and Shipping and Ocean Law Group (SHOC), Faculty of Law, University of Copenhagen.

[1] Directive 2009/31/EC of the European Parliament and of the Council of 23 April 2009 on the geological storage of carbon dioxide [2009] OJ L140/114 (Carbon Storage Directive).

[2] Council Directive 1999/31/EC of 26 April 1999 on the landfill of waste [1999] OJ L182/1 (Landfill Directive).

[3] Convention on the Prevention of Marine Pollution by Dumping of Wastes and Other Matter of 1972, as amended in 2006, available at www.imo.org/en/OurWork/Environment/Pages/London-Convention-Protocol.aspx (London Convention).

[4] Convention for the Protection of the Marine Environment of the North-East Atlantic of 1992, available at www.ospar.org/site/assets/files/1169/ospar_convention.pdf (OSPAR Convention).

[5] Convention on the Protection of the Marine Environment of the Baltic Sea Area of 1974 as updated in 1992, available at helcom.fi/wp-content/uploads/2019/06/Helsinki-Convention_July-2014.pdf (Helsinki Convention).

environment of the Baltic Sea area, has not done so. Thus, the legality of carbon storage in the Baltic Sea depends on the relationship between the Carbon Storage Directive and the Helsinki Convention.

The chapter first analyses the definition of waste in European and international waste law, showing that CO_2 may constitute waste.[6] It then presents the Carbon Storage Directive 2009/31/EC with its deviations from the otherwise applicable Landfill Directive 1999/31/EC[7] before it turns to international law.[8] It compares the approaches of the three conventions mentioned above and then analyses the conflict between the Carbon Storage Directive and the Helsinki Convention from the perspective of EU law.[9] The chapter concludes that, despite the permission to store carbon in the Baltic Sea under the Carbon Storage Directive, there is a certain risk that a relevant permit by the competent national authority might be declared unlawful by the Court of Justice due to its incompatibility with the Helsinki Convention.

II. Definition of Waste in European and International Waste Law

A. EU Law

In EU law, Directive 2008/98/EC on waste[10] defines 'waste' in its Article 3(1) as 'any substance or object which the holder discards or intends or is required to discard'. In line with the general meaning of a 'substance' as a type of solid, liquid or gas with particular qualities,[11] the notion of 'substance' covers all physical conditions, including liquid and gaseous. This is reconfirmed by the explicit exclusion from the scope of the directive of 'gaseous effluents emitted into the atmosphere' under Article 2(1)(a). CO_2 that is not 'emitted into the atmosphere' but instead captured before emission would thus principally fall within the directive's regulatory scope.[12]

The characterisation as waste, therefore, depends on the meaning of 'to discard', 'to intend to discard' (subjective waste definition) or 'to be required to discard' (objective waste definition), which the Court of Justice of the European Union generally interprets broadly to ensure a high level of environmental protection.[13] Neither is it necessary that

[6] Below, section II.

[7] Below, section III.

[8] Below, section IV.

[9] Below, section V.

[10] Directive 2008/98/EC of the European Parliament and of the Council of 19 November 2008 on waste [2008] OJ L312/3 (Waste Framework Directive).

[11] See *The Oxford Learner's Dictionary English*.

[12] See also MJ Mace, C Hendriks and R Coenraads, 'Regulatory challenges to the implementation of carbon capture and geological storage within the European Union under EU and international law' (2007) 1 *Int'l J of Greenhouse Gas Control* 253, 258. For a narrower view of the scope of application see S Much, 'Rechtsfragen der Ablagerung von CO_2 in unterirdischen geologischen Formationen' (2007) *Zeitschrift für Umweltrecht* 130, 134.

[13] See already Joined Cases C-418/97 and C-419/97 *ARCO Chemie Nederland Ltd v Minister van Volkshuisvesting, Ruimtelijke Ordening en Milieubeheer* and *Vereniging Dorpsbelang Hees, Stichting Werkgroep*

the waste holder gives up possession of the substance or object rather than undertaking a treatment operation himself,[14] nor is it necessary to undertake a recovery or disposal operation, which, however, serves as an indicator for characterisation as waste.[15] At the same time, neither the economic value of a substance nor the fact that a substance or object has no environmentally detrimental characteristics at all excludes a characterisation as waste.[16] Thus, the notion of 'to discard' can be defined as the submission of substances or objects to a recovery operation in the meaning of Annex II to the Waste Framework Directive or to a disposal operation in the meaning of its Annex I or to relinquish actual possession over them with the cessation of any further purpose.[17] Annex I lists different types of landfills (D 1) and deep injection (D 3) as disposal operations, amongst them the '(r)elease to seas/oceans including sea-bed insertion' (D 7). Thus, according to waste law, carbon storage, for example via injection into land or the sea-bed, would be regarded as a disposal measure and therefore as covered by EU waste law.[18]

Before the adoption of the 2009 Carbon Storage Directive, EU waste law, and in particular the 1999 Landfill Directive, was regarded as a major obstacle to carbon storage.[19] In principle, the Landfill Directive aims at the progressive reduction of landfilling of waste (as a last resort) and the prevention of leakages and negative effects on the environment and human health throughout the whole life cycle of a landfill. To this end, it sets up requirements relating to permits, waste acceptance, technical requirements in the operational and after-care phases, monitoring and reporting. The storage of liquid waste is completely prohibited.[20]

B. International Law: Basel Convention on the Transboundary Shipment of Hazardous Wastes

This approach to the definition of waste is reflected in international law. According to Article 2(1) of the Basel Convention on the Control of Transboundary Movements of Hazardous Wastes and Their Disposal,[21] 'wastes' are 'substances or objects which are disposed of or are intended to be disposed of or are required to be disposed of by the

Weurt+ and Vereniging Stedelijk Leefmilieu Nijmegen v Directeur van de dienst Milieu en Water van de provincie Gelderland ECLI:EU:C:2000:318, [2000] ECR I-4475.

[14] See already Case C-304/94 *Criminal proceedings against Euro Tombesi and Adino Tombesi* ECLI:EU:C:1997:314, [1997] ECR I-3561.

[15] *ARCO Chemie* (n 13).

[16] See eg Case C-9/00 *Palin Granit Oy and Vehmassalon kansanterveystyön kuntayhtymän hallitus* ECLI:EU:C:2002:232, [2002] ECR I-3533.

[17] See eg the definition in § 3 para 2 of the German Circular Economy Act (*Kreislaufwirtschaftsgesetz*; KrWG). English translation available at www.bmuv.de/en/law/circular-economy-and-safeguard-the-environmentally-compatible-management-of-waste.

[18] See also M Hellriegel, 'CO_2-Abscheidung und -Ablagerung – Teil 1: Anwendbarkeit und Anforderungen des geltenden Rechts' (2008) *Recht der Energiewirtschaft* 111.

[19] See eg Mace et al (n 12) 258.

[20] Landfill Directive (n 2) Art 5(3)(a).

[21] Basel Convention on the Control of Transboundary Movements of Hazardous Wastes and Their Disposal, 1673 UNTS 57 (Basel Convention).

provisions of national law'. As mentioned above, the notion of 'substance' is generally defined as a type of solid, liquid or gas that has particular qualities. Article 2(4) defines 'Disposal' as 'any operation specified in Annex IV to this Convention', which includes disposal operations under section A and recovery operations under section B. The three waste categories of 'to be disposed of', 'intended to be disposed of' and 'required to be disposed of' encompass more than the delivery to one of these methods. In any case, carbon storage, thus carbon to be injected and stored in sub-soil, would be included in the definition of waste. It could come under Annex IV A. D3: 'Deep injection (e.g. injection of pumpable discards into wells, salt domes of naturally occurring repositories, etc.)' or under Annex IV A. D7: 'Release into seas/oceans including sea-bed insertion'.

III. The EU Approach to Carbon Storage

In order to make the geological storage of CO_2 possible, the EU adopted the Carbon Storage Directive as part of the 2009 climate and energy package. According to Article 1, the Directive aims to enable the geological storage of CO_2 as permanent containment in order to prevent and eliminate negative climate effects and, at the same time, to prevent adverse environmental and health effects. In the case of storage in sub-seabed geological formations, in particular leakages could lead to devastating effects on the maritime environment, depending on the speed of the leakage.[22]

The Directive harmonises the administrative procedures across Member States in order to create legal certainty for investors that wish to develop CO_2 storage sites and construct installations for CO_2 capture and transport while, at the same time, it addresses environmental, health and safety concerns about the storage of CO_2.[23] It does so by amending not only EU waste law, where carbon storage is now excluded from the scope of application of the Waste Framework Directive[24] and also the Waste Shipment Regulation,[25] but also

[22] See eg R Purdy and R Macrory, 'Geological Carbon Sequestration: Critical Legal Issues' (2003) *Tyndall Centre for Climate Change Research Working Paper* No. 45, 4.

[23] See European Commission, *Report on review of Directive 2009/31/EC*, COM(2015) 576 final, 4; M Montini and E Orlando, 'Balancing climate change mitigation and environmental protection interests in the EU Directive on carbon capture and storage' (2012) 3 *Climate Law* 165, 171.

[24] Article 35 of the Carbon Storage Directive (n 1) amended Directive 2006/12/EC of the European Parliament and of the Council of 5 April 2006 on waste [2006] OJ L114/9, Art 2(1)(a), the predecessor of the Waste Framework Directive (n 10), accordingly. In Art 2(1)(a) Waste Framework Directive itself, the exclusion of 'carbon dioxide captured and transported for the purposes of geological storage and geologically stored in accordance with Directive 2009/31/EC of the European Parliament and of the Council of 23 April 2009 on the geological storage of carbon dioxide' is missing. There seems to be some uncertainty whether this is simply an error (as the Waste Framework Directive was not yet in force when the Carbon Storage Directive was adopted) or whether both Directives apply in parallel, see Triple, Ricardo-AEA and TNO innovation for life, *Study to support the review and evaluation of Directive 2009/31/EC on the geological storage of carbon dioxide (CCS Directive)* (Publications Office of the European Union 2014) 96. Germany, for example, has explicitly excluded carbon storage from its waste law regime, see Circular Economy Act (n 17) § 2 para 2 no 15. See also S Much, 'Die Behandlung von Risiken in der Gesetzgebung am Beispiel der Carbon-Capture-and-Storage-Technologie' in Jörg Scharrer et al (eds), *Risiko im Recht – Recht im Riskio* (Baden-Baden, Nomos 2011) 85, 98.

[25] See Regulation (EC) No 1013/2006 of the European Parliament and of the Council of 14 June 2006 on shipments of waste [2006] OJ L190/1 as amended by the Carbon Storage Directive (n 1) Art 1(3)(h).

EU water law[26] and other environmental legislation.[27] In fact, the Carbon Storage Directive predominantly covers the storage part of 'carbon capture and storage' (CCS), while the capture and transportation part is mainly dealt with by other legislation.[28] The Directive thereby follows a conservative approach and relies as far as possible on existing environmental law.[29] Geological storage of CO_2 is defined as the injection accompanied by storage of CO_2 streams in underground geological formations (Article 3(1)). Storage in the water column is not permitted (Article 2(3)).

According to Article 2(1), the Carbon Storage Directive applies in the territory of the Member States, their exclusive economic zones and on their continental shelves. Storage complexes shall not extend beyond these areas (Article 2(3)). Thus, the Directive allows storage on-shore and off-shore and covers relevant parts of the North Sea, the French, Spanish and Portuguese Atlantic coast, as well as the Baltic Sea. It does not apply to storages of CO_2 below 100 kilotonnes undertaken for research and testing purposes (Article 2(2)).

The Directive retains the right of the Member States not to allow for any storage in parts or the whole of their territory (Article 4(1)). Where storage is principally allowed, characterisation and assessment of the territory for a proper selection of storage sites are required in a three-step procedure pursuant to the criteria in Annex I (Article 4(3)). First, data must be collected relating to geology, hydrogeology, geochemistry, geomechanics, seismicity or the existence of wells or boreholes of the potential storage complex as well of domains surrounding the storage complex that may be affected, including population or valuable natural resources. Potentially interacting exploration or storage activities and the proximity of CO_2 sources or transport networks must also be explored. Second, a three-dimensional geological earth model of the candidate storage complex must be built. Any uncertainty with the parameters of the model or the model itself shall be assessed by developing a range of scenarios. Third, a characterisation of the storage dynamic behaviour, sensitivity and risk assessment based on dynamic modelling shall be carried out. A geological formation shall only be selected as a storage site if there are no risks of leakage and no significant environmental or health risks (Article 4(4)). Though adjusted to CO_2 storage, the principal approach is not that different from the waste law approach towards landfills, which also aims at preventing leakages and negative effects on the environment and to human health and establishes respective requirements concerning the location of the landfill, its geological conditions, and safeguards concerning the protection of soil and water.[30]

The exploration of potential storage sites requires an exploration permit. Exploration permits shall be granted on an open and non-discriminatory basis. Hereby, the permit holder shall have the sole right to explore the potential storage complex, and

[26] See, in particular, Directive 2000/60/EC of the European Parliament and of the Council of 23 October 2000 establishing a framework for Community action in the field of water policy [2000] OJ L327/1 as amended by the Carbon Storage Directive (n 1) Art 11(3)(j).

[27] For details, see Carbon Storage Directive (n 1) Art 31ff.

[28] Directive 2011/92/EU of the European Parliament and of the Council of 13 December 2011 on the assessment of the effects of certain public and private projects on the environment [2011] OJ L26/1 and Directive 2010/75/EU of the European Parliament and of the Council of 24 November 2010 on industrial emissions (integrated pollution prevention and control) [2010] OJ L334/17.

[29] Montini and Orlando (n 23) 172.

[30] See Landfill Directive (n 2) Annex I.

no conflicting uses shall be permitted (Article 5). Equally, storage as such, of course, requires a permit on an open and non-discriminatory basis, which allows for only one operator per site and ensures that no conflicting uses are permitted (Article 6). Priority for the granting of a storage permit shall be given to the holder of the exploration permit, provided that the application for a storage permit is made during the period of validity of the exploration permit.

The requirements for permit application, permit conditions and content again follow the logic of the Landfill Directive. The directives both require in their Articles 7 to 9 the technical (and financial) competence (and reliability) of the operator, the characterisation and quantity of the stored substances, an assessment of the expected security of the site, the adherence to the legal requirements of the directive, an (approved) accident prevention, monitoring and corrective action plan, a post-closure plan, notification requirements and financial security.[31] Financial security is part of the permit application, which shall ensure that all obligations, including closure and post-closure requirements, can be met (Article 19). The Carbon Storage Directive further requires a Commission review of the draft storage permits (Article 10). The operator has to inform the competent authority of all planned changes, irregularities or leakages, and the competent authority has to review, update or withdraw the permit. The permit has to be renewed after five years and every ten years thereafter (Article 11). In parallel to the Landfill Directive, the Carbon Storage Directive has (CO_2 stream) acceptance criteria and procedures. In particular, no waste or other matter may be added, and other (incidentally) associated substances shall be below levels that would adversely affect the integrity of the storage site or the transport infrastructure or pose significant risks to the environment or human health. The operator has to carry out a respective risk assessment and keep a register of the quantities and properties of the CO_2 streams (Article 12).

Moreover, both directives list monitoring and reporting requirements in the operational phase.[32] The Carbon Storage Directive requires the monitoring of the injection facilities, the storage complex and (where appropriate) the surrounding environment, a comparison between modelled and actual behaviour, the detection of significant irregularities, migration of CO_2, leakages, significant adverse effects, an assessment of the effectiveness of corrective measures and an update of the safety and integrity of the storage site (Article 13). Among others, the monitoring results have to be reported to the competent authorities (Article 14). The competent authorities have to carry out routine inspections of all storage complexes at least once a year until three years after closure and every five years until transfer of responsibility to the competent authority, and non-routine inspections in case of irregularities (Article 15). The operator has to immediately notify of leakages or significant irregularities and take the necessary corrective measures (Article 16).

In line with his closure and post-closure obligations, the operator remains responsible for monitoring, reporting and corrective actions in accordance with the post-closure plan, as well as for sealing the storage site and removing the injection facilities. In case of withdrawal of the permit, the competent authority becomes responsible but must

[31] The requirements in brackets only apply to the Carbon Storage Directive.
[32] Carbon Storage Directive (n 1) Art 13 and Annex II; Landfill Directive (n 2) Art 12 and Annex III.

recover the costs from the operator (Article 17). This again mirrors the post-closure obligations of the Landfill Directive.[33]

The responsibility for the storage site can be transferred to the competent authority after a minimum of 20 years in case all available evidence indicates that the CO_2 is permanently contained, all financial obligations have been fulfilled, the site has been sealed, injection facilities have been removed, and a report demonstrates the conformity with the modelled behaviour, the absence of leakages and its long-term stability. The report shall be submitted to the Commission. Regular monitoring may be reduced to the necessary level, which allows for the detection of leakages or significant irregularities. In the case of a leakage or a significant irregularity, costs can be recovered from the operator in case of fault (Article 18). To this end, the operator has to make a financial contribution to the competent authority before the transfer of responsibility (Article 20). Further, there are provisions on transboundary cooperation, registers, reporting and information to the public (Articles 24 ff).

Carbon capture and storage is part of the European Emission Trading System (ETS). Articles 11(4), 17(2) and 18(1) of the Carbon Storage Directive refer to the obligation of the operator or of the responsible party to surrender allowances pursuant to the ETS Directive 2003/87/EC in the event of leakage.

To what extent the Directive is able to reach its goals, which are in a certain mutual tension, such as combatting climate change (while still enabling a competitive European economy) through CO_2 storage and at the same time preventing negative (other) environmental impacts, in particular through leakages, is still difficult to predict.

In 2014, the Commission published a report on the review of Directive 2009/31/EC.[34] At that time, the number of CCS installations was much lower than expected when the Directive was passed, although CCS had been regarded as basically the only option available to reduce direct emissions from large industrial processes in the longer term.[35] Only one project in the Netherlands had been permitted and had practical experience with the Directive then, which had gone beyond exploration permits, whereas four projects were in the planning phase. In addition to that, two large CCS plants in Norway (linked to natural gas production) were in operation.[36] Permanent containment had not yet been fully demonstrated at a large scale. Results from research-scale storage sites and from projects in other countries, in particular from the two large-scale Norwegian projects that have been injecting CO_2 into saline aquifers under the North Sea since 1996, indicate that safe and long-term storage without leakage is possible.[37] The reason for the reluctance of industry has been seen in economic factors such as the lack of a commercial case for the technology due to low carbon prices. The resulting lack of experience has made it impossible to assess the effectiveness of the Directive towards its aims, but it has still been found fit for purpose.[38]

In the meantime, the interest in carbon storage has grown due to rising carbon prices and the emerging need to reduce emissions, in particular in fossil-intensive industries

[33] Landfill Directive (n 2) Art 13 and Annex III.

[34] COM(2015) 576 final.

[35] A policy framework for climate and energy in the period from 2020 to 2030, COM(2014) 15.

[36] European Commission (n 23) 3.

[37] ibid 4.

[38] bid 4–6.

such as cement production, which have basically no alternative. At the moment, projects are planned in Norway, Great Britain, the Netherlands, Denmark, France, Sweden, Ireland, Italy and Bulgaria, but none of them are in the Baltic Sea.[39]

As there is still a lot of uncertainty as to the environmental and health risks of carbon storage, commentators suggest strictly invoking the precautionary principle while applying the Directive, in particular with a view to the assessment of storage sites.[40]

IV. Approaches to the Subject Matter in International Law

Storage in sub-seabed geological formations also has to comply with international agreements on the protection of the seas, such as the London Convention, the OSPAR Convention and the Helsinki Conventions, which all prohibit the 'dumping of wastes and other matter'.[41]

A. London Convention and Protocol

The London Convention and Protocol on the Prevention of Marine Pollution by Dumping of Wastes and other Matter generally address the dumping of waste and other matter from man-made structures at sea. Hereby, the regulatory approach has changed over time. While the London Convention of 1972 blacklisted specific substances contained in the Annexes, the Protocol of 1996 (which replaced the Convention for its parties) codified a general prohibition of dumping and only allowed the dumping of substances that are specifically whitelisted in Annex 1, provided that a permit procedure (Annex 2) has been followed.

In line with the European and international definition of waste, Article 1(8) of the London Protocol defines 'wastes or other matter' as 'material and substance of any kind, form or description'. This covers principally everything or every substance to be dumped, irrespective of its form, be it solid, sludge, liquid, or gaseous,[42] which is not listed in Annex 1 (Article 4.1). The dumping of wastes and other matter listed in Annex 1 shall require a permit (Article 4.2). 'Dumping' includes any storage of wastes or other matter in the seabed and the subsoil thereof from vessels, aircraft, platforms or other man-made structures at sea (Article 1.4.1.3). Thus, carbon storage would, in principle, be covered by the London Convention and Protocol.[43] However, with an amendment

[39] See eg Reuters, 16 August 2023.

[40] Montini and Orlando (n 23) 176ff.

[41] Whether also the environmental obligations in the United Nations Convention on the Law of the Seas (UNCLOS), Part XII, Arts 192 ff., which generally prohibit maritime pollution, could be an obstacle to sub-seabed carbon storage depends on the risk of leakages and the harm caused to the marine environment, see eg J Friedrich, 'Carbon Capture and Storage: A new Challenge for International Law' (2007) *Zeitschrift für ausländisches öffentliches Recht und Völkerrecht* 211, 216ff.

[42] In addition to the general definition of waste, CO_2 deriving from the combustion of fossil fuels in industrial installations has explicitly been recognised as industrial waste under the Convention.

[43] At least as far as the geological storage is done by injection from vessels or man-made platforms and not by pipe-line from land-based sources, see eg Mace et al (n 12) 256. On the respective inconsistencies towards

to the Protocol of 2006,[44] the climate contribution of carbon storage was acknowledged and 'carbon dioxide streams from carbon dioxide capture processes for sequestration' were excluded from the total prohibition (Annex 1, 1.8). Instead, it was allowed under the condition that: (1) disposal is into a sub-seabed geological formation; (2) they consist overwhelmingly of carbon dioxide. They may contain incidental associated substances derived from the source material and the capture and sequestration processes used; and (3) no wastes or other matter are added for the purpose of disposing of those wastes or other matter' (Annex 1, 4.).

Annex 2 provides for certain requirements to be fulfilled, in particular, related to the selection and monitoring of dump sites. In addition, a risk assessment and management framework for CO_2 sequestration in sub-seabed geological structures was adopted[45] in order to ensure a precautionary approach towards the marine environment.[46] It basically requires a six steps risk assessment and management procedure, which includes a problem formulation with a critical scoping of scenarios and pathways to be considered, a site selection and characterisation on the basis of physical, geological, chemical, and biological data, an exposure assessment which is concerned with processes and pathways of (potential) CO_2 migration and leakage to the marine environment, an effects assessment on human health, marine resources, relevant biological communities, habitats, and ecological processes, a risk characterisation based on the likelihood of adverse effects based on different modelling assumptions, and a risk management which includes monitoring and mitigation measures also after CO_2 injection. Furthermore, in 2012 'Specific Guidelines for Assessment of Carbon Dioxide Streams for Disposal into Sub-Seabed Geological Formations' were adopted.[47] Finally, an amendment to Article 6 of the London Protocol allows the export of carbon streams for disposal, provided that an agreement exists between the respective States, which confirms and allocates permitting responsibilities.[48]

The International Maritime Organization (IMO) regards the London Protocol as the most advanced international regulatory instruments addressing carbon capture and sequestration in sub-sea bed geological formations.[49] However, from the EU Member States, the Baltic States, Croatia, the Czech Republic, Greece, Romania and Slovakia have signed neither the London Convention nor the Protocol. Hungary, Portugal and Poland have only signed the Convention.

its application to CO_2 storage, see also S Much, 'The Emerging International Regulation of Carbon Storage in Sub-Seabed Geological Formations' in R Caddell and R Thomas (eds), *Shipping, Law and the Maritime Environment in the 21st Century* (Witney, Lawtext Ltd, 2013) 255ff.

[44] Resolution LP 1.1 on the amendment to include CO_2 sequestration in sub-sea bed geological formations, available at www.imo.org/en/OurWork/Environment/Pages/CCS-Default.aspx.

[45] On the 1st Meeting of Contracting Parties under the London Protocol (30 October–3 November 2006) (Source LC/SG- CO_2 1/7, annex 3), available at www.imo.org/en/OurWork/Environment/Pages/CCS-Default.aspx.

[46] See eg Friedrich (n 41) 221ff.

[47] LC 34/15, annex 8, available at www.imo.org/en/OurWork/Environment/Pages/CCS-Default.aspx.

[48] See Resolution LP.3(4) on the Amendment to Article 6 of the London Protocol (adopted on 30 October 2009). In addition, on 11 October 2019 a Resolution on the provisional application of this amendment has been concluded in order to enable the transportation of CO_2 streams as the ratification process of the amendment was too slow, see Resolution LP.5(14).

[49] See www.imo.org/en/OurWork/Environment/Pages/CCS-Default.aspx.

B. OSPAR Convention

The OSPAR Convention for the Protection of the Marine Environment of the North-East Atlantic is a regional agreement which furthers the environmental objective of the London Convention and Protocol and is regarded as one of the most comprehensive legal frameworks for marine environmental protection. Contracting parties to the OSPAR Convention are the EU and all European States bordering the Atlantic Ocean.

OSPAR prohibits various types of pollution, including by dumping (Article 4 with Annex II). 'Dumping' means 'any deliberate disposal of wastes or other matter' (Article 1(f)).[50] In terms of cooperation across environmental regimes, the carbon storage discussion within the OSPAR framework built upon the negotiations of the London Protocol,[51] and as in the London Protocol, carbon dioxide streams from carbon dioxide capture processes for storage were excluded from the general prohibition of dumping in 2007 (Annex II, Article 3.2(f)).[52] Preconditions are that: (i) disposal is into a sub-soil geological formation; and (ii) the streams consist overwhelmingly of carbon dioxide. They may contain incidental associated substances derived from the source material and the capture, transport and storage processes used.

In addition, an exemption from the general prohibition of dumping from offshore installation was regulated under Articles 3.3 and 3.4 of Annex III. These amendments basically adopted the London Protocol requirements such as prior authorisation, risk assessment and management, the prohibition to add substances and the prohibition of storage in the water column. The importance of permanent storage without leakage was again emphasised.[53]

As the Carbon Storage Directive was meant to implement the (amended) international framework and was drafted in line with these international requirements,[54] it can be assumed, that neither the London Protocol nor the OSPAR Convention provide for any major obstacle to carbon storage in European waters. This is only different for those EU Member States that have ratified the London Convention but not the London Protocol.

C. Helsinki Convention

As the other two conventions, the Helsinki Convention on the Protection of the Marine Environment of the Baltic Sea prohibits pollution (introduction of substances) from all sources (Article 2.1 and Articles 5 ff) and the dumping of 'wastes and other matter'

[50] On the differentiation between land-based pollution and pollution from vessels and platforms and the related discussions on the admissibility of carbon storage before the amendment, see Friedrich (n 41) 224ff. See also Much (n 43) 272.

[51] See also Friedrich (n 41) 226.

[52] Sub-paragraph (f) was introduced by amendment to the Annex agreed by OSPAR 2007. The amendment will enter into force for those Contracting Parties which have ratified, accepted or approved it on the thirtieth day after receipt by the Depositary Government of notification of its ratification, acceptance or approval by at least seven Contracting Parties. Thereafter the amendment will enter into force for any other Contracting Party on the thirtieth day after that Contracting Party has deposited its instrument of ratification, acceptance or approval of the amendment.

[53] See also Much (n 43) 273.

[54] ibid 273f.

(Article 2.4(a) and Article 11). The contracting parties are the EU and all States bordering the Baltic Sea.

Injection in the sub-seabed is not expressly excluded, as the parties have never amended the relevant Annex V on 'Exemptions from the general prohibition of dumping of waste and other matter in the Baltic Sea area' in order to allow carbon storage. Thus, and following the above, carbon storage falls within the scope of application and under the prohibitions of the Helsinki Convention. Without an interpretation in line with the other marine protection agreements,[55] carbon storage remains prohibited in the Baltic Sea.

V. Conflict between EU Law and International Law

In the following, the chapter analyses, from the perspective of EU law, whether in the described conflict the Helsinki Convention or the Carbon Storage Directive prevails.

Since its famous decision in *van Gend & Loos*,[56] the Court of Justice has regarded EU law as an autonomous legal order *sui generis*, different from international law, and it has developed its own approach towards the relationship between EU law and international law:

In principle, the Court of Justice considers international agreements concluded by the EU as constituent parts of EU law.[57] This, however, depends on the conformity of the agreements with EU primary law.[58] An international treaty can never enjoy primacy over provisions that form part of the constitutional foundations of the Union.[59] Thus, such a treaty must not impact upon the very foundations of EU law, in particular, the autonomy of EU law and the competences of the Court of Justice,[60] and upon the fundamental rights which must be respected by all EU acts.[61]

[55] On the prospects of such an interpretation, see Tanaka (ch 14).

[56] Case 26/62 *NV Algemene Transport- en Expeditie Onderneming van Gend & Loos v Netherlands Inland Revenue Administration* [1963] ECR 1.

[57] Case 294/83 *Parti écologiste 'Les Verts' v European Parliament* ECLI:EU:C:1986166, [1986] ECR 1339, para 23; Opinion 1/91 *Draft agreement between the Community, on the one hand, and the countries of the European Free Trade Association, on the other, relating to the creation of the European Economic Area* ECLI:EU:C:1991:490, [1991] ECR I-6079; Opinion 1/17 *Comprehensive Economic and Trade Agreement between Canada, of the one part, and the European Union and its Member States, of the other part (CETA)* ECLI:EU:C:2019:34.

[58] This can be derived from Art 218(11) TFEU which allows for an opinion of the Court of Justice as to whether an agreement is compatible with the Treaties. This was reinforced by the Court in its *Kadi* ruling, Joined Cases C-402/05 P and C-415/05 *P Kadi and Al Barakaat International Foundation v Council and Commission* ECLI:EU:C:2008:461, [2008] ECR I-6351, paras 285 and 304, where the court declined the EU internal application of a binding UN Security Council Resolution due to its violation of basic constitutional principles of the EU legal order.

[59] *Kadi*, ibid para 300.

[60] See eg *European Economic Area* (n 52) paras 30-46 and 71; Opinion 1/00 *Proposed agreement between the European Community and non-Member States on the establishment of a European Common Aviation Area* ECLI:EU:C:2002:231, [2002] ECR I-3493, paras 11–13; Case C-459/03 *Commission of the European Communities v Ireland* ECLI:EU:C:2006:345, [2006] ECR I-4635, para 123; Kadi (n 58) para 282; Opinion 1/09 *European and Community Patents Court* [2011] ECR I-1137, para 76; Opinion 2/13 *Accession of the European Union to the European Convention for the Protection of Human Rights and Fundamental Freedoms*, ECLI:EU:C:2014:2454, para 201; Case C-284/16 *Slovak Republic v Achmea BV*, ECLI:EU:C:2018:158.

[61] *Kadi* (n 58).

International agreements concluded by the EU are binding upon its institutions and its Member States (Article 216(2) TFEU). They become constituent parts of EU law, even without explicit transformative legal acts,[62] and, from the perspective of the Member States, participate in the supremacy of EU law.[63] As international agreements are binding upon EU institutions, they precede secondary law which is created by these institutions and are thus located in the hierarchy of laws between primary and secondary law.[64] EU secondary law therefore must be interpreted in line with international law.[65] The same applies if all Member States but not the EU as such are bound by the international agreement.[66] If, however, only a few Member States are parties to an agreement, the same does not apply.[67] As the EU is a member of the Helsinki Convention, the Convention would, in principle, prevail over the Carbon Storage Directive.

EU secondary law which cannot be interpreted in line with an international agreement would, in principle, be declared invalid.[68] Incompatibility of secondary law with an international agreement can be argued in an action for annulment (Article 263 TFEU) as well as in a preliminary reference procedure (Article 267 TFEU), in case the international agreement or norm provides for an adequate benchmark and has direct effect.[69] Generally speaking, in order to have direct effect, the relevant provisions must

[62] See the landmark decisions of Case 181/73 *R & V Haegeman v Belgian State* ECLI:EU:C:1974:41, [1974] ECR 449 and Case 104/81 *Hauptzollamt Mainz v CA Kupferberg & Cie KG aA* ECLI:EU:C:1982:362, [1982] ECR 3641, para 13. See also, more recently, Case C-308/06 *The Queen, on the application of International Association of Independent Tanker Owners (Intertanko) and Others v Secretary of State for Transport* ECLI:EU:C:2008:312, [2008] ECR I-4057, para 53; Case C-63/09 *Axel Walz v Clickair SA* [2010] ECR I-4239, para 20; Case C-135/10 *Società Consortile Fonografici (SCF) v Marco Del Corso* ECLI:EU:C:2012:140, para 39; Joined Cases C-335/11 and C-337/11 *HK Danmark, acting on behalf of Jette Ring v Dansk almennyttigt Boligselskab* and *HK Danmark, acting on behalf of Lone Skouboe Werge v Dansk Arbejdsgiverforening, acting on behalf of Pro Display A/S*, ECLI:EU:C:2013:222, para 30; Case C-363/12 *Z v A Government department and The Board of management of a community school*, ECLI:EU:C:2014:159, para 73; Case C-464/14 *SECIL – Companhia Geral de Cal e Cimento SA v Fazenda Pública*, ECLI:EU:C:2016:896, para 95; Case C-224/16 *Asotsiatsia na balgarskite predpriyatia za mezhdunarodni prevozi i patishtata (Aebtri) v Nachalnik na Mitnitsa Burgas*, ECLI:EU:C:2017:880, paras 50–53; Case C-266/16 *Western Sahara Campaign UK v Commissioners for Her Majesty's Revenue and Customs and Secretary of State for Environment, Food and Rural Affairs*, ECLI:EU:C:2018:118, para 46; Case C-258/16 *Finnair Oyj v Keskinäinen Vakuutusyhtiö Fennia*, ECLI:EU:C:2018:252, para 20; Case C-83/17 *KP v LO*, ECLI:EU:C:2018:408, paras 21–25; Case C-15/17 *Bosphorus Queen Shipping Ltd Corp v Rajavartiolaitos*, ECLI:EU:C:2018:557, para 44.

[63] See eg S Vöneky and B Beylage-Haarmann, 'AEUV Art 216 Vertragsschlusskompetenz' in E Grabitz, M Hilf and M Nettesheim (eds), *Das Recht der Europäischen Union*, 60th edn (Munich, CH Beck, 2016) para 81.

[64] ibid para 82.

[65] See eg Case C-341/95 *Gianni Bettati v Safety Hi-Tech Srl* [1998] ECR I-4355, para 20; Case C-76/00 P *Petrotub SA and Republica SA v Council of the European Union* [2003] ECR I-79, para 57; Case C-245/02 *Anheuser-Busch Inc. v Budějovický Budvar, národní podnik* ECLI:EU:C:2004:717, [2004] ECR I-10989, para 42; Case C-431/05 *Merck Genéricos – Produtos Farmacêuticos Ldª v Merck & Co Inc* ECLI:EU:C:2007:496, [2007] ECR I-7001, para 35; *SCF* (n 62) para 51; *HK Danmark* (n 62) para 29; *Z* (n 62) para 72; Case C-395/15 *Mohamed Daouidi v Bootes Plus SL* ECLI:EU:C:2016:917, para 41; Case C-406/15 *Petya Milkova v Izpalnitelen direktor na Agentsiata za privatizatsia i sledprivatizatsionen kontrol*, ECLI:EU:C:2017:198, para 48; *Bosphorus Queen Shipping* (n 62) para 44.

[66] *Intertanko* (n 62) para 52; Case C-537/11 *Mattia Manzi and Compagnia Naviera Orchestra v Capitaneria di Porto di Genova*, ECLI:EU:C:2014:19, para 45.

[67] *Manzi*, ibid para 46ff.

[68] See Vöneky and Beylage-Haarmann (n 62) para 83.

[69] See, explicitly, *Intertanko* (n 62) para 45; Joined Cases C-120/06 and C-121/06 *Fabbrica italiana accumulatori motocarri Montecchio SpA (FIAMM) and Fabbrica italiana accumulatori motocarri Montecchio Technologies LLC, Giorgio Fedon & Figli SpA and Fedon America Inc v Council of the European Union and Commission of the European Communities* [2008] ECR I-6513, para 110; Case C-366/10 *Air Transport Association of America*

be precise, clear and unconditional, and they must not call for additional measures in order to enable individuals to rely upon these provisions.[70]

In this regard, however, the case law of the Court of Justice is somewhat inconsistent. The law of the World Trade Organization (WTO) has regularly been denied direct effect.[71] The same applies to the UN Convention on the Law of the Seas, which was not regarded to confer individual rights on ship owners.[72] Even Article 9(3) of the UNECE Convention on Access to Information, Public Participation in Decision-making and Access to Justice in Environmental Matters (Aarhus Convention), which addresses access to justice in environmental matters for members of the public and NGOs, was not regarded to be unconditional and sufficiently precise, as it requires the adoption of a subsequent concretising measure, detailing out the concrete requirements for members of the public and for NGOs.[73] Thus, the Court of Justice did not assess the validity of the EU law in question in the light of these agreements.

In contrast, the fact that the Convention on Biological Diversity (CBD) contains provisions which do not have direct effect, in the sense that they do not create rights which individuals can rely on directly before the courts, did not preclude review by the Court of Justice of compliance of a Community act with that agreement. The reason given was that the CBD is, unlike the other agreements, not strictly based on reciprocal and mutually advantageous arrangements.[74]

The prohibitions to introduce substances or to dump waste and other matter into the sea, the seabed or the subsoil primarily aim at the protection of the marine environment, and they are not strictly reciprocal either. Thus, it is well arguable, with all caution, that the Court of Justice would review the compliance of the Carbon Storage Directive with the Helsinki Convention. The relevant situation could be a permit for carbon storage by the competent national authority, which an environmental NGO challenges in the national court for incompatibility with the Helsinki Convention, and the national court might then initiate preliminary reference proceedings. In such a situation, the Court of Justice might come to the conclusion that the permit is unlawful.

and Others v Secretary of State for Energy and Climate Change [2011] ECR I-13755, paras 53–55; *Z* (n 62) paras 84–86; Case C-21/14 P *European Commission v Rusal Armenal ZAO*, ECLI:EU:C:2015:494, para 37.

[70] See only *van Gend en Loos* (n 56).

[71] For the annulment procedure see Case C-280/93 *Federal Republic of Germany v Council of the European Union* ECLI:EU:C:1994:367, [1994] ECR I-4973, paras 105–110; Case C-149/96 *Portuguese Republic v Council of the European Union* [1999] ECR I-8395, para 47; *Rusal Armenal* (n 64) para 38. For state liability actions see *FIAMM* (n 69) paras 111 and 120. For the preliminary reference procedure see eg Case C-377/02 *Léon Van Parys NV v Belgisch Interventie- en Restitutiebureau (BIRB)* [2005] ECR I-1465, para 39; Case C-306/13 *LVP NV v Belgische Staat*, ECLI:EU:C:2014:2465, para 44; *FIAMM* (n 64) paras 115–119. See also A Steinbach, 'Zur Rechtswirkung von WTO-Streitbeilegungsentscheidungen in der Gemeinschaftsrechtsordnung' (2005) *Europäische Zeitschrift für Wirtschaftsrecht* 331.

[72] See *Intertanko* (n 62) paras 54–64.

[73] See Joined Cases C-401/12 P to C-403/12 P *Council of the European Union and Others v Vereniging Milieudefensie and Stichting Stop Luchtverontreiniging Utrecht*, ECLI:EU:C:2015:4, para 55; see also Case C-543/14 *Ordre des barreaux francophones et germanophone and Others v Conseil des ministers*, ECLI:EU:C:2016:605, paras 49–56.

[74] See Case C-377/98 *Kingdom of the Netherlands v European Parliament and Council of the European Union* ECLI:EU:C:2001:523, [2001] ECR I-7079, paras 53f, which concerned Directive 98/44/EC of the European Parliament and of the Council of 6 July 1998 on the legal protection of biotechnological inventions [1998] OJ L213/13, which among others determined which inventions may or may not be patented; see also Case C-162/96 *A Racke GmbH & Co v Hauptzollamt Mainz* ECLI:EU:C:1998:293, [1998] ECR I-3655, para 47 concerning general rules on the termination of contracts under public international law.

VI. Conclusion

In principle, a broad definition of waste in European and international law which covers all 'substances or objects which are disposed of, intended to be disposed of or required to be disposed of', including gaseous and liquid substances, a permission of landfilling only as a last resort with a complete ban for liquid substances, and far-reaching bans for dumping of waste and other matter into the sea or subsoil, aims at a high level of protection of the environment. However, the importance of CCS as a necessary pillar to combat climate change has created the need to amend European and international legal frameworks and enable CCS. Hereby, detailed technical requirements aim at a balance between enabling CCS while at the same time ensuring a high level of environmental protection. Whether, in particular, the EU Carbon Storage Directive can achieve this aim still remains to be seen as the few European carbon storage projects are still in their infancy. Meanwhile, the aggravating climate change and rising carbon prices have increased interest in CCS projects, with the Helsinki Convention, however, still constituting an obstacle for CCS projects in the Baltic Sea. From the European perspective, the conflict between the Carbon Storage Directive and the Helsinki Convention, in principle, has to be solved in favour of the Helsinki Convention as international law, which is in line with EU primary law, precedes EU secondary law. However, CJEU case law is somewhat inconsistent as to which international agreements it applied as a benchmark for EU secondary law. Thus, the future of carbon storage in the Baltic Sea is difficult to predict.

INDEX

Printed in the USA
CPSIA information can be obtained
at www.ICGtesting.com
CBHW050100240824
R15508000001B/R155080PG13575CBX00001B/1

9 781509 972630